THE
MAKING
OF
POLITICAL
WOMEN

THE
MAKING
OF
POLITICAL
WOMEN

A Study of Socialization and Role Conflict

Rita Mae Kelly & *Mary Boutilier*

NELSON-HALL/CHICAGO

Library of Congress Cataloging in Publication Data

Kelly, Rita Mae.
The making of political women.

Includes index.
1. Women in politics—United States. 2. Sex role. 3. Women—Political activity.
4. Statesmen's wives—Biography. I. Boutilier, Mary, joint author. II. Title.
HQ1236.K45   301.41'2'0973   77-17081
ISBN 0-88229-290-0

We dedicate this book to all mothers,
but especially to our own,
Mary McKinnon Boutilier and Agnes Lorentz Cawley,
and to all daughters,
especially to Kathleen Theresa Kelly.

CONTENTS

ACKNOWLEDGMENTS

MANY INDIVIDUALS have contributed directly to the development of this work. We would like to thank Vincent Peter Kelly and Mary Lewis for their extensive contributions as co-authors of specific chapters. Margaret Ellen Cawley has contributed substantially with her knowledge of the sociological literature as well as by providing insightful criticisms and comments on the total effort. The exchanges of ideas with these individuals and other attendees at a panel on "The Cross-National Study of Political Women in Western Cultures" at the International Studies Association Convention in Washington, D.C., in 1974, was most helpful to us, as were the suggestions of Robert Manley. We would like to express special appreciation to various colleagues who have reviewed portions or all of the manuscript: Mary Carras, Marilyn Johnson, Coral Lansbury, Stanley Renshon, Lucinda San Giovanni, and M. Brewster Smith. The insightful comments of Marilyn Johnson, research director of the Center for the American Woman and Politics at the Eagleton Institute of Politics at Rutgers were helpful.

We would like to acknowledge also the various students who have assisted us in class and out, particularly Kathi Fiamingo, Mark Kosuth, Karen Smith, Roseanne Mirabella, Marie Bloomer, William Guidry, James Risimini, Pat Mueller, Frances Alford, and Judith Gizzi, all of Seton Hall University.

Camden College of the Arts and Sciences, of Rutgers—The

State University of New Jersey, provided one-third release time to Rita Mae Kelly to work on the manuscript, access to needed Xerox facilities, and also provided vital support for typing the final manuscript. A special thanks goes not only to the institution, but also to the specific individuals who made such support a reality: Dean Walter Gordon, Jon Van Til, Chairman of the Urban Studies Department, and the various secretaries, Doris Wentzell, Edith Mae Smith, Anna Mazza, Shirley Turco, and the work-study student, Jacqueline Brewer. Seton Hall University also provided the authors with assistance at needed points. The editorial comments of Mary Kay Ellis of Nelson-Hall helped make the book more readable.

Two of the women included in this study, Ella Grasso and Leonor Sullivan, completed the standard data form individually since relatively little biographical data had been published on them. Our gratitude for their cooperation is great.

At a more personal level we would like to thank all our non-academic friends and relatives, male and female, who have given us insights and motivation to pursue this study. Although we dedicate the book to mothers and daughters, we also learned much from our fathers, Lloyd G. Boutilier and John Francis Cawley, and are equally dedicated to the human development of sons. One of these sons, Patrick Joseph Kelly, like his father, Vincent Peter Kelly, has contributed substantially to this work by his cheerful patience, support, and understanding.

We also thank Plenum Publishing Company for releasing rights for those portions of Chapter 5 which were initially published in 1977 in *Sex Roles: A Journal of Research* under the title "Mothers, Daughters, and the Socialization of Political Women."

CHAPTER 1

Studying Women in Politics*

GROWING UP in the United States, in fact in any Western culture, can be confusing, even traumatic, for physically active girls with potential for leadership. The physical prowess of girls labels them "tomboys," while boys are called "athletes." As such young girls look for models to imitate, they find few. It is still generally true that boys, not girls, become the soldiers and entrepreneurs, the great scholars, "political men," and statesmen.

A girl's and a woman's sex and position within their families continue to define their lives. People explain and justify woman's nonparticipation in politics—and in other active careers involving policy-making and the leading of other human beings—by referring to her family responsibilities as societally more important and to the "weaker sex" theories based upon Freudian assumptions of psychosexual development. According to this latter view, "normal" women never develop an independent consciousness, intellect, or judgmental ability because their psychosexual development compels them to seek a submissive and subordinate posture before their husbands and fathers.

Surely, you say, we are more enlightened now. Psychologists would not support such views; the average person on the streets would not, nor would women themselves. Unfortunately, the old responses and their numerous derivative forms are not idle curiosities of the past. Even in the 1970s the age-old justifications

---

*Written by Rita Mae Kelly, Mary Boutilier, and Mary Lewis

are used to guide educational policies, to counsel high school and college girls, and to oppose women who seek policy-making and political careers. To give but one illustration, in 1970 Edgar F. Berman, liberal member of the Democratic Party's Committee on National Priorities, publicly asserted that "women were subject to raging hormonal differences which disqualified them for high public office."[1]

The nagging issues, therefore, remain: Are women somehow innately inferior politically? Are the responsibilities of family life and public policy-making roles really incompatible? To be a successful political woman must a woman deny herself a family entirely? Or at best wait until the children are grown or until her husband has died? If she has a family and still seeks leadership positions, will she be forced by circumstances to deny her family the traditional benefits politically nonactive women give? Is the "political woman" really an exceptional, "abnormal" phenomenon that the masses of women can never emulate, a twentieth-century aberration that historians will wryly note in future history books?

Our study examines these questions and issues in a time when industrialization, advanced technology, birth control, world wars, and coeducational systems have encouraged women to become involved in the economy. Many women have become scholars; some women have become soldiers; a few more have become revolutionaries; and an ever increasing number have become "political women"; a rare few like Indira Gandhi and Golda Meir have become heads of state. We directly explore these questions in this book by studying real women who became revolutionaries and elected political officials, and comparing them with each other and with women who engaged in politics only through their husbands. For each of these groups of women we systematically view the relationships they had with their parents during the formative years of their life, examining in the process aspects of the Freudian and more modern psychological view of female development. We also look at how these women viewed men, children, and family life; how these relationships affected their political behavior, decision-making, political thought, and political success. The final product will be, we hope, a unique contribution to an understanding of the nature of political women, and of the role of the family as an agent of social change.

This study delves into the subject matter of history, political science, psychology, and sociology in its search to synthesize and expand our knowledge of how family life, adult roles and constraints are linked to the development of political behavior in women. The study relies upon a qualitative comparative examination of biographical data. Because of its objectives, procedures, and content, the book has several unique features. It is the first, we believe, to compare systematically different types of women in politics and to identify and describe the socialization processes in their development. It is certainly the first to compare female revolutionaries and terrorists to elected political women and to the wives of famous political men. One of the most important features is that the results provide concrete examples and models of how real political women have dealt with *the* essential problem females must face: the impact of their sex upon the rest of their lives.

The basic purpose of this study is to try to reconceptualize current thinking—popular and that in the social sciences—about female political socialization, that is, the development of "political women." The historical divide that has separated most women from politics has had serious implications for social science research in this area. Almost all studies of female political socialization and female political participation have found no basis for distinguishing among the various types of female political behavior. We believe that this inability to discover processes underlying the political socialization of females has its source in an incorrect conceptualization of the nature of the phenomenon. For this reason this study seeks to develop a different definition of the problem and a different theoretical framework for exploring the political socialization of women. This framework is based upon the humanistic school of psychology associated with Abraham Maslow, Carl Rogers, A. Angyal, and Kurt Goldstein.[2] It is more directly derived from the theory of psychological needs and political efficacy elaborated by Stanley Renshon,[3] a follower of Maslow. This psychological tradition was chosen because it assumes that both males and females have equal needs, drives, and human natures. It is this critical assumption that has been lacking in much of the existing research and literature.

Our methods of approaching our task are both deductive and inductive. We start by developing a logical construct of what the humanistic psychological approach would lead one to hypothesize logically about political women. Next, through the use of biographical materials we examine the lives of thirty-six women who have actually lived and played a specific type of political role. Twelve of our subjects are wives of famous political men, men who were the chief executives of their nations. These women are Yvonne de Gaulle, Mamie Eisenhower, Mary Wilson, Nadezhda Alliluieva Stalin, Nina Khrushchev, Bess Truman, Pat Nixon, Jackie Kennedy, Lady Bird Johnson, Eleanor Roosevelt, Clementine Churchill, and Nadezhda Krupskaia, Lenin's wife. Another ten of our subjects are women who for the most part are clearly political achievers, women who have been involved in elective politics and held some of the most powerful and prestigious political positions in their countries. These women include Lady Nancy Astor, Leonor Sullivan, Margaret Chase Smith, Martha Griffiths, Ella Grasso, Indira Gandhi, Shirley Chisholm, Margaret Thatcher, Bernadette Devlin, and Golda Meir. To provide a broader base of the type of political behavior in which women as well as men engage we have included fourteen revolutionaries. These women are Alexandra Kollontai, Rosa Luxemburg, Halide Edib, Eva Broido, Angela Davis, Maud Gonne, Ekaterina Breshko-Breshkovskaia, Dolores Ibarruri (La Pasionaria), Countess Constance Markievicz, Vera Zasulich, Emma Goldman, Sophia Perovskaia, Ch'iu Chin, and Charlotte Corday.

These women represent three different categories of women in politics—what we call a focused sample: political wives, elected political women who supported the regimes in their countries, and the revolutionaries who opposed their governments. They were chosen because they filled specific specialized political roles, not because they were representative of women in general. (More detail on how and why these individuals were selected is given in Chapter Three.) Our task is to discover what they have in common and how they differ in the ways they were socialized and what effect these variations had on their adult behavior. By using real women who have actually played specific political roles we can systematically examine, if not test, the framework we propose. This instant feedback provides a corrective to the theoretical framework and ought to add additional insights that might not accrue from the abstract theory itself. The empirical use of real women gives "flesh and blood" illustrations for our abstract theorizing; it does not provide us, unfortunately, with the opportunity for hypothesis testing. We hope that the qualitative analysis of the biographies of these thirty-six women will generate hypotheses and insights for future research of a more quantitative, hypothesis-testing nature.

The need for a qualitative study of the socialization of political women is attested to by the fact that this present work could not have been written ten years ago. To have conceived of the possibility of two women (Indira Gandhi and Golda Meir) being the chief executives of their countries, India and Israel respectively, of a third (Margaret Thatcher of Great Britain) to be in direct line for such a position, of a woman (Ella Grasso) being elected on her own merits to the governorship of her state (Connecticut), of two women (Shirley Chisholm and Margaret Chase Smith) offering themselves as serious candidates for the U.S. presidency, was all so "absurd" that the mere suggestion would have met with laughter. And yet, today this study is not only possible but, we believe, essential. Existing literature on political socialization and female political behavior would not have led us to predicting these developments. Such women would have been considered historical aberrations. What makes their development so noteworthy is the degree to which they make us aware of how social change itself has overtaken our ability to conceive of it. Ten years ago these highly visible political women of today were not just beginning their careers. They were already long down the path of their development. The continual social science concentration on the "typical" and the "representative" (male or female) and the leaving of the atypical and unrepresentative to the students of biography and history has meant that the social system always appears to outstrip our ability to understand it. We plan to build upon what the biographers and historians have learned by systematically using a standard data collection form (see Appendix) for examining how the lives and socialization of these thirty-six political women compare and how well their development fits the pattern we outline in our theory.

Our theory of the socialization of political women is built upon four hierarchical stages of development. In other words, the typical pattern of human development is that stage one must have been successfully traversed in order to go on to stage two, and stage three must precede stage four. Stage one requires that a girl develop an activist, modern sex-role ideology which will enable her to conceive of the possibility for herself of adult roles other than wife, mother, and other roles that society has restricted to females. Stage two requires that the girl or woman in question attain a sense of personal control over her life-space, that is, over her day-to-day existence. Stage three requires that politics become salient to her and to her control over her life-space. Finally, stage four requires that the individual have a reasonably successful history of political participation at critical points in her life.

Rationale for Our Approach

As many scholars point out,[4] the socialization process is usually supportive of the status quo. Lower-class children learn beliefs, behaviors, and manners that tend to keep them in the lower class. Upper-class children learn what is needed to keep them in the upper class. The child's parents and environment, including his or her local community, school, church, and peer groups, teach and reinforce that which exists. Perceptions about sex roles are also learned. Kirsten Amundsen stated in 1971: "The belief in women's inferiority and unsuitability for certain types of activities is the greatest obstacle facing those who would organize women. . . . The values and postulates of sexist ideology appear to be quite effectively internalized in most women."[5]

As Amundsen states, the socialization of females generally supports the traditional view of women and their historical roles in life. If this is so, how then did some women become different? We would argue that the key to answering this question will be found in changes that have occurred and are occurring within the family structure and belief systems.

In order to present a clear rationale for our approach to the study of the socialization of political women, we review other explanations that have been offered for female political behavior or lack of it. We organize this discussion of alternative ways of explaining the political behavior of women around M. Brewster Smith's map of the classes of variables required to understand adult behavior (see Figure 1–1). We seek to demonstrate that the variables in Box I concerning our sociopolitical and cultural heritage and the interrelationship they have with the Box II variables concerned with socialization are the most relevant to understanding why women engage in politics in the manner they do.

Figure 1–1 depicts five classes of variables that need to be examined to explain human behavior. Box V involves the type of behavior to be studied, in our case various types of political behavior. The other boxes represent the diverse classes of variables that have been used by scholars to explain human behavior.

A few moments of thought on the five different classes of variables presented in Figure 1–1 should make it clear that most human beings have little or no control over three of the five classes of variables. They can have control only over the variables in class III (their current socioeconomic and biological self and personality processes and dispositions) and class V (their behavior). They can react to the other classes of variables, but not control them. Indeed, to the degree that one holds to a deterministic model of behavior, the class V (behavior) variables are simply the necessary results of all the previous events impinging on the individual over which he or she has no significant control. Obviously, the question of whether there is any real individual control over any of the factors leading to the behavior to be explained involves a philosophical issue, that is, the question of free will, and the consequences of free will for affecting and understanding human behavior. Such a philosophical discussion, however, is beyond the scope of this study.

Box V. Political Behavior

In broad terms, we see female political behavior as falling into three major categories, and types of women: (a) traditional nonparticipation in political and public life—the private woman, (b) participation in the local public life of society, sometimes as independent actor, but not in its national political life as an independent political actor—the public woman, and (c) participation in politics as an independent being even at the national level with no special mediation of that participation through males— the achieving woman, or, as we will call her for the purposes of this study, the achieving political woman. The rationale for this typology is presented in Chapter Two.

Under the heading of political behavior, then, we see a range of behaviors needing investigation and explanation. In this book we concentrate upon the similarities and differences in socialization experienced by: "private women" and "public women," as represented by a sample of political wives; and political women, as represented by a sample of elected officials and

Figure 1-1
Map of Types of Variables Relevant to Adult Political Behavior°

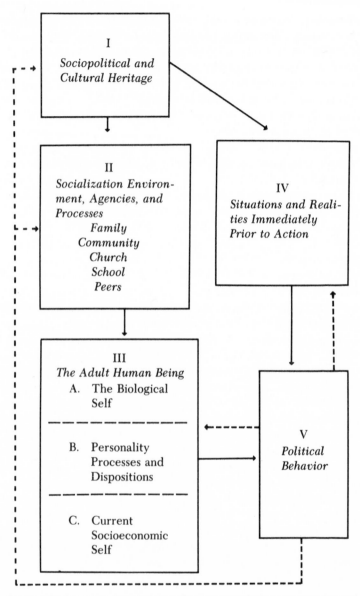

°Adapted from M. Brewster Smith, "A Map for the Analysis of Personality and Politics," *The Journal of Social Issues* 24 (July 1968): 17.

female revolutionaries. The variations identified in the lives of these women ought to enhance substantially our knowledge of why political women are more common now than in the past.

Although we do not dwell on this fact in this book, we believe that many of the socialization processes characterizing the political women in this study will also be common to women who have achieved outside the traditional family roles of mother and wife in other avenues of life, for example, in law, academia, business, or economics. The choice of a field for achieving will depend upon what becomes salient to an individual as a child and as a young adult. Whether or not a female will struggle to achieve outside of her family roles depends on the socialization process.

The other boxes in Figure 1–1 represent the various classes of variables which offer possible explanations for the political behavior women (or men) do ultimately engage in.

Box IV. Situations and Realities
Immediately Prior to Action

If we are seeking to explain behavior, one of the explanatory ingredients may be the class IV variables, that is, the present objective situations that cause a person to act one way or another. Here we can note some common assertions made about the political behavior of women. Angus Campbell and associates in *The American Voter* reported that the family burden of women reduced the vote rate of mothers in childbearing years.[6] Simply put, even at the lowest levels of participation, that of mere voting, concrete restraints resulting from one's adult role have more of an impact on women's political behavior than on men's. Opportunities for political behavior are fewer for adult women who have assumed the roles of wife and mother. For a woman with young children who are her daily responsibility, to vote may require more commitment than that required of a man with young children. He is out in the world; she is at home. He recognizes his duty as citizen and public actor; she recognizes hers as mother/ wife and private actor. He has a built-in baby-sitter; she must hire one or persuade some other family member (mother, father, in-laws, or husband) to baby-sit.

Such role restraints are traditionally cited to explain the lesser voting rates of women. Experience in the United States, however, suggests that at the level of political behavior which only entails voting, these role obstacles—the immediate prior antecedent factors—are surmountable for women. Facts indicating this are: (a) women in the past two elections have voted in numbers comparable to men (presumably without any overwhelming increase in the number of baby-sitters); and (b) a more recent study of five national elections between 1956 and 1972 has revealed that "fatherhood enhances vote turnout of younger men while motherhood does not affect the voting rate of younger women."[7]

It is when we look at more intense and extensive political participation that adult role restraints, inherent particularly in the role of mother, become significant. It may in fact not require a major alteration in assignment of familial duties to facilitate the woman's receiving time to leave the home to cast a vote, but the difficulties multiply rapidly as her time commitment to political activity becomes greater. A husband who cannot or will not help with the dinner dishes so she can go to an evening meeting is a concrete and real restraint that potentially active women do face. Trivial as this may at first appear to be, it is a situation that men who desire to be politically active do not encounter. If this hindrance alone were to dissuade the woman, one might indeed question her commitment but what of the woman who receives raised eyebrows from her neighbors and friends because she is regularly out to a party caucus while her young children are left to fend for themselves? The normative expectations about what constitutes a "good mother" and the control mechanisms employed to limit activity not normally associated with "good motherhood" can be very severe indeed. The ultimate depth and extent of this problem can be seen in women whose self-image and sense of personal worth have been undermined because they are made to feel that they are "neglecting" their primary responsibilities, husband and children.

"Strain and conflict (internal and external) are the normal result of attempting to combine noncongruent roles, as, for example, wife, mother, and legislator. The culture provides a fairly clear-cut hierarchy of values in which women can make choices and allocate time: children come first, husbands second, careers last, if at all."[8] And so a woman must usually wait to enter politics until her children are older. To achieve substantial and significant power normally requires years of involvement. Since women with young children often delay the beginning of their careers they are less likely to achieve real power. Some women, political achievers and revolutionaries, for instance, may be so intensely committed to the public realm that they can countenance the social disapproval of being labelled a "bad mother" in order to be politically active. Such a restraint does not arise for men, and male political achievers may indeed need less of a commitment; it is difficult, if not impossible, to estimate the number of potential female activists who are in the ranks of those who cannot or will not accept the possibility of being labelled a bad wife or mother.

Additionally, adult role imperatives which dictate to the vast majority of women that their primary orientation should be to marriage and family mean that careers in the legal profession —the primary path to politics and activism for males—are either not considered by women, or are considered a secondary commitment which only follows on settlement of primary ones. The geographic mobility of most women is dependent on their husbands, thus inhibiting their ability to move to areas of greater opportunity for involvement. Local political activity becomes for them the pivotal arena. Even there active women may be forced to interrupt their political careers because of the need to move elsewhere with their husbands.

The list of internal and external role constraints which must be overcome by women and which are not even remotely familiar to men could be added to greatly. In general, however, we argue that these class IV variables are only marginally determinant of adult political behavior. These variables only become pertinent long after basic sex-role perceptions and value commitments have developed. It is these latter factors which determine whether or not one will vote or be politically active. The beliefs and predispositions learned about the more basic orientations will weight how the individual will perceive the cost of actions. An activist woman for whom politics has become salient will not find that lack of a baby-sitter, uncooperative husband, or young children are sufficient to keep her from voting or possibly even from running for an office. The cost to her of not engaging in the behavior may be too high. The relative importance of these adult commitments may mediate the type of participation she may undertake; but they are not likely to negate completely an activist orientation. Conversely, for a woman with a very traditional female sex-role perception for whom politics has not become particularly important, the mere threat of rain might be sufficient to keep her away from the ballot box.

Although the situations immediately prior to one action or another (class IV) are not basically determinant, they do have an additive, cumulative effect on the already socialized self. A person's occupation and social position outside the family can have and usually do have a major impact on one's substantive interests and intensity of political views. Middle-class men do have a different type of cognitive life than lower-class men or women and most middle-class women.

> Insight into the political ramifications of complex social problems comes partly from education but, more importantly, from social experiences flowing from one's work. The daily dealings of upper occupational groups with legal, economic and technical problems [enables their members to] develop understanding of social and political processes and problems. The daily life of lower class men and of housewives does not. The lower class as compared to the middle class, and women as compared to men, have a deeper isolation from extra-familial concerns and activities and are resultingly less involved in the larger culture. For example, membership in the types of voluntary associations which have a positive effect on political activity is more frequent among the middle class than the working class. It also seems likely that the non-political organizations joined by middle class women will contain fewer politically interested persons than the organizations of middle class men.[9]

Once these differences in adults are noted, we are still left with explaining why they occurred to begin with. We are right back to attempting to identify those variables which led to the individual becoming the adult he or she is, back to the classes of variables specified by I and II and the interaction they have with the variables in III.

Box III. The Adult Human Being

Box III contains several subgroups of variables which separately and together have been used to explain female nonparticipation in political life: variables on the biological self, personality traits and dispositions, and the socioeconomic self.

The biological nature of humans has given rise to a variety of theories of human behavior. Because most of these theories place women in a subordinate, nonparticipating role, they have a special significance for our study. In terms of efforts to explain women's role or lack of it in producing social change, four broad biologically based theories are relevant: (1) those which attribute special abilities to one category of humankind over another because of anatomical, hormonal, or genetic differences; (2) those which emphasize reproductive vitality and degeneration; (3) those which rest on supposed natural instincts; and (4) those which stress the genius of exceptional individuals as the main forces of change.

Men and women differ from each other anatomically, hormonally, and genetically. These gender differences have led to sharply different perceptions of appropriate sex roles, identities, and, according to some, to different psychological categories of human beings.

The anatomical differences in size, reproductive organs, and physical strength have given rise to the "weaker sex" theories. Although these theories start with the fact that males tend to be physically stronger than females and hence ought to protect (or dominate) them, some theories have gone further than this. Herbert Spencer, for example, argued that the anatomical differences between the sexes and their differential rates of growth led to innate differences in intelligence. Because females grow faster on the average than males, and mature physically earlier, Spencer asserted that over time females developed a less complex and evolved brain, and that therefore their capacity for thinking abstractly and for logical analysis was sharply less than that of males.[10]

Doctors in the nineteenth century also saw a relationship between the female body and intellectual ability. In 1875 a Dr. E. A. Clarke in *Sex in Education* insisted that intense mental effort by women damaged their reproductive capacities, and that higher education for women thus endangered the human species.[11] Although Clarke did not declare that women were incapable of equal levels of intellectual activity, as Spencer did, it was just as devastating. Who would want to endanger the human species? Three-fourths of a century later Margaret Mead reversed this "weaker sex" argument. In *Male and Female* she agreed that aggressive, competent, and intellectually equal females could threaten societal reproduction. The consequent loss of the sense of superiority and dominance could lead to the sexual impotence of males which, in turn, would lead to a lowered reproduction rate for the species.[12] Although Mead's writings were known among academic circles, the opinions of the well-known baby care doctor, Benjamin Spock, were more widespread. He is quoted as saying, "Biologically and temperamentally, I believe women were made to be concerned first and foremost with child care, husband care, and home care."[13] Although his opinion has since changed, Spock for many years insisted that education only "confuses" women about their appropriate role and function in society.

None of the weaker-sex views have received acceptance among social scientists. Obvious deficiencies are the lack of empirical evidence to substantiate them and quite extensive contrary evidence. Maccoby and Jacklin, for example, in their extensive and comprehensive 1974 review of reported research findings on how the sexes differ found no support for the view that males and females differ in their overall intellectual abilities, analytic cognitive styles, or learning processes. Sex differences that have been definitely related to intellectual activity are the following: (a) girls have greater verbal ability than boys; (b) boys excel in visual-spatial ability; and (c) boys excel in mathematical ability. The variations in mathematical and verbal ability do not seem to be related to genetic determiners, however, while those found for visual-spatial abilities do seem to be.[14] In addition to the lack of evidence for "weaker sex" arguments based on genetic differences, the arguments themselves indicate the basic confusion behind naturalist explanations. If it is natural for females to be the weaker sex and to be less capable intellectually, then no amount of education ought to diminish this tendency.

Hormonal differences between the sexes also constitute sources for beliefs about the inferiority of women and for justification for excluding women from performing specific societal roles. As already noted, Dr. Berman questioned the suitability of women for high political office. The *San Francisco Chronicle* quotes Berman as saying: "Suppose we had a President in the White House, a menopausal woman President who had to make the decision of the Bay of Pigs. All things being equal, I would still have had a male JFK make the Cuban missile crisis decisions than a female of similar age who could possibly be subject to the curious mental aberrations of that age group."[15]

The various endocrine glands—the pituitary, thyroid, pancreas, and gonads (ovaries and testes)—produce the chemical substances called hormones. These substances control metabolism, primary sex characteristics, and growth rates. Whether or not they also produce particular personality characteristics, such as aggressiveness or mental aberrations, is unknown and the subject of great controversy. Some evidence exists indicating that "The injection of testosterone (the male hormone) in nonhumans increases aggressive behavior."[16] Furthermore, "Male monkeys which are at the top of the dominance hierarchies in their colonies tend to have the highest levels of testosterone."[17] Nonetheless, most scientists seem to have concluded that aggressiveness in animals is due to external stimuli and hunger needs, not to innate drives and instincts of aggression per se.[18] Psychologists generally conclude that aggressiveness in humans is a response to frustration, to the blocking of needs or goal-oriented behavior. Anthropologists like Margaret Mead have described societies where females are either as overtly aggressive as males or even more aggressive.[19]

Dr. Berman's pessimistic view of women's political capabilities stemmed from his interpretation of the effects of cyclical changes in estrogen levels and the positive-negative emotional states these changes produce in women. Studies do show that low estrogen levels can produce depression, anxiety, irritability, and aggressiveness in women,[20] but studies also show comparable effects on males when their androgen levels decline.[21] Moreover, studies of women in different societies and under varying circumstances reveal that the hormonal changes are probably not as critical in determining mood changes as psychological states related to role options. Yorburg's description of the findings of these studies is worth quoting here in full.

Women in nonliterate societies apparently did not experience premenstrual tension or postmenopausal depression (when estrogen levels decline), although in industrial societies both phenomena have been found in a variety of cultures. Postmenopausal depression is very closely related to role loss in industrial societies—the loss of the mother role, particularly, after the youngest child has left home. In traditional societies (nonliterate and agricultural) this role was not lost because adult children were not likely to move away from the village or family compound. The care of grandchildren in the days from the extended family was an important obligation of the middle-aged woman, an obligation that occupied her for the remainder of her relatively short life-span. In modern, industrialized society, women who are gainfully employed or who are otherwise very active and committed to nonfamily enterprises, are less apt to experience postmenopausal depression than women who live more traditional lives.[22]

In sum, although hormonal differences certainly do exist between the sexes, no firm evidence exists indicating that these hormonal variations are the primary determinants of personality traits and behaviors.

In her search for the sources of social change, Betty Yorburg concluded that studies of human genetics are also of small assistance.[23] The chief genetic difference between male and female, according to her, is the presence of the XX (female) versus the XY (male) chromosomes. The second X chromosome appears to provide females with protection against diseases, malnutrition, other forms of physical deprivation, and against being the transmitter of genetically caused defects. Genetic differences seem to be linked to the personality traits of aggression and passivity. Studies have reported that a slightly higher proportion of males who are violently aggressive have an extra Y chromosome (chromosome pattern XYY).[24] "Researchers have also reported greater passivity and lower virility in males who have sex chromosomes X, X, and Y."[25]

While these findings obviously need to be investigated further, we must keep in mind that most aggressive men, criminals and others, have normal chromosome patterns. We also must remember that, although the anatomical and genetic differences might be ostensibly useful in "explaining" the historical nonparticipation of women in politics, they offer little insight into why women are active, participating, and aggressive beings in the twentieth century. Presumably, the anatomy and the hormonal and genetic composition of women have remained essentially stable. No proof exists that the female of the species has had major evolutionary biological changes or mutations that can possibly explain her altered status and behavior. In addition, it is far from clear that in human societies aggressiveness is as important for political behavior as personality characteristics such as competitiveness, striving for dominance, self-esteem, need for achievement, and other factors which have not been found to be genetically related to sex. Moreover, with regard to aggression, it has been found that, although females aggress against others less than males, "they do not yield or withdraw when aggressed against anymore frequently than males do."[26] When leadership is achieved as the result of performance and skill rather than as the result of seizure by physical force, the greater aggressiveness of males ought not handicap females.

The traditional split between the male and female worlds has given rise to other views of how the instincts of each differ. Women are said to have a weak sex instinct, a weak instinct for aggression, and a strong maternal instinct. Traditionally males have been said to have instincts opposite those of women. With regard to the supposed differences in sex instincts, cross-cultural research has revealed that even historically not all cultures have held the same views. For example, in the Arab world women were considered to have stronger sex drives than men.[27] The supposedly greater instinct of human females for nurturance and "maternal" behavior has not been confirmed by direct empirical evidence either. Cross-cultural studies do show that "aggression is largely incompatible with child care, and that the process of caring for children moderates aggressive tendencies [even in males]."[28] But no data support the view that there is hormonal priming of females to a more nurturant role. The fact that the female gives birth and historically has breast-fed her child has meant that the child-caring role has been a female one. While there is obviously a biological connection, it is not at all clear that being female means that one is "maternal" and naturally desires children and a nurturing role.

It is evident that most supposed instinctual differences between the sexes do not explain basic behavior differences which occur in society. When the same instinctual drive can be attributed to both sexes or be used to explain the same and different types of behavior for both sexes, then clearly the naturalness of the "natural" instinct and its linkage to one of the sexes is non-existent. Indeed, several decades of research have not only challenged these popular views of instinctual differences between the sexes, but have also led to the denial that innate instincts really exist.

The confusion manifest in the area of instinctual drives requires that much more research be done to learn how personality traits associated with masculinity and femininity are related to anatomical, hormonal, and genetic differences. Until there is some manner in which to be able consistently to predict and anticipate behavioral differences between the two sexes on the basis of these factors, they will remain speculative, polemical weapons used to "explain" everything, even the most contradictory of phenomena.

We also have no evidence indicating that politically active women are geniuses or an exceptional subcategory of females. Some students of social change (e.g., Thomas Carlyle, Gaetano Mosca, Vilfredo Pareto, Robert Michels, Arnold Toynbee, and John Stuart Mill) have attributed unique initiating powers to specific individuals or social subcategories. These theories have usually excluded women as being part of the "creative" and "innovating" elite. The theories have applicability to our discussion of social change essentially only to the extent that they have been popularized to justify the position that women engaging in political behavior are somehow "exceptional" personalities or persons of unique genius or genetic composition. This view provides a supposedly reasonable basis for arguing that women of achievement are indeed the exception to the rule, and not viable role models for children. Illustrations of the efforts taken to maintain this view include the Greek hetaerae. These women were the only ones in ancient Greek society who were given high status with males. But they were foreigners, prisoners of war, or abandoned Greek girls. Special training was instituted to make them accomplished in the arts, philosophy, and general knowledge of their times. The purpose of the training was to provide interesting and stimulating social and sexual companionship to the privileged Greek males. The "abnormality" of their origins, however, fostered the view that it was impossible for most Greek women to become like them. Indeed, the prevailing beliefs about the hetaerae were such that almost no self-respecting Greek woman would want herself or her daughters to become like them. Once again we have evidence in this illustration of the basic flaw in all the strictly biological deterministic arguments. There is absolutely no foundation for supposing that the hetaerae were anatomically, hormonally, or genetically different from other women. Certainly an environmentalist explanation of the differences between the hetaerae and the ordinary Greek woman would make more sense than some speculative assessment of organic differences.

Before leaving the discussion of biological theories it is

worth stressing one aspect of female existence that does give some empirical foundation to the "weaker sex" theories. Until the twentieth century there was an extreme paucity of knowledge about medicine in general and female sexuality and gynecology in particular. This ignorance had serious consequences for women's health. In the middle of the nineteenth century Catherine Beecher stated that "the *standard of health* among American women is so low few have a correct idea of *what a healthy woman is*."[29] The topic of female invalidism was prevalent throughout the century. Beecher noted: "In my wide circle of friends and acquaintances all over the land out of my family circle, the same impression is made. In Boston I cannot remember but one married female friend who is perfectly healthy. In Hartford, Conn., I can think of only one. In New Haven, but one. In Brooklyn, N.Y., but one. In New York City, but one. In Cincinnati, but one. In Buffalo, Cleveland, Chicago, Milwaukee, Detroit, those whom I have visited are either delicate or invalids. I am not able to recall, in my immense circle of friends and acquaintances all over the Union, so many as *ten* married ladies born in this century and country, who are perfectly sound, healthy, and vigorous."[30] The women Beecher was speaking about were generally of the upper and middle classes. Lower-class women often did not have the luxury of invalidism. If a woman worked, it was a minimum of ten hours a day with at best a half hour off for meals. Once her work day was finished, she could go home to clean, wash, cook, to be mother and wife. No wonder such women were said to have little or no aggressiveness or sex instinct!

Medical ignorance, high birth rates, and high death rates might well have contributed to keeping most women out of public life. If so, the historical lack of political participation of women might well have some physiological rather than biological foundation. The industrial, technological, and medical advances of the late nineteenth and early twentieth centuries produced the means needed for the masses of women to move beyond constant concern with physiological problems. Some of the startling changes that have occurred in the lives of women since 1900 can be seen from the following statistics: in the late 1800s the average mother had five or six children and several stillbirths and/or miscarriages; in the 1970s the average mother has two or three children and almost no stillbirths or miscarriages. Today's American woman also does not usually work hard physically immediately before and after childbirth as previously. The improved water supplies, the development of polio, measles, and other vaccines, pure food and drug laws, wonder drugs such as penicillin, balanced diets, and generally better housing and medical care have also sharply reduced the physical strain mothers suffered just to keep their children alive. Substantially fewer women today bury their offspring, removing another major source of physical and psychological debilitation.[31] The institutionalization of education for children until their mid-teen years in most western societies has further reduced the physical and emotional burdens of motherhood. The number of days per year that mothers need to supervise their children is also minimal now compared to past centuries. One could also add that the physical burdens of keeping a house have diminished enormously.

On the basis of our review of biological theories attempting to explain women's role in society we must conclude that reliable and valid empirical evidence supporting a biologically deterministic view of sex roles is nonexistent. The evidence that does exist tends rather to support the conclusion that the state of human knowledge about biology is more determinative of expectations and behavior than the biology itself. The biology and physiology of women appear to have no direct effect on female potential for political behavior once basic control over their physical health and their life-space is obtained. Because most women in advanced industrialized, urbanized societies have by the 1970s attained at least the option of exercising personal control over their bodies, we can no longer look to either biological or physiological differences to explain sex variations in political participation. Within these nations, furthermore, because of the large numbers of women now active publicly and politically, explanations for the behavior of political women can no longer rest upon the view that such participants are "exceptional," "abnormal," or special geniuses. To account for them in this way would be to assert the existence of a new category of super beings. We believe more earthly, comprehensible theories for this social change are available.

Another important component of Box III, The Adult Human Being, involves personality traits, processes, and dispositions. The differences between the male and female societal roles have given rise to the view that males ought to be masculine and females ought to be feminine. In the biologically deterministic view sex roles and personality traits are directly determined by gender. Differences in personality between the sexes have typically been said to be as follows: feminine personalities are more passive rather than aggressive; they are dependent, conforming, obedient, suggestible, nurturing to others, sympathetic and empathetic to others, highly verbal, more sociable, more popularity- than achievement-oriented, and sexually restrained. Masculine personalities are said to be the opposite.

As already noted, Maccoby and Jacklin's exhaustive review of reported studies of sex differences did not find personality traits, other than aggressiveness, to be biologically based. But the stereotypes remain and must be addressed.

The thrust of the biologically based theories, the "weaker sex" theories derived from them, and even the more sophisticated Freudian theories, is that the personality characteristics of "normal women" tend toward masochism, passivity, vanity, jealousy, submissiveness, and a limited sense of justice. Of particular interest for this study of political women, the "normal woman" is said to have less of a superego than a "normal man," to be less capable of sublimation, and to be less concerned about social issues and problems. From the start, then, according to these theories, we are informed that any type of political woman must have abnormal or at least atypical personality characteristics. At the minimum these characteristics include independence, assertiveness, a sense of justice, the ability to make moral and independent political judgments, and at least a reasonable ability to engage in abstract, theoretical thinking.

Although research on personality traits of males and females is now receiving great emphasis in the fields of psychology and sociology, the literature on the formation of personality traits leading one to politics almost totally comprises studies of males. Thus the literature of the psychology of politics is not helpful because it has ignored women. Scholars following the Maslowian human development "self-actualization" school of thought, such as Jeanne Knutson,[32] have devoted almost no attention to female political behavior. The index of Knutson's book contains entries for neither "sex," nor "females," nor "women." The most that political psychologists have done to date on the subject of women is to note, like Greenstein, that "an adequate theory must account for the psychological underpinnings of political sex differences, understood in terms of sex roles in the society, how they develop, and what maintains them."[33]

Much of the political science literature treating personality as an important variable has stressed the Freudian psychoanalytic approach.[34] Although it seems reasonable on the surface to assume that this approach would add insights to our knowledge of social change by providing knowledge of how the nontypical political women developed, we have found that it does not. According to Freud, the path to normal womanhood begins with the pre-Oedipal recognition by little girls that their clitoris, their "little penis," is a totally useless organ in any love relationship with their mothers. Equally important, with this recognition of the "castration" of the "little penises," little girls must choose whether to renounce or pursue the pleasure of masturbating their clitorises.[35] As Juliet Mitchell puts it:

> After her recognition of castration, the girl has three courses open to her, only one of which is "normal." With her self-love already shattered by her "lack," her hostility to the mother (who was supposed to be phallic but who was discovered to be likewise castrated) can make her turn from women and womanhood altogether; in which case, debasing and despising women, as men do, she is liable to become inhibited and neurotic. Or she can refuse to abandon the pleasures of her clitoris; if so, she remains at the pre-Oedipal "masculine" phase. Finally, if by exploiting her passive instinctual impulses—that is, the passive aims of her sexual drive—she can transfer her sexual attentions from her mother to her father, she can want first his phallus, and then by the all-important analogy, his baby, then the man again, to give her this baby. Thus she becomes a little woman. This transference from mother to father is the girl's "positive" Oedipus complex and, as it is the first correct step on her path to womanhood, there is no need for her to leave it.[36]

Although what follows is an oversimplification, Freud's discussion of the psychological development of the normal woman leads to the "logical" deduction that to be an "abnormal," politically active woman, one would have to be either neurotic or someone who never stopped masturbating her clitoris. Needless to say, it would be difficult to base a research project on this type of premise! Additionally, such an approach makes so many negative assumptions about politically active women that it is doubt-ful that at the end of the study the most "objective" scholar could conclude such activity is normal. The normative bias is so great in the premises of Freudian analysis and the empirically substantiable propositions so few that in this area it does not ap-pear to hold any independent value. As Roy Schaffer has pointed out in the *Journal of the American Psychoanalytic Association:*

> Freud was clearly not appreciating two factors, one being the part played in the girl's development by the example of the *active nurturant mother* who has her own sources of pride and consolation, and the other being the part played by the great variety of positive environmental emphases concerning girls and women. His attention was fixed on the decisive part played in the girl's development by one set of unconscious equations: my lost penis = father's actual penis = the baby given me by father's penis.[37]

In practice, studies linking political behavior to psychoana-lytic theories seldom discuss masturbation or even go back to very early childhood. For example, E. Victor Wolfenstein in his study of three revolutionaries, Vladimir Ilich Ulianov (Nikolai Lenin), Leon Trotsky, and Mahatma Gandhi, outlined a set of propositions about the male revolutionary personality based upon events occurring in the adolescent years. In brief, his prop-ositions are that the revolutionary personality develops as the re-sult of (1) the strain of highly ambivalent father-son relationships exacerbated during adolescence; (2) the son basing his claim to manhood on continuous rebellion against paternal authority; (3) the son directing all hatred against established authority and all love toward the revolutionary brotherhood; and (4) warding off consciousness of the underlying psychological concerns by blending them into an overarching ideology, delineating revolu-tionary identity and goals.[38]

In spite of the reductionist nature of Wolfenstein's research and conclusions, we thought it might be worthwhile to apply the logic of his proposition to the revolutionary women chosen for our project, but in a preliminary study, we found no comparabil-ity. According to Wolfenstein, the male revolutionary develops as the result of sharp exacerbation of natural, common relation-ships that all sons and fathers go through. For daughters to be-come revolutionaries, however, it would seem that they would have to go completely counter to the normal pattern of psychosexual development as the Freudian view describes it. Not only would the process of personality development have to differ from the normal, but also the entire structural pattern of family relationships would have to alter from that described by Freud.

The Freudian theory of female personality development, in spite of much recent feminist opposition and general revision of it, has retained its hold not only in popular thinking but also among numerous psychologists. In 1967 in the *Archives of General Psychiatry,* Leon Salzman noted: "Myths and outworn theories die slowly and reluctantly. The notion that an individual's character structure is bound to biology and that the psychology of the female is largely dependent upon the presence of a female reproductive system belongs to this class of one-sided theories which still dominate a great many notions of female psychology."[39] Whatever the virtues and vices of Freudian theory in general, we had to conclude that it offers no viable theoretical framework for a study of the political socialization of women and their role conflicts.

We assume that, compared to traditional women, politically active women will be more assertive, competitive, concerned with social justice, and more likely to possess personality traits that historically have been considered "masculine." Having made this assumption, however, we do not intend to go further. We are not so much interested in describing and analyzing personality traits in general, but rather in ascertaining if, how, when, and under what conditions an understanding of personality traits and processes helps us to explain adult female political behavior or lack of it. Although we feel an understanding of personality traits is important for understanding politics, this work is not a study of such traits. Our study is concerned with how real political women and political wives developed the traits and behavior patterns they did, not how either their psychology and personalities varied or how women in general vary from each other or from men.

The last major component of Box III, The Adult Human Being, concerns the socioeconomic self. Historically women have received the socioeconomic status of their husbands and fathers. Even in the 1970s the class status of women is not determined primarily by their own behaviors. In the late 1960s less than two percent of all American working women earned more than

$10,000 a year.[40] Obviously if sociologists applied the same criteria to women as they do to men in assessing class and social standing, almost all American females would fall in the lower-middle or lower class.

In spite of the fact that women seldom determine their own class and socioeconomic standing, income and socioeconomic status are critical in determining the scope and type of life-chances a girl-child will have. Historically, women from higher socioeconomic classes have been better educated, better traveled, and have had better health care and, therefore, better health than poorer women; middle-class and, to a lesser extent, upper-class women have also tended to be the chief political participants and promoters of women's liberation. However, since the middle and upper classes have also produced most male political participants, we cannot argue that class status itself is a major determinant of female participation.

Box I. Sociopolitical and Cultural Heritage

Box I refers to one's cultural and sociopolitical heritage that provides the broad environmental framework of a human being's existence. This heritage and the institutions it fosters shape our belief systems, our expectations of what is possible, permissible, and approximate as well as what is materially feasible. The two key aspects of this heritage that have systematically affected the development of political women are the sex-role ideology inherited from our Greco-Judeo-Christian tradition and the type of family institutions this tradition and various types of economies have produced.

Sex-Role Ideological Heritage

In the twenty-five centuries between Classical Greece and the twentieth century the themes of the eternal "woman question" have continually recurred. Almost all these themes, many of which were still believed and espoused in the twentieth century, derive from the philosophies of the ancient Athenian Greeks regarding women and their proper sphere in the social order. Although the realities of women's lives underwent changes due to new economic and social conditions in later centuries, the attitudes and policies formulated by the Greeks toward women (with the addition of Christian doctrines in the later Roman period) withstood all efforts at change and themselves acted as a conservative force to retard the social, economic, and political development of women.

Long before the Greeks, the assemblage of myths had differentiated the nature and functions of the male and female, but under the influence of Greek rationalism this distinction took on a semi-scientific aura of certainty, truth, and justice. The major theses of this Greek doctrine are: (1) males and females are opposite in nature, the reconciliation of which brings order and harmony to society; (2) similarly, the roles of males and females are opposite and complementary in accord with the design of Nature. Society's needs can be divided into two distinct spheres which agree with the nature and capabilities of the two sexes; (3) the Outdoor sphere, comprising heavy labor, military activity, and deliberation over the protection and livelihood of the society, is assigned to the male, while the Indoor sphere, where less strength but a greater share of love and nurture is required, is relegated to the female; (4) the Outdoor nature of the male makes it appropriate for him to engage in the Public, political, visible, and official activities of his society; woman's Indoor nature excludes her from the above and places her in the Private, publicly invisible functions; (5) the Public sphere, concerned with the survival of the Polis and the freedom of its members, is more dignified and sublime and more important than the Private sphere, which is concerned with the most common of animal needs, the survival of the species—a care of slaves and even beasts; (6) the male is stronger, more courageous, superior; the female weaker, deficient, irrational, inferior.

The value judgments the Greeks put on the roles played in their society by males and females were negative for women. Xenophon believed that the relationship between a husband and wife was one of teacher and pupil, and that even in matters which were under her control and supervision, the husband was more knowledgeable. If the husband taught well and his wife learned well, he would have freedom to do other important things.[41] Aristotle too referred to marriage as a convenient reconciliation between opposite functions with each sex assigned distinct duties to perform. But he made it clear that there is no equality in this division of responsibilities. Again and again in the first book of the *Politics*, Aristotle discussed the inequality of men and women, referring to women as weaker, without authority, and subject to their husbands. The implications of this distinction between the Private and Public levels of life have received notice from Hannah Arendt. In *The Human Condition* she writes: "According to Greek thought, the human capacity for political organization is not only different from but stands in direct opposition to that natural association whose center is the home (*oikia*) and the family."[42] The Greek philosophical heritage says politics, women, and the family do not mix.

The doctrine of the Greeks regarding the Public/Private realms in society, and the value judgment made on the significance of each, contributed strongly to the past and present powerlessness of women to control their lives and to attain full citizenship. Let us use T. H. Marshall's formulation of the essential rights of citizenship[43] as a standard:

Social rights—the right to a modicum of economic welfare and security; the right to share to the full in the social heritage, and to live the life of a civilized being according to the standards prevailing in the society;

Civil rights—liberty of person; freedom of speech, thought, and faith; the right to own property and to conclude valid contracts; the right to justice;

Political rights—the right to vote and the opportunity to hold office.

As citizens Athenian women enjoyed the benefits of the first of these categories of citizenship rights. With regard to the second category, while protected by the laws of the city, women were considered "incompetent" to achieve these privileges on their own behalf. From the third category of rights they were excluded altogether. During her entire lifetime a woman was under the tutelage of a male, a *kyrios* (guardian). This would be her father or another adult male appointed upon the father's death, usually a close relative. On the marriage of the woman the function of *kyrios* was assumed by the husband although the father still retained certain claims, such as over the dowry and the right to terminate the marriage of his former ward. Married usually before reaching the age of seventeen to a man who was usually at least thirty (or in the case of a widower perhaps much older), an Athenian girl would then assume the role which it was believed the gods intended for her—that of providing for the survival of the species. It was commonly suggested by Greek writers that the sole purpose of cohabitation was the begetting of children. The concept of love in marriage was not widely ac-

cepted as significant in antiquity. It is notable that in the most famous Greek work on love, Plato's *Symposium*, there is only one
mention of love between husband and wife. Demosthenes once
categorized women in the following three groups: "wives to bear
us children, courtesans to be our companions, and prostitutes for
our physical needs."[44]

The Greek concept that the political rights of women citizens should be exercised on their behalf by the male members of
their families held steadfast to the early decades of the twentieth century, even in the face of vast social, economic, and
cultural developments which were to modify woman's status in
society in significant ways. The basic motive behind the united
front maintained by western societies against the award of any
privileges which would give women any modicum of self-de-
terminism was the preservation of the family as the one constant
in a world in which other institutions were subject to a multitude
of modifications and fates. This can be seen by the arguments
used in the nineteenth and early twentieth centuries against suffrage. The rhetoric, not only of the big business interests—especially the liquor industry—which had joined forces to defeat
women's suffrage, but also of women of good intentions, was that
the family, the very fabric of society, would be endangered if
women were to enter the voting booth.

Up to this point the philosophical heritage of Plato has not
been discussed. But it is he who espoused in ancient Greece what
has remained throughout history the minority view of what the
appropriate sex-role ideology ought to be. In the fifth book of
the *Republic* Plato develops the argument that the major differences between men and women are that men are generally
stronger and that women bear children. Once this is said, the
individual differences among the members of each sex are so
great that it is absurd to assign tasks merely on the basis of sex.
He suggests that to do so on the basis of hair length would be no
more ridiculous. In keeping with the principle of the *Republic*
that natural ability should determine what one's role in society should be, Plato concludes that women too must be scruti-
nized and placed in occupations where each will function most
effectively. Men and women who have similar natures and abilities should be allowed the same pursuits. Plato, of course, recognized the irreconcilable nature of the Public and Private
realms for women. Therefore, in order to free qualified women

for service to the state, he advocated the abolition of all traditional familial relationships and the establishment of communal
life for those who administer the state, his Guardian class. Only
when freed from the realm of necessity could women participate
in responsible positions of leadership.

Although the ancient Greek philosophies laid the foundations for both the majority and minority sex-role ideologies of
the western world, the effect of Roman tradition added variations to the themes. The open mingling of Roman wives with men
at public festivities and their presence at private social gatherings led to denunciations of them as wanton and indiscreet by
Greek writers. The explanation for this divergence of views on
women's social roles seems to be a difference in attitude toward
the family. In Rome, particularly in Republican times (500-30
B.C.), the social importance of the family was exaggerated by its
political significance. Political partnerships and trade-offs were
frequently embodied by political marriages. A man's success was
generally determined by his wife's family connections as well as
his own. Fathers and husbands alike used their women to influence, persuade, and affect voting policies. Many of these women
became shrewd political analysts of their own accord, but influence was always informal and unofficial. In contrast, the Athe-
nians made every effort to break down the political importance
of the family, requiring that a man be identified by his neighborhood rather than by his kinship. Sociologists refer to the
Athenian male as "family avoidant" in his personal life—preferring the company of courtesans and other men in his social relationships over that of his family.[45]

Relationships between marriage and politics comparable to
those of the Roman era have been noted in American politics. Gore Vidal in an essay on the Adams family referred to the
"commitment of the required hypergamy,"[46] where the male
politician became upwardly mobile and politically more acceptable through marriage. What often seems to occur in American
political marriages is that the men, marrying at the threshold of
their political careers, gain access to money and influence
through their marriage to a woman from a more prestigious family. Historically, in turn, the economically and socially more distinguished family developed access for creating or maintaining
political power. The degree to which this practice is widespread
in the United States and elsewhere is an empirical question. Nev-

ertheless, the use of wife, daughter, a mother, or indeed the whole family for political advancement, is a centuries-old Roman contribution to the western cultural heritage.

Although no gains were made by women in obtaining official public rights in the Roman era, women did make considerable headway in achieving private civil rights—to hold title to property, to make contracts, to sue for divorce. The impact of Roman law on medieval Europe was considerable; and although Germanic tribal customs which maintained the legal incapacity of women prevailed in the early Middle Ages, women's private rights increased during that period under the stimulus of Roman ways.

The breakup of the Roman Empire in the fourth century and the diffusion of new peoples into its former domains brought about an uneasy modification of Roman institutions by a Christian outlook and Germanic tribal conditions. This resulted in an initial decrease in the status of women which later centuries only partially restored. Most significant to a study of the political development of women is the establishment of theological doctrines about the functions and place of women in Christian society.

In theory Christianity offered a new and unique status of spiritual equality to women while in reality it promulgated a patriarchal and male-centered doctrine which provided a justification for women's inferior social, political, and religious status, even to the present day. Constance Parvey has shown that "The later Church . . . inherited two seemingly widely divergent messages: the theology of equivalence in Christ; the practice of women's subordination. In attempting to reconcile them, it maintained a status-quo ethics on the social level through the subordination of women, and it affirmed the vision of equivalence on the spiritual level by projecting it as an otherworldly reality."[47] The epistles of the apostle Paul reflect his Greco-Semitic upbringing at the time of the birth of Christ. He accepted the Hebrew mythology of the creation, holding that while man was made in the image of God, woman was made in the image of man and to be a helpmate to man. He preached that women were to take a subordinate place in the family, subject to the authority of their husbands in all things. Positions of leadership in the new church were to be denied women, as was the right to voice their ideas and feelings in church. He recommended celibacy to those who would spread the new gospel but admitted that marriage was preferable to sin caused by sexual desire.

While Paul's attitudes can be understood as representative of the social institutions of his day, the application of his doctrines to the vastly changed social and economic conditions of later centuries must be viewed as a reactionary vehicle to maintain the status quo. Parvey has recently commented: "These passages have not only had an impact on the later epistles within the New Testament but they have provided the shape for the fundamental religious and social attitudes toward women in both the Eastern and Western churches to the present day. These references have been used as proof texts for explaining why women should be prohibited from priestly and liturgical roles, and they still constitute today a major justification for maintaining women in a subordinate role in the Church and in society at large."[48]

In the thirteenth century, St. Thomas Aquinas called on Greek science in an attempt to provide a scientific, rational basis for Christian doctrine and practice. He accepted the Aristotelian notion that the female was a deficient male and stated that in the reproductive process the female existed only as a passive instrument, the "active" principle being supplied by the male. The female, he argued, is weaker morally as well as physically, a condition resulting from her sexual nature, and is in every aspect inferior and subordinate.[49] Aquinas's low esteem of women led him to reject the view that Mary was the "Mother of God" and that she was immaculately conceived. On this particular point, however, Aquinas was found to be heretical by his own church. Nonetheless, Thomism was adopted as the official Catholic philosophy for centuries.

With the spread of Christian doctrine through medieval Europe, the conditions which had offered women in the Roman world a degree of control over their lives—ease of divorce, control over property and wealth—were subordinated to strict dogma or regulations regarding women's functions in the family and their relationships to their husbands. The only escape was from marriage altogether, to the convents where, free to control their minds and bodies, many women developed into scholars and creative thinkers and writers.

The Renaissance witnessed an increase in material prosperity. This development and the presence of strong female rulers on the thrones of England and Spain and the influence of wise queens on the male rulers in France (where by Salic Law succession was limited to males) necessitated a reconsideration of the role of women in public life. Influenced by the humanism of the Renaissance, many scholars developed more enlightened attitudes toward the mental capabilities of women. Erasmus, the most famous humanist of his day, blended a curious respect for women with a belief in their primitive inferiority. The failure to educate women, he believed, allowed their worst faults—shallowness, vanity, and capriciousness—to go uncorrected, thus rendering them incapable of providing their sons with the proper moral education.[50]

While the literature of the intelligentsia was generally supportive of women and the trend toward their education, in the popular literature of the Elizabethan period there was agitated discussion about the fair sex. That this furor was caused by the increased social status of women is seen by the topics of this literature: the rule of women, the education of women, the position and proper behavior of women, the dress of women, the character of women. The most notorious attack on the rule of women was issued by John Knox in *The First Blast of the Trumpet Against the Monstrous Regiment of Women*. Published during the reign of Mary Tudor, he charged that the rule of woman was "repugnant to nature, contumelie to God, a thing most contrarius to his reveled will and approved ordinance, and finallie it is the subversion of good order."[51] It has long been realized that his attack on Mary was as much in opposition to the rule of a Catholic as to a woman, yet when the Protestant successor, Elizabeth, came to the throne, Knox refused to retract his disapproval unless the queen would admit that her rule was the result of chance circumstance rather than the natural right of a woman. Many came to the defense of Elizabeth, but their arguments are interesting; for example, Bishop Aylmer chose to give his support to Elizabeth by claiming that God sometimes chooses to work through weak instruments.[52] Thus, no major ideological support was forthcoming to help pave the way for the active participation of women in political life. With few exceptions all who entered the debate agreed that it was the plan of the Lord that women be subject to their husbands. Yet, in practice, the paternal authority over upper-class wives and children was weakened as governments extended their powers in an effort to break the strength of the aristocracy.

The late seventeenth century and the eighteenth century were of great moment in the history of women in two strikingly contrastive grounds, both significant for contributing to the emergence of the "modern" woman. First, the model inaugurated by the Renaissance of the Lady, the woman of social grace, freed from the labors of the household and dependent on her husband for support, was embellished and perfected in the court of the French kings at Versailles. Second, from France too radiated the concepts and ideals for which bloody revolutionary wars were to be waged at the end of the eighteenth century. In the nineteenth and twentieth centuries women would demand a share in the rights promised to men as a consequence of those revolutions.

During the seventeenth century the focus of attention of the privileged woman turned increasingly from the household to the social realm. Several factors contributed to this change. The function of the nobility was transformed at this time in the face of the rise of the professional army. No longer serving an important military function, the energies of the aristocracy were increasingly devoted to social functions. The court of Louis XIV at Versailles was the pacesetter in this regard. Increasing numbers of servants, not only among the rich but the middle class as well, gave women greater leisure to pursue their imitation of High Society. Women could more easily divert their attention from their families as homes were built differently, larger and with greater compartmentalization, and often with two stories. This gave women the privacy required to devote hours each day to the toilette. In salons and drawing rooms, undistracted by the needs of her children, a woman could direct her total energy to the life of a Lady of Society, to the endless hours of gossip and idle chatter while her husband joined his male companions in the more masculine pursuits of drinking and gambling.

Among the intellectual elite, status was achieved not only by wealth and the symbol of that wealth, fashion, but also by familiarity with and the ability to discuss the important intellectual issues of the day. Thus, the salon, often hosted by a bright and witty woman, became the center of lively debates on the important and often revolutionary ideas of the great thinkers of the day. The brothers de Goncourt, who wrote a history of woman's increasing influence in the eighteenth century, described her social role in the following passage: "In the language of the age, everything was expressed, no longer in the husband's name but in his wife's. Service was carried on in the woman's name: people went to see Madame, they went to Madame's reception, they dined with Madame, Madame's dinner was served. These were new expressions; their mere existence gives a sufficient idea of the decrease of the husband's authority and the progress of his wife's."[53] Woman's influence and power in the social aspects of western culture had grown steadily since the Renaissance and by the close of the eighteenth century the women of the upper classes were the arbiters of what was fashionable in literature, the arts, and fashion. This status, however, did not alter significantly the prevailing sex-role ideology as it applied to women's place in the home and their exclusion from politics.

While rationalism was an acceptable and desirable trait in the male, the same quality in the female was still seen as unfeminine. Women were warned by Fordyce in his *Sermons to Young Women* that men did not find wit in women attractive and suggested that they emphasize their prettiness and delicacy.[54] Dr. Gregory's *A Father's Legacy to His Daughters* cautioned against a display of reason and intelligence lest it appear to threaten men's superiority.[55] Rousseau gave authority to such views in his treatise on education, *Émile*. Although he saw how the true nature of men was cruelly constrained and imprisoned by tradition, social mores, and institutions, he believed that the established status and function of women was the "natural" one. Their subjugation and subordination to men were not repressive but "romantic." His attitudes, like those of Freud, Spock, and other "scientists" of later centuries, reflected those of Xenophon and Aristotle: males and females are opposites, but complementary; the male is active, the female passive; the male powerful and rational, the female weak and without reason. Influenced by Pauline doctrine, Rousseau believed that women existed to serve, please, console, and nurture men. Like Dr. Spock of the twentieth century, Rousseau warned women against developing their minds rather than adhering purely to the practical, "a woman of wit is the scourge of her husband, her children, her friends, her servants, of everybody. In the sublime elevation of her fine genius, she disdains all the duties of woman."[56]

The intellectual fervor and political activism of the eighteenth century did not fail to elicit the reaction and participation of women. In England and on the Continent women played an important role in the cultivation not only of sociability but of ideas as well. The women of the salons heard, challenged, and won the respect of the greatest minds of the era. In England these women intellectuals were called "bluestockings." They frequently educated themselves and supervised the intellectual training of their daughters. Most of the bluestockings deferred to the traditional definition of femininity and woman's role, encouraging education for the edification of high moral character and the development of sensibility. A few, like Mary Astell and Catherine MacCauley Graham, believed in the true equality of males and females and called for the reordering of society. They held that once equal educational opportunities were achieved for women, barriers to women's participation in public and political life would be removed.

Although the bluestockings in England knew their place, in France many of the intellectual women of the salons translated their theories and ideas into political action when the revolution broke out. They joined in an uneasy alliance with the women of the masses to win liberty for all. They expected not only to share equally in the fruits of the labor but to share the labor as well. Willing and expecting to assume functions of active duty and leadership, they were distressed (as were young American women during the Civil Rights movement in the 1960s) to find that French men expected them to serve the revolutionary cause in supportive, traditional female roles, but not in leadership or combat.

When the National Assembly was formed in 1789 and it became clear that the rights of women were not to be increased, revolutionary feminists went before the Assembly and condemned their representatives: "You have destroyed all the prejudices of the past, but allow the oldest and the most pervasive to remain, which excludes from office, position and honor, and above all from the right of sitting amongst you, half the inhabitants of the kingdom."[57] A major leader of these feminists, Olympe de Gouges, wrote the *Declaration of Rights of Women and Citizens* in response to the insensitivity of the revolutionary leaders to the needs of women. A strong statement on the natural right to share in all the privileges and responsibilities of public life, it demanded access to employment, public office, and decision-making for women. She and other feminists who continued to oppose the revolutionary leadership were fated to die by the guillotine. In 1792 French law gave the franchise to all adult males except servants. Political expression on the part of women continued to be deemed unnatural.

Women in America too found their hopes for political freedom dashed by the conservative sex-role ideology of the revolutionary leaders. The Declaration of Independence stated that all men were created equal. Though men often argue that the word "man" subsumes "woman," political history clearly belies the assertion. The restriction of the franchise in the Constitution of 1789 to white, propertied males was retained until the Fourteenth and Fifteenth amendments gave the right to vote and political freedom to black males. These amendments, though referring to "persons" (the Fourteenth) and "citizens" (the Fourteenth and the Fifteenth), were ruled by the U.S. Supreme Court as not applying to women. Only in 1920 did American women receive the right to vote. French women were not enfranchised until 1945.

In the 1800s industrialization and urbanization became intensified. Women and men both were forced into new economic roles. More and more women became educated. One might expect that the changes would have had an immediate impact upon the progress of women to achieve full status as human beings in western societies. However, as long as any culture can adjust and compensate for serious attacks on its stability and traditions, it will do so, and revolution can usually be avoided. Victorian society of the nineteenth century responded to the changing conditions of the day with the creation of a Cult or Ideal of Womanhood which on the surface glorifies women and women's role, while at the same time serving to keep most women subordinate and in their place.[58] The dynamics and/or origin of such cults and ideals are not fully understood, but it is clear that women are either the initiators or full advocates of their development. In the nineteenth century the Victorian ideal of woman evolved—chaste, pious, subordinate, delicate, modest, genteel, and domestic. Care for the home and children assumed an importance which it never had before in the history of the family. The true irony of this is that with the help of hired servants and the availability of manufactured products homemaking was easier than it had ever been.[59]

The Cult of True Womanhood served not only to rationalize middle-class life for women but also to stave off any threat to the traditional family by the presence of large numbers of working women in the factories. The continued propagation of the doctrine that woman's place is in the home created tensions between working men and women, between working women and their families, and ambivalent feelings about their proper role in working women themselves.

In a totally different direction, ideal societies were proposed and utopian communities established in which the traditional attitudes about women were replaced by claims to sexual, social, and economic equality. In the United States the followers of Robert Owen founded their community, New Harmony, in Indiana. Promising women equality, they were able to attract feminists like Frances Wright to join them. Owen's son led a successful campaign at the Indiana Constitutional Convention in 1850 to insert provisions for married women's ownership of property. Another feminist, author Margaret Fuller, frequently visited Brook Farm, a transcendentalist commune which later turned to Fourierism, a community "system" in which the family was viewed as fostering and forcing unnatural relationships.

These attempts to find the perfect society were eventually overshadowed by Marxism. Marx too had a solution for oppressed women, and men as well—a communal society run for and by the workers of the world. In his identification of the cause of oppression of women, in his views on private property and the family, Marx was a successor to Plato. Their respective solutions, though both claiming to provide for the liberation of women, were radically different. Plato would institutionalize an intellectual elite while Marx called for an end to elitism altogether.

Socioeconomic and technological changes clearly produced conflict between the dominant Greco-Judeo-Christian sex-role ideology and the changing life situations of women in the western world. While the forces of modernization came to be hailed as virtuous for the development of males, making them into "modern men," care was taken in most countries to restrict the impact of these forces upon women. Studies of the position of women in various western countries in the twentieth century clearly reveal the critical importance of sex-role ideology.

Gail Warshofsky Lapidus in her article entitled "Modernization Theory and Sex Roles in Critical Perspective" stresses that modernization is not a systemic process, in which change in one or more sectors induces interrelated changes in all other segments of the social system. "These evolutionary and systemic assumptions, the legacy of the imagery of the 19th century biological sciences, have distorted the analysis of social change more generally and of its effect on women's roles as well."[60] She concludes, "the Soviet experience suggests that the character of the development process, rather than the fact of development per se, is decisive in shaping women's roles. Cultural norms and political choices and capabilities become more significant than socioeconomic determinants. Both the desire and the capability to alter existing societal arrangements become central."[61]

Alexander Groth has reported the strong relationship between the political ideologies underlying social movements and governments and their connections with the options for women. He writes: "The political orientation of a regime is frequently more important in determining the woman's place in her society than is economic development. Japan under the rule of the militarists and Germany under the rule of the Nazis provide striking examples of social systems in which high levels of industrialization and modernization were combined with the relegation of women to inferior status. In both countries, the autocracies managed to reverse previous trends under parliamentary regimes in the 1920s and reverse them despite the continuing, even accelerated, progress of economic development, industrialization and urbanization."[62]

As Groth notes, the more authoritarian, politically conservative ideologies tend to stress the subordinate role and status of women. Nazism, for example, was instrumental in reversing progress German women had made during the Weimar Republic. Under Nazism and the "Kinder-Küche-Kirche" philosophy the sex-roles were sharply segregated; and as Yorburg points out, "In the labor camps and in youth organizations, girls were taught the age-old peasant virtues and values—obedience, hard work, service to males, and, now, service to the state."[63]

In Spain during the Franco regime the established Catholic Church and the politically conservative Fascist government reaffirmed the traditional status of women. Even as of 1974, the law forbade young women to leave their fathers' homes except to get married or become nuns. Moreover, a married woman could not "hold a job, open a bank account, apply for a passport, sign a legal contract, or obtain legal custody of her children without her husband's written permission."[64]

Socialist movements have tended to take the Platonistic view that women are equal to men. In the countries where socialists have had power this ideology has led to legislation promoting political, legal, and economic equality. According to Yorburg:

> Where socialist governments have made systematic attempts to abolish formal religion, the changes in the roles of men and women have been the most rapid and most dramatic, particularly among the young in urban areas and regardless of the strength of preexisting religious and philosophical orientation.[65]

We must add, however, that in many socialist countries such as the Soviet Union a retrenchment has occurred over time with regard to the role of women. Legislation alone is insufficient to produce women's liberation.

Our review of the Greco-Judeo-Christian sex-role ideological heritage and the political status of women leads us to conclude that for the masses of females, cultural and political norms are not only essential environmental determinants of their political development, but the means of their having personal control over their life-space. The Industrial Revolution has been critical for women because it has provided the needed economic, material, and technological base for gaining such control. But studies show that a cultural belief system supporting the movement of women from the private realm to the public realm is also an absolute prerequisite if politically active women are to develop. In essence, the beliefs humans hold about themselves, the social order, and their ability to change that order are major factors determining individual behavior and reactions to objective reality and social myths. Values that have recently given rise to new definitions of womanhood are secularism, which replaces religious control over human affairs with human control over it; humanism, which gives dignity to all persons, regardless of sex; egalitarianism, which stresses the equality of all; rationalism, which questions tradition and stereotypical thinking; and individualism of human personalities, regardless of sex. These values and beliefs, although affected by the underlying material and technological bases of societies, have a clearly liberating effect upon human behavior.

The Box I variables are critical to the study of political women because the sociopolitical and cultural heritage which they reveal largely determine the legal, educational, economic, and political opportunities that will be available to women. For most women throughout history the effects of the sociopolitical and cultural heritage have been so powerful that even the thought of participating in the political system as a competitive, independent actor never really occurred to them. But for a minority of women in history the minority sex-role ideology à la Plato was the heritage received. It was this group that led the feminist causes and sought political participation. This minority has obviously increased substantially in the twentieth century. In our search to discern why, we found the most plausible answer in the interrelationship between socioeconomic change and the family, the institution which historically has defined the place and role of women.

The Family and Political Women

The technological and economic foundation of our society and the striving of the masses for equality of condition, status, and experience, rest upon industrialization. The mass production needed to provide sufficient goods and services to meet basic human needs and human "wants" did not exist before the Industrial Revolution. Although this material foundation has ramifications as important for the lives of men as women, the effect of industrialization upon the family has had the greatest impact on the lives of women. As Thompson has noted, "Each stage in industrial differentiation and specialization struck also at the family economy, disturbing customary relations between man and wife, parents and children, and differentiating more sharply between 'work' and 'life.'"[66] This disturbing of the family has given rise to several different types of families in terms of the role and status of women.

An important study of these changes was reported in *The Symmetrical Family* in 1973 by Michael Young and Peter Willmott. It is the proportionate increase in what Young and Willmott call the "Stage 3" family[67] that enables us to understand the development of political women in the twentieth century.

During the preindustrial period the family was a unit of production. Men, women, and children worked together in the home and field. The male was the unchallenged center of authority, even though the domestic economy, like the peasant economy, supported a way of life that made the home and the woman within it central. Subordinate, often beaten, usually illiterate, and a legal minor, the woman of the Stage 1 preindustrial family worked with her spouse, but seldom was considered equal to him.

The Stage 2 family arose with the wage economy; the family as the unit of production for society was torn asunder, as men, women, and children alike were pulled by the factory bell from the home, away from each other. As the nuclear family unit was disrupted, the ties between husband and wife weakened, while the ties between mother and daughter were strengthened. According to some scholars on the history of the family,[68] the extended family with its stress on the female ties was fostered by women as a defense against their lowered status in the Stage 2 family. The men still ruled in the public realm and controlled the finances, even those monies earned by the women. In contrast to the Stage 1 type of family, however, the individual wage earner was stressed, not the family as a collective unit of production. The life-space of men and women began to differ even more sharply than in Stage 1. Alienation from spouses, the home, and families grew for males as well as alienation from work. According to Young and Willmott, the extended family (consisting of different generations and family members additional to parents and children) of this period can be viewed as a type of trade-unionism for women. Sisters, grandmothers, and aunts could provide the insurance needed when the woman was ill, when she or her husband was earning too little money, when the children needed care or supervision while the mother needed to work. Men during this period did not usually help with "women's work." The Stage 2 family was a disrupted family where the battle of the sexes was common.

The Stage 3 family is a development essentially of the twentieth century. This family, called by some "the symmetrical family," indicates a return to the family as a collective unit in the economy. Instead of being a collective unit of production, however, it has now become a collective unit of consumption. This type of family is, like the Stage 1 family, centered around the home, particularly while the children are young. Also like the

Stage 1 family, it is nuclear rather than an extended family. The husband and wife are the linkages, and not the grandmothers, mothers, and daughters. Isolated from the trade-unionism type of supports that the extended family gives, the husband and wife of the Stage 3 family must rely on each other. Sex roles become less segregated. Both husband and wife earn money; both raise the children; both participate in decision-making; and both perceive a basic human equality between the sexes and their roles. This is not to assert that the Stage 3 family assumes a complete similarity in sex roles. The roles are not identical, but rather symmetrical. It is not a unisex family; it is a family based upon companionate love, mutual esteem and respect, and assumptions of equality of human needs, desires, and aspirations. It is a type of family that seems to have been most rare in history. We believe it is this type of family (and the societies which allow and encourage such families to develop) that permit the girl-child to develop her full human potential. It is this type of family that is likely to perpetuate what was historically the minority sex-role ideology of equality between the sexes.

All three of these types of families have surely existed throughout history; indeed, there are undoubtedly other types of families as well. The point we wish to make is that the proportion of the families at each of these stages at various times in history has varied substantially. Young and Willmott stress strongly that it is only in the twentieth century that the proportion of Stage 3 families has been sufficiently large to have an effect upon the society as a whole. We think their substantial increase is directly related to the increase in the number of political women appearing in the twentieth century.

We anticipate that each of these family types will have different sex-role ideologies and will socialize their girl-children quite differently. For any child, parents and family filter the heritage of the past. They, not the heritage, socialize the child and place him/her in a particular religious, community, school, and peer-group setting. The family's sex-role ideology will largely determine the life-space a girl-child will have and the amount of control the parents will assist her in obtaining over it. The explanation of why this woman rather than that one is likely to become a political actor, then, ultimately must revolve around the interaction between the sex-role ideological heritage the girl receives and the education and other skills and competencies she attains. It is for this reason that the remainder of the book is devoted to elaborating a theoretical framework for developing a typology of political women based upon an understanding of sex-role ideology, control over one's life-space, and the type of political salience women experience; and to identifying the socialization conditions and processes most typical of each political type. Chapter Two details the theoretical relationships we see between the development of political efficacy, sex-role ideology, control over one's life-space, political salience, and types of political women. Chapter Three introduces the actual women whose lives we have investigated and places them in the typological classification. Chapter Four reviews various approaches to the study of socialization and examines their utility in studying social change. The necessity for changes in the sex-role ideology of the institutions socializing girls is also discussed. Chapter Five analyzes the relationship between family structure, the development of sex-role ideology, and political women. Chapter Six elaborates our view on how socialization patterns and processes are linked to females' developing a sense of personal control and political salience. Chapter Seven provides our general conclusions regarding the questions of how, why, and under what circumstances some women become political beings. This last chapter also discusses the implications of this study for further research and for public policy.

Notes

1. Cited by Kirsten Amundsen, *The Silenced Majority* (Englewood Cliffs, N.J.: Prentice-Hall, 1971), p. 84. See also the *San Francisco Chronicle*, July 31, 1970, p. 17.

2. Abraham Maslow, "A Theory of Human Motivation," *Psychological Review* 50 (1943): 370–396. Maslow, *Motivation and Personality* (New York: Harper and Row, 1954). For systematic attempts to apply Maslow's theory to the study of politics, see James Davies, *Human Nature and Politics* (New York: John Wiley and Sons, 1964); and Jeanne Knutson, *The Human Basis of the Polity* (Chicago: Aldine-Atherton, 1972). See also Carl Rogers, *On Becoming a Person* (Boston: Houghton Mifflin, 1961); A. Angyal, *Foundations for a Science of Personality* (New York: Commonwealth Fund, 1941); and Kurt Goldstein, *The Organism* (New York: American Press, 1939).

3. Stanley Allen Renshon, *Psychological Needs and Political Behavior: A Theory of Personality and Political Efficacy* (New York: The Free Press, 1974).

4. Roberta Sigel, "Assumptions About the Learning of Political Values," *The Annals of the American Academy of Political and Social Science* 361 (September 1965): 1–9; Richard Dawson, "Political Socialization," *Political Science Annual* I: 2–84, ed. James A. Robinson; Fred I. Greenstein, "Personality and Political Socialization: The Theories of Authoritarian and Democratic Character," *Annals of the American Academy of Political and Social Science* 361 (September 1965): 81–95.

5. Amundsen, p. 130.

6. Angus Campbell, A. Converse, D. Stokes, and W. Miller, *The American Voter* (New York: John Wiley and Sons, 1960). This carries over in other responsibilities of citizenship as well as voting. Women for instance can receive exemption from jury duty simply on the basis of child-care problems whereas men are not allowed such exemptions. Leo Kanowitz, *Women and the Law: The Unfinished Revolution* (Albuquerque: University of New Mexico Press, 1968), p. 29.

7. Patricia Taylor, "Sex Differences in Voting Turnout: The American Voter Reconsidered," paper presented at the Northeastern Political Science Association Convention, November 1974, Saratoga Springs, New York.

8. Jeane Kirkpatrick, *Political Women* (New York: Basic Books, 1974), p. 230.

9. Taylor, p. 10. See also S. M. Lipset, *Political Man* (Garden City, N.Y.: Doubleday, 1960), pp. 191–97.

10. Betty Yorburg, *Sexual Identity: Sex Roles and Social Change* (New York: John Wiley and Sons, 1974), p. 50.

11. E. A. Clarke, *Sex in Education* (New York, 1875).

12. Margaret Mead, *Male and Female* (London: Gollancz, 1949).

13. Cited by Janet Chafetz, *Masculine/Feminine or Human?* (Itasca, Ill.: F. E. Peacock, 1974).

14. Eleanor Emmons Maccoby and Carol Nagy Jacklin, *The Psychol-

ogy of Sex Differences (Stanford, Calif.: Stanford University Press, 1974), pp. 351–52.

15. The *San Francisco Chronicle,* July 31, 1970, p. 17.

16. Yorburg, p. 29.

17. Ibid.

18. M. F. Ashley Montagu, ed., *Man and Aggression* (New York: Oxford University Press, 1968).

19. Margaret Mead, *Sex and Temperament in Three Primitive Societies* (New York: Morrow, 1955).

20. William J. Goode, "A Theory of Role Strain," *American Sociological Review* 25 (1960): 383–96.

21. William E. Knox and Harriet F. Kupferer, "A Discontinuity in the Socialization of Males in the United States," *Merrill-Palmer Quarterly* 17 (1972): 251–67.

22. Yorburg, p. 29.

23. Ibid., p. 15.

24. Johannes Nieke, "Klinefelter's Syndrome and the XYY Syndrome," *Acta Psychiatrica Scandinavica,* 1969, Supplement: 209; M. D. Casey, D. R. Street, L. J. Segull, and C. E. Blank, "Patients with Sex Chromation Abnormality in Two State Hospitals," *Annals of Human Genetics* 32 (1968): 53–63.

25. Yorburg, p. 16.

26. Maccoby and Jacklin, p. 355.

27. Yorburg, p. 16.

28. Maccoby and Jacklin, p. 372.

29. Catherine Beecher, "Letters to the People on Health and Happiness," cited in Nancy F. Cott, *The Roots of Bitterness: Documents of the Social History of American Women* (New York: E. P. Dutton and Co., 1972), p. 264.

30. Ibid., p. 265.

31. Robert Smuts, *Women and Work in America* (New York: Columbia University Press, 1959).

32. Jeanne N. Knutson, *The Human Basis of the Polity: A Psychological Study of Political Men* (Chicago: Aldine-Atherton, 1972). See also J. C. Davies, *Human Nature and Politics* (New York: John Wiley and Sons, 1964).

33. Fred Greenstein, *Children and Politics* (New Haven: Yale University Press, 1965), pp. 126–27.

34. See, for example, the following: E. V. Wolfenstein, *The Revolutionary Personality* (Washington, D.C.: American University, Center for Research in Social Systems, 1966). H. D. Lasswell, *Psychopathology and Politics* (New York: The Viking Press, 1960), and *Power and Personality* (New York: The Viking Press, 1948). Erik Erikson, *Young Man Luther* (New York: W. W. Norton & Company, 1958); *Childhood and Society*, rev. ed. (New York: W. W. Norton & Company, 1963); and his *Identity: Youth and Crisis* (New York: W. W. Norton & Company, 1968). Gustav Bychowski, *Dictators and Their Disciples* (New York: International Universities Press, 1948). T. W. Adorno, E. Frenkel-Brunswik, D. J. Levinson, and R. N. Sanford, *The Authoritarian Personality* (New York: John Wiley and Sons, 1950). Those interested in a more general discussion of the uses of psychoanalysis in the study of history and political figures should see Benjamin B. Wolman, ed., *The Psychoanalytic Interpretation of History* (New York: Basic Books, 1971).

35. The primary sources used in this study for Freud's view on the psychosexual development of girls are his "Some Psychical Consequences of the Anatomical Distinction Between the Sexes," 1925, in the *Standard Edition of the Complete Psychological Works of Sigmund Freud*, translated and under the general editorship of James Strachey in collaboration with Anna Freud, assisted by Alix Strachey and Alan Tyson (London: The Hogarth Press and the Institute of Psychoanalysis, 1964 edition, hereafter cited as *S.E.*), Vol XIX; "The Three Essays on the Theory of Sexuality," 1905, *S.E.*, Vol. VII; "The Dissolution of the Oedipus Complex," 1924, *S.E.*, Vol. XIX; and "Female Sexuality," 1931, *S.E.*, Vol. XXI.

36. Juliet Mitchell, *Psychoanalysis and Feminism* (New York: Pantheon Books, 1974), p. 96.

37. Roy Schaffer, "Problems in Freud's Psychology of Women," *Journal of the American Psychoanalytic Association* 22 (1974): 464.

38. Wolfenstein, pp. 1–3.

39. Leon Salzman, "Psychology of the Female: A New Look," *Archives of General Psychiatry* 17 (August 1967): 195.

40. Amundsen, p. 8.

41. Xenophon, *The Economics*, 7: 11–43.

42. Hannah Arendt, *The Human Condition* (Chicago: University of Chicago Press, 1958), p. 24.

43. T. H. Marshall, *Class, Citizenship, and Social Development* (Garden City, N.Y.: Doubleday and Co., 1964), pp. 71–72.

44. Demosthenes, *Neaera*, 122.

45. Philip Slater, *The Glory of Hera* (Boston: Beacon Press, 1968), p. 12.

46. Gore Vidal, "Adams, The Best People: I," *New York Review of Books*, March 18, 1976, pp. 18–20.

47. Constance F. Parvey, "The Theology and Leadership of Women in the New Testament," in Rosemary R. Ruether, ed., *Religion and Sexism* (New York: Simon and Schuster, 1974), p. 146.

48. Ibid., p. 125.

49. St. Thomas Aquinas, *Summa Theologica*, II-II, 70, 3.

50. Erasmus, *Institutio Christiani Matrimoni* (Basel: Froben, 1526).

51. John Knox, *The First Blast of the Trumpet Against the Monstrous Regiment of Women* ([Geneva, 1550] Westminster, England: Constable, 1895), pp. 11–12.

52. Quoted in S. R. Maitland, *Essays on the Reformation in England* (London: Rivington, 1849), pp. 214–15.

53. Edmond and Jules de Goncourt, *The Woman of the Eighteenth Century* ([Paris, 1862] London: George Allen and Unwin, 1928), pp. 246–48.

54. James Fordyce, *Sermons to Young Women* (London: T. Cadess, 1814), I, pp. 147–48.

55. John Gregory, *A Father's Legacy to His Daughters* (London: W. Strahan, 1774), pp. 30–31.

56. Jean-Jacques Rousseau, *Émile* ([Amsterdam, 1762] New York: D. Appleton and Co., 1895), p. 303.

57. Quoted in Sheila Rowbotham, *Hidden from History* (London: Pluto Press, 1973), p. 67.

58. Barbara Welter, "The Cult of True Womanhood, 1820–1860," *American Quarterly* 18 (1966): 151–74.

59. Betty Friedan, *The Feminine Mystique* (New York: Norton, 1963). See especially pp. 33–68 and 233–57.

60. Gail Warshofsky Lapidus, "Modernization Theory and Sex Roles in Critical Perspective," in *Women in Politics*, ed. Jane S. Jaquette (New York: John Wiley and Sons, 1974), p. 245.

61. Ibid., p. 254.

62. Alexander Groth, *Comparative Politics: A Distributive Approach* (New York: The Macmillan Company, 1971), pp. 188-89.

63. Yorburg, p. 149.

64. Ibid., p. 125.

65. Ibid., p. 150.

66. E. P. Thompson, *The Making of the English Working Class* (London: Gollancz, 1963), p. 416.

67. Michael Young and Peter Willmott, *The Symmetrical Family* (New York: Pantheon Books, 1973).

68. Ibid., pp. 90–92.

Chapter 2

Political Efficacy and Women

T HE DEVELOPMENT of an ideological commitment to a political system which legitimizes universal adult participation, if only for a majority of males, is a phenomenon of relatively recent origins. In the late 1950s and early 1960s it was commonplace to assert that such a commitment stems from broad historical changes occurring with urbanization, industrialization, and economic development.[1] More recently the importance of cultural norms, institutions, and ideological beliefs has also been stressed,[2] particularly as factors relevant to female political participation. Changes in the traditional belief systems regarding the female role and position in life (the sex-role ideology) appear to be essential to the development of individual female political activity.[3]

Figure 2-1 graphically depicts our view of how individual political development is related to the macro forces of social change. In essence, we hypothesize that the sources of socioeconomic modernization cited by Lipset in *Political Man* (economic development, industrialization, and urbanization) are broad indicators of the national technological and economic development needed to produce politically active individuals on a wide scale, but that a series of linkages between the macro socioeconomic forces of modernization and the politically independent individual actor must exist before this transformation can occur.

The model depicts two major variables which mediate the

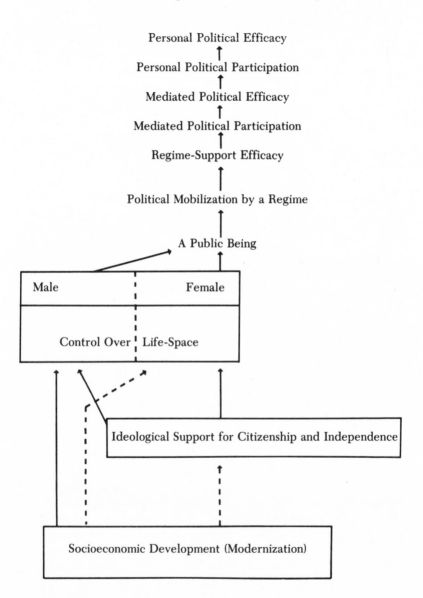

Figure 2-1
The Development of Political Efficacy

Personal Political Efficacy

Personal Political Participation

Mediated Political Efficacy

Mediated Political Participation

Regime-Support Efficacy

Political Mobilization by a Regime

A Public Being

Male	Female
Control Over	Life-Space

Ideological Support for Citizenship and Independence

Socioeconomic Development (Modernization)

modernization forces: personal control over life-space and ideological support for a person's subgroup to have independence in socioeconomic and political realms. Before we can systematically identify the independent variables likely to produce independent political actors, we must first identify the life-space in which individuals live, and then find the major linkages between the life-space and the forces of individual modernization. It is at the interface between the individual's life-space and politics that the key to understanding political efficacy lies.

The term "political efficacy" is often used by political scientists, but unfortunately its meaning is not always clear. The three most common uses of "political efficacy" stress efficacy as a *condition* of participation. The definitions are: (1) it is a norm of democratic societies that citizens ought to participate in governing and to feel that those in authority will be responsive to this participation; (2) it is a set of predispositions which includes the confidence that one's behavior will be heeded by other political actors; and (3) actual behaviors that demonstrate personal efficacy (the citizen not only feels efficacious, but has actually demonstrated competence in deeds). The usage which we believe is most correct and the one upon which this study is based is that proposed by Stanley Renshon in *Psychological Needs and Political Behavior: A Theory of Personality and Political Efficacy*. Utilizing the theory of motivation and human development proposed by Abraham Maslow,[4] Renshon defines political efficacy as "the belief that one has sufficient control over political processes to satisfy the need for control in relevant life areas."[5] In contrast to the other definitions, Renshon's assumes that those people who participate in politics do so in order to fill a human need, to become more capable of controlling events affecting their own lives. They do not engage in politics only if they are already competent and confident that others will heed them. In other words, because political efficacy is directly derived from the psychological need for personal control over one's life-space, it is a motivating force for political behavior: one seeks to extend one's control; if politics becomes salient to the person's life-space, then he or she will attempt to engage in political behavior. Moreover, as Figure 2-1 shows, Renshon's concept suggests to us that individuals can experience several types of political efficacy depending upon the motivation for political participation.

We would like to stress that we see a complex interaction

between the need for personal control and the gaining of competence to actually exercise that control. All human beings undoubtedly have a psychological need for control over their life-space; however, during early childhood, in particular, such needs can be suppressed or diverted through the socialization process. Though the need itself can never be fully extinguished, its fulfillment can be stymied if proper competence-training and opportunities for fulfilling the need are not available. Ultimately, as Renshon notes, the politically efficacious person—male or female—is one who believes that he or she has enough control over political processes, enough competence, to use politics as an arena to fulfill his or her personal need for control over the life-space. The need is a motivating force, but competence training and periodic fulfillment of the need (reinforcement) are essential if a person is to continue to be strongly motivated by the need.

Control over Life-Space

The concept of life-space can most simply be defined as the physical and social reality of an individual's day-to-day existence, objectively and as self-perceived. The model in Figure 2-1 as well as the historical relationship between the family and the two sexes suggests that the immediately relevant life-space differs for men and women and for subgroups of males and females. Because the relevant life-space for individuals differs, socioeconomic modernization will affect such subgroups differentially and will produce different patterns of political behavior. As Renshon points out, the variable "control over life-space" has three dimensions, all of which must be addressed. The first dimension concerns the *need* for such control. Abraham Maslow has suggested that human beings have five need levels arranged in a hierarchy. These are: (1) physiological, (2) safety, (3) love, (4) self-esteem, and (5) self-actualization. According to Renshon, the need for personal control over one's life-space develops as part of the second level of Maslow's need hierarchy. Only after the physiological needs are reasonably well satisfied (level 1) can an individual develop his or her safety needs, the need to be safe from harm, to have an orderly, secure world, and to have control over relevant aspects of that world (level 2). Moreover, because this need for personal control over life-space is part of the basic need hierarchy, "it serves as an organizing need for subsequent need satisfaction. That is, the potential to fulfill love, self-esteem, and self-actualization needs are dependent (for most people) on obtaining personal control."[6] It should be obvious that different individuals will have different levels of need for personal control. Moreover, those with a low need level will seek less control than those with a high need level. Those with high need levels will seek greater control unless their abilities and beliefs about their abilities are so poorly developed or thwarted that the need itself becomes thwarted and/or reduced.

The second dimension of personal control over one's life-space refers to the person's belief in his or her ability to shape his or her life.[7] This dimension is based upon two types of abilities: first, "the ability to acquire and successfully utilize a variety of skills and pathways to reach personal goals, and second, the ability to engage in successful reality testing."[8] Implicit within both aspects of this dimension is the assumption that the prevention of individuals and minority groups from obtaining specific skills will lead to a lower level belief in having personal control and a thwarting of the need for personal control in selected areas of life. In other words, the social structure and the socialization process can raise or lower the expectations that a person has for personal control over areas of his or her life-space, thereby eliminating growth of skills. This effect is accomplished by either promoting or inhibiting the person's belief in his or her competencies and expanding or restricting the scope of that person's interpersonal and institutional relationships. Changes in social values over time might also influence one's sense of personal control. In one sense the social structure may be viewed as a reward distribution system which reflects the dominant social values. Limits in personal control beliefs might also occur because an individual's attributes or skills do not coincide with prevailing values or perceived needs.

The third dimension of the variable control over one's life-space refers to the scope or "extent of the life-space area that the individual seeks to affect."[9] The scope can be narrowly or broadly circumscribed. It is obviously at least partly determined by the person's beliefs and actual abilities to exercise personal control. The scope might also be defined by the existing life-space of the individual within a given social structure. Or the scope might be determined by the individual comparing himself or herself to members of reference groups who actually live in different types of life-spaces but who have comparable beliefs and abilities to control the life-space. In this latter instance, one would expect intensive effort at social change to make either the life-space or the existing social structure more amenable to this person's gaining control.[10]

There is a definite relationship between these three dimensions of control over the human life-space. The theory assumes that all individuals have some type of need for personal control if they have reached the second level of Maslow's need hierarchy. The theory also assumes that this need can be thwarted by punishment and lack of reinforcement when individuals seek to develop skills and abilities to gain control. It also assumes that selected aspects of a person's life-space, such as those pertaining to politics, can be defined by the culture and, through socialization, by the individual as something that individuals within a certain subgroup category do not have the right or capacity to control. In other words, it is consistent within this theoretical framework to assume that women have the ability to exercise extensive and meaningful control in some aspects of their life-spaces, but that they do not have it in others. A major task of social scientists is to try to determine why some aspects of the life-space are systematically excluded from female control, and why most women do not object violently to that exclusion.

The nature of a person's life-space, the day-to-day existence, can expand or contract in a variety of ways. It seems reasonable to assume that the path of expansion of both the human life-space and the need for control over it will be related to Maslow's need hierarchy: that is, a person will need to gain control over the physiological aspects of his or her life-space before progressing to gaining control over aspects of life external to those specific aspects. This assumption is important, particularly in light of the historical and biological nature of the roles of mother and wife. A woman who cannot control the number of children she will have or when she will have them does not have control over the physiological aspects of her life. She cannot choose a career outside the home because she has no control over what the nature of her day-to-day existence, her life-space, will be. She knows that the decisions about allocating her time and energy will not be hers to make. A lack of control over such decisions can lead to a severe reduction in one's beliefs about abilities to gain control over other aspects of the life-space. Additionally, the lack of reliable child care will produce a similar effect on women. For example, economic independence requires, unless one is wealthy by inheritance, some form of intellectual or physical labor. If that labor is not a reliable, predictable commodity, whether due to one's own condition or to the burden of child care, then efforts to assert personal control over the economic aspects of the life-space will not succeed. Employers do not wish to hire unreliable individuals. The female child whose parents do not wish her to be frustrated might be discouraged from developing in her a desire to work—an activity which could lead to her being in direct conflict with the system. As S. Goldberg has argued in *The Inevitability of Patriarchy* in 1973, parents often seem to socialize children to exaggerate basic biological differences so that girls will not be doomed to face failure and disappointment as adults. It seems that parents often provide (a) different definitions of needs to be satisfied according to the sex of their children and (b) alternative contexts for their satisfaction.

Pursuing the logic of this argument further, the containment of the female (or male) life-space to selected aspects of the human condition will strongly encourage restrictions in other areas such as politics. In other words, a human being can be viewed as having a variety of actual and potential life-spaces that are arranged in a hierarchical fashion that are directly related to Maslow's need hierarchy. For an individual to seek control not only of his or her personal life-space but also control over policies affecting other people's lives would require that the person be at a fairly high level in the life-space hierarchy—with beliefs and abilities to match the scope.

All this might be a fancy way of saying that an illiterate beggar seldom seeks to become a king or a president! But we do not think so. We think it means that we have to be very specific about how the various life-spaces of individuals differ when generalizations about political behavior and achievements are being made. To understand variations in individual political behavior and to identify the sufficient as well as the necessary conditions for high levels of political participation, specific aspects of the human life-space must be examined.

The nature of a human being's life-space and the three different dimensions of control over that life-space are, in turn, determined. For social change to occur something must happen to alter, first, the life-space of sub-groups within a society and, second, the dimensions related to a particular individual's gaining personal control over his or her life-space. The nature of the life-space can change as the result of socioeconomic, technological, and other scientific changes. The nature of the female life-space has obviously changed as the result of advanced knowledge about physiology, birth control, good health, industrialization, and advanced technology, both as applied to women's traditional household work and as a means of opening nonhousehold areas of employment to women. Nonetheless, this type of change is not enough. There must also be within the intellectual life-space in which a girl or a woman lives the belief, the expectation, that she herself actually exercises control over her personal life-space. Such a belief is an ideological support for personal citizenship and independence which filters and shapes the effect of the broader modernization forces.

Ideological Support for Citizenship and Independence

The role of ideology as a moving force of history has been debated by many. Those who have studied the behavior of women in the twentieth century have reached a general consensus "that certain ideologies can predict the values and behavior of women with remarkable accuracy."[11] As Jean Lipman-Blumen has pointed out, these systems of belief about the appropriate behavior of women with respect to men and children "shape the destiny of women in ways never imagined by Freud."[12] These beliefs are not explicitly taught, but rather passed on through implicit expectations, assumptions, rewards, and punishments.

In the western world of the mid-1970s the variety of sex-role ideologies is considerably larger than in earlier historical periods. For the sake of simplicity and clarity, however, we present here the starker contrasts between the more traditional sex-role ideology and the more modern sex-role ideology. According to Lipman-Blumen, the traditional sex-role ideology in its simplified form is "the belief that under ordinary circumstances women belong in the home, caring for children and carrying out domestic duties, whereas men are responsible for the financial support of the family."[13] The more modern ideology (she calls it the "contemporary ideology") is "that the relationships between men and women are ideally egalitarian and that husbands and wives may share domestic, child-rearing, and financial responsibilities."[14]

The difference between how these ideologies would have women relate to the external public world is straightforward. Women with the modern ideology obviously would be more likely to become political women. Because of the power of the self-fulfilling prophecy, we also believe the nature of the sex-role ideology will have a direct impact upon the level of need a girl develops for personal control, the type of beliefs and abilities (competencies) she will develop, and the scope of the life-space she desires to control. All these factors are directly related to whether or not and how a particular woman will participate in politics.

In 1955 Maurice Duverger described the political behavior of women as follows: "Women . . . have the mentality of minors in many fields, and, particularly in politics, they will accept paternalism on the part of men. The man–husband, fiancé, lover, or myth–is the mediator between them and the political world."[15] We agree with Duverger that this statement describes rather well the political behavior of women who hold the traditional sex-role ideology and operate within the traditional female life-space. That ideology prescribes that the female shall relate to the public, political realm precisely in this way. It is a highly predictable form of behavior, and is represented in our model by the concepts of mobilized and mediated participation and mobilized and mediated political efficacy.

Most social scientists now recognize a need to distinguish between political activity mobilized by a regime and that initiated by individuals.[16] The enfranchisement of an entire subgroup of the population such as females is obviously mobilization by the regime. The vast bulk of the subgroup population seldom is a participant in the politicking leading to the mobilization.

It is also recognized that the characteristics of those who initiate political activity tend to be quite different from those who simply respond to regime-mobilized activity.[17] In other words, having been pulled into the political system does not necessarily make one an independent actor.

Our model goes further than this to suggest that once an individual is mobilized, several different types of political efficacy are sequentially experienced. The first type of efficacy would be a feeling of being competent in actively supporting the regime that mobilized the individual. Since being political is a new experience, an individual could feel quite exhilarated and important in acting out his or her regime-supporting feelings of efficacy. However, as time passes and the patron-client relationship and other factors provide the mobilized persons with both greater control over their life-space and greater experience in political participation, a higher level of political efficacy will tend to develop. The regime-mobilized sub-group will become more open to developing what Mathiason and Powell call "mediated political efficacy."[18] Individuals will make more personalized demands upon the regime in order to extend further their control over their life-space. In other words, the mobilization by the regime of this sub-group will tend to raise the expectation level of its members for additional personal control over their life-space.

A time lag between the mobilization and the rise in the need level will obviously exist. Moreover, all individuals within the sub-group will not be affected at the same rate or intensity. Therefore substantial variations in the need level will exist and indeed perhaps even increase. It is our contention that the initial political consequence of an increase in the need level, once it does occur, will be a more intensified form of mediated political participation and a greater sense of political efficacy based upon this mediated participation.

Kendall Baker in his study of socialization in West Germany found "the rather interesting situation in which seventeen-year-old boys and girls feel almost equally efficacious, but the former are far more likely to plan to implement their feelings with activity. Apparently, therefore, a strong sense of political efficacy does not necessarily result in a desire to take an active part in politics."[19] Baker's finding and the large body of literature asserting that women participate in politics through their husbands or fathers suggests to us that the way in which individuals participate is strongly affected by their historical and current life-space. Women historically have not participated directly in the political system. The expectation of most women has been, and still appears to be, that their demands will be mediated through the males of the polis. Hence, to the extent that they believe they can get males to present their demands to the system, they could feel politically efficacious, that is, as possessors of sufficient control over political processes to satisfy the need for control in relevant life areas, without becoming independent political actors at all! They feel a sense of mediated efficacy because of being a member of a collective, the family unit. Such political efficacy ought not, however, be confused with the higher level of efficacy, *personal political efficacy!* It is this latter type of efficacy that leads individuals to try to become members of political elites.

It is worth noting that the mediated form of political participation permits a maximum reduction in cognitive dissonance. According to Leon Festinger, *"two elements are in dissonant relation if considering these two alone, the opposite element would follow from the other."*[20] Such dissonance produces uncomfortable tension which people try to reduce or avoid. The mediated participation allows the woman to perform the required behavior of voting and expressing political opinions that the new civic duty requires; it also permits her to relate in the traditional fashion to her husband or father as the traditional sex-role ideology requires.

As politics becomes included in a woman's day-to-day existence, it is possible that she will begin to expand her definition of her life-space to include political activity. The greater her intellectual and emotional involvement in political activity, the more likely she is to develop a greater need for personal control over that aspect of her life-space and to develop further the beliefs and the abilities required to exercise that control. The vital question is: what types of political activity will this woman tend to seek and/or be permitted to seek? Constantini and Craik's 1972 study of Republican and Democratic party leaders in California suggests that she will seek political activity that will parallel the pattern and style of behavior women have within the family structure relating to their husbands.

> The public office versus intraparty career styles and the self-serving versus public-serving motivational patterns reflected in the present data bear marked resemblance to often noted sex-role differences in the family. The male party leader, like the husband, is more likely to specialize in the instrumental functions of the system involved (whether party or family)— that is, in those functions related to the external world. The female party leader, like the wife, tends to specialize in expressive functions or those concerned with "the 'internal' affairs of the system, the maintenance of integrative relations

between (its) members." In general, she is relegated to, or relegates herself to, a supportive role of more or less selfless service to her family or party, while the male partner or co-partyist pursues a career in the outside world.[21]

The effect of the sex-role ideology upon female political behavior is clearly direct and very strong. Even when the need for exercising personal control in the political arena becomes strong enough to push women into political leadership activity, the activity they choose or are forced to choose is guided by male-female relationships within the family structure! The effect of the sex-role ideology and structural-functional constraints derived from it are so strong, in fact, that female political leaders who are definitely independent actors like men are rare. Werner found, for example, that between 1917 and 1964 only seventy women had served in the United States Congress. Over half of these attained their office after relatives had been elected to Congress; and about half were appointed or elected to fill a vacancy that was usually due to the death of the husband.[22]

In sum, at this point in history only a very rare handful of women seem to have reached the highest levels of personal political efficacy that enables them to strike out as political leaders, independent in their own right. Even those who have successful experience in political participation seem to have that experience in traditional female types of ways. The purpose of our theoretical model is to understand and explain how and why some women have actually reached the highest levels of participation and efficacy. The rarity of the occurrence makes the process by which it occurs exceptionally difficult to identify and to study. By the same token the rarity makes the importance of such a study even greater.

Ideal Types of Female Political Behavior

Models of political behavior popular in the 1970s in the social sciences stress what Verba and Nie[23] call the standard socioeconomic model. The major categories of variables examined are (a) social circumstances, usually measured by the subject's socioeconomic status, (b) position in the life cycle, (c) race, (d) the voluntary associations one belongs to, (e) one's party affiliation, (f) the type of community one lives in, (g) one's civic attitudes, (h) how conscious one is of one's ethnic or social group, (i) the extent of one's partisanship, and (j) the substantive content of one's political ideology. These variables obviously offer significant insights into political socialization and behavior; however, they are incapable of distinguishing between male and female behavior of individuals who score similarly on subcategories of these variables. For example, take the Kennedy family. The males—John, Robert, and Edward—are clearly political men; the females— Eunice, Joan, Ethel, Rose, Pat, Jacqueline—are occasional public figures who only support the political activities of their sons, brothers, and husbands. Yet the men and women are likely to be very similar if not identical on the above variables. If male behavior is "explained" by variations found within and among these variables, why are these variations not useful in explaining variations between the sexes within each of these subcategories?

Throughout all cultures the male has historically been the public being, the female the private, nonpublic being whose place is in the home. This ideological definition of the male and female life-space *precedes and outweighs all other categories* of variables usually analyzed by social scientists studying political socialization and political behavior. One's socioeconomic status, educational level, political ideology, memberships in voluntary associations, and so on cannot contribute to a person's becoming a part of the political elite if entrance into such an elite is considered to be wrong for the role one is "supposed" to play in life.

Most of the more discriminating political-behavior variables, such as socioeconomic status (SES) and level of education, are indicators of a person's level of achievement and involvement in the public realm. Most women do not, however, have an *achieved* socioeconomic status; the SES achieved by their husband or father is *ascribed* to them. Moreover, relatively few women have attained high levels of education. According to U.S. Bureau of the Census data for December 1974[24] only 10 percent of U.S. females twenty-five years of age or older had completed college; only 3 percent had begun—not necessarily had completed—some type of graduate or professional work. At the graduate level women also tend to get their degrees in education, the arts, or the humanities. Even in the 1970s relatively few women specialize in the social sciences, the physical sciences, law, business or management, or other professional fields.

One consequence of these academic choices is that those women who do work—regardless of level of educational attainment—tend to work in staff and supportive positions. The U.S. Department of Labor's *Handbook on Women Workers* for 1975 revealed that only 5 percent of all women workers held managerial or administrative positions. In 1970 women represented only 4.7 percent of all lawyers in the country—albeit almost double the 2.4 percent they represented in 1960. The extreme concentration of females into a few occupations and their exclusion from others are further illustrated by the fact that "in 1973 more than two-fifths of all women workers were employed in ten occupations: secretary, retail sales, bookkeeper, private-household worker, elementary school teacher, waitress, typist, cashier, sewer/stitcher, and registered nurse."[25]

Given the sharp sex differences in education and in the types of occupations worked in, common sense forces us to ask if the "standard socioeconomic model" of politicization applies to females. How can it adequately explain or predict female political behavior if the scores given to men on SES and level of educational achievement, for example, mean something different for women? What is either the theoretical significance or the empirical import of such variables when they are not indicators of achievement but rather are indicators of one's private relationship to another person? Or to the opposite sex in general?

If the standard socioeconomic model of political behavior is not appropriate for studying female political socialization and behavior, what model is more appropriate? What model can lead to theoretical significance? Because so many women still have not become full public beings, we must use a theoretical framework concerned with the process of human and psychological development per se, not with what might or might not have already occurred in terms of achievement in the public realm of life. As stated earlier, we believe that the core of such a theory has been presented by Stanley Renshon who bases his conception of the socialization process upon the psychological school of human development in the tradition of Abraham Maslow. If this need theory of human development has applicability to the real world and therefore to political efficacy, it should be possible to develop a set of ideal types that would distinguish among women in terms comparable to those of the theory. We turn to this task now by establishing ideal types for women engaging in politics.

Dimensions of the Typology

Our typology is organized around three dimensions, which in turn are related to the socialization process (see Figure 2-2). The first two dimensions are (a) the traditional, passive, versus modern, activist sex-role ideology, and (b) the extent of control over one's life-space. For the purposes of visual presentation we combine these two dimensions as follows: (1) traditional, passive sex-role ideology with little or some control over one's life-space; (2) traditional, passive sex-role ideology with great control; (3) a moderately activist modern sex-role ideology with little or some control; (4) a moderately activist modern sex-role ideology with great control over one's life-space; (5) a strongly activist modern ideology with little or some control; and (6) a strongly activist modern ideology with great control. The third dimension, the nature of political salience, finds its origins in an elaboration of the Maslowian need theory.

The need theory of political efficacy assumes that politics becomes salient to a person to the extent that it is perceived to be relevant to that person's life-space. According to Renshon, three types of salience can be isolated: "(1) the political system may be seen as the only source capable of supplying certain benefits in the forms of either goods or services [political-reward salience]; (2) the decisional outputs of the political system may be viewed as interfering with the pursuit of an individual's values and goals [political-punishment salience]; or (3) the political system may become salient because the individual believes he has an obligation as a citizen to pay attention to the process of the political system [political-obligation salience]."[26]

As Figure 2-2 depicts, the essential prerequisite for the development of any independent elite political behavior in women is a moderately activist modern sex-role ideology. The key dimension for women is the ideological one. Without some break in the traditional belief that politics is male and none of their concern, no amount of personal control or political predilection will produce adult elite political behavior in women. Further, the type and scope of political behavior engaged in depends on the extent of control a woman has over her life-space and the nature of the political salience. By analyzing and comparing women on these dimensions, a useful typology of female political behavior can be developed. In developing this typology, we will discuss three basic categories of women which we call the private woman (the traditional nonpolitical women), the public woman° (the emerging political women), and the achieving woman (in-

---

°We realize that to some readers the phrase "public woman" will call forth the image of an immoral woman or a prostitute. To these individuals we wish to note that such perceptions are derived from an outmoded and most undemocratic

Figure 2-2
Typology of Female Political Behavior

Sex-Role Ideology & Extent of Control over Life-Space	Type of Woman	Political Salience		CIVIC OBLIGATION
		REWARD	PUNISHMENT	
1. Passive/Little or Some Control		Not directly applicable	Not directly applicable	No sense of political efficacy: almost all public behavior mediated by males; vote at most and then as a male dictates
2. Passive/Great Control		Not directly applicable	Not directly applicable	Regime-support efficacy; in politically active families, perhaps mediated efficacy
3. Moderately Activist/Little or Some Control		Regime-Support or mediated political participation and efficacy locally and nationally; civic volunteer	Alienation/withdrawal, or intermittent supporter of non-status quo causes	Regime-support or mediated efficacy

64

	ACHIEVING	PUBLIC	PRIVATE
4. Moderately Activist/Great Control	Mediated efficacy and participation nationally, but personal efficacy and participation locally	Mediated efficacy and participation as a revolutionary	Regime-support or mediated efficacy and participation
5. Strongly Active/Little or Some Control	Mediated usually, but not by choice	Revolutionary, but as a terrorist/agitator or rank-and-file crusader	Regime-support or mediated efficacy
6. Strongly Active/Great Control	Strong sense of personal political participation and efficacy at all levels, especially at the national level	Member of revolutionary elite; theorist, organizer, strategist	Mediated efficacy; but latent personal political participation & efficacy

cluding elected women among the national political elite and famous female revolutionaries).

The Private Woman

The private women are characterized by a traditional, passive sex-role ideology, and politics is salient to them only at the level of civic obligation. The amount of control they have over their life-space is somewhat irrelevant, essentially because the sex-role ideology they hold would prevent them from behaving nontraditionally unless absolutely forced to do so. Compared to the general category of achieving woman, the private woman would appear to share a common disdain, avoidance, and lack of interest in acquiring authority positions and power in general. As Jeane Kirkpatrick has noted, "while legal barriers to women's participation in political life have been abolished, cultural norms have preserved the definition of politics as 'man's work.' Politics is a male world in the sense that presidents, senators, congressmen, mayors, judges, virtually all important political actors, are men. And male incumbency creates an expectation of male incumbency in the same way that nurses are women creates the expectation that nurses will be, *are* women."[27] More conventional in their expectations concerning sexual differentiation of roles, traditional private women will tend to internalize almost totally the cultural definitions of masculinity and femininity. They will have been most fully socialized into the culturally arranged sex roles. Politics is a man's business; they are women; thus, politics is none of their business.

It has been repeatedly documented that men are more likely to participate in politics than women.[28] In 1976 of *all* public offices in the United States only 4 to 7 percent were held by women, even though women represented about 53 percent of the voting population.[29] This finding has been substantiated time and again in a wide variety of countries. Indices used to measure political participation ranging from running for office to talking to others about politics, or even to wearing political buttons, would indicate that women are generally less likely than men to

---

belief system. For centuries males have been referred to as public men and public figures with positive connotations being conveyed. It is time, we feel, to end these simplistic but powerful forms of verbal and institutional sexism. Part of our effort at reconceptualizing how we think about achieving political women includes reconceptualizing what we think when we hear "public women."

partake in all political activity. To the vast majority of women, politics has been perceived as having minimal impact on their primary area of concern, the family. And yet, more recent studies in the United States have shown a marked tendency for voting to increase among women. As the easiest measure of political interest, the diminution of voting differences between men and women is employed by proponents of the women's movement as confirmation of the changing role of women and the impact of the movement on society.[30]

Although the women's movement and the developing role of women have undoubtedly contributed to the increase in women's voting, we wish to suggest an alternative explanation of at least some portion of this change. We believe the greater voting turnout of the traditional, nonpolitical woman is the result of her reacting in a conventional manner to some external incentive. Any sense of political efficacy that might be felt from such voting would be of a regime-support nature derived from performing a civic obligation or an obligation to one's husband or father; it would not be a sense of political efficacy derived from feelings of personal political competence. According to our view, politics has been perceived as having minimal impact on their primary area of concern, the family. And yet, more recent studies in the United States have shown a marked tendency for women within the western cultural heritage.

Earlier we specified three levels of political efficacy: regime-mobilized efficacy, mediated political efficacy, and a sense of personal political efficacy. In the case of traditional women who have voted for the first time, even out of a sense of civic obligation, the voting act itself is a simple response to a regime-mobilized attitude. Taught by the society and government that the honors and privileges of citizenship require one to participate and vote, women do begin to engage in this political behavior, but only as an acceptance of their civic duty. The results of this regime-mobilized support and participation are hardly likely to be disruptive and harmful to the purposes of the regime or to males in general. The resulting sense of regime-supportive political efficacy is also hardly likely to instill in these women a sense of the potential of politics for rewarding and punishing. If these women do not vote, they may experience a sense of guilt because they have not fulfilled their proper duty as citizens. However, such women are not likely to be motivated to greater political activity, for the simple act of voting will relieve them of civic obligation and thus of the impetus to be active.

To summarize, the expectation stemming from our theory is that traditional women will perceive the political system as having little or no impact on their social and physical life-space. They will be inactive in this arena. They will continue to be uninterested in politics. Even within this group, those who see the political system as having limited salience will follow a civic-obligation model and thus will perceive their functions in minimal participatory terms (voting). The degree of salience will derive from outside, passively received sources, that is, from pertinent male figures in their lives or from the male-dominated political culture.

Many political wives are "private women." It might be asked: how can women who at certain points in their lives (for example, campaign time) literally live and breathe politics be considered as traditional, nonpolitical women? Many political wives may simply be traditional women who have happened to marry men who were then or subsequently became engaged in politics. The civic-obligation model could readily explain these women's concern with politics. More significantly, the origins and intensity of the salience of politics to them—their husbands—may explain the apparent greater political interest attributed to them. Perhaps a fictitious scenario of the political wife will clarify our point:

A young woman socialized in a strict sex-role orientation meets and marries a young lawyer. His career affords advancement by way of a political route. The status of his family is determined by his career. The wife's status is a residual of his status. She accepts her position as the nurturing, supportive helpmate willing to do whatever she can to advance his career. Politics is reward-salient to him and his wishes are salient to her. He is interested in politics; she must at least publicly share his interest (but she must not independently or competitively express any interest). His commitment to political activity may be all-encompassing; hers must be as intense toward him and his needs. If he needs public exposure, she will head the March of Dimes. If he is unable to speak to a women's club, she will. While he campaigns, she campaigns. The demands on her may be highly political in nature, but they are derivative of her relationship to her husband, not to the political system directly.

The political wife, then, may be political solely because she is the wife of a political man. The opportunities to be more actively involved in politics derive from her primary role, that of wife. The exigencies of this role formulate unusual expectations of her by the outside world, but she is fundamentally unaltered relative to her personal world. Once again, passive acceptance defines this particular traditional woman's response. These private women are publicly known but are not public beings. They do not want their private life-space converted into public property.

For the traditional, private woman the duties of a political wife may lead to severe personal and family conflict. Thrust into the public spotlight, she may resent the lack of privacy normally associated with the wife and mother roles. Most of the time she is expected simply to follow and to mimic her husband's positions. At other times she must represent him in unfamiliar situations; after a few incidents she may wonder whether the supportive wife and political spokesperson roles are compatible.

The Public Woman

The kind of political activity springing from civic obligation obviously does not apply to all wives of political men. Many of these women, along with numerous women in the population at large, will have moved to what we call the "public woman" stage of political development. This type of woman, generally characterized by a moderately activist, modern, sex-role ideology, will engage in many different types of political behavior depending upon the amount of control she has over her life-space and the nature of political salience she experiences. The public woman tends to see politics as being relevant to her life-space, but will stop short of any political behavior which will directly challenge or interfere with her roles as wife/mother. As Figure 2-2 shows, however, women with an activist sex-role ideology and control over their life-spaces can also experience the salience of politics as a mere civic obligation. Politics need not become important to a person just because of changes in ideology or life-space. These changes indicate only that it is more probable that politics will become reward- or punishment-salient.

As previously noted, in addition to regime-mobilized efficacy, there is what Mathiason and Powell have termed "mediated political efficacy" and mediated political participation. At this level of participation and efficacy, the individual's internal needs and motivations are the impetus. The individual starts to view the political system as capable of giving reward or punishment. Once politics does become reward- or punishment-salient, political participation is no longer seen simply as an obligatory act thrust upon one by the culture and society, but rather as a means of achieving some individually held purpose. However, for most public women, in spite of the internal personal impetus for participation, some actual or perceived barrier prevents them from participating in politics as an independent actor; therefore, participation must be through some other person who represents a collective unit to which one belongs. For women the collective unit is likely to be the family and the mediator is likely to be their husbands or fathers. Public women with a moderately activist, more modern ideology but little or some control over their life-space are the most likely to experience mediated efficacy regardless of the type of political salience. Those for whom civic obligation is the reason for political activity are more likely to remain at the regime-support efficacy level while those experiencing punishment salience from the political system tend to become so alienated that they withdraw. For all ostensible purposes they behave just like traditional nonpolitical private women.

Some public women may have attempted to expand their opportunities to become legitimately involved in the male domain of politics by marrying men they know to be interested in political careers. Unable to ignore completely the sex stereotyping of politics as male or to deny their own personal attraction to politics, they may have sought out men who could provide them with an opportunity to fulfill these seemingly contradictory desires. For such women, being a political wife might entail very little role conflict. It might also serve as a transitional phase to their own future independent political participation and activity should their husbands die. Such women would work with a reward-salient model of the political system, first as public women through the mediated participation of the male and later, as their own participation increases, in rejecting the definition of the political world as exclusively male. Over time, some of these women develop a sense of *personal political efficacy*, enabling them to become independent political actors, such as senators and congresspersons.

In general, what we call public women are women who might be found organizing voter registration drives, working long and hard within a political party, lobbying for more consumer-protection legislation, demonstrating against a war, protesting abortion laws, and fighting for welfare reform. They may be liberal or conservative, young or old, married or single, but they share one element. They have been sufficiently aroused by an issue, policy, controversy, or whatever, to step outside the confines of their primary roles, at least for a short period of time, and to see themselves as possessing opinions and positions that should be conveyed to others.

Public women differ from achieving women in the nature and intensity of their commitment to their chosen public sphere. They also differ in the type of life-space they have and the amount of control they have over that life-space. Public women with traditional female educations (in education, nursing, the humanities) and a civic volunteer–homemaker life-space often legitimize their entrance into the political sphere by focusing on issues which have been linked to traditional female concerns—children, health, education, welfare, moral issues, and so forth. Historically, women have been at the forefront of such popular movements as anti–child labor, prohibition, abolition, and unionization. Thus, women with a moderately activist ideology and sufficiently great control over their life-spaces have been able to exercise personal political efficacy locally and even at the state level as independent actors. So long as the wife/mother roles are "under control" and protected, the public women with a political reward-salience will be independent politically. Because it is so difficult to maintain control over the homemaker life-space from a distance, and because the experiences and knowledge obtained as a civic volunteer are less applicable at the national and international political levels, public women will usually stop short of striving to become achieving political women—women with a strong sense of personal political efficacy regardless of level of government, the age of their children, their marital status, or any other lack of role convergence.

The extent of control over one's life-space also has an impact upon those public women subject to the punishment-salience of politics and possessing a moderately activist sex-role ideology. Women with this type of salience and also a strong sense of obligation as wife/mother are likely to allow their political behavior to be shaped by males, particularly husbands. Thus there may be revolutionaries who, although competent, experienced, and politically efficacious while working with their husbands, still operate politically within the male-mediation framework. Since the husband generally determines the place of residence, the political beliefs and connections, and the wife's activity seldom deviates from the husband's, that woman, though engaged in revolutionary behavior, would be no more independent or personally politically efficacious than any other public woman with a reward type of political salience. Both types are politically active and reasonably competent; they both also stop short of individual initiatives that might alter their marital sex-role relationships.

It might be asked at this point how the typology applies to unmarried women. The question is difficult to answer primarily because there are few examples of female politicians who never married. Logically, however, unmarried women have the same options of ideology and control over life-space as married women. Those with a traditional or moderately activist ideology are likely to have wanted to marry but were unable to do so. If their single state is viewed by them as a "failure," then they are not likely to enter politics where the threat of male rejection is continual. Also, the single woman with a strongly activist ideology and reward-salience but little or some control over her life-space is not likely to have sufficient skills and interpersonal contacts to compete successfully in the politics of any western democratic society. Since most political persons are married and social interactions often do not include single people, even single women with strongly activist ideology and great control over their life-space might find entrance into the political elite more difficult than comparable married women. Additionally, married nonpolitical women and male politicians might feel more hostility to single women than married women, particularly if the single woman has a strong anti-male, anti-family component in her ideological views. When all is considered, the likelihood of single women with reward-salience achieving membership in the national political elite seems lower than that of married women. For those with a punishment-salience who choose revolutionary activity, such obstacles would be fewer. Even among revolutionaries, however, the single female can remain a public woman.

It is the extent to which public women are willing to allow their ideas and values to be mediated by others, particularly males, and are *able* to be successfully independent politically that determines the chief difference between our ideal types of public and achieving political women. These ideal types of women differ in the range of influence they seek and in their intensity and consistency of commitment to political activity. The public women do not strike out on their own as independent political actors for either one of two reasons: (1) their need for and ability to exercise personal control over their life-space and their definition of their life-space have not expanded to encompass independent political decision-making, or (2) the structural and ideological barriers within the society to independent female participation are still so strong that the individual woman cannot see how she can overcome them. Often these two obstacles to the entering of public women into the realm of achieving women are related. In order to expand one's life-space to include the thought of achieving in politics, specific competencies and abilities must be developed, and obstacles related to adult female roles must be removed. For most public women these requirements mean that their children must be grown, and continual successful participation in civic volunteer groups must occur.[31]

The difference in family roles for men and women, particularly that the women bear the children, affects how they spend their time: a career for men, and homemaking for women, at least during the children's earliest years. This helps to explain why women are usually older on the assumption of their first political office, have shorter political careers, rise to less elevated political positions, and have not accumulated the power their male counterparts have. Though these factors may explain some variations between political males and females, they do not help to explain why so many public women never conceive of the possibility of a political career. They will volunteer their time and energy, but would never consider running for or seeking appointment to public office, at least a national public office. Once again the intensity of the commitment comes into play. Although both public and achieving political women foresee "good" coming from political activism, although both have broken away from the passive, receptive orientation of traditional women, public women retain the conventional priority of values and hierarchy of demands—husband and children first, self and public life or career second. The traditional sex-role socialization has been stronger for the public women; their ability to reject or alter it is less than it is for achieving women. The acceptance of a political career entails the possibility of severe role conflict. The political role or career calls for a devotion of time and energy normally reserved for her spouse and children. It also requires a different definition of the self and a different style of adult role-playing.

The wife/mother role is diffuse, affective, particularistic, and supportive in nature. In social relationships, too, women are often consigned to diffuse rather than specific, clearly established, and contractually binding rights and duties. Wife and mother are clear examples of the diffuse nature of the relationships, but even in occupational realms (secretaries, for example), women have duties as an "office wife" which are not required in male relationships. In fact, in business and in government it is not unheard of for some bosses to expect sexual relations as part of the well-paid "secretary's" duties. In addition, "the sphere of women is expected to be characterized by particularistic morality more than by universalistic morality, by intense personal loyalty more than by principles."[32] Wives and mothers are expected to love and support husbands and children regardless of their behavior. Similarly, they are expected to sacrifice themselves and their desires for the good of the major social institution which historically has defined the female self—the family. The male orientation to self-interest, advancement, and achievement even at the risk of straining family ties is culturally more acceptable for it establishes his status in the male sphere.

Because the wife/mother role is so diffuse and affective, a political career demanding a specific allotment of energies will create extreme cross-pressures on women, certainly more cross-pressures than on men. Knowing such problems arise, many public women will simply avoid them by refusing to seek wider political involvement. The identification of self with the female, personalized, private sphere of children and husband conquers the tendencies toward identification of self with a wider community. Sex-role socialization triumphs over any inclinations towards a more inclusive and public definition of self. Committed though she may be, the public woman, when faced with the inevitable conflict between family obligations and political ones, retreats into the culturally accepted role. Political efficacy has been fostered, but sex-role identification remains stronger. Cultural norms form the basis on which one evaluates oneself as "good" or "bad." Cultural approbation is afforded to the woman who is a good wife and mother but not to the woman who is a good public official at the expense of her family. In fact, the achieving woman's ego must be very strong to risk the social disapproval aimed at the wife and mother who would "abandon" her husband and children to seek her own gratification and success. Achieving women seemingly have gained the ego strength to ignore this criticism whereas public women have not.

A vital difference between public and achieving women seems to be that the achieving woman stresses self-esteem and self-actualization goals and uses internal criteria to evaluate herself, while the private and public women place greater value upon belonging and conforming to the prevailing culture.[33] This difference, perhaps more than any other, undergirds what Karnig and Walter have identified as the major problem in equalizing female political representation in local politics in the United States—the problem of recruiting women to be political candidates.[34] In their 1975 study of municipal elections in 774 U.S. cities over 25,000 in population they concluded: "The chief obstacle women encounter in achieving equitable council representation is apparently the shortfall of woman candidates. Since women have been candidates in at most 20 percent of the most recent council races, they have conceded at least 80 percent of the council posts to men. When women do run, they win in nearly 50 percent of the contests."[35] Such figures ultimately mean that less than 10 percent of all local government positions are held by women. Such figures also demonstrate the tremendous impact the type of sex-role ideology a woman holds has upon her political behavior. In the twentieth century ideological biases about sex-roles and the socialization processes leading women to refuse to become candidates might well be the greatest barriers to equalizing the proportion of females in the political elite. Overt discrimination against female candidates appears minimal in comparison.

The importance of the ideology is seen in its effect upon the female's definition of her self and her relevant life-space. Before the *self* of the self-significance, self-respect, and self-esteem of Maslow's fourth need level and the self-actualization of his fifth need level can be perceived as being related to politics, the girl or woman must have an expanded definition of her self and her life-space. Many women may be affected by the women's movement without ever extending their life-space to include politics. As a result of the women's movement many proliberation females may derive a sense of belonging from sources other than their private families, and they may even achieve a sense of self-esteem from activities not currently receiving cultural approval, but these changes will not make them into "political women." The fact that more women in the United States have not accepted the challenge of political office endorses our belief that current adult options cannot even be perceived if women have not achieved childhood control and extension of life-space to include the public and political realm as a source of self-esteem.

A final comment should be made concerning the relationship between public and achieving political women. In individual cases these types may only be temporarily distinct. That is, the transition for women from the less political to an independently active political sphere may require small steps and the public issue route may be the first in this progression. Recruitment into politics for most women seems to entail a slow, ego-strengthening process. The rewards of participation in a public arena must begin to compensate for the lessening of the gratification found in total identification of self with the success of husband and children. For this to occur women will need to assume more totally the responsibilities of the creation of their own status and being.

The Achieving Woman

Theoretically, the typology suggests that women with little or some control over their lives are or can be achieving women. In practice, however, except for those women for whom politics has had a punishment-salience, we doubt that this ideal type has, or ever had, an empirical referent. The category of achieving political woman should ideally consist only of women with a history of past successful political participation and a strong sense of personal political efficacy. But how can a woman with only some control over her life-space, regardless of her sex-role ideology, attain the successful history of participation that will lead to a strong sense of political efficacy? In societies where the sex advantage in politics goes to males—which is all—women usually need both luck and skill to enter the national political elite. A strongly activist sex-role ideology cannot substitute for or diminish the failure to obtain the skills or experience seen as necessary for assumption of high political office. Political opportunity may knock on the door of the inexperienced male but it is less likely at this time that political rewards will be offered to the inexperienced and unskilled female.

The typology does offer an empirical referent for those with a strongly activist sex-role ideology with some control who hold a punishment-salience attitude. Terrorists and agitators usually reject the traditional sex-role ideology. Not requiring social approval for the success of their political activities, their skills and competencies can be different from elected political elites. Without skills, educational training, and experience needed to develop the competencies required to use politics to extend their control over their life-spaces, the terrorists and agitators resort to violence and agitation which require less formal training and traditional, "acceptable" political skills. The absence from this category of real political women other than terrorists and agitators suggests that the nature of abilities one has acquired and can employ becomes more critical as one approaches the sense of personal political efficacy and national elite political levels.

Women who have strongly activist sex-role ideologies and great control over their life-space can experience the salience of politics as civic obligation. These women, who probably would be achievers in nonpolitical fields, will usually experience mediated political efficacy too. They might well, however, have a latent sense of personal political efficacy that could be activated under specific conditions.

For the purposes of this study, we have limited the meaning of "achieving political woman" to those individuals who have achieved national fame or notoriety for their political behavior; that is, we have limited it to famous terrorists/agitators and to those women with a strongly activist sex-role ideology and great control over their life-spaces, engaging in two types of activity: (1) women elected to a public office, having successfully competed against men within an existing political system; or (2) women who have been political as part of a revolutionary elite opposing the existing political system. Although many women may have voted, given money to a party or candidate, canvassed and campaigned at election time, they do not move themselves from the public to the achieving political woman category on the strength of these activities. According to our definition, achieving women have in common their ability to handle the lack of "professional convergence"[36] in their joint roles as wife/mother and politician. At the very least some reordering and alteration of family responsibilities results from these political obligations. Or, as is the case for so many revolutionaries, such responsibilities are rejected.

In light of our theory of individual political development, the ideal type categorized as achieving political women—except for the terrorists/agitators—will represent those who have actually attained a high need and ability level for personal control over their life-space. The life-space will have expanded to encompass politics. As an ideal type, the achieving political woman will also have reached the highest level of political efficacy: personal political efficacy. An important question is: Did her sense of personal political efficacy come before or after she became an elected public official?

The theoretical framework outlined in this chapter specifies that independent political participation must be engaged in before one attains a sense of personal political efficacy. We maintain that this order—first, participation; then, efficacy—might mean that many women might not attain a sense of personal political efficacy until after they are elected. The great numbers of female officials initially appointed or elected to fill vacancies (caused by death of a husband or relative) who later became independent political actors attest to this progression. Our theory would lead us to hypothesize that these women would have to engage in the role of congressperson or whatever, for a time, as an independent actor before gaining the highest level of political efficacy. In other words, whether or not an elected woman in national politics will have a higher sense of political efficacy than a public woman who remains at the state or local political level or who is seeking but has not yet won office is an empirical question. The answer depends upon what socialization and behavior patterns the particular woman has experienced. In cultures that deny females the right of holding political office, structural barriers and obstacles can overrule internal need levels and abilities. In some societies and some historical periods, it may be more important to be married to a popular male politician in order to be elected than to be an independent political actor with a high sense of personal political efficacy.

These theoretical considerations lead to the hypothesis that the resocialization as an adult to become an independent actor will have occurred more frequently among the elected women in our study than among the revolutionaries. Elected women with a strong sense of personal political efficacy and revolutionaries will tend to be those who have developed a strongly activist sex-role ideology, and who have attained an expanded life-space with educational training and resultant competencies during early childhood and adolescence. Appointed women and, particularly, elected women who came to political office in their middle-age after the death of their husbands, will be more likely to have the more traditional sex-role ideology. We anticipate that such elected women who allowed their political beliefs and behavior to be mediated by their husbands for so long will have had a less consistent socialization pattern than that of the revolutionaries and the elected political women who became personally efficacious when very young. Resocialization will have been needed to get them to become independent political actors. Hence, the elected/mediated public type of political women are likely on the average to be older than the revolutionaries and the elected/personal efficacy achieving women in terms of when they first began their independent political careers. Some women, such as Lurleen Wallace (elected governor of Alabama in 1966), who were actually elected to political office but as a figurehead for their husbands, will never have attained a sense of personal political efficacy because they were never independent political actors. Such women who are used by their husbands may hold a high public office by virtue of having been elected. They do not, however, fulfill the qualifications for inclusion in our ideal type of "achieving political woman."

Because of the potential for overlap, it is worthwhile to clarify more sharply how the elected achieving political woman with a strong sense of personal efficacy differs from, first, the public political woman and, second, the revolutionary woman.

The public and achieving women are similar in that both have broken into the traditionally male sphere while traditional, private women have not. Both types of political women have demonstrated a stronger, more personalized sense of political efficacy than most other women. Achieving political women go beyond public women, however, in that their concrete political goals are more inclusive and extensive. The public and achieving political women differ in the intensity of their attraction to the political system. The vision of the achieving women is wider and the field of activity widens accordingly. Second, the achieving political women more often settle the conflict between the role of wife/mother and the role of political officeholder or actor on the side of the political role. They may be able to do this only because the expectations of the mother/wife role have lessened (e.g., the children are grown and the husband is willing to "fend" for himself), but even the willingness to foster the possibility of role conflict suggests a greater intensity and activist orientation than that of the public women.

The revolutionary women contrast with the elected, achieving political women essentially in the direction of the political salience experienced. They are the women who got involved in politics outside the established political system in an effort to overthrow it. In their eyes, "the government is not so much a means to a problem solution as it is the problem itself."[37] Politics has not merely assumed a new position in the value hierarchy but has become dominant. Other roles are adjusted to its demands. The extreme forms of political behavior might be occasioned by the resistance of the political system itself. Under different circumstances, the revolutionary woman might have been an achieving political woman.

The combination of high political salience, a modern, activist sex-role ideology, and great control over an expanded lifespace for the revolutionaries and the elected women who develop a strong sense of personal political efficacy early, suggests that the socialization characterizing these women might most accurately reflect the kinds of experiences needed to get greater numbers of women involved in high levels of political activity. Until there is an increase in the number of visible female role models among the political elite, major deviations from traditional sex-role socialization patterns may be necessary. Major variations in the traditional socialization process will be needed to create a number of political women. The direction of the political salience, whether it supports or rejects the regime, may very well be dependent on factors of the macro type and outside the control of the emerging political women.

In conclusion, we believe that under the heading of political behavior there is a range of behaviors needing investigation and explanation. Through the use of the political typology we have established a foundation for explaining and predicting female elite political behavior. In Chapter Three we place into six categories thirty-six women who have participated in elite politics at the national level in their respective countries. The remainder of the study investigates the socialization process that has fostered women with such varying types of political behavior. As we have previously stated, we believe that many of the socialization processes affecting the political woman also affect those women who have achieved in other avenues of life traditionally not considered feminine, such as business, banking, academia, and so on.

Notes

1. See, for example, Seymour Martin Lipset, *Political Man: The Social Bases of Politics* (Garden City, N.Y.: Doubleday and Company, 1960), and his "Some Social Requisites of Democracy: Economic Development and Political Legitimacy," *American Political Science Review* 53 (March 1959): 69–104; Philips Cutright, "National Political Development: Measurement and Analysis," in *Politics and Social Life: An Introduction to Political Behavior,* ed. Nelson W. Polsby, Robert A. Dentler, and Paul A. Smith (Boston: Houghton Mifflin, 1963), pp. 771–780. For general discussions on modernization, see: Ioan Davis, *Social Mobility and Political Change* (New York: Praeger Publishers, 1970), pp. 11–46; Daniel Lerner, *The Passing of Traditional Society: Modernizing the Middle East* (Glencoe, Ill.: The Free Press, 1958), pp. 43–75; Donald J. McCrone and Charles F. Cnudde, "Toward a Communications Theory of Democratic Political Development: A Causal Model," *American Political Science Review* 61 (March 1967): 72–79; Alex Inkeles, "The Modernization of Man," in M. Weiner, ed., *Modernization* (New York: Basic Books, 1966), and Inkeles and David M. Smith, *Becoming Modern* (New York: John Wiley and Sons, 1974); Samuel Huntington, "The Change to Change: Modernization, Development, and Politics," *Comparative Politics* 3 (April 1971): 283–322.

2. Alexander Groth, *Comparative Politics: A Distributive Approach* (New York: The Macmillan Company, 1971); Lucian W. Pye, *Politics, Personality, and Nation Building* (New Haven: Yale University Press, 1962); Barbara Jancar, "Women Under Communism," in *Women in Politics,* ed. Jane S. Jaquette (New York: John Wiley and Sons, 1974), pp. 217–242; Gail Warshofsky Lapidus, "Modernization Theory and Sex Roles in Critical Perspective: The Case of the Soviet Union," in Jaquette, pp. 243–256.

3. Jean Lipman-Blumen, "How Ideology Shapes Women's Lives," *Sci-*

entific American 226 (January 1972): 34–42; Alice P. Wrigley and C. Shannon Stokes, "Sex-Role Ideology, Selected Life Plans, and Family Size Preferences," a paper presented at the annual meeting of the Southern Sociological Society, Washington, D.C., April 1975.

4. Abraham Maslow, *Motivation and Personality* (New York: Harper, 1954).

5. Stanley Allen Renshon, *Psychological Needs and Political Behavior: A Theory of Personality and Political Efficacy* (New York: The Free Press, 1974), p. 75.

6. Ibid., p. 73.

7. Ibid., p. 43.

8. Ibid., p. 44.

9. Ibid., p. 45.

10. In sum, we would suggest that much of the so-called "revolution of rising expectations" is based on the overwhelming sense of deprivation of the people who have the chance to compare their meager life-opportunities with those of others.

11. Lipman-Blumen, p. 34.

12. Ibid.

13. Ibid.

14. Ibid., p. 35.

15. Maurice Duverger, *Political Role of Women* (Paris: UNESCO, 1955), p. 129.

16. See, for example, Richard Rose and Harve Mossawir, "Voting and Elections: A Functional Analysis," *Political Studies* 15 (June 1967): 200–201; Balder Raj Nayar, "Political Mainsprings of Economic Planning in the New Nations: The Modernization Imperative Versus Social Mobilization," *Comparative Politics* 6 (April 1974): 341–366; Karl W. Deutsch, "Social Mobilization and Political Development," *American Political Science Review* 55 (September 1961): 493–502; René Lemarchand and Keith Legg, "Political Clientelism and Development: A Pre-

liminary Analysis," *Comparative Politics* 4 (January 1972): 149–178.

17. Sidney Verba and Norman H. Nie, *Participation in America: Political Democracy and Social Equality* (New York: Harper & Row, 1972). For a brief discussion of the different characteristics of participants and nonparticipants and of different types of political participants in the U.S., see pp. 95–101.

18. John R. Mathiason and John D. Powell, "Participation and Efficacy: Aspects of Peasant Involvement in Political Mobilization," *Comparative Politics* 4 (April 1972): 305.

19. Kendall L. Baker, "Political Participation, Political Efficacy, and Socialization in Germany," *Comparative Politics* 6 (October 1973): 87.

20. Leon Festinger, *A Theory of Cognitive Dissonance* (Stanford, Calif.: Stanford University Press, 1957), p. 13.

21. Edward Constantini and Kenneth H. Craik, "The Social Background, Personality and Political Careers of Female Party Leaders," *Journal of Social Issues* 28 (1972): 235.

22. E. E. Werner, "Women in Congress: 1917–1964," *Western Political Quarterly* 19 (1966): 16–30.

23. Sidney Verba and Norman Nie, *Participation in America*, Chap. 1, esp. pp. 18–22.

24. U.S. Bureau of the Census, *Current Population Reports*, P-20, No. 274 (December 1974), p. 15.

25. U.S. Department of Labor, *Handbook on Women Workers* (Washington, D.C.: U.S. Government Printing Office, 1975), p. 91.

26. Renshon, p. 76.

27. Jeane Kirkpatrick, *Political Woman* (New York: Basic Books, Inc., 1974), p. 14.

28. Lester Milbrath, *Political Participations: How and Why Do People Get Involved in Politics?* (Chicago: Rand McNally & Company, 1965), p. 135.

29. Marilyn Johnson and Kathy Stanwick, *Women in Public Office: A*

Biographical Directory and Statistical Analysis (New York: R. R. Bowker Company, 1976), p. xx.

30. Kirsten Amundsen, *The Silenced Majority* (Englewood Cliffs, New Jersey: Prentice-Hall, 1971), p. 81.

31. Kirkpatrick, pp. 59–84.

32. Jessie Bernard, *Women and the Public Interest: An Essay on Policy and Protest* (Chicago: Aldine-Atherton, 1971), p. 26.

33. Recent studies of proliberation and traditional women have found similar differences. John Mahoney, for example, concluded on the basis of his study, "An Analysis of the Axiological Structures of Traditional and Proliberation Men and Women," *Journal of Psychology* 90 (1975): 37, "that thus, in general, it seems appropriate to argue that proliberation females struggle for significance and respect, in order to fulfill the Maslovian (being)-needs, while the traditional female confronts problems of acceptance, which corresponds to Maslow's concept of belongingness and love needs. The needs to belong and love are subordinate to esteem in Maslow's hierarchy, again suggesting that proliberation females are more self-actualizing than traditional females." Other students of the female personality and female involvement in the women's liberation movement have reached similar conclusions. See C. Cherniss, "Personality and Ideology: A Personological Study of Women's Liberation," *Psychiatry* 35 (1972): 109–125; M. G. Fowleder and H. K. Van de Reit, "Women, Today and Yesterday: An Examination of the Feminist Personality," *Journal of Psychology* 82 (1972): 269–276; J. Joesting, "Comparison of Women's Liberation Members with Their Non-member Peers," *Psychological Reports* 29 (1971): 1291–94.

34. Albert K. Karnig and B. Oliver Walter, "The Election of Women to City Councils," *Social Science Quarterly* 56 (March 1976): 605–613.

35. Ibid., p. 610.

36. The concept of "professional convergence" is derived from the work of Heinz Eulau and John Sprague, *Lawyers in Politics: A Study of Professional Convergence* (Indianapolis: Bobbs-Merrill, 1961).

37. Renshon, p. 78.

CHAPTER 3

Types of Female Political Participation

THE VIRTUE of formulating ideal types is that the sharpness of the contrasts often helps us to perceive reality more accurately. A vital issue for us now is the empirical question of whether or not real women exist who conform to the ideal types we have formulated. It is our task in this chapter to demonstrate that these types do indeed exist and that they can be distinguished in reality. In demonstrating the existence of our ideal types we will, in essence, be concentrating upon stage four of our developmental model, that is, on the nature and direction of political salience and behavior of the females as adults. In the subsequent chapters, we will seek to demonstrate that the political behavior associated with each type included in the study is fundamentally rooted and grounded in the socialization processes in their families.

To date no one has done a study of the socialization of women who have become active in national and international politics. We believe that if we concentrate upon such a group, considerably more will be learned about the potential for future participation by women than if a random sample of the female population, adult or child, is examined. Random samples are representative of existing reality. Unless such samples are studied longitudinally over time or contain representatives of several generations, insights about social change will not be forthcoming. And, even if several generations are studied (if our

---

°Written by Rita Mae Kelly, Mary Boutilier, and Vincent P. Kelly

theory outlined in Chapter Two is correct), then it will still be unlikely that sources of social change will be identified. Social change seems to begin among select pockets of people. The odds of including sufficient numbers of such persons and having the wisdom to recognize them from the rest of the random, representative sample are low indeed.

For our study we have limited our subjects to what is called a focused sample, in this case, women who have attained a specific political status: female revolutionaries, elected female legislators or major political executives, and the wives of political men. All are members of the female elite in politics. The new role for women is exemplified in the revolutionaries and elected female politicians. The lives of the political wives represent the ultimate form of political participation that most women were expected to have and indeed could have traditionally.

Table 3-1 lists the women selected within the three ideal types. The adult behavior of the elected women was found to vary with regard to the age some women began their political careers and the manner in which they related to their husbands and children. Some elected women, such as Margaret Chase Smith, had a strong tradition in their adult lives of having their political participation mediated by their husbands. We call these women the elected/mediated group. They seem to be public women types who were resocialized in their adult life. Another group of women, exemplified by Golda Meir, participated as their own persons from the beginning of their political lives. We call these women (clearly of the achieving political woman type) the elected/personal efficacy group. The revolutionaries also evidence different types of adult behavior. Some, such as Nadezhda Krupskaia (Lenin's wife), are public women subject to the punishment aspect of political salience. The other revolutionaries are famous, achieving political women but with varying amounts of control over their life-spaces. Some of these women personally engaged in terroristic acts and/or were agitators—anarchists. The others were more theoretically inclined; administrators/achievers, if you will. Those whose fame stemmed primarily from their acts of violence and/or anarchist activities we label "terrorists." The other revolutionaries who may have advocated violent overthrow of government, but did not become famous for their personal violence we call the "revolutionaries." Again, it is anticipated that these variations in adult behavior will be directly related to early socialization patterns.

Figure 3-1
The Women Studied

Name	Year of Birth	Year of Death	Country
The Private Women			
1. Yvonne Vendroux de Gaulle	1900	—	France
2. Mamie Doud Eisenhower	1896	—	U.S.A.
3. Nina Petrovna Khrushchev	?	—	U.S.S.R.
4. Thelma Patricia Ryan Nixon	1912	—	U.S.A.
5. Nadezhda Alliluieva Stalin	1903	1932	U.S.S.R.
6. Elizabeth (Bess) Truman	1885	1972	U.S.A.
7. Gladys Mary Baldwin Wilson	1916	—	Great Britain
The Public Women			
1. Clementine Hozier Churchill	1885	—	Great Britain
2. Claudia Alta (Lady Bird) Taylor Johnson	1912	—	U.S.A.
3. Jacqueline (Jackie) Bouvier Kennedy	1929	—	U.S.A.
4. Nadezhda Konstantinovna Krupskaia (Lenin's wife)	1869	1939	U.S.S.R.
5. Anna Eleanor Roosevelt	1884	1962	U.S.A.
The Elected/Mediated Women			
1. Nancy Witcher Langhorne Astor	1879	1964	Great Britain
2. Margaret Chase Smith	1897	—	U.S.A.
3. Leonor Kretzer Sullivan	1904	—	U.S.A.
The Elected/Personal Efficacy Women			
1. Shirley St. Hill Chisholm	1924	—	U.S.A.
2. Bernadette Devlin	1947	—	N. Ireland
3. Indira Nehru Gandhi	1917	—	India
4. Ella Tambussi Grasso	1919	—	U.S.A.
5. Martha Wright Griffiths	1912	—	U.S.A.
6. Golda Mabovitch Meir	1898	—	Israel
7. Margaret Hilda Roberts Thatcher	1925	—	Great Britain
The Revolutionaries			
1. Ekaterina Breshko-Breshkovskaia	1844	1934	Russia

Figure 3-1
The Women Studied

Name	Year of Birth	Year of Death	Country
2. Eva Broido	1876	1941	Russia
3. Angela Davis	1944	—	U.S.A.
4. Halide Edib	1878	1964	Turkey
5. Maud Gonne	1866	1953	Ireland
6. Dolores Ibarruri (La Pasionaria)	1895	—	Spain
7. Alexandra Kollontai	1872	1952	Russia
8. Rosa Luxemburg	1871	1919	Russia, Germany, Poland
9. Constance Markievicz	1876	1927	Ireland
The Terrorists			
1. Charlotte Corday	1768	1793	France
2. Ch'iu Chin	1875	1908	China
3. Emma Goldman	1869	1940	U.S.A.
4. Sophia Perovskaia	1853	1881	Russia
5. Vera Ivanovna Zasulich	1849	1919	Russia

Although the women studied do not constitute a random, representative sample, we have tried to reduce arbitrariness in selection in several ways. First, the private and public women types are represented solely by the wives of twentieth-century chief executives of major political powers. The wives of Lenin,[1] Stalin,[2] and Khrushchev[3] are included from the Soviet Union. Breshnev's wife was not included due to an almost total lack of information on her. Indeed, Khrushchev's wife is quickly dropped from our analyses as we progress because of the paucity of data on her. The wives of the American presidents are represented by Eleanor Roosevelt,[4] Elizabeth (Bess) Truman,[5] Mamie Eisenhower,[6] Jacqueline Kennedy,[7] Lady Bird Johnson,[8] and Pat Nixon.[9] The wives of heads of state of Western European powers are represented by Yvonne de Gaulle,[10] wife of the first president of the Fifth French Republic, Gladys Mary Wilson,[11] and Clementine Churchill,[12] wives of British prime ministers.

The elected women are chosen essentially for their achievements. The elected/mediated efficacy group consists of three women who are clearly outstanding political figures: Margaret Chase Smith[13] was a U.S. congresswoman and senator for over thirty years and the first serious female candidate for the nomination for the U.S. presidency from a major party; Lady Nancy Astor[14] was the first woman elected and seated in the British Parliament, a position she then held for twenty-five years; and finally we include Leonor Sullivan,[15] a U.S. congresswoman for almost twenty-five years. Few women exist in the world with comparable political credentials.

The elected/personal efficacy group are also outstanding political figures who have commanded reputations and/or positions of authority second to none, at least to very few: Indira Gandhi,[16] elected prime minister of India from 1965 to 1977; Golda Meir,[17] prime minister of Israel from 1969 to 1975; Ella Grasso,[18] formerly a congressperson and since 1974 governor of Connecticut, the first woman ever elected governor in her own right of a U.S. state; Martha Griffiths,[19] congresswoman from the Seventeenth District of Michigan (Detroit) for close to twenty years; Shirley Chisholm,[20] one of the first black women elected to the U.S. House of Representatives and, along with Margaret Chase Smith, one of two American women from the major parties who has offered herself as candidate for the U.S. presidency; Margaret Thatcher,[21] member of Parliament for many years, head of the Conservative Party in Great Britain since the summer of 1975 and, hence, at this writing, in line to become Britain's first female prime minister; finally, there is Bernadette Devlin,[22] probably the youngest woman elected to the British Parliament and a famous Irish rebel.

Although some device might exist for obtaining a more representative sample of outstanding elected elite political women, we are confident these women would be within the sample universe. In general, they represent the ultimate form of political participation achieved by anyone—male or female. If the socialization patterns and adult behaviors of these achieving women do indeed differ from those of the private and public women studied, then we will know a great deal about what changes are likely to be needed to increase their number.

The revolutionaries selected also tended to be well-known in their time as important political figures. The specific individuals are: Ekaterina Breshko-Breshkovskaia,[23] a member of the Social Revolutionary party and known as the "Little Grandmother of the Russian Revolution"; Eva Broido,[24] a Russian Marxist and Menshevik; Maud Gonne,[25] member of the Irish revolutionary movement who formed the Daughters of Erin to show that women could fight for freedom as well as men; Halide Edib,[26] one of the very few Turkish female revolutionaries, writer for the leading Young Turk newspaper *(Tanine)*, and the only woman member of the general congress of the Turkish Hearth, a secret organization which supported nationalism; Alexandra Kollontai,[27] a Russian Marxist, Bolshevik, the commissar for social welfare in Lenin's first Soviet cabinet, and the first woman in the world to be accredited as a minister to a foreign country; Rosa Luxemburg,[28] leading political figure in the Polish, Russian, and German Social-Democratic movements, one of the main proponents and theoreticians of the German Left, and one of the founders of the German Communist Party, considered the intellectual equal of the revolutionary theorists of her time (Nikolai Lenin, Leon Trotsky, Karl Kautsky, Karl Liebknecht, and George Plekhanov); Angela Davis,[29] a black American who has gained fame in the 1970s by advocating revolutionary Communistic views; Constance Markievicz,[30] an Irish revolutionary, the first woman ever elected to the British Parliament (she was in jail at the time of her election and unable to take her seat, even if the members of Parliament would have admitted her; she also was the first woman elected and seated in the Irish Parliament, and minister of labor after the Irish revolution); and finally Dolores Ibarruri[31] (La Pasionaria), the Spanish revolutionary who became the heroine legislator of the Spanish Civil War and internationally famous as an outspoken Communist opponent of Generalissimo Francisco Franco and the Nationalists.

Our selection of the revolutionaries and terrorists was necessarily more personalized than the selection of the political wives or the elected political women. Severe language barriers existed simply because there were not very many famous female revolutionaries that we were aware of from English-speaking countries. Since one of the authors (Rita Mae Kelly) had written her doctoral dissertation on a Russian terrorist/revolutionary, Vera Zasulich, and could read Russian, a large number of Russian female revolutionaries were included. The Russian women chosen are among the most famous female participants in the Russian revolutionary movement. The Turkish revolutionary, Edib, is also clearly one of the, if not the most important female political figure of the Turkish Revolution. Maud Gonne, Countess Markievicz, and La Pasionaria were also highly important political figures in the revolutionary movements of their respective countries.

The terrorists/agitators are represented by five people: Sophia Perovskaia,[32] one of the founders and leaders of Zemlia i Volia and Narodnaia Volia, a terrorist who planned and implemented the assassination of Tsar Alexander II in 1881; Vera Ivanovna Zasulich,[33] the attempted assassin of General Trepov, the governor of St. Petersburg in 1878, and later one of the founders and leaders of Russian Marxism and Menshevism; Charlotte Corday,[34] who in 1793 stabbed Jean Paul Marat, a French Jacobin, in his bathtub; Emma Goldman,[35] a well-known American agitator/anarchist; and Ch'iu Chin,[36] member of the Chinese Restoration Society, the chief revolutionary organization in Chekiang in 1906, and founder of the *Chinese Women's Journal*, who was beheaded for complicity in the assassination of a provincial governor. Again, we claim no representativeness for this sample of terrorists/agitators. We only know of their existence and have been able to obtain the needed biographical data on them.

We believe that the women selected for our study represent the range of political behavior in which people engage. We also think that if patterns or variations in the data exist in these ideal types and subgroup types of political women, then we will have found considerable support for our theory of both social change and the socialization of political women—enough support to encourage others to investigate the question of political socialization and social change from the perspective we propose.

To obtain comparable data on the subjects of our study, a standard form was developed (see Appendix). This form allowed us to compare systematically existing historical and biographical data gathered on these women. The available information for each subject was reviewed independently by the two authors and for most subjects at least one outside reader and coder was asked to complete the data form. Due to language and financial barriers, only one person read the Russian subjects. However, both authors went over each item on the standard data form for these and all subjects. The evidence used to justify each coding was reviewed. Where disagreements arose over the proper coding, further evidence and clarification from the original documents were sought. This review process was continued until both authors agreed that the proper code had been given. Since the data sources were of a multiple nature (biography, autobiography, questionnaire), every effort was made to verify every factual piece of information by using more than one source. Items on the form which required some interpretation on the part of the coder (that is, were not a simple matter of fact, such as how many years of formal education the subject's mother had) were completed only if the evidence was unquestionable, could be given direct citation from a passage of a major source, and had unanimous agreement among all readers. The authors' operating procedures and working norms established a very conservative check on the reporting of findings. All benefit of the doubt was toward "non-reporting" when a difference in information or interpretation was found to exist. The coding procedures thus heightened the probability of incurring the Type II or beta error, that is, accepting a null hypothesis—in effect saying no relationship exists when in fact one does. As a consequence of this decision, precise measures of inter- and intra-coder reliability were not deemed necessary and indeed would have proved redundant since 100-percent agreement was necessary for a finding to be cited. (The authors are aware that in experimental and "path-breaking" research the normal procedure is to risk incurring the Type I or alpha error more often than the Type II error. However, the use of biographies prepared by others made, in our judgment, the requirement of the beta error more preferable.)

Our study is exploratory. Its objectives will be obtained if the study is "productive of hypotheses, even if not proof."[37] The use of such diversely collected biographical data, the relatively small number of cases, and the use of retrospective, comparative design obviously means we are not testing the stated hypotheses. The occasional application of statistical tests in Chapters Five and Six (the Student's t) must be viewed in terms of the limitations of the sample and design. Our occasional use of scales, percentages, and tests of significance are presented *only to help clarify the patterns and trends discussed among our subjects* and to provide the reader a suggestive guide for interpreting trends based upon a small number of cases. We seek to determine the "goodness of fit" of the existing biographical data for real elite women with the hypotheses we have formulated. We feel that even with the limitations in the design our efforts are more likely to reveal the processes actually needed to socialize real political women than studies done on random, representative samples of elementary, secondary, or college students or even of women in general which may well meet more adequately the rigorous scientific requirements usually established for such studies.

The Private Woman:
The Tradition-Bound Wife of a Political Man

Winston Churchill once wrote that "there is no doubt that it is around the family and the home that all the greatest virtues, the most dominating virtues of human society, are created, strengthened and maintained."[38] It is not surprising that women, who have traditionally found their essential meaning tied to this institution, would not lightly jeopardize their actual status in this realm for potential status in the political system. This section deals with a category of women who have reaffirmed the importance of the family versus politics, a group who have not consciously chosen to place so great a significance on politics that it might endanger the stability of their own families. Yet, for these private women, politics has encroached on the importance of the family and at times endangered its very stability: these are the tradition-bound wives of political men.

It might appear at first that referring to political wives as private women is contradictory. Recalling the fundamental distinction which the Greeks made between the public and private realms, no greater contrast could be possible than that between the life of politics and the life of a traditional wife. The political half of this category puts one in the public realm, demands that one consider the wider community, and insists that one's ultimate value derives from the contributions one makes to the growth and enhancement of the polis. By contrast, the wife half of the category suggests just the opposite. The family, especially the nuclear family, is the quintessence of the private group. The privatization of the nuclear family cuts it off from the tradition in which the family was one in a complex network of wider groupings such as the clan and the tribe. Finally, the wife in the nuclear family has been historically viewed as a figure who loses her independent adult status when she marries. Proof of this loss is found in the law of coverture: "By marriage, the husband and wife are one person in law; that is, the very being or legal existence of the woman is suspended during the marriage, or at least is incorporated and consolidated."[39] In substance, then, women who married were consigned to primary concern with the private world of the family and were so far removed from the public that even their independence as a potentially public political entity was questioned.

Here we consider seven women who have attempted to fulfill the demands of the role of political wife in a traditional, private-woman type of way. We have restricted the women chosen for this category to those who were the wives of the chief executives of their respective governments. Surely, here all the conflicting forces affecting the "political wife" must reach their apex. To the extent that men who achieve the highest political position in their countries are subjected to the maximum in pressure to devote all their time and energy to the public realm, so too must the wives of such men contend with a variety of pressures that wives of lesser political figures could hardly even countenance. The "private" wives in our study are Gladys Mary Wilson, wife of the former British prime minister; Mamie Eisenhower, Bess Truman, and Pat Nixon, wives of United States presidents; Yvonne de Gaulle, the wife of the first president of the Fifth French Republic; Nadezhda Alliluieva, Joseph Stalin's wife; and Nina Khrushchev, wife of Nikita Khrushchev. Both Stalin and Khrushchev were heads of the U.S.S.R. and the Communist Party of the Soviet Union.

Our first question of these seven women must be whether it is possible to be the wife of the chief executive officer of a country and not "like" or be interested in politics. Obviously, there is a definitional problem involved in the use of the word "politics." One could conceivably be very much interested in the politics of international affairs, the political ramifications of a policy, but not be interested in electoral politics. This may, indeed, be an important theoretical and definitional distinction, but it is one that is not easily handled at an empirical level, for when one says that she is or is not interested in politics, or that politics is or is not salient to her, the fine distinctions are not made. There is, however, seemingly universal understanding as to the general meaning of the term. At some point, the constant regression to primary principles must end. Thus, it is assumed for our purposes that the concept of politics for the women involved in our study evokes similar symbolic images. Accordingly, the assumption of the researchers is that "politics" evokes the same or similar meanings. Nevertheless, whenever and to the extent that finer distinctions can be made, they will be made.

Because they live their entire lives with men whose existence is tied to politics, political wives could never be completely unaware of politics. One might suggest, however, that it is entirely possible to be aware of politics and yet dislike it intensely. Indeed, this seems probable for women who want to devote their lives to the private world of family and friends. The strains of a husband's career on a marriage in terms of mobility factors, time commitment, energy allotment, psychological pressures, and innumerable others can be very great. This appears to be so true that two-career marriages are rare and, if for no other than structural reasons, seemingly unstable. Of course, the society can either enhance or diminish the structural inhibitions to a two-career marriage; and the more rigid the sex-role differentiation, the greater are the societal restraints against the occurrence. However, some careers put more strains on a marriage than others.

A political career is unique in that it involves all the strains cited before and heightens the problems by forcing the public limelight on them. Rather than being worked out in privacy and obscurity, the interactions between husbands and wives with a high public visibility get widespread coverage. The political man is public property as perhaps no other kind of man is. The "servant of the public" is not just an idle image. Consequently, since we make certain assumptions about the package nature of a marriage relationship, the wife also becomes public property. Led to this situation not by choice but by the exigencies of their husbands' careers, political wives may find adjustment very difficult indeed. In the October 7, 1974, issue of *Time* there was an extended article on the ordeals of a political wife in which an anonymous source who happened to be the doctor for a great number of wives of Washington politicians estimated that no more than 3 percent or 4 percent of the political wives genuinely enjoy what they are doing.

There's a lot of resentment under the surface. They always start out with 'my dear, darling husband' and how much he's doing for Cayuga County or wherever the hell he comes from. But if you listen long enough, you find out she doesn't give a hoot about Cayuga County. If you really establish rapport with one of these wives, she will come right out and tell you how horrible her life is.[40]

A good example of a wife who is political only because of her relationship to a political man is YVONNE DE GAULLE. She, of all the wives included in this study, has made the most concerted effort to remain out of the public realm. She has carried her preference for anonymity to such an extreme that she has refused to grant interviews or even to pose for pictures.[41] It is claimed that she could spend the whole day in Paris shops without ever being recognized.[42] This, of course, made our research on her extremely difficult. Even such public sources as *Who's Who in France* had little of the normal public information one might expect to find on such a figure. Consequently, there are gaps in our information on Yvonne de Gaulle. She was never anxious to share any of her husband's political life and seemed always desirous of devoting all her time to him—the private man and husband—and to his children. "Yvonne never felt the need to share more of her husband's public life than was absolutely essential."[43] On at least one occasion, she tried to convince him to give up politics. Clark has described Yvonne de Gaulle as a shy and retiring woman who always kept "aloof from politics."[44] Her self-proclaimed mission in life was "to make a happy home for ... [her] husband."[45] Her rejection of the limelight finds its origins not simply in her shyness; it stems also from her resolution to "do nothing which could possibly detract from the attention which she feels should be paid to General De Gaulle alone."[46] Indeed, the reason she gave her husband for her hesitation concerning his continuation in politics was her feeling that this activity might somehow diminish the exalted place he would have in French history. Her dislike of leaving her own comfortable home and living in the impersonal presidential palace was combined with her interest in her husband's ultimate reputation.

Despite her attempts to be completely divorced from the public realm and remain in the private world of the family, she has had a few minimal public activities which have been closely associated with her primary concern of the family. She has been instrumental in the establishment and workings of the Anne de Gaulle Foundation, named for her daughter, who was retarded and died at an early age. The connection between public duties and the responsibilities of private family life is clear. The traditional female concern with children, especially sick children, is present. The reasons for her interest in this public foundation and working for it appear very personal and highly related to her private family.

Yvonne de Gaulle's public interests also have been directed toward an almost puritanical watchfulness over the moral climate within her immediate environment, which in the case of the wife of the president, includes the government. During De Gaulle's tenure, Madame De Gaulle was known to have objected to the decay of public morality as evidenced by violent or erotic films and revealing fashions for women. The wives of some cabinet ministers were intimidated to the point that they were "afraid to dress in a daring way."[47] She was also vociferous in her objections to divorce and showed her disdain for divorced persons, even, or especially, if they were high governmental officials.

Very similar to Madame De Gaulle in her attitude and behavior toward politics is GLADYS MARY WILSON, wife of the former British prime minister Harold Wilson. Mary Baldwin knew very little about politics when she married Harold Wilson and seemingly her interest did not increase appreciably after that. She felt that her primary task was to keep a comfortable home for her hard-working husband. "This she always regarded as her real responsibility, rather than attempting to enter into the daily happenings of high-powered professional responsibilities."[48] Mary Wilson even wanted her husband to give up politics altogether and return to his career as a teacher at Oxford. Although her preference for the relatively quiet life of the wife of an Oxford professor was not realized, she was able to personally avoid a great deal of unwanted publicity. Harold Wilson has said of the minimal public role his wife played, "After all, she didn't choose this kind of life, and I always try to protect her from things she suffers just because she married me."[49] While Mary Wilson has tried to avoid the limelight, she strenuously objected to being treated simply as a politician's wife. In 1964 when she finally began to accompany Harold Wilson on the campaign trail, she refused to follow the Laborite tradition of wearing red on election day, saying, "I am a woman first and a politician afterwards, and red doesn't suit me."[50]

Joseph Stalin's second wife, NADEZHDA ALLILUIEVA, was difficult to classify. She did not oppose Stalin's role as a public figure. Indeed, at times she seemed excited to be the wife of the Bolshevik who ruled the U.S.S.R. Yet she did not have a public or political life of her own. She worked as a clerk-typist in Lenin's secretariat for a while, but did not have what could be called a separate career. Her most significant political act was the taking of her own life in 1932. But the motivation for suicide seems to have been quite private.

Alliluieva is an example of a girl who struggled to become a public woman, but who was unable to rise above the structural constraints imposed on her by her marriage and station in life. Married at the age of sixteen to a man twenty-two years her senior, she was, as her daughter states, "like a tiny sailboat drawn to a giant, ocean-going steamer."[51] She could never quite catch up to Stalin or to the people who surrounded him when he became the chief executive of the party and the country. The daughter of a mechanic, she was not as cultured or educated as they were. She had a great need to exercise control over her own life, but neither the sex-role ideology with which she was raised nor her position as Stalin's wife permitted her the opportunities she needed to become her own person. "She longed to work on her own and hated being 'first lady of the kingdom.'"[52]

Some commentators assert definitively that she never really loved Stalin. How could she, they ask. He was old enough to be her father, pockmarked and swarthy-looking, while she was a raving beauty.[53] But her daughter believed that she loved him and that she was a good family woman with a strong sense of duty. Her daughter did not believe that Alliluieva would ever have left her father. Her duty was to be his wife; she often left the children to be with him. She took her job as head of the household affairs very seriously. Her husband, Joseph Stalin, came first.

Her daughter suggests that the impetus for committing suicide came from her mother's anger and frustration over Stalin's attitude toward her as a person. At a banquet in honor of the fifteenth anniversary of the October Revolution the night before she killed herself, Svetlana reports, "My father merely said to her, 'Hey, you. Have a drink!' My mother screamed, 'Don't you dare "hey" me!' And in front of everyone she got up and ran from the table."[54] She shot herself a few hours later. Some people said she was mentally unbalanced. We think she is an example of the multitudes of women in the world whose unmet need for personal control over their own lives leads to self-inflicted mental and physical wounds and, sometimes, death. She was a private woman who desperately wanted to be something else.

A Russian political wife who appears to fit the ideal type of

private woman more like Yvonne de Gaulle and Gladys Wilson is
NINA PETROVNA KHRUSHCHEV. She, too, is so shy and retiring that there is scant information, even of the most basic kind,
on her. In an attempt to compile simple information for the W.
Randolph Hearst publication *Ask Me Anything,* a team of researchers asking questions about Nina Khrushchev and her family "had been met with blank stares or banal generalities."[55] It
was noted by the team during the 1957 visit that Nina Khrushchev's picture had never appeared in a Russian periodical. The
obscurity surrounding her extended to the point that the team
could not learn her first name! In one of our sources on Nikita
Khrushchev the information on his wife is revealing. These are
some of the characteristics and actions attributed to her:

1. Nina Khrushchev is credited with having lowered her
husband's high consumption of alcohol.

2. She stopped him from wearing a military uniform.

3. She was a very good housewife and mother.

4. She was said to have designed a country house outside of
Moscow and had it constructed based on models of homes she
had seen during her visit to the United States.

5. During the 1959 visit by U.S. Vice-President Richard M.
Nixon, she cooked one of the meals.

6. She is taller than the average Russian.

7. She dresses simply.

8. On one occasion, "she mentioned that the bloody purges
must end."[56]

The first deals with the private habits of her husband, the second and seventh with dress or fashion, the third, fourth, and fifth
with the customary female roles of wife, mother, and homemaker. The sixth is a physical trait: she is tall. It is only the eighth
item that is directly connected with the public/political realm.

In the final analysis, it is her absence from the political and
social scene, as evidenced by the lack of public knowledge about
her, which leads us to classify Nina Khrushchev as a traditional,
private woman.

BESS TRUMAN is the first private type of American political wife included in our study. The themes which are to be repeated in reference to women who marry public men and whom
we have classified as traditional, private women run through her
life. Although Harry S. Truman was a henpecked man in his own
home,[57] the realm of Bess Truman's authority and influence

seems to have been restricted to that private world. She was un-interested in transforming private power into political power. Even the influence and sway she exercised over Harry Truman appears to have been in traditional female areas. The stories of his verbal excesses are many. The occasions on which his wife tried to break him of this habit are probably as numerous. On one occasion, Truman had publicly told certain voters to "go to hell." He was then told by his wife if he could not talk "politer [sic] than that in public, you come right home."[58] The public and po-litical consequences of this sort of behavior are minimal indeed. The potential for significant political clout is left unrealized. Being close to the source of political power does not necessarily lead to participation in the exercise of that power.

With regard to the wider world, Bess Truman

> carried out her public functions dutifully and correctly, dis-playing neither zest, flair, nor pleasure. She had not sought the role. If it had been her choice, she would not have gone to the White House. She did not want her daughter to be a First Lady; and if she had had a son, she would not have brought him up to be President.[59]

She saw the public world of her husband's life as an imposition on her privacy and urged him to leave public life to return to In-dependence, Missouri, after completing the unexpired term of Franklin Delano Roosevelt.

Bess Truman is perhaps best described as a woman for whom politics was positively distasteful. Born into the genteel world of wealth, she disliked many of the qualities associated with political careers. "She was a robust, strong-willed, clear-headed, no-nonsense woman."[60] She clearly preferred her ac-quaintances and friends from Independence to those of the Washington circle. Not interested in promoting her husband's political career, she spent most of her time and energy on tradi-tional female concerns. Her greatest passion appears to have been bridge. She was known to have on occasion transported her entire Missouri bridge club to Washington to continue a game.[61]

The case of MAMIE EISENHOWER is also familiar to most Americans; she, too, illustrates well that the ideal type of private woman exists in the United States. As Borzman puts it, "Mamie made no attempt to influence her husband; it was not her place, she believed, to participate in the affairs of the government."[62]

Even after Dwight Eisenhower's election to the presidency, Mamie Eisenhower thwarted attempts to make her more visible by refusing interviews, making no speeches, and granting no press conferences. "On one thing she was determined: that was to remain in the background and not attempt to shine in Ike's reflected glory."[63]

The fact that Mamie Eisenhower had never voted in a national election before 1948 indicates two things: (1) that she was basically disinterested in politics, and (2) that her husband's status in the military removed him—and her—from participation in politics. When his status changed suddenly, she did not drastically alter her attitudes or behavior. Mamie Eisenhower, like Mary Wilson and Yvonne de Gaulle, did not enjoy large parties or formal entertaining, and even had a fear of crowds. She did not want or encourage her husband to try for the presidential nomination in 1952. When the necessities of the presidential race required her to talk to reporters, she did not talk about politics.[64]

THELMA PATRICIA NIXON shows a general similarity to the other political wives discussed thus far. Her insistence on privacy and isolation from public view left most Americans to wonder what she really was like. Levin has written of Pat Nixon:

> she is self-effacing, to the point of bluntness—that rare woman who loathes talking about herself, who seems to regard the use of the first person pronoun as self-indulgent, and, in general, prunes her thoughts to a single sentence where others would feel constrained within a long paragraph.[65]

She, like so many political wives, was not a leading star, but a supporting actor; it was in this supportive role that she found her purpose.[66]

Pat Nixon appears to be the totally private woman who was indeed pushed into the limelight which held little enticement for her. Her reticence extends even to her own internal family relations. David Eisenhower, her son-in-law, has said of her, "It's really unusual to be talking about her—she never talks about herself. I kind of worry about her because she never lets any of us know what troubles her."[67] And yet, ever since Richard Nixon's first campaign for Congress, this totally private woman has been at her husband's side willing to do whatever she could for him. It was said of her during the 1960 presidential campaign that she was the ideal candidate's wife, for she accompanied her husband on every trip and avoided all political subjects.[68]

Pat Nixon has had to face many severe personal disappointments related to her husband's career. They began as early as the scandal that necessitated the "Checkers" speech, when Nixon was running for the vice-presidency, and continued through the bitter disappointment of the 1960 loss of the presidential election. Of this defeat, Pat Nixon said, "We deserved to win. We won in 1960, but the election was stolen from us."[69] Another great trial was Richard Nixon's loss in the 1962 election for governor of California, an election in which she did not wish her husband to participate. Finally, there came the ultimate disgrace of his resignation from the presidency and the need of a pardon for his activities during his own administration. Pat Nixon has known the sorrow associated with public life. Her response to this sorrow was to find refuge in her private life and to remove herself from public view and the political arena.

One journalist sums up her attitudes about the presidency this way: "Pat, of course, would never stand in her husband's way. He knew that she did not share his passionate affinity for politics despite the fact that she had served faithfully at his side during his House and Senate campaigns."[70] Pat Nixon has stated her own position in unmistakable terms: "I want to be a wife and mother, not a public figure."[71]

For these seven political wives, politics was not personally salient save for its connection with their husbands. None received personal gratification from the purely political behavior but rather grounded her acceptance of the exigencies of politics in devotion to husband and family. These wives let the requirements of political life interfere as little as possible with their private lives and, when politics did intrude, resentment, resignation, and a sense of the inevitable surrounded their assent to its demands. The length of their interest in politics, its consistency and persistence, the range and levels of interest are all functions of their relationship to their husbands. The origin of their minimal interest in politics is found in their marriage; their success or failure in political behavior reduces to the success or failure of their husbands, and without this connection the political system would seemingly lack all salience for them. They do represent real-life forms of our ideal type of the private woman.

The Public Woman:
The Political Wife with a Moderately Activist Sex-Role Ideology

The political wives who appear to be real-life representatives of our "public woman" ideal type are Jacqueline Kennedy, Lady Bird Johnson, Clementine Churchill, Nadezhda Krupskaia, and Eleanor Roosevelt. These women represent those who have remained traditional in their relationships with their husbands and families and have clearly given the family top priority in their lives, but who have also embarked upon public activities of their own. Unlike the traditional women who were thrust into the public limelight because of marrying men whose private lives were necessarily public, these women envisioned some role for themselves beyond that in the private family. Some even have chosen some forms of political involvement as a means of self-expression.

Of the five women in this category JACQUELINE BOUVIER KENNEDY is closest in behavior to our private women. Jacqueline Kennedy, however, was never able to maintain the anonymity common to the "private woman." Followed constantly and relentlessly by the press, Jacqueline Kennedy during and after her marriage to Jack Kennedy was almost instantaneously recognized by everyone, everywhere. Nor was this public "notoriety" always necessarily thrust upon an unwilling recipient. Particularly during her White House years Jackie Kennedy made personal appearances on TV which were not strictly necessary to further her husband's career. Yet her usual practice was to remain uninvolved in political action. Mary Gallagher, her personal secretary, has noted that even during the height of the 1960 presidential campaign, "Only around Jacqueline was there serenity and a sense of regal aloofness from the grubby details of politics."[72]

In many respects Jackie Kennedy's attitudes and behavior stand out in sharp contrast to the other Kennedy wives and sisters. As Gallagher observed, "Jackie did not relish politics. She did not get a thrill as the Senator did, in hearing a crowd outside his window cheering him. . . . Jackie was a reluctant campaigner. She did not take to politics as the other Kennedy women did—the candidate's mother, sisters, sister-in-law."[73]

Another writer confirms the picture of Jacqueline Kennedy

as a person who sought to keep at least part of herself away from public view.

> Though public interest would follow her every move, the First Lady was to retain a core of privacy which would enable both the President and herself to relax and be replenished. Here, in this shelter, she fulfills to her own satisfaction her primary roles of wife and mother. Mrs. Kennedy's special qualities, enhanced by experience in the years ahead, will continue to benefit her husband, her children, and the nation.[74]

Once again the theme of the family-centered private woman who has been drawn into the public limelight is stressed.

Much of the publicity that Jackie Kennedy received while in the White House was associated with functions which strict sex-role stereotyping would designate as feminine. Probably the most widely remembered of these activities was the redecoration of the White House. "When Jackie's love of interior decorating turned to the White House, she worked harder and longer and more painstakingly than anyone could imagine. And that was because she wanted to. If anyone had tried to stop her from redecorating the White House, he would have had a hard time."[75] What more could one expect from a dutiful and loving wife and mother than that she convert a house into a home? Even the cultural and historical renovation, which was publicly hailed as her contribution to the public life of the nation, was entirely in keeping with the functions traditionally expected of women. Not politics, power, and the grubby side of campaigns, but the cultured, refined, and noncontroversial aspects of public life; these were the First Lady's concerns.

Another way in which Jackie Kennedy gained much publicity related to yet another female concern—fashion. It is not an exaggeration to say that Jackie Kennedy literally dictated fashion in the Washington circle, if not in the country, for some time. The interest in what she wore, the length of her gown or dress, the nature of her hair style, the type of her hats, went on and on. Surely this was not independent of her personal interest in this area, but just as surely this is an area in which the First Lady of the nation is expected to be interested and involved.

Unlike Eleanor Roosevelt, who hated the protocol and the ceremony associated with social functions, and who feared that her position as First Lady would prevent her from her own personal active involvement in issues she found important, Jackie Kennedy loved and relished this aspect of White House life. Never a slave to the staid tradition of White House entertaining, she brought an opulence and elegance which had not been seen before.[76]

Although we have suggested that Kennedy fits the private-woman mold of political wife better than Eleanor Roosevelt, one should not underestimate the differences between Jackie Kennedy and self-effacing wives like Yvonne de Gaulle, Mary Wilson, and Mamie Eisenhower. These latter women forswore publicity and the limelight; they were motivated by the simple desire to be a helpmate for their famous husbands and never to outshine them. Jackie Kennedy was not so disposed. This was particularly true of environments in which she felt comfortable. Thus when the Kennedys visited Paris, Jack Kennedy, the president of the U.S., could humorously remark, "I do not think it altogether inappropriate to introduce myself. I am the man who accompanied Jacqueline Kennedy to France."[77] One who might not have found this statement particularly funny was Yvonne de Gaulle, a woman who would do nothing to detract from the attention to her husband.[78]

LADY BIRD JOHNSON is more clearly a public woman. Her attitudes toward politics and public life were more ambiguous than Jackie Kennedy's. Lady Bird Johnson had the opportunity to be with her husband through an entire range of political positions and jobs, and her own relationship to each of these seems to have constituted a developmental process itself. The Johnsons were married in 1934 and, when a congressional seat became available in 1937, Lyndon B. Johnson decided to run for it. He did consult with his wife on this matter before he made up his mind. However, Lady Bird Johnson recalls, "I think his own decisiveness should get almost the entire credit for that [deciding to run]."[79] Although the decision to run seems to have been his, the money was hers. The campaign costs were expected to be about $10,000; the day after the decision was made Lady Bird Johnson called her father, and the sum was placed at LBJ's disposal.

As the wife of a congressman, Lady Bird Johnson found the social functions enjoyable and even received personal delight from ushering constituents about the Capitol, for it meant "she would not be lonely while he spent long hours on his job."[80] Her initial entries into politics were dictated by her concern for her husband and his career rather than some profound and personal interest in politics. It was not until she came to operate her husband's congressional office while he was in the Navy that she found some personal growth and development flowering from her involvement. She recalls that running his office was "the best thing that ever happened to me, because after about three or four months I felt for the first time that, if it were necessary, I could make my own living and that is a good feeling to have. But best of all, it gave me a greater understanding of Lyndon."[81] Significantly, the best part of this experience was not the revelation it afforded about the how and why of politics, but the opportunity it gave her to come to understand better what she perceived to be her first obligation, her husband. It was at this time that she decided to acquire a business to act as a cushion for her husband's unpredictable political career. Her business ventures were primarily in communications and in ranching. Thus, even though Lady Bird Johnson had sufficient time and independence to start businesses, it was not politics and the political arena that attracted her attention. She did not actively campaign or speak on LBJ's behalf until his 1948 Senate campaign.

Once Lyndon Johnson achieved the presidency, Lady Bird Johnson was constantly interviewed and her relationship to her husband became a source of widespread interest. She always answered such queries in a most wifely manner. For instance, she is quoted in *Vogue* as saying, "I became all I am in response to Lyndon."[82] When asked by a *New York Times* reporter if the White House had changed her personality, she replied, "I tried to learn how to dress better. How to look better. That pleases my husband. And what pleases him, pleases me."[83] Again in response to a *New York Times* interview Johnson explained that as the wife of the president she "attempts to provide a secure 'pleasant little island' where he can work, relax without being bothered by questions."[84]

The one issue with which Lady Bird Johnson was probably most frequently associated during the presidency of her husband was that of beautification. Needless to say, this is one of those issues to which women, and political wives in particular, are likely to devote their time and for which the normative structures of the culture afford them positive reinforcement. Undoubtedly, it is the societal counterpart to the idea of personal fashion and beauty, factors usually associated with the females of the society. In a discussion of her interest in the beautification program, Johnson commented that beautification begins "as everything should begin—right at home."[85] Perhaps unlike other political wives because of her own financial independence and the lack of wealth on the part of her husband, Lady Bird Johnson contributed in an unusual way to her husband's political career, but nevertheless the motives and values behind this activity seem to be those of women with a moderately activist sex-role ideology, that is, as the helpmates and supporters of their husbands.

The adjectives so often used to describe Yvonne de Gaulle, Mary Wilson, Mamie Eisenhower, and Pat Nixon—quiet, shy, self-effacing, retiring, totally devoted wives and mothers—certainly do not fit the person of ELEANOR ROOSEVELT. Writing of her earliest entry into the public realm, Lash has stated: "Eleanor had never shunned work, but the war [World War I] harnessed her considerable *executive abilities* to her always active sense of responsibility. The war gave her a reason acceptable to her conscience to free herself of the social duties that she hated, to concentrate less on her household, and plunge into work that fitted her aptitudes. Duty now commanded what she could take pleasure in doing."[86] (Italics ours.)

Perhaps the most noteworthy thing about Eleanor Roosevelt's political involvement is that it did not so much complement Franklin Delano Roosevelt's actions as compensate for them; she was severely hurt by his affair with Lucy Mercer.[87] While FDR was running for vice-president with Cox, she granted an interview in which she clearly distinguished between her own interest in politics and that of her husband. Asked if she was interested in politics she said:

> Yes, I am interested in politics, intensely so, but in that I think I am no different from the majority of women only that, of course, I have followed my husband's career with an interest that is intense because it is personal. But I have never campaigned for him. I haven't been active in politics in any way, and so you see there isn't much of a story to be found in me.[88]

It was not long, however, before she was campaigning with FDR in that 1920 election. Although this meant a great personal sacrifice, she acquiesced to his wishes. In order to do so she had to place James, their twelve-year-old son, in a boarding school where he promptly became ill. Despite her natural desire to go to her son's bedside, she again complied with FDR's request that she remain with him on the campaign trail. She did, writing to a friend, "I am going gaily on."[89]

After the campaign Eleanor Roosevelt returned to school herself and also became very active in the League of Women Voters. Later, after FDR was stricken with polio, she often became his stand-in at social and political events. As to her motivations, Lash again makes a very important point:

> As it became clear that Franklin would not return to public activity for a long time . . . Eleanor had to become actively involved in Democratic politics in order to keep alive Franklin's interest in the party and the party's interest in him . . . . and beneath the implacable promptings of conscience, there now were also the stirrings of ambition—the desire to show that she could succeed in this man's world of politics—and, even deeper, a repressed but sweetly satisfying awareness that the fate of the man who had hurt her so deeply now depended upon the success she made of her work for him.[90]

The duration and range of Eleanor Roosevelt's interest in the public, political realm is extensive indeed. She was involved in a wide variety of public causes: the Women's Trade Union League, the American Foundation to get the U.S. into the World Court, the fight for the child labor amendment. She fought for prison reform, against discrimination toward Negroes, and for an active role for women in the Democratic Party machinery. She supported movements to help delinquent black girls and to block the State Department's reorganization, and so on. Her Democratic Party work and organization over the years would require an extensive volume just to describe. What is most interesting to note is the degree to which she could see politics as so independent of her husband that when FDR won the governorship of New York but Al Smith lost the presidency, she was upset, saying, "If the rest of the ticket didn't get in, what does it matter? No, I am not excited about my husband's election. I don't care. What difference can it make to me?"[91]

In 1932 Eleanor Roosevelt had mixed feelings about her husband's nomination to the presidency, as did Mamie Eisenhower later. What is totally different about these similar responses is the motivation behind them. Eleanor Roosevelt feared FDR's victory and assumption of the presidency not because it would thrust her into the public limelight, as was Mamie Eisenhower's thought, but rather because she feared that the pomp and traditional responsibilities of the position of First Lady would prevent her from continuing her own public and political activity. "She did not wish to be shielded from the world but to take part in it and change it. . . . She feared that all these things would become impossible once she was First Lady, that she would become a prisoner of protocol and tradition."[92] Eleanor Roosevelt does not seem to fit the traditional mold of political wife at all. Indeed, it appears that under suitable circumstances at the appropriate time and place Eleanor Roosevelt might easily have assumed some elected political position herself.

CLEMENTINE CHURCHILL, the wife of the former British prime minister, resembles Eleanor Roosevelt in a number of ways. In fact her friendship with Eleanor Roosevelt led to many meetings and mutual projects for these two famous women. Like Roosevelt, Churchill was always deeply involved in her husband's political career and campaigned vigorously for his election. She has even been called "his chief election aid[e]."[93] On one occasion she said of her own campaign activity that "someone has got to speak up about him, and who, if not his wife."[94] She, of course, also performed the functions of the wife of the prime minister as the social entertainer par excellence. But Clementine Churchill's activity, like Eleanor Roosevelt's, went beyond that normally associated with the wife of the chief executive. The circumstances of World War II made the utilization of the services of women a necessity at all levels of society. Both she and Eleanor Roosevelt were very interested in the war effort and particularly the part the women were playing in it. On several occasions she made her own decisions about which areas she would visit despite the dangers associated with the visits and her husband's objections. Clementine Churchill was especially interested in the hospitals and the hostels the young women were living and working in during the war. In addition, because of Winston Churchill's concern with national affairs, she often handled his election in his home constituency; she even wrote her own speeches.[95]

There is little doubt that Churchill could have had a significant and worthwhile political career of her own. "Clementine wished she could have been an M.P. on her own and she had the ability for it."[96] She was personally active in Conservative Party politics, and was the president of the Woodford Conservative Association. There was even talk in 1952 of having her run for Winston's old seat when he suffered his stroke.[97]

Despite the obviously strong personal character and ability of Clementine Churchill, the reasons for her involvement in politics were very similar to those of the political wives who saw their role as complementary rather than fully independent of that of their husbands. A longtime friend of the Churchills has indicated the motivation behind the primary activity of her life. "I honestly think she is the ideal wife. If a wife loves a husband enough to sink herself completely in him, in what interests him, and in his work, ignoring her own advancement except through him—that is the perfect relationship of husband and wife. . . . Her husband has always been the most important thing in her life."[98] Thus, although Clementine Churchill might have had more of the personal qualities and interests to allow her to be an independent political actor than many of the wives studied, she nevertheless still found her roles as wife and mother the most important. "In spite of Clementine's possessing a distinct personality of her own, her sense of dignity would never allow her temperament to create domestic turmoil that would intrude into her husband's public or private life."[99]

NADEZHDA KRUPSKAIA is best known as the wife of Lenin, the Father of the Russian Revolution and first head of the Union of Soviet Socialist Republics. But Krupskaia was no ordinary "First Lady." The very title was considered bourgeois by the early Russian Marxists. As McNeal states, "Women were comrades, not decorative possessions now, and an experienced party member like Krupskaia could better serve the cause as a responsible official in her own right than by shaking hands in reception lines."[100] Krupskaia contributed substantially to the Russian revolutionary movement and later participated as an administrator in the newly formed Soviet government.

Krupskaia's father had been radical for his time; he encouraged her interest in social issues and education. In her early twenties she became a teacher of basic subjects to adult factory workers, an unusual occupation for a woman at that time. She saw the squalor and suffering caused by poverty and ignorance. Her involvement in revolutionary activity began before meeting Lenin in 1894, and became increasingly more intense after their marriage in 1896.

She became Lenin's assistant, secretary, and executive manager for development of the underground Russian Social-Democratic Workers Party while she and Lenin lived in Western Europe. There was no doubt, however, who was the leader, thinker, and boss, and who was the follower, secretary, and subordinate. She clearly worked under his direction. After the Bolshevik revolution, she became a noted Russian educationist. She became a member of the commissariat of education and contributed substantially to the party's plan for popular education for what at the time was basically an illiterate population. In 1921 she became head of Glavpolitprosvet (Main Committee of Political Enlightenment), which had a budget of a million rubles and an organization of about 475,000 people.[101] After Lenin's death in 1924, though her moral authority was eulogized, her actual influence dwindled. The formal honors sharply increased, however. At the Fifteenth Party Congress in 1927 she became a member of the Central Committee of the Communist Party. In 1929, at the age of sixty, she was given the Red Banner of Labor; in 1931 she was named an honorary member of the Academy of Science; in 1933 the Order of the USSR and the Order of Lenin were bestowed upon her. In 1936 an honorary doctorate of pedagogical science was awarded to her. Politically, her highest elective position came in 1935 at the age of sixty-six, when she was elected to the All-Union Congress of Soviets, the legislative assembly of the USSR, and in 1937, when she was elected to its successor, the Supreme Soviet, and to that body's inner circle of the Presidium. McNeal notes "these honors were but baubles, signifying only that Lenin's widow gave her blessing (and his) to the regime of Stalin, who had arranged it all."[102]

McNeal also notes that "her place in the Soviet pantheon is secure, below Lenin and nobody else. Krupskaia remains the symbol of the liberated woman, the devoted spouse, the loving mother—in sum, the bride of the revolution."[103] In spite of the phrase "liberated woman," this quote and Krupskaia's life place her more clearly in the traditional category of public woman than the other revolutionaries discussed below, even though she never had any children. Throughout most of her life she was Lenin's helpmate, not an independent political actor. Although the cultural and historical context was different, Krupskaia's relationship to political activity and to her husband was rather similar to that of Eleanor Roosevelt. Both had husbands who promoted their wives' political activities; both had husbands who had love affairs that hurt their wives considerably. Both made historically important contributions to their respective countries. Yet both did so from the traditional stance as the wife of a famous male politician. Although it is not totally inconceivable that Krupskaia would have become a famous revolutionary if she had not married Lenin, we strongly doubt it. The adult role of support that she played with Lenin is most similar to the role which her own mother played with her father, who wandered throughout Russia for many years in part because of his political views. If Krupskaia had not married Lenin, she probably would have married someone else to whom she would have devoted her considerable talents and energies. She and Lenin were married by a Russian Orthodox cleric; and although she later sharply opposed religion of any sort, she always remained a firm advocate of the traditional family structure and, essentially, of traditional male-female relationships in society. Her views of women's place in society in no way match the type of social change desired by many of her contemporary female revolutionaries, such as Alexandra Kollontai (see below).

Our public women are clearly different from the private women in their attitudes toward nonfamily activity and politics. The wives described as public women find much more joy and pleasure in their public roles. Public and political functions add an important, usually desired, dimension to their lives; this contrasts sharply with the political wives designated as private women. Political wives of the public-woman type may have begun their political lives because of political husbands and their demands, but they quickly found this activity to their liking. Politics for them has been mediated by a male at its origins but as they personally spoke, appeared in public, organized, campaigned, fought and contributed in whatever way they could, they gained confidence and interest. Mediated efficacy led to a personal sense of efficacy. Given the appropriate adult opportunities, they might well have become elected political women on their own.

The Elected Woman with Mediated Efficacy

For this study the concept of achieving political woman has been restricted either to women elected to a major public office, and possessing a strong sense of personal political efficacy, or to those engaging in revolutionary political behavior. In terms of our ideal types, girls become achieving political women as a result of having developed a strong sense of personal efficacy very early in life. There are women, however, who have the characteristics of public women but who have achieved national elected office. These women seem to have been resocialized to develop a strong sense of efficacy after being married for several years or after their husbands have died. Most of these elected women with public-woman characteristics married men with political aspirations. The husbands' participation seems to have heightened the wives' mediated sense of efficacy and increased their personal participation to such an extent that politics became not only salient to them, but also a career aspiration. The women studied in our group designated as the elected/mediated women—Nancy Langhorne Astor, Leonor Sullivan, and Margaret Chase Smith—are resocialized women. Their sense of mediated efficacy was changed after marriage to a sense of personal political efficacy. Although these women are a subcomponent of our ideal type of public woman, for ease of reference we will distinguish these elected public women from the political wife/public woman by calling them "elected/mediated" women. Such a distinction will convey the difference in political behavior and allow us to stress more sharply the importance of resocialization for such women in becoming achievers in politics.

The first woman elected and actually seated in the British Parliament, NANCY WITCHER LANGHORNE ASTOR, was born in the United States. Her father was something of a tyrant who dominated a submissive wife. The father's sister, however, was a strong-willed woman who provided a positive female role model. Her Aunt Lewis shattered the social expectations of what a young lady could do. She founded the first school for "colored people" in Virginia and she herself served as principal and teacher. Nancy Astor developed a strong will and independent mind. She was an early and ardent suffragette. However, it was not until her marriage to her second husband, the Briton Waldorf Astor, that she became involved in politics.

Waldorf Astor belonged to a wealthy and influential family. He had held various ministries in addition to running the family-owned newspaper, the *Observer*. It was at his suggestion and insistence that she entered political life.[104] Indeed, it may have been that he was utilizing his wife to retain a seat in the House of Commons. When his father died, the seat from Plymouth became vacant. Too busy with the family business and the *Ob-*

server, he encouraged his wife to run for her late father-in-law's seat. Elected in 1919, she remained in the House of Commons twenty-five years, allowing her husband to retain some influence there.

Nancy Astor's personal political history does not demonstrate much personal initiative in substantive political issues. Outside of a futile attempt to promote legislation to prohibit alcohol and a brief trip to Moscow, she seems to have performed mainly feminine tasks in Parliament. Most often she played the role of hostess, welcoming new women members into government service and encouraging more women to run for office. Other than prohibition, no independently espoused political issue can be linked with the name of Nancy Astor. Twenty-five years in the House of Commons appear to represent more the fulfillment of expectations associated with her uniquely political husband and family than any independently and individually held desire to seek political office.

Her political involvement did not conflict with her family obligations to any substantial degree. Indeed, had she not acceded to her husband's wishes the potential for familial conflict might have been greater. Nancy Astor gave birth to six children while a member of Parliament. She had achieved her seat before the birth of her first child. Of course, her husband's wealth facilitated this freedom from the obligations of cooking, housekeeping, and child care.

Politics seems to have been a central interest in family life for the Astors, since four out of her five sons went on to political careers of their own. It was at her husband's insistence that she finally retired in 1947; but with her sons grown she felt restless and confined. Accustomed as she was to public recognition and social and personal political activity, staying at home was difficult for her. When she tried to continue her political life by involving herself in her sons' political activities, they demanded that she desist. One of her sons, Jackie, even forbade her to speak to members of his constituency.[105]

The insistence of Astor's husband that she retire, and the conflicts stemming from one of her son's homosexual activities and attempts at suicide, led to a series of separations from her husband, and almost to the dissolution of the marriage. At length, however, she acquiesced to the wishes of her husband and sons. Her action was reminiscent of her mother's role, and she once said: "Very early in life I sensed that she [mother] had the stronger character. But father had the power. He held the purse strings."[106] Thus, both Astor's entry into and her exit from politics were mediated by the men in her life.

LEONOR SULLIVAN's initiation into the U.S. political arena was mediated by her marriage to a man who was already active in politics. When asked at what age she first got involved in politics, Leonor Sullivan answered simply, "When I married."[107] She states that her marriage to John B. Sullivan was instrumental in getting her involved in politics, for her husband was active already and it seemed the appropriate thing to do.

She married relatively late, at thirty-seven, and had no children. Accordingly, she could spend the major portion of her time working in her husband's congressional office. After his death she worked for another congressman for a year before deciding to run for Congress herself.

In twenty-three years in the House of Representatives, Leonor Sullivan achieved a position of influence in the Congress. As chairperson of the Merchant Marine and Fishing Committee, she was the seventh woman to head a standing committee.[108] It is contended by some that she was the most powerful woman member of Congress in 1974.[109]

Leonor Sullivan gives personal testimony to the fact that in her case political salience was originally male-mediated. Writing about how she helped her husband in his political life, she says:

> I felt it was my responsibility to help the public know him as I did and I believe I was successful. Later this association with politics was very valuable when I became a candidate myself. After my husband's death I made this work my life—perhaps taking on more responsibility than was needed—but it kept me in the Congress for twenty-three years to date.[110]

Much of the tone of her response is reminiscent of that so frequently given by political wives. She began her political activity as a wife interested in helping her husband in his career. It is significant that after twenty-three years as representative from the Third District of Missouri, she still identifies herself and signs her letters as Leonor K. (Mrs. John B.) Sullivan. Despite the power of her political office, she has never demonstrated a "feminist" approach to politics. In fact she was the only congresswoman to vote against the Equal Rights Amendment![111] Gentle, kind, and ladylike, Leonor Sullivan represents the public woman who has, through circumstance, evolved into an elected official.

Although MARGARET CHASE SMITH had engaged in public life as member and president of the State Federation of Business and Professional Women's Clubs and as Republican committeewoman from Somerset County in Maine, "it was really her marriage to Clyde Smith that determined her career in politics."[112] At the time of their marriage in 1930, Clyde Smith was already very much involved in politics. In fact, the couple had a rather unusual courtship. She says: "Mostly we went campaigning. Anyone who ever spent any time with him ended up going campaigning."[113] When they married, Clyde Smith was fifty-four, his bride thirty-three. The fact that they had no children in their ten years of married life together meant that the couple could be more involved in politics as a team. Relieved of the cross-pressures of motherhood and public life, Smith and her husband could literally make politics their entire lives. Persuaded to run for Congress in 1936, Clyde Smith won and took his seat in the House of Representatives. In April of 1940 Clyde Smith suffered his second heart attack. In doubt as to whether he could manage to survive the upcoming election, his physician suggested to him that he tell his constituents of his illness and that his wife would file in his place if his illness proved disabling. On the very day that Clyde Smith released this plan to the press, he suffered a fatal heart attack. Despite the fact that Margaret Chase Smith had never run for office, the death of her husband and his wish to have her assume his seat propelled her into four campaigns in seven months. This did not mean she had party support. In fact, just the opposite was the case. First she had to wage a campaign in a primary, win an election to fill her husband's unexpired term, and then less than six months later get the nomination and be elected to Congress in her own right. Of her four victories she said, "I'd been taught by my husband to do it right. None of the elections was even close."[114]

Margaret Chase Smith spent more than twenty-five years in the House and the Senate. Her decision to run for the Senate was one based on a clear idea of her own personal qualifications for the post. Her personal political participation clearly had raised her sense of personal political efficacy. "Unusual" must be the label used to describe her political career *once she became a political actor.* Early in her political life she was assigned to innocuous congressional committees but by the time of her retirement she was the ranking Republican on the Senate Armed Services Committee—hardly a typically traditional female concern. In addition, Smith made it publicly known that she was seeking the presidential nomination and would accept the vice-presidency. Aside from the presidential campaigns of early suffragettes representing minor fringe parties, no woman had ever before aspired to such a high position in a major party.

As a realist, Margaret Chase Smith knew that her bid for the presidency could not possibly be successful at that time. Yet as a representative of American women in general she demonstrated that it is every woman's right to aspire to as high a responsibility as she is capable—if she wants to. More women will want to when they realize that success in politics for a woman is a real possibility.

Her record of being present at consecutive roll calls is remarkable in the Senate. It reflects her sense of moral responsibility to vote on every issue on behalf of her constituency, regardless of the difficulties in arranging her own schedule or in attending to other political matters in committees. This behavior was most uncommon among her colleagues—all of whom were men.

Smith's courage to be different and to follow the dictates of her conscience showed in other ways as well. In response to the 1950s witch-hunt for Communists led by Senator Joseph McCarthy, she delivered her now famous "Declaration of Conscience." A most impolitic move was this. She had called to task a member of her own party; she had risked an attack from the very forces using these scare tactics; and significantly, she had questioned the "gentlemanly" rules and procedures of the hallowed halls of the Senate by noting how "we smear outsiders from the Floor of the Senate and hide behind the cloak of Congressional immunity and still place ourselves beyond criticism on the Floor of the Senate."[115]

One need not doubt the salience of politics to Margaret Chase Smith, but its origins, direction, and intensity had all been initially contingent upon her husband's involvement. It is impossible to predict how different her political behavior would have been under other circumstances. It is a fact, however, that this highly visible and respected politician did not actively embark on her political career until after the death of her husband. She is a public woman resocialized into a formidable, achieving, political woman.

The Achieving Woman:
The Elected/Personal Efficacy Group

The next group of subjects represents those women who developed a strong sense of personal political efficacy as children. They began their careers independent from those of their husbands. The motivation and impetus for intense participation in politics come from their personal experiences and beliefs; the mediation of males in their political activities is essentially nonexistent. At least, the assistance and encouragement from males are not sharply different from what one man might give to another. In other words, these women begin with the assumption that both sexes are created equal. The family, while important and a vital part of their lives, is not an impossible obstacle to political participation. Nor are husbands. The women studied who represent this type are Martha Griffiths, Ella Grasso, Shirley Chisholm, Margaret Thatcher, Indira Gandhi, Golda Meir, and Bernadette Devlin.

MARTHA WRIGHT GRIFFITHS spent eighteen years representing the Seventeenth District of Michigan (Detroit) in the House of Representatives. Her stance on many public issues marked her off from all other congresspersons. Martha Griffiths has been oriented toward significant and powerful committees. As a member of the House Ways and Means, Economic Progress, and Urban Affairs committees, she has been in a position to initiate and to support important legislation helpful to her constituents and to the nation at large.

Unlike Smith and Sullivan, Griffiths did not assume the political position vacated by the death of her husband. Her path to political office certainly was closer to the traditional male pattern. She graduated along with her husband from the Michigan Law School in 1940, and both entered the legal department of the American Automobile Insurance Company. Martha Griffiths next opened her own law firm which her husband later joined. Since the majority of political leaders in the United States are recruited from the legal profession, Martha Griffiths' interest in law was likely to have made politics personally salient to her. This does not mean, however, that her husband was uninfluential in the development of her political career. In 1946 a Detroit lawyer, Phoebe Moneybean, telephoned Griffiths and told her that she must run for the state legislature. Martha Griffiths backed down, but when she explained the call to her husband, he said, "Call her back right now and tell her you've just started running."[116] She did precisely that. Obviously, the thought of a political career was not repugnant to Martha Griffiths, but the potential for role conflict between her position as wife and politician had to be mitigated before she would acquiesce to pursuing her political interest. Her husband's enthusiastic support provided the necessary impetus. This pattern was repeated when Martha Griffiths moved from the state level to national politics. She states, "Hicks convinced me that I should run for Congress."[117]

For Martha Griffiths the degree of conflict between the traditional family orientation of the female and the nontraditional political orientation of the female politician appears to have been precariously balanced throughout her public life. Griffiths managed this conflict by limiting the impact of the political realm on her private life. At the point at which the political aspect would seriously interfere with her sex-stereotyped role as woman, she would try to lessen the contradiction between the two. Thus she declined an opportunity to run for the U.S. Senate on the grounds that as a senator she would have to travel all over Michigan and would therefore have no homelife at all. During her tenure in Congress, Griffiths maintained close ties to her home and husband; it was her practice to fly home to Michigan every weekend during the periods Congress was in session.

Martha Griffiths was one of the sponsors of the Equal Rights Amendment. This fact demonstrates her own awareness of the difficulties women have to face when they wish to undertake nontraditional roles and occupations. As a woman who had undertaken a career that was generally reserved for men, she personally suffered from the external and internal cultural restraints often unrecognized by many women themselves. Martha Griffiths handled the tensions produced by the conflict between her career and her wifehood by limiting her political activity to certain times and places and her activity as wife to others. In a real sense she was able to "render unto Caesar that which is Caesar's."

ELLA GRASSO stands out among U.S. female political leaders. Although there had been four other female governors, three of them rose to the top state position on the basis of her marriage to the former governor. Ella Grasso was the first woman elected to the governorship without the benefit of a husband's incumbency. She made it on her own.

Her path to the governorship of Connecticut covered twenty-two years of standing for election at various levels of government. Although she was fortunate to have been a member of the Democratic Party during the chairmanship of John Bailey, who was particularly committed to promoting women in the party, the decisions about her career have been hers. Ella Grasso's range of political activity has been limited by her own concern for travel time and distance, and she has been most satisfied with political offices that did not require her long or continual absence from home. Indeed, part of her reluctance to represent the Sixth District of Connecticut in the House of Representatives was that it necessitated her being away from her home and family. As she herself noted, "I hate not sleeping in my own bed."[118] Thus we have another woman for whom familial concerns were a key factor in the definition of her political career.

Ella Grasso began her political career in 1952 when she first ran for the Connecticut state legislature. Already married and the mother of a three-year-old girl and a one-year-old boy, Grasso was blessed with an extended family which allowed her to participate in politics without feeling as if she had abandoned her husband and children. She acknowledges that without this support system she would never have committed herself to such extensive political activity. "My husband was always very helpful. And we shared many of the tasks I might have had to assume alone. I was very lucky because I had parents who lived right across the street and I had uncles and aunts all around. My children were living in a familiar neighborhood ... where their mother had been born. So it was almost like a little enclave, and I had no qualms."[119]

Although Thomas Grasso was not particularly interested or active in politics himself and did not necessarily encourage his wife to begin her political career, he was instrumental in this development insofar as he did not object and did not oppose her political activity. Her career is predicated on the acceptability of her ambitions to other members of her family. Better able to combine her private life as wife and mother with her public life at the state level, she did not seek to run for Congress until 1970, eighteen years after her entrance into politics. One might expect such a delay had she lacked the party support, or if she had been an independent spirit, "an outsider" who "did not get along because she would not go along," but this is hardly the case. As legislator and secretary of state Ella Grasso "paid her dues in backroom party chores: she canvassed, wrote Democratic planks and speeches, [and] served as floor leader in the legislature."[120] Epitomizing the party loyalist, Grasso could well have anticipated a congressional seat earlier than she achieved it. It was the family consideration which led her not to enter Congress until she was nearly fifty years old; she would never consider going off to Washington while her children were still young and at home. The fact that her children had grown up and her husband had retired may have facilitated her taking on the congressional post, but it also meant that her power potential in the Congress was severely limited. The years of "internship" necessary to acquire political power were no longer accessible to her.

Grasso frankly stresses the priority of her family in her career: "I measure all these events in my life by what my family was doing at the time."[121] Seeking the governorship of Connecticut reflects this pattern as well. Unhappy with being separated from her home and family so much, she did not establish a very impressive record during her two terms in Congress. It is probable that the governorship will cause her less conflict. She will again be closer to her home and family just as in the first eighteen years of her political career when she worked at the state level. Grasso is a successful political woman who has continued to be a loving wife and mother.

SHIRLEY CHISHOLM is another woman who developed a strong sense of personal political efficacy early in life. To be a black and a woman in Congress is unusual enough, but to have declared herself a candidate for the presidential nomination of a major political party makes her unique indeed.

During her college years Shirley Chisholm attended a few New York City political clubhouse meetings in the Seventeenth Assembly District. Attending club meetings when there was a speaker she wanted to hear, she constantly asked unwelcomed questions which challenged officeholders. She violated implicit norms of racial separation as well as norms of political power. Recalling her actions, Chisholm writes, "One night I tried another challenge. I walked in the room and right past the rows of people waiting, black on one side and white on the other, and up on the dais."[122] Such actions were unprecedented in local politics. While the direct results may have been minimal at the time, they do indicate an unusual independence of spirit and a sense of personal political efficacy at a very early stage in her political activities.

This independence of spirit and her self-ascribed role as a "shaker-upper of the system"[123] was not restricted to opposition to the white power structure. It was even used against the man Chisholm acknowledged as her practical political mentor. She began to have a more concrete and positive orientation once she became the political protégée of Wesley McD. Holder, founder of the Bedford-Stuyvesant Political League (BSPL), a political club organized to get black people elected to public office. Chisholm wrote of her apprenticeship under Holder:

> I learned politics from him. He would explain to me what was happening in politics, what maneuvers the white politicians were making and what they meant, how the deals were being made. I absorbed his sophistication on how the system works, how some people are kept out and others kept in.[124]

She learned her lesson so well that she even challenged Holder for the presidency of the BSPL. She lost that fight but it clearly showed that she was an independent force to be reckoned with. No male mediator was going to subordinate and direct her political activities for his rather than her purposes.

Never one to underestimate her own abilities, in 1964 Chisholm called upon the Unity Democratic Club to support her nomination as the state assemblyperson. She writes:

> I wanted it and I told the club I felt I deserved it. This was unwelcome news to the county organization, and it did not appeal very much to some of the people in my own club. Some of the men fancied the nomination themselves. Others, who had a taste of how I operated—a little woman who didn't know how to play the game or when to shut up—didn't want to see me in a position of any more importance than I already had. For my part, I was not interested in listening to any reasons why I shouldn't run. By then I had spent about ten years in ward politics and had done everything else but run for office. Starting as a cigar box decorator, I had compiled voter lists, carried petitions, rung doorbells, manned the telephone,

stuffed envelopes, and helped voters get to the polls. I had done it all to help other people get elected. The other people who got elected were men, of course, because that was the way it was in politics. This had to change someday, and I was resolved that it was going to start changing right then. I was the best-qualified nominee, and I was not going to be denied because of my sex.[125]

Chisholm's experiences in ward politics are common to innumerable women. Often recognized as the backbone of the major political parties and political clubs, women have been willing to perform the necessary menial tasks. What makes Shirley Chisholm unique is that she consciously decided to advance beyond this type of work to a political career, thereby challenging the sex stereotyping so prevalent in the division of political labor. She was so successful at the state level of politics that she soon was elected to the U.S. House of Representatives. Not the kind of person to be awed by her famous and powerful colleagues, she promptly announced, "I have no intention of just sitting quietly and observing. I intend to speak out immediately in order to focus attention on the nation's problems."[126] Asking for three key committee appointments (Education and Labor, Post Office and Civil Service, and Foreign Affairs), she only managed to have herself appointed to the Agriculture Committee. Public protest did lead to her being put on the Veterans Affairs Committee but she was still unable to obtain her preferred committee assignments.

The meteoric nature of Shirley Chisholm's advance to national prominence violates many of the expectations associated with political careers in general and women's political careers in particular. That a woman with less than two full terms in Congress could seriously declare herself a candidate for the presidency and receive 151.95 out of the 3,016 total delegate votes at the 1972 Democratic National Convention seems incredible. Yet Shirley Chisholm did precisely that.

Unusual and nontraditional as her political career is, there are factors in Representative Chisholm's adult life that facilitated her success. First, she did not marry until after the completion of her education, when she had already begun a career and was active in politics. Second, she has no children. Third, she has a very supportive husband who is willing to accommodate his career to hers. "When his wife ran for Congress and for the Presidency, he took a leave of absence from his job with the New York City Bureau of Medical Services to be her chauffeur, research her speeches, and 'see that she eats on time.'"[127] Having a supportive spouse when engaging in political battle is an asset to all aspiring politicians.

MARGARET HILDA ROBERTS THATCHER could have become prime minister of Great Britain if the Conservative Party had won the 1977 national election. Until Margaret Thatcher became the head of the Conservative Party in the summer of 1975, no woman had ever ascended to the position of head of the "loyal opposition." Her accomplishment is the result of a unique set of political circumstances and her own unusual character. Despite the fact that she herself had earlier said she did not think that the Conservative Party was ready for a woman chief, nor would it be likely to welcome a woman during her lifetime,[128] the convergence of several factors led to her rise to power.

Edward Heath's performance as Conservative Party chief had not been particularly noteworthy or effective. A change seemed in order. The two most likely male challengers declined to become candidates for the position, saying that they did not wish to place so great a strain on their families and wives. In other words, these men felt a conflict between their political careers and their responsibilities as husbands and fathers. This unpredictable occurrence left Thatcher in an excellent position to challenge Heath. She had once before contended against Heath and three other male candidates; her showing at that time was good enough to demonstrate that she was a viable candidate. Her own strength of character and determination did the rest.

As Patrick Cosgrave, political editor of the Tory weekly *Spectator*, observed, "To be leader of the Conservative Party you have to want to be leader more than anything else."[129] Margaret Thatcher did want to further her political career more than anything else. She has been described as "a steely, strong-minded woman of disciplined ambition and impressive intelligence"[130] and as "a woman . . . who possessed the necessary ruthlessness and single-mindedness."[131] These personality traits indicate how Thatcher has arrived where she is.

The achievements of Margaret Thatcher are her own rather than the result of some male's influence or advice. Having graduated from Oxford with an M.A. in chemistry, Thatcher first became a scientific researcher. She soon decided to take up law instead, and specialized in tax and patent law. Eventually, she became interested in politics. "By the time she met her husband, Dennis Thatcher, she was out in the world, bitten by the political bug and the youngest woman candidate in the 1950 election."[132] She had already entered national politics by running for the House of Commons. Although she lost that election to a man who, in fact, was an unbeatable Labourite, the experience confirmed her choice of politics as her major area of interest. Nevertheless, she withdrew from active politics after this election and in 1953 became a mother. As one critic humorously observed, "Conveniently twins, all over at once."[133] Margaret Thatcher waited six more years before she again ran for and won a seat in the House of Commons. By then her children were ready for school and she herself was again ready for an independent career. Her role conflict was sufficiently resolved.

Margaret Thatcher's interest and success in politics are independent of her husband's or family's interest. She had begun her political career before her marriage. Having a husband and children to care for interrupted her political activity for almost nine years, yet once her career had recommenced her family ties in no way inhibited her steady progress within the Conservative Party.

Margaret Thatcher's performance as a member of Parliament cannot be described as that of a "feminist." One political commentator noted that Thatcher's victory was "no triumph for women's lib" for she is "contemptuous of that sort of nonsense."[134] Unlike Shirley Chisholm, she has seldom questioned or challenged the party line. She has no great record of outstanding impassioned speeches nor of controversial debates. She generally votes as a conventional conservative and has not been particularly identified with specific issues. As a result she has received relatively little attention from the media. The one exception, however, may have been during her term as minister of education and science under the Heath government. At that time she advocated abolishing the free-milk program for schoolchildren. Although a mother of school-age children herself, she alienated many lower-class mothers whose children benefited from the program.

The persons of Indira Gandhi and Golda Meir stand out among our political women not only in terms of their international stature but also because of the extreme degree of their devotion to the political world. To become the head of a political party and the chief executive of a nation is not an aspiration of even most political men. To find two women who have achieved this height is unusual enough but to add that both the nations they represent are in the throes of enormous social, political, and economic change is to heighten the extraordinary nature of these occurrences.

INDIRA GANDHI was almost destined to become politically interested and influential because of her childhood family. Living in a family which included one of the key figures if not the most important single individual in the emancipation struggle of India with Great Britain—Jawaharlal Nehru—could not be without impact.

> With the atmosphere in the country what it had been since her childhood, and especially with the Nehru family's involvement in politics, no child of Jawaharlal's could have insulated herself from her surroundings to such an extent as to become a dancer or an interior decorator or a conventional historian [these are all professions Gandhi is quoted as having preferred to politics]. At the same time, however, her sense of commitment to her family—as a daughter, a wife, and mother—prevented Indira from throwing herself into politics with anything resembling the near total abandon that her father had displayed when he joined the independent movement in his youth.[135]

It is noteworthy that for Nehru, being a son, a husband, and a father had not prevented him from throwing himself so totally into politics that he could write in his autobiography, "In spite of the strength of my family bond I almost forgot my family, my wife, my daughter."[136]

Indira Nehru's marriage to Feroze Gandhi not only caused private family problems but became a cause célèbre when her engagement was publicly announced. Coming from a most prominent family, and a Kashmiri Brahmin girl, she was expected to have a husband from her racial group, religious affiliation, and social status. Feroze Gandhi did not match in any of these. The public outcry was great indeed. Nehru was forced to issue a public statement that he had been convinced of the maturity of his daughter's choice and that even Mahatma Gandhi had given "his blessing to the proposal."[137] Throughout, Indira "stood like a rock in her unyielding determination to marry the man of her choice against the concerted opposition of her entire family."[138]

Needless to say, a woman who could withstand such familial and public pressure could handle the role conflicts associated with being a wife/mother and politician. Feroze Gandhi also had political ambitions and ultimately was to serve as a member of Parliament. Theirs was not a totally happy marriage, however. In part this was due to the fact that they were "two personalities, equally headstrong and strong-willed, highly individualistic, and prepossessing."[139] Feroze Gandhi was reminded even while he was a prominent member of the party and Parliament of his "subsidiary status," and was "either condemned to anonymity or to condescending recognition."[140] Being the husband of the political "understudy" of the prime minister was not an easy role for such a proud man to play. It is interesting that the corollary of this position, that of the political wife, is not seen in a similar light. Eventually their class differences and divergent political careers led to their living in separate quarters.

Gandhi's relationship to her children appeared to be very warm and avidly assumed. She could not conceive of the possibility of marrying and not having children. Though fragile, she systematically built up her strength during her pregnancies. She gave birth to two sons. Often away from her children, she has always contended, "It is not the amount of time spent with the children that matters as much as the manner of spending it."[141] She relishes the account of her encounter with the mother of a friend of her son Sanjay. She relates how "once when Sanjay was quite small a nursery school friend of his came to our house with his mother. The mother, a society lady of some means, commenting on my public work, remarked that I could not be spending much time with my sons. This hurt Sanjay, and before I could think of a reply he rushed to my rescue with the words: 'My mother does lots of important work, and yet she plays with me more than you do with your little boy!' It seems his little friend had complained about his mother's constant bridge-playing."[142]

From the very earliest days of her youth, politics was a great concern of Indira Gandhi. She can recall how at the age of four she sat on the lap of her beloved grandfather in court and watched him and her father tried and sentenced to prison. Yet, when she was first urged to run for an elective office in 1946, when she was assured of a seat and a possible cabinet post after independence was obtained, "she was not tempted. Her children needed her more than the Uttar Pradesh assembly."[143] This reluctance was repeated some four years after independence when Gandhi's children were now older and had entered good schools. This time an elective office was rejected because "she felt that her father, past sixty and as Prime Minister, lonely and bowed under the weight of running a country of India's size and problems, was entitled to her time and attention to the exclusion of all ambition on her part."[144] Thus, even though the jobs of being a housekeeper and a hostess were personally distasteful to her, she took on the tasks of managing Nehru's household, was his secretary and companion. One might wonder, given the degree to which such a position afforded her immediate access to and influence over the most politically important man in India, her father Jawaharlal Nehru, whether in this particular choice it was not just a happy coincidence that her female nurturant roles converged with her political-power orientation.

The experience of being her father's hostess and constant companion was one with enormous political content and consequence. This opportunity not only allowed her to be his understudy and to become aware of the internal workings of politics in India, but it also gave her first-hand contact and personal knowledge of key world leaders.

Gandhi's first elective position was one on the Congress Working Committee, the organizational rather than the parliamentary wing of the Congress Party. Despite the fact that she could have secured appointment to this position without standing for election (fourteen of the twenty-one members were traditionally nominated by the party's president, and U. N. Dhebar, president of the Congress Party, was amenable to nominating her), she chose rather "to accept the rough-and-tumble of elective politics."[145] In this office her presence was rarely directly felt and she went almost completely unnoticed by the press and public. Dedicating herself to the women's department of the party, not entering into the general debate, and keeping her presence conspicuously low-keyed meant "most people in the press and the party still regarded her as Nehru's daughter and gave almost no heed to her new role as a political leader in her own right."[146]

In 1959 Indira Gandhi was elected to the post of president of the Congress Party. The party leaders had anticipated that this action would give them a more direct line to Nehru, and that Gandhi would act as a mere channel of political communication. Her use of the position surprised everyone.

> Even those who cynically believed she had been given the post because of accident of birth, later acknowledged that she proved to be a dynamic leader of the aging organization. Under her the party took several difficult and controversial steps and at times appeared to lead the government rather than to act, as it had tended to do previously, as its handmaiden.[147]

Indira Gandhi's rejection of another term as president of the Congress Party can be attributed to two factors: first, her husband and father were both ill, and she wanted to be free to give them her personal attention; second, as official leader of the Congress Party she resented having to rely on the power and prestige of her father to handle an obstructionist and recalcitrant wing of the party. She was constantly reminded that it was the authority of her father and his prestige that gave her the political clout that she had. "For a proud self-willed person like Indira that must have been galling."[148]

In May 1964 Nehru died. Indira Gandhi's immediate impulse was to withdraw completely from politics. But her strong sense of personal political efficacy made this impossible. Tempted as she might have been to go to England and live with her two sons, who were studying there, no tremendous amount of persuasion was needed to dissuade her from this course. The contemplation of leaving the country may have been politically motivated for she "mentioned to some friends, she felt that entering politics after a period of absence from India might discourage the public impression that she was there merely as her father's daughter."[149] The new Prime Minister Shastri invited her into his cabinet. Despite the fact that she could have chosen to be foreign minister she asked for the less prestigious post of minister of information and broadcasting. The public explanation of this selection—"she was conscious of her administrative inexperience"[150]—was borne out by her handling of the position. Her contributions were "singularly unimpressive" and "her contributions to the deliberations of the Cabinet ... were from all accounts small and inconsequential."[151]

A series of circumstances in early 1966 led Gandhi from this minor post to that of prime minister. Shastri had died unexpectedly and two of his rivals, Desai and Nanda, began almost immediately to contend with each other for the post. Gandhi, however, devised a strategy whereby she appeared not to be actively seeking the prime ministership but rather simply showing herself available should the office seek her. "Her attitude was that the Congress President had urged her to offer herself for leadership; and she had agreed because she felt it was her duty to do so."[152]

The assumption of the top political office finally permitted the convergence of the public and private person. In office Prime Minister Gandhi found a way of breaking the hold on the public mind that she was merely the daughter of India's first leader after independence. The 1971 war with Pakistan finally and perhaps irrevocably established her difference in style and approach from her father. Many believe that "had he been Prime Minister in 1971 . . . he would have hesitated and procrastinated in the face of the military threat."[153]

More recently Gandhi cast aside yet another shadow of her father's continuing eminence, that of self-imposed restraints on the exercise of personal power. Nehru certainly had as extensive power as his daughter but many of the authoritarian and corrupt practices associated with her government were never employed or even contemplated by Nehru. Her critics note that "her years of power have witnessed a distressing debasement of political values . . . a staggering increase in corruption at all levels including the top, callous misuse of authority and a sharp decline in administrative efficiency."[154] Undoubtedly, the imprisonment of her political opponents in 1975 heightened this perception.

Indira Gandhi has never known the feeling of the inappropriateness of concern with politics that the vast masses of women have experienced. From the earliest day of her life she was exposed to the direct effect of political actions on her private family life. Her political apprenticeship extended through forty-nine years of personal relationships to politics before becoming prime minister. The intensity of her involvement cannot be denied. Her ascendancy to power may have been through the paths of her father's influence but there can be no doubt that she has been an independent political actor or that her sense of personal political efficacy is strong. Being the political understudy of one's father is quite different from being a stand-in for one's husband. In the

1970s Indira Gandhi was one of the most powerful and politically astute women in the world.

In her recent autobiography GOLDA MEIR eloquently expresses the dilemma faced by every working wife/mother. The political woman faces the horns of this dilemma much more than the woman who has been forced to work because of family necessity and can afford no qualms over accepting necessity. Meir writes:

The fact is that I have lived and worked with men all my life, but being a woman has never hindered me in any way at all. It has never caused me unease or given me an inferiority complex or made me think that men are better off than women—or that it is a disaster to give birth to children. Not at all. Nor have men ever given me preferential treatment. But what is true, I think, is that women who want and need a life outside as well as inside the home have a much, much harder time than men because they carry a heavy double burden. . . . And still to this day I am not sure that I didn't harm the children or neglect them, despite the efforts I made not to be away from them even an hour more than was strictly necessary. They grew up to be healthy, productive, talented and good people, and they both are wonderful parents to their own children and wonderful companions to me. But when they were growing up, I knew that they deeply resented my activities outside our home.[155]

Golda Meir's assessment of her adult role conflict also demonstrates that it is the role of mother rather than that of wife which appears to cause the most difficulty in adjustments with the public roles. In speaking of her marriage she notes, "What I do regret—and bitterly so—is that although Morris and I remained married to each other and loving each other until the day he died in my house in 1951 (when symbolically enough I was away), I was not able to make a success of our marriage after all."[156] The tone here is, however, markedly different from the regret expressed about her children. Regret is the theme in both instances; but clearly Morris was an adult who had freely chosen to marry such a political person. She was not an unknown commodity, and while Morris Meir might not have had all his needs fulfilled, he was capable of understanding her claim, "I had to be what I was, and what I was made it impossible for him to have the sort of wife he wanted and needed."[157] The children were not able to understand this necessity. All they knew was that their mother was not at home, that she was "a public person, not a homebody."[158]

No amount of public acclaim and appreciation appears to have soothed the personal feeling of guilt Meir experienced relative to her children. This guilt stemmed from the criticism she received from her own mother and sister for not devoting herself totally to her children. Reminded constantly of her separation from her children especially when she was required to travel, Meir writes that "my guilt was overwhelming."[159]

Throughout this discussion in her autobiography, Golda Meir carries the burdens of the expectations of others about mothers. She regrets that her husband's needs were not satisfied and recognizes that they could have been had she been a homebody. She recognizes her own need to be a public person; yet she knows that there is no way to escape the guilt of not being with her children. Although she would not sacrifice her own need to be a public being to that of her children's demands on her time, how many women with less acutely felt need to be public must have succumbed to these social exigencies? The conflicting demands on women of home and work are more often settled on the side of home, particularly when the work is of choice rather than of economic necessity. Some of the emphases put on the development of the kibbutzim in Israel may be the direct result of this conflict. It is certainly connected in Meir's mind; she writes that here is an environment "where life is organized to enable them [women] to work and rear children at the same time."[160]

Golda Meir achieved a sense of personal political efficacy very early in her life. The origins of her interest in politics and of her public action to achieve some personally held goals date back to her early youth. Unlike Indira Gandhi, for whom politics was intimately a part of her childhood family, Meir's own family life had not had this direct political content. Although her family's migration from Russia had been motivated by what could be called political reasons, the oppression they suffered in Russia was more closely associated with their religion. Once in the United States the family's immediate plight seemingly had less to do with this factor. Neither her father nor mother was actively involved in the political realm. Neither was even particularly concerned with the degree to which their family's situation was due to a public rather than a private cause.

Golda Meir's account of what she herself terms "my first public work" indicates the extent to which the source of this concern was personally derived. In the fourth grade Golda Meir and Regina Hamburger (later Medzini) established an organization they called the American Young Sisters Society to raise money to pay for textbooks for the poor students in their class. At eleven years of age Golda appointed herself chairperson of this group, rented a hall, and sent out invitations. She, her sister Clara, and Regina held a meeting which raised money for books. Though praised by her parents, the initiative for this action came from this eleven-year-old child. Thus a child of eleven reached a level of personal political efficacy most adult women will never reach.

Meir demonstrated the same independence of spirit toward her family when she went to work at an early age. She was "determined never again to ask . . . [her] parents for money."[161] As a result of her mother's refusal to allow her to pursue an education with a nontraditional content, her father's agreement that "it doesn't pay to be too clever . . . men don't like smart girls,"[162] and finally her mother's attempt to find her a husband, the die was cast. Golda Meir was not going to remain in that family situation. At the age of fourteen she ran away from home to live with her sister Sheyna in Denver. She herself notes the monumental importance of this move: it "was a turning point in my life because it was in Denver that my real education began and that I started to grow up."[163]

In Denver Meir became involved in lengthy discussions with Zionist friends of Sheyna—much to the dismay of her sister who tried to assume the domineering position previously held by her mother. Meir resisted all attempts to keep her out of these discussions and activities, and when she found them too restrictive, she simply picked up and left the home of her sister. Time and time again she demonstrated an indomitable will. It is important that she always measured her private concerns by a wider public one. Even when faced with a choice between her future husband and going to Palestine, she could countenance giving up the man she loved for her ideals and public concerns. Of this situation Meir writes: "The idea that I might have to choose between Morris and Palestine made me miserable, and for the most part I kept to myself, working for the Labor Zionists in my free time—making speeches, organizing meetings, raising funds. There was always something that took precedence over my private worries and therefore served to distract me from them—a situation that was not to change much in the course of the next six decades."[164]

Given this start it is not difficult to understand that a short time after the marriage of Golda and Morris Meir, she was traveling about the country raising money for the Labor Zionist Party. Going to Palestine, joining the Merhavia Kibbutzim, being elected by the kibbutz to represent it at the 1922 national convention, were all natural progressions in her life. The one four-year hiatus in this public life, years spent in Jerusalem trying to make a home for her husband and children were "the most miserable . . . [she] ever experienced."[165] The cause of the misery was not the lack of money or the poor living conditions but as she says,

> the constant feeling that I was being deprived of just those things for which I had come to Palestine in the first place. Instead of actively helping build the Jewish national home and working hard and productively for it, I found myself cooped up in a tiny apartment in Jerusalem, all my thoughts and energy concentrated on making do with Morris' wages.[166]

Despite Meir's attempt to reconcile herself to the life of the private housewife in Palestine, she was unsuccessful. When offered a position with the Histadrut (the General Federation of Jewish Labor) which would have required a great deal of traveling about Palestine and even to other countries, she hesitated but finally decided that her efforts to suppress her public instincts had been a failure. Though as noted above she would be driven by guilt for the remainder of her public career because of absence from her children and the sadness she caused Morris, she jumped at the opportunity. The position in the Histadrut was to be followed by many others including minister of labor for the state of Israel, minister to the Soviet Union, and fund raiser for the new state of Israel in the United States. Golda Meir personally raised $50,000,000 for Israel in the U. S. She records that David Ben-Gurion said to her at that time, "Someday when history will be written, it will be said that there was a Jewish woman who got the money which made the state possible."[167] Finally in March of 1969 she became prime minister of Israel. None of these career stages is particularly surprising or unexpected given Meir's early achievement of personal political efficacy.

Born in Northern Ireland, BERNADETTE DEVLIN has been a civil rights activist, marcher, demonstrator, organizer, pamphleteer, and public speaker on behalf of the Catholics in Northern Ireland. Elected to the British Parliament in 1969, Bernadette Devlin clearly achieved this position as the result of her own sense of personal political efficacy. Although the origin of her interest in politics is closely associated with her youthful remembrances of her father[168] and the stories he would tell her as a child, he had no direct connection with her election to political office: he died when she was only nine. Nor did the legislator Devlin come to this office by way of a husband or his interest in or holding of office. Of all our elected political women Bernadette Devlin was the only unmarried one. In her life, the radical nature of the break from the pattern of the "normal political woman" as a married, older woman with grown children is enhanced further by the fact that Bernadette Devlin in August of 1971 gave birth to a child out of wedlock. She refused not only to marry the child's father but even to identify him. It is difficult to imagine a more "outrageous" and explicit rejection of norms for appropriate female behavior both in the public and in the private realm. Devlin did marry in the mid-1970s (to Michael Mc-Aliskey, a schoolteacher).

Certainly no private-public role conflict has yet prevented Devlin's initiation of political actions of the most intense nature. Demonstrations, riots, rabble-rousing, and public display are all part of her political repertoire, and she has even been imprisoned for her activities. Her interest in politics dates back to her earliest years when the bedtime stories told by her father were of English-Irish conflicts. The songs and nursery rhymes she learned "developed an unconscious political consciousness"[169] which fully blossomed during her years at Queens University where she joined among other clubs, the Irish Democratic Club, the Gaelic Society, and the Republican Club. Although this statement suggests that a gap in political awareness and concern might exist, such is not the case. At twenty-two Bernadette Devlin was elected to Parliament. By then she had had literally twenty-two years of politically salient life. No private adult role can or seemingly could ever interfere with this public activity. Although she lost her seat in Parliament in 1974, she still is an active leader of the Irish Committee for Socialist Progress and continues promoting her "anti-imperialist" struggle against the British.

The Revolutionaries

The revolutionaries are a group of women with strong personalities, unusually high skills, and advanced educational training. As children all were considered rebels by their parents. All began their political involvement early, indicating a strong sense of personal efficacy. All were much more politically inclined than their first husbands or lovers. They range in their socioeconomic origins from a daughter of a coal miner to a descendant of a Russian tsar. Included in our study are Alexandra Kollontai, Eva Broido, Ekaterina Breshko-Breshkovskaia, La Pasionaria (Dolores Ibarruri), Halide Edib, Angela Davis, Maud Gonne, the Countess Constance Markievicz, and Rosa Luxemburg.

ALEXANDRA KOLLONTAI became a Russian Marxist in 1896. She is one of the few noted Russian female revolutionaries who is a feminist as well as a revolutionary. After the split in the Russian Social-Democratic Workers Party in 1903, she became an avid Bolshevik and was close to Lenin. In 1905 she started a variety of feminist organizations in St. Petersburg and became more intimately involved in the women's international socialist movement. After the October 1917 revolution, Kollontai was appointed commissar for social welfare in Lenin's new Soviet cabinet, replacing Countess Panina, who had been arrested and imprisoned by the Bolsheviks. In 1918 Kollontai was relieved of her duties in the commissariat, and between 1919 and 1922 she was head of the Central Department of Women's Education. In 1922 she joined the People's Commissariat of Foreign Affairs and soon became the first woman in the world, we believe, to become an accredited diplomatic minister to a foreign country. In her career as a Soviet diplomat, she served as a minister to Norway and to Sweden. She was elevated to the rank of ambassador to Sweden in 1943, and conducted the Soviet-Finnish armistice negotiations in 1944. She died in Moscow on March 9, 1952.

⋅⋅ At the age of sixteen and against her parents' wishes, Kollontai married her second cousin, a handsome, dashing fellow. Though she loved him she soon found herself being stifled by 'love's tyranny."[170] He did not object to her working on political and economic problems, but he had no interest in joining her in them. Intellectually they had little in common. Then, in 1898, only a few years after her marriage, she and a childhood girl friend decided to enroll in a university. Kollontai divorced her husband, left her young son with her parents, and went to the University of Zurich. Nonetheless, Kollontai felt that the roles of mother and revolutionary were compatible. She felt that her son was her responsibility, not her husband's nor her family's, though she left him with her parents and at school when she felt it was best for his welfare. But when possible, she preferred to have her child at home with her, for they were quite close.

While Kollontai was at the University of Zurich, she became a confirmed Marxist and revolutionary. In a work written later, *Love and Friendship*, she articulated how she conceived her revolutionary mission. From early youth she felt she had a mission in life, but was not sure what that mission was. Only after her marriage did it become clear to her:

> My mission would be to struggle against unfairness in the sexual question . . . to teach women not to put all their hearts and souls into the love of a man, but into the essential thing—creative work. . . . Love must not crush the woman's individuality, not bind her wings. If love begins to enslave her, she must make herself free, she must step over all love tragedies, and go her own way.[171]

She was careful to note that she was not preaching "free love," but rather freedom from love. In her opinion, friendship was a more sociable emotion than sexual love.

Though she thought promiscuity was a bourgeois phenomenon, she did have other liaisons. She even tried to marry again. In 1917 before the Bolshevik revolution she was sent by Lenin to Helsingfors to arouse the sailors to revolt. While there she met and fell in love with a dashing sailor several years her junior, Fedore Dubenko. In spite of her dislike for the constraints of the marital role, and against the protests of her son and her best friend, she agreed to have their relationship legalized. At that time she was minister of social welfare and Dubenko was chairman of the Central Executive Committee of the Baltic fleet. She agreed to marry him because he took her refusal as a sign that she felt superior to him. To ease his mind she consented, but bureaucratic inefficiency prevented the relationship from reaching legal status.

Shortly after their effort to marry, Dubenko was arrested.

He had entrusted ships to officers of the old regime who then turned the ships over to the Germans. When he was arrested, Kollontai was very upset and staged public protests on his behalf. To many this display represented feminine weakness. Some even wanted to arrest her. She was forcibly removed from her position as minister of social welfare over the matter. Never again did she hold such a high position in the Soviet government. Instead, because of her mastery of eleven languages, she became involved in diplomatic affairs.

EVA BROIDO joined the Russian Social-Democratic Workers Party in 1899. For close to twenty years she dedicated herself to the dangerous, clandestine work of a professional revolutionary. During this period she spent much time either in prison or in Siberian exile. She took an active part in the February 1917 revolution, becoming the secretary-general of the Menshevik central committee. After the Bolsheviks defeated the Mensheviks, she left Russia in 1920 to settle with her husband and children in Berlin, where she helped publish the Menshevik journal, *The Socialist Courier*. In 1927 she returned to Russia. It is believed that she was either imprisoned or shot by Stalin in 1941.

Broido married twice—for love. The first turned out to be a mistake. In her memoirs she described the first marriage as follows: "The three years of our marriage were the three most unhappy, most miserable of my life. . . . He suffered from a hereditary nervous disposition and plagued me with unbearable, morbid jealousy. During these three years I bore him two children, we lived on the scanty allowance sent by his mother and we were hopelessly in debt."[172] She sought diversion in political circles and became involved with the Jewish Social-Democrats. In 1896 her husband was placed in a hospital in Berlin, giving her an opportunity to study socialist ideas more deeply. After reading Bebel's *Woman and Socialism*, she was convinced of her destiny. Taking her children with her, she left her husband for a revolutionary career. Back in St. Petersburg, she met Mark Broido, who became her de facto husband and revolutionary colleague for the rest of her life.

Broido had several children and was devoted to them. They went everywhere with her, even to the hard labor camps of Siberia. On rare occasions she left them for short periods with her mother, but she never seemed to consider seriously the possibility of giving them up. From 1909 to 1912 she gave up her deep involvement in revolutionary activity to support them. Her husband was in prison at the time. This is the only time, however, that she appeared to feel it necessary to choose between the needs of her children and her revolutionary interests.

EKATERINA BRESHKO-BRESHKOVSKAIA was a rebel almost from birth in 1844 in Russia. But thanks to her parents' willingness to support her efforts to help the peasants and to help her be trained as a teacher, these rebellious tendencies were delayed in their development into revolutionary activity for close to three decades.

At the age of twenty-five with her parents' blessings Breshko-Breshkovskaia married a liberal, broad-minded, generous young nobleman. Both he and her father willingly assisted her in the late 1860s and early 1870s in her efforts to help the peasants. Together they established a cooperative bank and a peasants' agricultural school. After a short time, however, their activities aroused hostility among the more conservative nobles. They and their like-minded friends were denounced to the minister of the interior as a band of conspirators against the government. Her father, considered a dangerous rebel, was fired from his position. Several friends were sent to Siberia without trial for these "political" activities. She and her husband were put under police surveillance and their school and bank closed. Enraged by these injustices, and unwilling to acquiesce quietly in the destruction of her work, Breshko-Breshkovskaia announced she was going to become a revolutionary. Her husband refused to join her, and they separated forever. As far as we know she formed no other liaisons but devoted her life exclusively to the work of revolution.

At the age of thirty she became involved in the "To the People" movement as a Russian populist; she was arrested, tried among those in the "Trial of the 193," and sentenced to hard labor in Siberia. After twenty-two years of imprisonment, she returned without a passport to the revolutionary underground in European Russia, where she helped create the Social Revolutionary Party. In 1903 she toured the United States, successfully seeking funds and support for her cause. Back in Russia in 1907, she was arrested again, but was not tried until 1910 in St. Petersburg. At the age of sixty-six she was imprisoned once more. In 1917 at the advent of the first Russian revolution, Alexander Kerensky, then minister of justice in the provisional government, set her free and brought her to St. Petersburg, where again she became active in the Social Revolutionary Party as a member of the new government. Her admirers affectionately called her "the Little Grandmother of the Russian Revolution."

Breshko-Breshkovskaia is the only revolutionary in our study who consciously chose to leave her child forever to engage in political activity. She suffered from this decision, but she chose to be one of the "fighters for justice rather than mothers of the victims of tyranny."[173] As a child and youth Breshko-Breshkovskaia had been told she would outgrow her wish to rebel and to escape traditional life after the attainment of love, marriage, and children. "Now they argued: 'Yes, you have remained unchanged by husband and home, but you will succumb to the command of Nature. With the birth of a child will come the death of your revolutionary ideals. The wings you have used for soaring high in the air among the clouds you will now use to shelter your little one.' And I gave birth to a little one. I felt that in that boy my youth was buried, and that when he was taken from my body, the fire of my spirit had gone out with him. But it was not so. The conflict between my love for the child and my love for the revolution and for the freedom of Russia robbed me of many a night's sleep. I knew that I could not be a mother and still be a revolutionist."[174]

LA PASIONARIA (DOLORES IBARRURI), the daughter of a Spanish coal miner, was too frail to work in the mines as did her father, mother, brothers, and sisters. Instead she was allowed to go to normal school but, because of lack of money, she had to leave school to work as a servant in the homes of the wealthy. To escape this form of drudgery she married a poor young miner who happened to be a socialist. The poverty in which the couple lived was heart-rending. When she had her first baby, the new mother was so undernourished that she was unable to produce sufficient milk to feed the child. At one point she said, "Only love for my baby kept me alive."[175] The desperate woman had to borrow money to buy food and medicines, but soon she had to borrow again to buy a baby's coffin. Reflecting on this traumatic experience she later wrote: "Do you understand the pain, the bitterness, the desperation we mothers have in our hearts when we cannot feed our children or cure their sickness, when they die before our eyes because we have no money for doctors or medicines?"[176]

Soon after her child died, she abandoned the Catholic religion in which she had been reared and became a militant Marxist. Her husband's political activities and socialist beliefs now seemed insufficient for her. She craved justice and vengeance against a system that had caused her and her neighbors and family to suffer so much for so long. Once when the Guardia Civil, the state police force, came to arrest Señor Ibarruri for his antigovernment acts, he meekly surrendered. His wife became furious with him: a true revolutionary would either fight or go into hiding. Surrender? Never. She protested so vigorously to the authorities that they feared she would stir up public sentiment against the government; her husband was quickly released. But Ibarruri was not interested in only her own problems. She dedicated herself to helping other desperate families, and became increasingly involved in politics. She became one of the founders of the Communist Party in Spain, and at the age of twenty-two helped foment the general strike of 1916 by making bombs and supplying arms to the workers. She was arrested many times but with each arrest her fame and popularity grew. The beleaguered monarchical government feared correctly that imprisoning her would only arouse greater public animosity. The prestige of La Pasionaria, "the passionate one," became so great that she organized a march of 30,000 women and children to a government prison to demand the release of all political prisoners. Armed guards stood before the gates. Alone and without any weapon Ibarruri walked up to an officer and imperiously commanded that he open the gate to let her in and then to give her the keys. Dumbfounded, he complied, and the woman proceeded to release all of the prisoners before the startled eyes of the prison guards and amid the acclaim of the cheering crowd.

The Ibarruris were blessed with another child, a boy. But the bonds of marriage weakened as the wife's commitment to revolutionary activity increased. Finally the couple drifted apart altogether. After the abdication of the king and the fall of the government, La Pasionaria went to Madrid to take part in the formation of the new Republican government, reluctantly leaving her child in the care of his grandmother. However, whenever it was feasible, the mother kept the child with her. She even tried to resign her post in Madrid so she could return to the Basque country to be with him. But she was elected to Parliament and was needed to help temper some of the abuses of the new government. When the Nationalists rebelled, starting the bloody Spanish Civil War, La Pasionaria undertook a major role in resisting Franco's Fascist forces. Fearing for the safety of her only child, she sadly sent him to the Soviet Union and totally devoted herself to the struggle against the Fascists. Most of her energies were spent in writing articles for the press and traveling about the country giving impassioned speeches to the army and the people. Her words became the battle cry of the Republican forces: "No pasaran" (They shall not pass). But she used more than words: on occasion she commanded a machine gun in battle. Rumors circulated that Ibarruri had even killed a Nationalist soldier by biting him on the throat. True or untrue, the story nevertheless enhanced her reputation as a fearless woman.

When Franco, with the aid of German planes and Italian troops, finally crushed the Republican forces, La Pasionaria had to flee the country. Her new country of residence was the Soviet Union, where she continued to write and speak in favor of the Republican cause and Communism. In 1977, after the death of Franco and several requests for amnesty, she returned to Spain, stood for Parliament, and was elected to office.

HALIDE EDIB, a Turkish revolutionary, was a remarkably traditional Muslim woman in her relations with both her father and her husband. Around the turn of the century she married a man who was the same age as her father, her intellectual mentor. Her husband, Abdulhak Adnan-Adivar, a well-known mathematician and scientist, encouraged her to produce some of her revolutionary writings. Both were active in the Kemalist movement headed by Mustapha Kemal, who later took the name Ataturk. She assisted her husband in assembling his monumental work, *The Mathematical Dictionary*. She led the life of a traditional Turkish woman, was seldom seen in public, and had almost no contact with other men. Not long after her marriage she had a nervous breakdown. She found the isolation of her role difficult. In 1910 she divorced her husband after he took another younger wife, as was customary among wealthy Muslims. She could not bear the polygamous relationship. This was an insult to her sense of dignity. Her new freedom gave her renewed vigor and desire to live independently on her own. She became dedicated to and involved in the cause of revolution. When she left her husband, she took her children with her.

In 1901 Halide Edib became the first Turkish woman to receive a Bachelor of Arts degree. The Constitutional Revolution in 1908, basically of a nationalist, liberal nature, stirred her to write for the leading Young Turk newspaper, *Tanine*. Her articles advocated the emancipation of Turkish women as well as the general revolutionary cause. Her writings were considered to be an inspiration to the revolutionary soldiers; during the War of Liberation she herself was a soldier, first an army corporal and then a sergeant, but in 1909 she was forced to flee Turkey because of the sultan's reaction to her activities. In 1912 she participated actively in the nationalist movement, serving as the only woman member of the general congress of the Turkish Hearth, a secret organization. In 1922 she rode at Ataturk's side during the victorious reentry of Turkish troops into Izmir. After the revolution, she lived alone which was very unusual for Turkish women, taught school to support herself, and continued to help further the emancipation of Turkish women. Edib was the first Turkish woman to address an open mass meeting. She played a major role in Ataturk's effort to get women to rid themselves of their face veils, to make polygamy illegal, and to achieve equal rights for women before the law.

One of the advantages of youth is the complete abandon with which one can throw oneself into those things that seem so important at the time. With no accumulation of expectations about what can't be done, and no adult limitations, youth can afford to be "irresponsible." Of course, what is deemed irresponsible by older adult values can be judged highly responsible by the youth. Such appears to be the case with revolutionaries in general and ANGELA DAVIS in particular—a black American born in Birmingham, Alabama, in 1944. Undoubtedly, she considers it the height of irresponsibility for black Americans to continue to work in a system that she believes to be irreversibly committed to their continued servitude, if not extinction.

Angela Davis has just begun her fourth decade of life and yet the account of her activities, political travels, and political contributions reads like that of a person of many more years. She has taken part in meetings, demonstrations, and rallies in no fewer than five different countries (United States, France, West Germany, East Germany, and Cuba); she has been at various times a member or a sympathizer with numerous politically radical groups including the Students for a Democratic Society, the Black Panther Political Party, and the Communist Party. She has organized political activity around causes such as the Black Student Union at the University of California and the Rap Brown and Huey Newton defense funds; been a founder of the "Liberation School" for the Panthers and the Student Non-Violent Coordinating Committee; attended the Black Congress and the Conference to Found a United Front Against Fascism; been the prime fund raiser for the Soledad Brothers and the Bobby Seale–Erica Huggins Defense Committee, and a general coordinator of a variety of black radical activities. As a result of these activities she has created many enemies who would not mourn her death. Time and time again in her autobiography, Davis contemplates the possibility of an early violent death. The sources of danger appear to be everywhere. Even within the black movement itself there are groups who have not liked her politics, particularly her Communist Party affiliation. Of course the official law-enforcement agencies of the United States are none too friendly either. Despite her acquittal on murder charges for allegedly having supplied the guns used by Jonathan Jackson in the San Rafael shoot-out, her fear of official harassment and persecution has not lessened substantially.

There is no question that Angela Davis considers herself to be a revolutionary. Indeed, the major reason she gives for having joined the Communist Party in July 1968 was: "I needed to become part of a serious revolutionary party."[177] Her commitment to black liberation and general leftist politics is of long standing and relentless intensity. No adult role conflict has interfered with this commitment and many personal alliances have been made because of ideological similarity. Davis is not likely to be swept off her feet by romantic love; nor is she likely to abandon her political activity for the private life of housewife/mother.

Davis is not married nor does she have any children. She has been linked romantically with two men—a German student, Clemenz, whom she at one time thought of marrying, and George Jackson, a black American political activist. Although Davis does not write at any length about her relationship to Clemenz, she does note that she went to Germany to meet his parents. Unexpressed and yet implicit in her discussion is a note of exasperation over the racial difficulties she experienced during this visit because of the prejudices of the German society. Davis' critique of the German society and its racism is given particular emphasis because of its contribution to the dissolution of her relationship with Clemenz. A personal, private matter in her adult life was interpreted in a political manner. Davis gives primacy to the public, not to the private. Limitations on choice and freedom are considered to be of public origin, not the result of private failure.

The case of George Jackson even more clearly illustrates the penetration of the public into the private world of Angela Davis. The conditions under which Davis came to know George Jackson were publicly determined. Jackson was a prisoner. He was attempting to organize black inmates and make them politically conscious of their oppression. Even while Davis was in the New York City House of Detention and Martin County jail she was distributing, against official orders, the work of George Jackson entitled *Soledad Brothers.*

The implication of the prosecution's case was that Davis had been injured by the death of Jackson as a love-struck woman and that she was acting on her feelings in a public way. At the same time the prosecution was claiming that Davis had brought the guns because of a "passionate love for George Jackson ... that knew no bounds, no limitations, no respect for human life."[178] In contrast, Angela Davis considered Jackson's death a political murder—merely one in a series of publicly encouraged acts against the Soledad prisoners and the black radical population. In our judgment Davis did not displace private grief onto a public object. For Davis the political world had by now become completely integrated with the private world. The two had become inseparable. She is a woman with a strong sense of personal political efficacy.

ROSA LUXEMBURG was born a Polish Jew in the tsarist Russian empire. She became a leading political figure in the Polish, Russian, and German social-democratic revolutionary movements. In addition to being a great orator and a popular leader, she was a well-known theoretician both of macro economics and of party organization. Historians consider her one of the main spokespersons and theoreticians for the German Left and one of the founders of the German Communist Party. Her writings opposing the bureaucratic rule of Bolshevism and its rejection of democracy became a rallying point for Marxists and Socialists opposed to Bolshevism. In turn, the Bolsheviks elevated her ideas to an "ism" and fought them vociferously. She was brutally murdered by forces of the German state and became a martyred figure.

Rosa Luxemburg married only once. It was a marriage of convenience to a young German so that she could obtain German citizenship. She and her legal husband rarely had any contact with each other. The major love of her life was a revolutionary colleague, Leo Jogiches, who became her common-law husband. He was an unsurpassed organizer, a clever and forceful debater, and a dedicated, devoted worker for the socialist cause. Though she never allowed him to dictate to her on theoretical or other revolutionary matters, she was totally submissive to him in their personal monetary matters. On the one hand, she was totally independent and free; on the other, she was dependent and "wifely." Clara Zetkin, who knew both Luxemburg and Jogiches well, said of him: "He was one of those rare men who can tolerate a great personality in the woman by his side, working with him in a loyal and happy comradeship, without feeling her growth and development as a limitation on his own personality."[179] When this relationship lost its romantic flavor, both remained friends, but passed on to other affairs. Luxemburg never had children, probably because of a hip disease.

MAUD GONNE was born to an English mother and Anglo-Irish father in London in 1866. Her parents belonged to the upper-middle class. The mother, a beautiful and gentle person, died when Maud was only four, but the young girl retained fond memories of her. Her father, an officer in the British army, took his children with him on duty assignments wherever he could. So when he was assigned to a command in Ireland, he took his daughters with him to live in the lovely mansion that belonged to his family. In his official post the father prevented his soldiers from harassing the local inhabitants. His daughters acquired his sympathy toward the impoverished Irish. At that time the English landlords found it more profitable to concentrate the cultivation of their large landholdings in the hands of a small number of farmers. Until that time the traditional custom was for the absentee landlord to appoint agents to rent out the lands. The agents charged so much that the original renters had to sublet and divide the land; these smaller sections were even further subdivided and let out to other tenant farmers. Thus families had lived on tiny plots of land for centuries without ever being able to accumulate wealth; they were barely able to raise enough to pay the rent and feed themselves. Now many of the tenant families were being forcibly evicted. With no place to go, the poor tenants resisted desperately. But their shacks were burned down and they were often shot or arrested if they refused to leave. The girls observed many instances of such exploitation and cruelty toward the poor, but the experience made a much greater impression on the elder daughter, Maud. Her heart went out to the poor Catholic Irish and, identifying with them, she became resentful of the wealthy Protestant Anglo-Irish landlords and the government that permitted such injustice. Her father eventually resigned from the army in disgust with the government's policies and tried, unsuccessfully, to run for public office.

The elder girl assumed a sort of parental responsibility toward her young sister, especially during the father's absence. She was very fond of her father and spent a great deal of time in serious discussions with him. He treated her as an equal, and she gladly served as a social companion to him by accompanying him to formal dinners and dances. When he had to leave for long periods, the father hired private companion-tutors for his daughters. Young Maud Gonne spent a good deal of time in France with one such tutor, from whom she acquired some of her liberal ideas as well as fluency in French.

Years later she returned to the south of France to recuperate from a lung condition she acquired in Ireland's damp, chilly winter weather. She met and formed a lasting friendship with a patriotic young Frenchman who shared her hatred of the English government. They made a pact to aid each other in any way they could in their mutual fight against England. He even gave her a gun, which she agreed to keep. Although she eventually became an advocate of the violent overthrow of the government by force, she could never bring herself to use a gun against anyone. Instead, Gonne worked for the cause of Irish freedom by editing a journal and writing articles explaining the Irish cause against England to Europeans and the rest of the world. She also managed to raise funds for the support of the revolutionary movement.

When Gonne met Arthur Griffith, one of the central figures in the Irish resistance to English rule, she volunteered her services. Griffith rejected her offer; he was suspicious that she might be an English spy; he also thought that, because she was beautiful and gentle in manner, she would be of little value to his party. Besides, none of the Irish political parties accepted women. Disappointed but determined to continue to work for Irish independence, Gonne decided to form her own political party for women. She traveled about England and Ireland speaking on the Irish question. Gonne was a highly effective speaker, and her poignant description of the sufferings of the poor evicted tenants she had seen as a young girl won the sympathy of many of the English people who heard her. A wave of protest grew against the abusive policies of the British toward their Irish subjects, who were also supposed to be citizens of Great Britain. For her opposition to the eviction policy and her pursuit of land reform law, Gonne became widely acclaimed as a friend and champion of the oppressed. Local government authorities often tried to prevent her from speaking at public gatherings by banning specific meetings. She refused to obey and continued to speak out publicly whenever she could. As a result she was arrested on a series of petty charges and imprisoned several times.

An intelligent and cultured woman, Gonne became friendly with many of the famous writers of the Irish literary renaissance. William Butler Yeats proposed to her several times, but she would consent only to act in some of his plays. In the title role of the play *Cathleen nee Houlihan*—a name symbolic of Ireland itself—Gonne was an outstanding success. Along with Yeats and several others she formed a society for the study of the occult and attended a number of seances. She even reported having recurring dreams and visions of a gray woman who beckoned to her.[180] Gonne believed that the mysterious figure was the ghost of an ancient queen of Ireland who was communicating to Gonne that she had a mission of destiny to fulfill. She frequently used the title "Servant of the Queen" in reference to herself. The queen, of course, was not the queen of England but rather Ireland itself—Cathleen nee Houlihan.

In spite of her belief in a sort of pagan mysticism, Gonne converted from Anglicanism to the Roman Catholicism of her adopted Irish countrymen. She seemed to have little interest in or understanding of the theological differences between the two religions. Her choice of Catholicism was based more on cultural preference; it seemed somehow "natural" to her to be a Catholic in Ireland.

At the age of thirty-six Gonne married a man who bore

many superficial resemblances to her own father. John MacBride was a handsome, young Irish officer in the British army. Sympathetic to the Irish cause, he left the army to become involved in revolutionary activity. The major leaders of the revolutionary movement, however, neither liked him nor trusted him. He had a bad reputation as a braggart, a drinker, and a carouser. The couple traveled on speaking tours together in the United States to gather money and public support for the Irish cause. They were both convincing speakers and their trips were highly successful. Their marriage, however, was not. They soon separated, but in keeping with Catholic precepts neither ever remarried. Mac-Bride sought new adventures traveling in Europe for a few years. By coincidence and without his wife's knowledge, MacBride returned to Dublin a few days before the Easter Rebellion of 1916. He took no part in the preparations and was not even aware of the plot until the fighting began. Experienced soldier that he was, he immediately joined in the battle on the side of the rebels. When the short-lived insurrection was over, MacBride was arrested, tried, condemned, and executed along with Patrick Pearse and the other leaders of the rebellion. MacBride achieved instant immortality as a martyr for Ireland; and, ironically, Gonne—as she preferred to be called—gained the sympathy and admiration of Irish women everywhere as the widow of an Irish hero. Masses of men and women clamored to see and hear her wherever she went. Many women who had formerly remained aloof from politics because they thought it was "man's work" now came in great numbers to join the political organizations she had formed. At last the ordinary Irish woman began to develop the consciousness that she too was an "Irishman" and had a stake with her sons, husband, and father in Irish independence.

COUNTESS CONSTANCE GORE-BOOTH MARKIEVICZ was another intelligent, cultured woman to support the Irish revolution. The daughter of an Anglo-Irish aristocrat, she was born in London, where the family frequently returned to participate in English court society. Most of her time was spent, however, on her family's large estate. Unlike most of the wealthy landlords who owned and controlled all the farmland in Ireland, her father was neither an absentee landlord nor did he blatantly exploit his tenant farmers. For generations the family had the reputation of showing genuine concern for the welfare of their tenants; the family never condoned nor took part in the massive eviction of poor from the land. On the other hand, neither of her parents was particularly active in political or benevolent social causes. Lord Gore-Booth in fact showed little interest in overseeing his huge landholdings; he preferred to go on long voyages of scientific exploration to places like the Arctic. In the meantime Lady Gore-Booth continued her role as leader of polite Anglo-Irish Protestant society in her area of the country. She even played a prominent role in making arrangements for the visit of Queen Victoria to Ireland.

At the age of eighteen Constance Gore-Booth was formally presented to the queen at Buckingham Palace. But the athletic, outgoing, high-spirited girl preferred the simpler life of the Irish countryside to the courtly manners of London social life. She loved to be with the poor Catholic Irish tenants on her parents' estate. The poor affectionately described her as "wild but kind."[181] On one occasion she stayed at the cottage of an expectant mother doing her chores so that the woman could stay in bed both before and after the baby was born. Another time she spent several days and nights personally taking care of a sick tenant until he came through the most critical part of his illness. The poor accepted the girl as one of their own, while her parents tolerated what they considered to be an extreme form of charity. They knew that she could not be dissuaded.

Educated in the traditional manner for aristocratic young ladies of that time, the Gore-Booth sisters were well trained in the arts and humanities: music, art, language, and literature were stressed as the appropriate "graces" for young ladies. Both girls indeed grew to be lovely and gracious women. Constance Gore-Booth, being the more adventurous of the two (after traveling in France and Italy to view the works of the great masters), went to London to develop her interest and unusual talent for art. There she met and fell in love with another art student, Count Markievicz, a handsome, witty, and talented Polish aristocrat living in exile. They soon married and pursued their mutual interest in art and the theatre together. Settling in Dublin, the couple became active in the Abbey Theatre group in company with such famous playwrights as Sean O'Casey and W. B. Yeats. The count wrote several plays which were well received, partly due to the acting talents of his wife. The countess also appeared in some of

Yeats's plays and even wrote a few herself. Although not revolutionary in content, the plays delved seriously into some of the current political and social issues. Eventually the countess became convinced that the Irish people were entitled to independence and the only way to obtain it was through open revolt.

Although the count was also sympathetic to the Irish cause, his main concern was with Polish nationalism, since his own country was under siege by Russia. He traveled frequently on the continent working on behalf of the Polish cause. Gradually he and his wife spent more and more time apart; nevertheless, they maintained their mutual esteem and affection.

The countess offered her own services to the cause of Irish liberation, and, like Maud Gonne, was rejected. As the daughter of an aristocratic landlord she was considered English and not Irish. The main reason for her rejection, however, was simply that she was a woman. Markievicz then decided that she would serve the movement by becoming a teacher and fomenting the ideals of liberty among the youth, especially girls. Traditionally, Irish women had left the concerns of politics and war to men. The countess sought to change that; but with growing frustration she found that she had little success in interesting the girls in the new ideas she presented. Reports about what she was trying to do reached government officials; she was arrested for advocating sedition and the school was closed.

Next she turned her efforts to instilling revolutionary ideas and sentiments in young boys. She formed a boys' club, somewhat similar to the boy scouts but more militaristic. Here she met with great success. In addition to evoking national and ethnic pride through Irish history and literature, she began training the boys in the tactics and skills of guerrilla combat under the guise of boyish games. Eventually Markievicz won the trust and respect of the rebel leaders, such as Patrick Pearse, who was also a teacher. She was invited to participate in the planning of the ill-fated Easter Rebellion of 1916. Skilled in the use of guns and rifles, Markievicz was made second in command of a mission to capture and then hold one of the government buildings in the heart of Dublin. Although under constant attack by British troops, Markievicz and her companions successfully defended their position until the inevitable order of surrender came from Pearse. All of the tiny band of conspirators were tried and condemned to death. Markievicz and Eamon De Valera, however, were not executed. He was an American citizen; she was the wife of a Polish citizen and, accordingly, was also considered a foreign national. Besides, since Britain was involved in war with Germany, the execution of a woman might have swayed the opinion of neutral nations, such as the United States, against Britain.

Upon her release from prison, the countess was acclaimed as a heroine of the Irish people. The British government began proceedings to deport her as an undesirable alien, but since she had been born in England, Markievicz was able to make the government's case appear ludicrous. She then threw herself back into the struggle for Irish liberation. She openly preached defiance against English rule, and again strove to interest Irish girls, wives, and mothers in the revolutionary movement—urging them, if not to join it, at least to understand it, to appreciate it, and to support it. The authorities attempted to prevent her from making public speeches by banning public meetings at which she was scheduled to appear. Invariably she disobeyed the order and was arrested and imprisoned. So great was her popularity that, without her knowledge and while she was in prison, she was nominated for a seat in Parliament. While still in prison, she received official notification from the British prime minister that she had been elected—the first woman in the history of Britain—to be a member of Parliament. The countess, however, refused to take the required oath of allegiance to the queen. Thus she was never allowed to take her seat nor to speak in Parliament. Later, however, when the Dael, the traditional legislative body of Ireland, was reconvened for the first time in centuries, Countess Markievicz became the first woman member. This time she served actively in her elected office and was also appointed minister of labor in De Valera's new cabinet. In this capacity she organized workers' unions and farmers' cooperatives, and instituted social welfare programs for the poor.

While vestiges of odious British rule remained, Markievicz and her companions continued to press for full independence from England. When they rebelled again in 1918, England was still involved in a desperate struggle with Germany. Desirous of avoiding an additional conflict, England was finally willing to concede self-rule to Ireland but with the proviso that six of the thirty-two counties remain under British control and that the country be partitioned. Without arms and wearied from struggle, Michael Collins and most of the rebel leaders were willing to accept Britain's terms for peace and liberty. De Valera and Markievicz, the sole surviving leaders of the 1916 rebellion, indignantly denounced the treaty; anything less than complete independence and self-rule for all of Ireland would be tantamount to surrender. De Valera and Markievicz resigned from the Dael in protest. Civil war among the Irish themselves ensued, lasting until 1922, when the bitter fact of partition was finally accepted and two separate nations were formed on Irish soil.

Weakened by strenuous physical activity and long periods of imprisonment, Markievicz became less active in politics. She suffered from a series of minor illnesses until, in 1927, she became gravely ill. Her faithful husband returned from the Continent to be at her side during her final struggle. When death came, all citizens of the new nation of Eire mourned. Her outstanding contribution to the cause of Irish freedom was publicly acknowledged at her funeral. Without the foresight, leadership, and dedication to the training of Irish youths for combat and the heroic example of the Countess Markievicz, there could have been no uprising in 1916 and no successful rebellion in 1918.

The Agitators/Terrorists

It is one thing to advocate the overthrow of a government and quite another to take weapon in hand and kill a person face-to-face. The fame of five of our subjects is directly related to this personal willingness to assassinate officials of the establishment. Although they were initially separated from our other revolutionaries primarily because of this violent behavior, they differ from them in other significant ways as well. Only one of them was legally married and that was because she was forced to be by her parents as a teenager; and only one, the same one, had children. As will become evident in our further discussion, these five women also experienced a socialization process different than did the other revolutionaries. Our terrorists are Charlotte Corday, Vera Ivanovna Zasulich, Sophia Perovskaia, Ch'iu Chin, and Emma Goldman.

CHARLOTTE CORDAY was sent to a convent by her father at a very tender age due to the death of her mother. It was here that she learned of the French revolutionary movement and came to sympathize with it. Each act of repression against the revolutionaries caused her much personal suffering. When she identified Jean Paul Marat, a Jacobin, as the key source of the torture and bloodshed, she stabbed him to death in his bathtub in 1793. She was executed shortly thereafter at the age of twenty-five. Although Corday was acquainted with young men, she apparently knew none of them terribly well. She never married and, of course, had no children. To her the words "liberty," "peace," and "justice" were "living beings of flesh and blood, beings whom she loved; to her they were what children's names are to a mother."[182]

VERA IVANOVNA ZASULICH was involved at almost every major ideological and organizational turning point in the Russian revolutionary movement. In 1878 she attempted to assassinate the governor-general of St. Petersburg. After her trial and acquittal, she became hailed as the "heroine of the revolution" and was compared to Charlotte Corday, the heroine of the French Revolution. Later, she came to oppose terroristic acts and helped found Chernyi Peredel' (Black Repartition Group). In 1883 she collaborated with George Plekhanov and Paul Axelrod in founding the Emancipation of Labor Group. Through her activities and writings she became one of the founders and leaders of Russian Marxism and the Social-Democratic movement in Russia. A close colleague of Nikolai Lenin, Julius Martov, Leon Trotsky, and Peter Struve at the turn of the century, she became one of the editors of *Iskra* and *Zaria*, the important ideological and organizational organs of the Russian Marxists. Opposing Lenin at the Second Congress of the Russian Social-Democratic Workers Party in 1903, she became one of the founders and leaders of Menshevism. From 1905 ill health kept her involvement in revolutionary affairs at a minimal level.

In her mid-twenties Zasulich began living with Lev Deich, who became, in effect, her common-law husband. So far as we know he was the only lover she ever had. After a few short years with her, he was captured by the Russian police and imprisoned. Only after twenty years of separation did they meet again; both had changed to such an extent that they did not resurrect their intimate relationship. Thus Vera spent most of her life living on the periphery of families not her own. She was constantly haunted by the feeling of not belonging, of being an outsider, just as when she was a small child. The revolutionary movement and her revolutionary colleagues were her life.

In 1871, at the age of eighteen, SOPHIA PEROVSKAIA became "the soul of the Chaikovskist group"[183] in St. Petersburg. The Chaikovskists combined the anarchism of Mikhail Bakunin and the socialism of Peter Lavrov. They were the initiators of the Russian populist movement. In 1878 she became one of the founders and leaders of the *Zemlia i Volia* (Land and Freedom) party; in 1879, when that party split into two groups, she joined and became a leader of the *Narodnaia Volia* segment, which (partly inspired by Zasulich's act of terrorism in attempting to kill the governor-general of St. Petersburg) made political terrorism and the destruction of absolutism its chief aims. On March 1, 1881, she, herself a daughter of another governor-general of St. Petersburg and a descendant of the Russian tsars, along with several other conspirators, assassinated Tsar Alexander II. With three men who had a part in the assassination, she was hanged on April 3, 1881. Her name was commonly invoked as an inspiration to other revolutionaries in the decades that followed.

Since her early childhood, Perovskaia had hated her father. As a young woman this hostility was reflected in her openly expressed low opinion of male intelligence and reliability. Usually she ignored men as inferior beings unworthy of even her interest, much less her favors. In her late twenties, however, she fell madly in love with a fellow leader of *Narodnaia Volia*, Andrei Zheliabov. Good-looking, virile, daring, a man of peasant extraction, he swept her off her feet. Together they planned the tsar's assassination. After her lover was imprisoned, Perovskaia arranged for the implementation of the murder plot. They were hanged together for the deed. She was twenty-eight years old.

Our only Chinese representative, CH'IU CHIN, dreamed of being like Perovskaia as a small girl. The push to implement that dream came when her parents forced her to marry a very conventional and dull son of a wealthy merchant. She felt so entrapped and useless in her subservient role that it became unbearable. After seven years of marriage and three children, at the age of twenty-eight she divorced him, left her children, and went to Tokyo in 1903.

In Tokyo she and other Chinese radicals published a revolutionary journal, conducted demonstrations, and studied marksmanship and how to make bombs. In 1906 she returned to China and joined the Restoration Society, the chief revolutionary organization in Chekiang. At the same time she also established the

Chinese Women's Journal. In 1907 she took a position as teacher and headmistress in a girls' school in Shaohsing, and became the leader of the revolutionary forces in the area. She tried to build a girls' army and openly discussed revolution, but the girls were not interested. In 1908 her distant cousin and revolutionary associate Hsu assassinated the provincial governor and was executed. Ch'iu Chin was immediately suspected of complicity, quickly arrested, and beheaded.

EMMA GOLDMAN, who was born in Lithuania, part of the tsarist empire, emigrated to the United States in her early teens. Her political consciousness was aroused by the execution of anarchists for the Haymarket disturbance of 1886 in Chicago. Shortly after the executions, she moved to New York City from Rochester, New York, and became involved with anarchists. She dedicated her life to their cause, becoming a well-known agitator and speaker. It was with Alexander Birkin, one of her anarchist colleagues and her lover, that she planned the death of a well-known capitalist. She ultimately did not participate because they had only one gun and insufficient money for both to take the train to where the man was to be killed.

Goldman's experience with the opposite sex was not joyous. Her father beat her as a child; she was sure he hated her. At the age of six she engaged in sexual play with a peasant boy of about twelve years of age, and when she was twelve, she was sexually assaulted by a hotel clerk. As a result of her childhood experiences, Goldman confided, she always felt a twinge of repugnance for the act of intercourse. This did not, however, preclude her having an active sex life with a variety of partners. It did mean that she could never fully enjoy the intimacy of sexual or marital love. Love, she felt, was precious but very rare. In 1887 at the age of eighteen she married Jacob Kersner, a Russian Jew, who turned out to be impotent. Less than a year later she divorced him. She later remarried him and divorced him again. What she disliked most about marriage, or any personal liaison, was being tied down with specific responsibilities. An anarchist in her personal as well as her political activities, Goldman could not bear any restrictions for long. She wrote, "The struggle to maintain my own individuality and freedom was always more important to me than the wildest love affairs."[184]

Goldman's adult life was almost entirely male-centered. She seemed to need the approval of men, perhaps because she felt her own father had never loved her. In any case Goldman achieved one satisfying and lasting relationship with a man who perceived marriage and government much the same as she did, the anarchist Alexander Birkin. Goldman had no children. To do so she would have had to have an operation. She suppressed "this need," she said, to work for the children of the world.

Conclusion

These thirty-six women clearly represent a broad spectrum of the type of political behavior women engage in. In looking at their adult lives we see no evidence that the achieving women are biologically different from the private or public women. We do see sharp differences in the sex-role ideology held by these women and in the type of political efficacy and the control over their life-spaces they had and sought. The political women, particularly those with a strong sense of personal political efficacy, do not seem able to limit their activities to their families. When they try, they are miserable. Private women, however, find selfless devotion to the family to be a great joy.

Much of the literature on women and politics in the early 1970s stressed how important motherhood was in deterring female political participation. The lives of our real-life women suggest, however, that being a mother or wife is not the major obstacle to political behavior. (Additional empirical support for generalizing this conclusion beyond our thirty-six women has been provided by a 1976 study of 3,298 of all 3,562 women holding public office at any governmental level in the United States. This study states, "Just as the 'typical' woman in office is married, she is also a mother—and a mother of as many children as any other woman her age."[185]) The major obstacle to participation is a sex-role ideology that requires women to be subordinate to as well as supportive of their husbands. The women in our study who became politically active (1) waited until their husbands died, (2) had husbands who strongly supported their efforts, or (3) did not get into any long-term family involvement with men at all. Children sometimes delayed, but they did not deter, the achieving women from having a political career. Motherhood itself cannot be considered the main deterrent to female political behavior. Belief about what being a mother and a wife requires of women is another matter, however. The socialization to particular sex-role ideologies and behavior patterns is the key to understanding why the women described here differ.

Notes

1. The initial citation on each of the individuals included in our study will be a short summation of the major sources from which the biographical information on these women was gathered. For Lenin's wife, Nadezhda Konstantinovna Krupskaia, the sources were chiefly: Vera Dridzo, "Nadezhda Konstantinovna," *Novyi Mir*, No. 2, February 1957, pp. 162–176; S. Bobrovskaia, *Lenin and Krupskaia* (New York: Workers' Library Publishers, 1940); Nadezhda K. Krupskaia, *Moia Zhizn'* (Moscow: Proletarii, 1925); L. Stal, *Nadezhdaia Konstantinovna Krupskaia* (Moscow: Gosudarstvennoi izdatel'stvo, 1928); Nadezhda K. Krupskaia, *Memories of Lenin*, trans. E. Verney (London: M. Lawrence, 1930); *Soviet Woman: A Citizen With Equal Rights*, a collection of articles and speeches (Moscow: Cooperative Publishing Society of Foreign Workers in the U.S.S.R., 1937); Robert M. McNeal, *Bride of the Revolution: Krupskaia and Lenin* (Ann Arbor: University of Michigan Press, 1972).

2. Svetlana Alliluyeva, *Twenty Letters to a Friend*, trans. Priscilla Johnson McMillan (New York: Harper & Row, 1967); Elizabeth Lermolo, *Face of a Victim*, translated from the Russian by I. D. W. Talmadge (London, 1956); Maxim Litvinov, *Notes for a Journal*, ed. E. H. Carr (London, 1955); H. Montgomery Hyde, *Stalin: The History of a Dictator* (New York: Farrar, Straus & Giroux, 1971).

3. Roy MacGregor Hastie, *The Man from Nowhere* (New York: Coward-McCann Inc., 1961); William Randolph Hearst, Jr., Frank Conniff, and Bob Considine, *Ask Me Anything: Our Adventures with Khrushchev* (New York: McGraw-Hill, 1960).

4. Alfred Steinberg, *Mrs. R: The Life of Eleanor Roosevelt* (New York: G. P. Putnam's Sons, 1956); Anna Eleanor Roosevelt, *The Autobiography of Eleanor Roosevelt* (New York: Harper & Row, 1961); *Who's Who in America* (Marquis), Vol. 31 (1960–61); Joseph P. Lash, *Eleanor and Franklin* (New York: W. W. Norton and Company, 1971).

5. Merle Miller, *Plain Speaking: An Oral Biography of Harry S. Truman* (New York: G. P. Putnam's Sons, 1974); Bert Cochran, *Harry Truman and the Crisis Presidency* (New York: Funk & Wagnalls, 1973); Alfred Steinberg, *The Man From Missouri: The Life and Times of Harry S. Truman* (New York: G. P. Putnam's Sons, 1962).

6. Alden Hatch, *Red Carpet for Mamie* (New York: Henry Holt & Co., 1954); Sol Borzman, *The First Ladies* (New York: Cowles Book Company, 1970).

7. Jacqueline Bouvier Kennedy and Lee Bouvier, *One Special Summer* (New York: Delacorte Press, 1975); Mary B. Gallagher, *My Life With Jacqueline Kennedy* (New York: David McKay Company, 1969); John H. Davis, *The Bouviers: A Portrait of an American Family* (New York: Avon, 1970); Mary Van Rensselaer Thayer, *Jacqueline Bouvier Kennedy* (Garden City, N.Y.: Doubleday and Company, 1961).

8. Lady Bird Johnson, *A White House Diary* (New York: Holt, Rinehart and Winston, 1970); Marie Smith, *The President's Lady* (New York: Random House, 1964); Sol Borzman, *The First Ladies;* R. Angelo, "Life Without the Presence," *Time,* May 21, 1973, p. 41; H. Brandon, "Talk with the First Lady," *New York Times Magazine,* September 10, 1967, pp. 47–49; D. McConathy, "Wife-Power," *Vogue,* June, 1975 p. 110; R. A. Sohalov, "Rare Bird," *Newsweek,* November 2, 1970, p. 114.

9. Edwin P. Hoyt, *The Nixons: An American Family* (New York: Random House, 1972); Henry Spalding, *The Nixon Nobody Knows* (New York: Jonathan David, 1972); Judith Viorst, "Pat Nixon Is the Ultimate Good Sport," *New York Times Magazine,* September 13, 1970, pp. 25–27; Kandy Stroud, "Pat Nixon Today," *Ladies' Home Journal,* March, 1975, p. 77; Phyllis Lee Levin, "The Private Pat Nixon," *Vogue,* October 15, 1972, p. 85; Trude Feldman, "Mrs. Nixon Tells How She Brought Up Tricia and Julie," *McCall's,* March, 1969, p. 74; Jessamyn West, "The Real Pat Nixon: An Intimate View," *Good Housekeeping,* February, 1971, pp. 67–70; Wenzola McLendon, "The Unsinkable Pat Nixon," *McCall's,* October, 1973, p. 84; Jean L. Black, "The Pat Nixon I Know," *Good Housekeeping,* July, 1973, p. 72; Edward Clark and Alfred Eisenstaedt, "Lovely Aspirants for the Role of First Lady," *Life,* October 10, 1960, pp. 150–57.

10. Aidan Crawley, *De Gaulle: A Biography* (New York: Bobbs-Merrill Co., 1969); Alden Hatch, *The De Gaulle Nobody Knows: An Intimate Biography of Charles de Gaulle* (New York: Hawthorn Inc., 1960); Brian Crozier, *De Gaulle* (New York: Charles Scribner's Sons, 1973); Pauline Frederick, *Ten First Ladies of the World* (New York: Meredith Press, 1967); Phyllis Feldkamp, "Places," *Atlantic Monthly,* May, 1967, pp. 114–18; Edward Behr, "The Silent First Lady of France," *Saturday Evening Post,* January 18, 1964, p. 65; "His Lady," *Newsweek,* April 25, 1960, pp. 45–46; Stanley Clark, *The Man Who Is France* (New York: Dodd, Mead & Company, 1960).

11. Stella King, "The Housewife at No. 10," *New York Times Magazine,* February 7, 1965, p. 43; Leslie Smith, *Harold Wilson: The Authentic Portrait* (New York: Charles Scribner's Sons, 1964); Dudley Smith, *Harold Wilson: A Critical Biography* (London: Robert Hale

Limited, 1964); Anthony Howard and Richard West, *The Road to Number 10* (New York: The Macmillan Co., 1965).

12. Jack Fishman, *My Darling Clementine: The Story of Lady Churchill* (New York: David McKay Company, 1963).

13. Frank Graham, Jr., *Margaret Chase Smith: Woman of Courage* (New York: The John Day Company, 1964); Rudolf Engelbarts, *Women in the United States Congress, 1917–1972* (Littleton, Colo.: Libraries Unlimited, 1974); Hope Chamberlain, *A Minority of Members: Women in the U.S. Congress* (New York: Praeger, 1973); Margaret Chase Smith, *Declaration of Conscience* (Garden City, N.Y.: Doubleday, 1972); Peggy Lamson, *Few Are Chosen* (Boston: Houghton Mifflin Co., 1968).

14. Maurife Collif, *Nancy Astor: An Informal Biography* (New York: Dutton, 1960); Elizabeth Langhorne, *Nancy Astor and Her Friends* (New York: Praeger, 1974); Christopher Sykes, *Nancy: Life of Lady Astor* (New York: Harper & Row, 1972).

15. Engelbarts, *Women in the U.S. Congress;* Lamson, *Few Are Chosen;* Chamberlain, *A Minority of Members;* Susan and Martin Tolchin, *Clout: Womanpower and Politics* (New York: Coward, McCann and Geoghegan, 1974). A great deal of the information on Congresswoman Sullivan came from a written questionnaire which she graciously completed in the fall of 1975.

16. Krishan Bhatia, *Indira: A Biography of Prime Minister Gandhi* (New York: Praeger Publishers, 1974); Anand Mohan, *Indira Gandhi: A Personal and Political Biography* (New York: Meredith Press, 1967); Frederick, *Ten First Ladies of the World.*

17. Golda Meir, *My Life* (New York: G. P. Putnam's Sons, 1975); Peggy Mann, *Golda: The Life of Israel's Prime Minister* (New York: Coward, McCann and Geoghegan, 1971); Marie Syrkin, *Golda Meir: Israel's Leader* (New York: G. P. Putnam's Sons, 1969).

18. Lamson, *Few Are Chosen;* Chamberlain, *A Minority of Members;* Engelbarts, *Women in the U.S. Congress;* Tolchin and Tolchin, *Clout;* "The Year of the Woman," *Newsweek,* Nov. 4, 1974, pp. 20–22. The bulk of the data on Ella Grasso came from a questionnaire she kindly completed for us in December 1975.

19. Lamson; Chamberlain; Engelbarts; Tolchin and Tolchin.

20. Shirley Chisholm, *The Good Fight* (New York: Harper & Row,

1973); Chisholm, *Unbought and Unbossed* (Boston: Houghton Mifflin, 1970); Lamson; Chamberlain; Engelbarts; Tolchin and Tolchin.

21. Christopher Hitchens, "Downstairs Upstairs," *New York Times Magazine*, June 1, 1975, p. 6; Auberon Waugh, "Letters from Europe," *Esquire*, June, 1975, p. 72; "The Company She Keeps," *Time*, March 3, 1975, pp. 46–47; "A Tough Lady for the Tories," *Time*, February 24, 1975, pp. 30–31; "Britain's 'La Pasionaria' of Privilege," *Time*, February 17, 1975, p. 46; Anthony Le Jeune, "The Tories' Big Gamble," *National Review*, March 28, 1975, pp. 338–339; Russell Lewis, *Margaret Thatcher: A Personal and Political Biography* (London: Routledge & Kegan Paul, 1975).

22. Bernadette Devlin, *The Price of My Soul* (New York: Knopf, 1969).

23. V. M. Zenzinov, "Rannyi gody E. K. Breshkovskoi," *Novyi Zhurnal* (New York: Kn. 60), pp. 179–195; *Babushka E. K. Breshko-Breshkovskaia o samoi sebe* (Petrograd: Izdatel'stvo 'Narodnaia Vlast,' 1971); Ekaterina Breshko-Breshkovskaia, "Iz moikh vospominania," *Vestnik russkoi revoliutsii*, 1905, No. 4, pp. 187–224; Alice Stone Blackwell, ed., *The Little Grandmother of the Russian Revolution: Reminiscences and Letters of Catherine Breshkovsky* (Boston: Little, Brown and Company, 1919); Lincoln Hutchinson, ed., *Hidden Springs of the Russian Revolution: Personal Memoirs of Ekaterina Breshko-Breshkovskaia* (Stanford, Calif.: Stanford University Press, 1931).

24. Eva Broido, *Eva Broido: Memoirs of a Revolutionary*, Vera Broido, translator and editor (London: Oxford University Press, 1967).

25. Maud Gonne MacBride, *A Servant of the Queen* (London: Purnell & Sons, 1938).

26. Halide Edib, *The Memoirs of Halide Edib* (New York: The Century Company, 1926).

27. Isabel de Palencia, *Alexandra Kollontay: Ambassadress from Russia* (New York: Longmans Green & Co., 1947). Alexandra Kollontai's own writings: *The Basis of the Woman Question* (Moscow, 1906); *Love and Friendship* (Moscow, 1919); *A Letter to a Young Comrade* (Moscow, 1919). See also Louise Bryant, *Mirrors of Moscow* (New York: Thomas Seltzer, 1923).

28. Little is known about Rosa Luxemburg's early life. Most material has been taken from Paul Frölich's *Rosa Luxemburg: Her Life and*

Work, trans. Edward Fitzgerald (New York: Howard Fertig, 1969); J. P. Nettl, *Rosa Luxemburg* (London: Oxford University Press, 1966).

29. Angela Davis, *An Autobiography* (New York: Random House, 1974); Marc Olden, *Angela Davis* (New York: Lancer Books, 1973); Angela Y. Davis, *If They Come in the Morning* (New York: New American Library, 1971); *Angela* (North Hollywood, California: Leisure Books, 1971); Charles Ashman, *The People vs. Davis* (New York: Pinnacle Books, 1972).

30. Jacqueline Van Voris, *Constance de Markievicz: In the Cause of Ireland* (Amherst: University of Massachusetts Press, 1967).

31. Dolores Ibarruri, *They Shall Not Pass* (New York: International Publishers, 1966); Ibarruri, *The Women Want a People's Peace* (New York: Worker's Library Publishers, 1941).

32. Nik. Asheshov, *Sofiia Perovskaia: materialy dlia biografii i kharakteristiki* (Petersburg: Gosudarstvennoi izdatel'stvo, 1921); Vera Finger, *Zapechatlenii Trud* (Moscow, 1921); L. Tikhomirov, *Sofiia Lvovna Perovskaia* (Geneva, 1899); David Footman, *Red Prelude: The Life of the Russian Terrorist Zhelyabov* (New Haven: Yale University Press, 1945).

33. Vera Zasulich, "Vospominania," *Byloe*, 1919, No. 14, pp. 89–107. Zasulich is the most intensely studied of the women because one of the authors chose her for the subject of her doctoral dissertation. See Rita Mae Cawley Kelly, "The Role of Vera Ivanovna Zasulich in the Development of the Russian Revolutionary Movement," Diss. Indiana University, 1967. A complete, annotated listing of all of Zasulich's writings are on pp. 310–318 of this dissertation.

34. Michael Corday, *Charlotte Corday*, trans. E. E. Buckley (New York: E. P. Dutton, 1931); Margaret Goldsmith, *Seven Women Against the World* (London: Methuen and Company, 1935).

35. Emma Goldman, *Living My Life* (Garden City, N.Y.: Garden City Publishers, 1931); Richard Drinnon, *Rebel in Paradise* (Chicago: University of Chicago Press, 1961).

36. Mary B. Rankin, "The Revolutionary Movement in Chekiang: A Study in the Tenacity of a Tradition," in Mary C. Wright, ed., *China in Revolution: The First Phase, 1900–1913* (New Haven: Yale University Press, 1968), pp. 319–361; Mary B. Rankin, *Early Chinese Revolution-*

aries: Radical Intellectuals in Shanghai and Chekiang, 1902–1911 (Cambridge, Mass.: Harvard University Press, 1971).

37. Samuel A. Stouffer, *Social Research to Test Ideas* (New York: The Free Press of Glencoe, 1962), p. 231.

38. Winston Churchill quoted in Fishman (n. 12), p. 374.

39. Sir William Blackstone, *Commentaries* 433, quoted in Leo Kanowitz, *Women and the Law: The Unfinished Revolution* (Albuquerque: University of New Mexico Press, 1968), p. 35.

40. "The Relentless Ordeal of Political Wives," *Time*, October 7, 1974, p. 16.

41. Feldkamp, p. 116.

42. Behr, p. 65.

43. "His Lady," *Newsweek*, April 25, 1960, p. 46.

44. Clark, p. 57.

45. Ibid., p. 89.

46. Behr, p. 65.

47. Ibid.

48. Leslie Smith, p. 58.

49. Ibid., pp. 77–78.

50. Ibid., p. 202.

51. Alliluyeva, p. 93.

52. Ibid., p. 100.

53. Lermolo; Hyde, pp. 168–69.

54. Alliluyeva, p. 108.

55. Hearst, Clark, and Considine, p. 61.

56. Hastie, p. 111.

57. Cochran, p. 226.

58. Ibid.

59. Ibid.

60. Ibid., p. 227.

61. Ibid., p. 226.

62. Borzman, p. 324.

63. Hatch, p. 182.

64. Ibid., p. 242.

65. Levin, p. 85.

66. West, p. 67.

67. Eisenhower quoted in Jean L. Black, p. 72.

68. Clark and Eisenstaedt, p. 150.

69. Stroud, p. 77.

70. Spalding, p. 298.

71. Nixon quoted in Spalding, p. 298.

72. Gallagher, p. 43.

73. Ibid., p. 44.

74. Thayer, p. 127.

75. Gallagher, p. 159.

76. Ibid., p. 174.

77. Quoted in Gallagher, p. 177.

78. Behr, p. 65.

79. Marie Smith, p. 57.

80. Ibid.

81. Ibid.

82. McConathy, p. 110.

83. Brandon, p. 47.

84. Ibid.

85. McConathy, p. 110.

86. Lash, p. 287.

87. Ibid., p. 342.

88. Ibid., p. 343.

89. Ibid., p. 347.

90. Ibid., p. 375.

91. Ibid., pp. 427–28.

92. Ibid., p. 466.

93. Fishman, p. 53.

94. Ibid., p. 52.

95. Ibid., p. 255.

96. Ibid., p. 341.

97. Ibid., p. 345.

98. Ibid., pp. 370–71.

99. Ibid., p. 14.

100. McNeal, p. 183.

101. Ibid., p. 196.

102. Ibid., p. 288.

103. Ibid., p. 296.

104. Sykes, p. 187.

105. Ibid., p. 505.

106. Ibid., p. 21.

107. Questionnaire filled out by Leonor Sullivan.

108. Morrigene Holcomb, *Women in the U.S. Congress* (Washington, D.C.: General Research Division, 1975), p. 10.

109. Tolchin and Tolchin, p. 70.

110. Sullivan questionnaire.

111. Tolchin and Tolchin, p. 70.

112. Graham, p. 27.

113. Ibid., p. 26.

114. Ibid., p. 33.

115. Margaret Chase Smith quoted in Graham, p. 179.

116. Lamson, p. 90.

117. Chamberlain, p. 262.

118. "The Year of the Woman," *Newsweek*, November 4, 1974, p. 21.

119. Tolchin and Tolchin, p. 99.

120. "The Year of the Woman," p. 21.

121. Tolchin and Tolchin, p. 99.

122. Chisholm, *Unbought* . . . , p. 42.

123. Chamberlain, p. 332.

124. Chisholm, *Unbought* . . . , p. 51.

125. Ibid., pp. 63–64.

126. Chamberlain, p. 335.

127. Ibid., p. 337.

128. "Britain's 'La Pasionaria' of Privilege," *Time*, February 17, 1975, p. 46.

129. Cosgrave quoted in Christopher Hitchens, p. 21.

130. "Britain's 'La Pasionaria' of Privilege," *Time*, February 17, 1975, p. 46.

131. Ibid.

132. Hitchens, p. 6.

133. Ibid.

134. LeJeune, p. 339.

135. Bhatia, p. 133.

136. Nehru quoted in Bhatia, p. 71.

137. Mohan, p. 146.

138. Ibid., p. 144.

139. Ibid., p. 210.

140. Ibid., p. 211.

141. Ibid., p. 194.

142. Ibid.

143. Bhatia, p. 133.

144. Ibid., p. 134.

145. Ibid., p. 144.

146. Ibid., p. 145.

147. Ibid., p. 148.

148. Ibid., p. 159.

149. Ibid., p. 168.

150. Ibid., p. 169.

151. Ibid.

152. Ibid., p. 181.

153. Ibid., p. 261.

154. Ibid., p. 266.

155. Meir, pp. 114-15.

156. Ibid., p. 112.

157. Ibid., p. 122.

158. Ibid., p. 118.

159. Ibid., p. 115.

160. Ibid., p. 114.

161. Ibid., p. 42.

162. Ibid., p. 43.

163. Ibid.

164. Ibid., pp. 64–65.

165. Ibid., p. 100.

166. Ibid., p. 101.

167. Ibid., p. 214.

168. Devlin, p. 35.

169. Ibid.

170. Palencia, p. 33.

171. Cited by Palencia, ibid., p. 137.

172. Broido, pp. 10–11.

173. Blackwell, p. 39.

174. Ibid.

175. Ibarruri, *They Shall Not Pass*, p. 60.

176. Ibid., p. 76.

177. Angela Davis, *Autobiography*, p. 187.

178. Ashman, p. 9.

179. Frölich, p. 28.

180. MacBride, passim.

181. Van Voris, p. 66.

182. Corday, p. 45.

183. Franco Venturi, *Roots of Revolution* (New York: Alfred A. Knopf, 1960), p. 480.

184. Drinnon, p. 23.

185. Marilyn Johnson and Kathy Stanwick, *Women in Public Office: A Biographical Directory and Statistical Analysis* (New York: R. R. Bowker Company, 1976), p. xxxii.

CHAPTER 4

Socialization, Social Change, and Sex-Role Ideology

U
NTIL THE TWENTIETH century most women had been private persons whose lives were determined by their role within the collective unit of the family. Even in the 1970s in a modern country like the United States of America most women still follow the old Greek practice of separating concern for the home and the family and concern for politics. In 1977 at the national level—the level we are most concerned about—only one woman (Patricia Harris) was a member of the federal cabinet. No woman has ever served on the Supreme Court; in 1976, about 1 percent of the 675 federal judges were women; and less than 4 percent of the 535 members of Congress were women—all nineteen of these were in the House of Representatives. In the same year, thirty-six states of the United States had no female representative in Congress.[1]

The fact that political participation has been rare for women has given rise to basic questions about those women who are politically active. Where did they come from? How did they arrive at the positions they did? What were the circumstances under which they developed? What factors explain their development?

Several of these questions have already been addressed in Chapter One. There we considered the explanatory models which attribute female nonparticipation to a theory of their being the "weaker sex," an idea refuted in that chapter. The very existence of the political women described in Chapter Three eliminates that simplistic argument. Theories based on nature cannot explain the appearance of political women unless these women are considered mutations of the species (an absurdity, most will agree). Thus, there must be something in the nurture and socialization of these women which explains their development. The previous chapter has examined how the achieving political women differ from the private women and public women in their adult behavior relative to the political system and their families. This chapter begins the discussion of why they differ; that is, it begins the analyses of those factors and conditions that must exist for achieving political women to develop.

Questions to Be Answered

Socialization processes leading females to become political actors such as legislators and revolutionaries must be atypical since the product, a female member of the political elite, is also atypical. We are dealing with socialization processes that have produced a major type of social change. Most studies of socialization, however, have stressed how individuals are incorporated into the status quo and how socialization processes maintain the status quo.[2] Rather than bind ourselves into an inappropriate conceptual framework which would necessarily limit our investigation, we begin with Fred Greenstein's approach to the major ingredients in the socialization process: we ask about the female elite included in our study, "Who learns what from whom under what circumstances and with what effects?"[3] We assume that achieving political women will have learned quite different things from quite different types of mothers, fathers, peers, and institutions under rather different circumstances than nonpolitical women.

Greenstein defines political socialization as "all political learning, formal and informal, deliberate and unplanned, at every stage of the life cycle, including not only explicitly political learning but also nominally nonpolitical learning of politically relevant social attitudes and the acquisition of politically relevant personality characteristics."[4] This definition which incorporates informal, unplanned, and nonpolitical learning and also draws attention to personality characteristics and their development, is most suitable for our study. It is to these types of learning that we look for meaningful answers about how these unusual women became the people they did.

As a guide to what ought to be included in a study of the socialization of women in politics, the framework provided by Greenstein has been used. He asserts that in any socialization study five major elements must be considered: (1) Who is learning? (2) What is learned? (3) Through which persons or institutions (agents of socialization) does the individual learn? Does the individual learn only what the socializing agent intends to teach or is the agent a source of unintentional, informal learning? (4) What are the circumstances or conditions under which certain types of learning occur? and (5) What are the effects of what is learned? In our study we seek to answer each of these questions for women who have not been socialized to continue the status quo.

Who Learns?—And with What Effects?

In the 1960s the major political socialization studies concentrated almost solely on middle-class white children. It is not surprising that the findings of such studies were homogeneous, showing a national norm of children with positive images of America and its government. Traditional and "proper" national norms, attitudes, and behavior among these children were already differentially acquired according to sex. Boys almost always were found to be more politically knowledgeable, more active, and more expectant of an active participatory role. Girls seemed to be developing into relatively traditional private beings with the expectation that their involvement in political affairs, if any at all, would be mediated by intervening males— fathers, brothers, or husbands.[5]

After the riots in the late 1960s, several scholars began to study black children and poor white Appalachian children. To their surprise the rosy picture of positive transmission of the prevailing political culture was not occurring in these groups.[6] Changing the sample of people changed the picture!

For our study we have limited our subjects to what we call a focused sample, women who have attained a specific political status: female revolutionaries, elected female legislators or major political executives, and wives of political men. By concentrating only on these elites we can try to discover what specific variations in learning content and circumstances led to their becoming the politically active persons they did become. By specifying who learned, we can eliminate guessing about what effects such learning will have. We already know the effects, at least in the general terms in which we are interested; what we want to know is what produced them.

What Is Learned?

The question of what types of learning and what specific substantive content is relevant to political behavior is of critical importance to the study of political socialization. Greenstein identifies three general topics of learning as being of interest: learning connected with the role of citizen—which political party, which ideology one should follow; learning connected with the relationship of the citizen to the state—whether or not to be loyal to it and to consider it a legitimate governing body; and learning connected with recruitment to and performance of specialized political roles.[7] Most women seem to have developed the first two types of political learning, but almost none have mastered the last type of learning. Our study deliberately focuses on identifying the substance and circumstances of the learning needed for women to have attained specialized political roles. We are interested in the first two types of learning only to the extent to which they add to our knowledge of what is necessary for women to become independent political actors in specialized political roles.

A common way of organizing "what is learned" in political socialization studies is the classification scheme for the levels of the political system and basic political orientations developed by David Easton and Robert Hess, and espoused by other scholars such as Jack Dennis. Stressing the importance of socialization for maintaining the existing political system, they assert: "No system is able to maintain itself for any length of time without educating its young politically. Each new generation emerges upon the political scene as a tabula rasa upon which a political system must seek to imprint its images if it is to persist."[8] Conceptually their schema is as follows:

Levels of the Political System	Basic Political Orientations		
	Knowledge	Values	Attitudes
Community			
Regime			
Government			

In this schema the community refers to a "collection of persons who share a division of political labor."[9] It includes learning of nationalism, patriotism, territoriality, and general concepts of which categories and types of people in the world have the "right" to make political decisions for persons living within a geographical area. For example, Americans learn at a young age that Canadians, Russians, Germans, Japanese, and other individuals from other countries ought not make our political decisions for us, for they are of a different political community. The term "regime" refers to the constitutional order, the "rules of the game," the general structure of authority. The term "government" refers to the administration holding power at a given time, the political party, individuals, and the policies they enact. Concern for what is learned at the governmental level would involve wanting to know why and how children learn to affiliate and identify with a particular political party or national political figure.

Our revolutionaries are distinguished from the nonrevolutionaries by their nonsupport of the regime. While both the female revolutionaries and the elected officials reject the general norm of the political community that males are to be the primary active political beings, the revolutionaries reject the validity of the regime as well. Except for Krupskaia, our political wives generally question nothing at these two levels and are concerned essentially with which political party they will support, which individuals they will follow, and which policies are supportable.

At first glance it might seem that our study of female political elites would fall into the "government" level of the Easton-Hess schema. If one stresses within the community level of the schema as Easton, Hess, and Dennis do, the status quo, nationalism, patriotism, and territoriality, such a conclusion might be correct. It is our contention, however, that although we must deal with all three levels of this schema, we are most basically concerned with the community level of this Easton-Hess-Dennis hierarchy. Most women learn somehow that they are not to be among that "collection of persons who share a division of political labor." Women most certainly are patriots and nationalists, and belong to old and new nations. However, they also learn something else—something that subordinate males learn as well: they learn that they will not be recruited to elite political roles. Easton, Hess, Dennis, and their followers have tended to restrict the community level of their schema to studying how new nations are built, or how nationalism and patriotism are fostered. But we must take quite literally the definition that the community level of the political system specifies in the value system "that collection of persons who share a division of political labor." Throughout history the value systems have systematically excluded women from being considered legitimate members of that collectivity, even though they reside within the same territory as their male spouses and fathers.

The systematic exclusion within each political community of females and other subordinate males has had, of course, direct effects upon the regime-level aspects of the political system. Because regime-level support for the political system involves the rules of the game and the structure of authority, which in turn also involve beliefs about what types of persons can become members of the political elite, to some extent we are concerned with aspects of this level too. If a political community at its ideological core excludes females from active participation in the polis, obviously the country's constitution and other written and unwritten rules will also exclude them. The governmental level will contain no females if neither the political community nor the regime levels permit their acceptance.

It seems clear to us that the study of social change requires a broadening of the Easton-Hess-Dennis definition of community-level values. An analysis of the implications of the definition to the groups residing within a territory is also needed. Recognizing that we are expanding and, hence, distorting their definition we stress that all three levels of the schema must concern us. The values of the political community and the regime (written and unwritten norms) about female political participation and the nature and number of female role models within the political system are all vital factors needing our attention.

Although political socialization has become a relatively popular field of study, very little information exists about the socialization of political elites. Indeed, to our knowledge little of substantive, comparative nature exists on male political elites, to say nothing of female political elites.[10] Given the unusual nature of our thirty-six women, there is not available an existing body of knowledge or theory to guide us in studying the socialization process that led to their emergence. Although we hope to have made substantial progress in this area, our conclusions will have to be considered exploratory and tentative until additional verification is completed.

In essence, it is our contention that the development of an independent political woman proceeds through the following broad, general stages: first, as a child she develops the belief that an activist, independent, nontraditional sex role for herself is feasible. Second, as a child she develops (learns to have), and throughout her life cycle maintains, a need to have independent, personal control over her life-space. She finds it psychologically untenable to have her economic, intellectual, political, and other types of existence determined primarily by a male or, for that matter, another female. Third, once the need for personal control over her life-space is realized, she learns that politics is important as a means for fulfilling that need—and other needs. Fourth, in order to pursue a political career as an adult, she must have learned that she will be positively rewarded, not be punished or suffer severe role conflicts for participating. In other words, prior to committing her life to politics, she must have some history of successful political participation. At some point she must decide that participating as an independent actor is more rewarding personally than not participating. If these four separate stages of learning and development occur, an independent female political actor will have come into existence. As the small number of independent female political actors indicates, traversing these paths of development is neither simple nor easy.

Through Which Persons and Institutions Does the Individual Learn?

There exists in the political socialization literature a major debate about which agents of socialization are most important. Such prestigious political scientists as Gabriel Almond and Sidney Verba definitely state that the educational system is the most critical socializing agent.[11] Demonstrating the influence of Talcott Parsons and structural-functionalism on their thinking, Almond and Verba maintain that structures closest in nature and kind to the political system are likely to have the greatest impact in the socialization process. Because the family is characterized by the ascriptive, specific, particular, affective, and self-oriented pattern variables, and the political system is characterized by achievement, diffuseness, universal, affectively neutral, and collectivity-oriented patterns, the political system, they argue, is further removed from the family than is the educational system. Hence, the school is given more importance than the family as the agent of socialization into the political culture.

Robert Hess and Judith V. Torney also reach a similar conclusion. "From the viewpoint of the totality of socialization into the political system, these results indicate that the effectiveness of the family in transmitting attitudes has been over-estimated in previous research. ... Aside from party preference, the influence of the family seems to be primarily indirect and *to influence attitudes toward authority, rules, and compliance*"[12] (italics ours). Other scholars, however, such as Herbert Hyman,[13] Stanley Renshon,[14] James Davies,[15] and Kenneth Langton[16] have argued that the family and peer group are more important than the educational system. They particularly stress the importance of the family.

To a large extent the debate over which agents of socialization are more important results from ambiguity about what aspects of learning are being influenced, and whether or not the focus of attention is upon maintaining the existing political system and status quo, or understanding individual conformance to, or deviance from, the status quo. The school represents society's institutionalization of the transmission of formal knowledge and information. Hence, if substantive beliefs and information are being studied one would logically anticipate that the school would be better equipped for this type of socialization than the family. At the cognitive level of socialization most families cannot compete with the schools. The schools are obviously important for cognitive socialization, which includes knowledge of political boundaries, the constitution, political history, and so on.

There are two other major types of learning, however, in which the schools cannot so easily compete with the family and the peer group. These two types are the affective and psychomotor dimensions of socialization. The affective dimension, which obviously is related to values and attitudes in the Easton and Hess schema, is related to emotional ties formed early. It is especially influenced by the individuals with whom the child first comes into contact. Most political socialization studies concentrate upon the acquisition of political attitudes and specific types of knowledge. Hence, the critical role of the school and peer groups is stressed. One of our major theses is that much of the "learning" particularly relevant to politics for females is set and finished before the school and/or peer groups become important. For our study the noncognitive dimensions of socialization and to some extent perhaps even the nonpolitical types of learning are critically important for females.

Prior to this study, students of political socialization have not stressed the psychomotor aspects of political socialization. Yet political scientists are aware of the close relationship between activity in the political arena and nonpolitical learning and personality development. Dean Jaros, for example, stressed that parents are primarily responsible for personalities of children. "They establish patterns of decision-making and ways of interacting with the outside world. Parental behavior patterns become a standard or norm against which much that the child subsequently encounters can be evaluated. In short, many general features of the child's life-style are determined in the parental environment."[17] Hess and Torney also note the strong relationship between family structure and parental behavior and activity among children.[18] In addition, they comment that "Group membership and activity seem to be related to political activity, but apparently only because the child who is active tends to be active in several areas of endeavor."[19] The children, in other words, have learned, physically and neurologically as well as cognitively, a certain way to handle time and to relate physically to the external world. The school and their peers do not seem to have "taught" them this type of psychomotor behavior. Although it seems commonplace to assume that political participation is determined more by the cognitive dimension than the psychomotor, we do not believe this assumption is correct. People learn their adult roles in stages. Higher-order cognitive content comes, according to Jean Piaget,[20] at later stages of development than psychomotor and affective learning. Greenstein and other political scientists have also found that until the age of about ten most children cannot be said to have a real cognitive understanding of politics. Yet by this time they have expectations about whether or not they will participate in politics and even how they will participate.[21]

It is our expectation that by concentrating on the families of our subjects we will learn why these women broke with the tradition of nonparticipation in politics for females, or in the case of the private political wives, why they maintained it. This does not mean that we will ignore the school or the peer group. Both are important. However, we believe that specific conditions must exist within the family structures of small girls for them to grow up with an activist sex-role perception and predisposition. Moreover, we further assert that without the development of this activist sex-role perception and psychomotor foundation for activism, few girls will become independent active political beings. The other agents of socialization, such as the church, school, peer groups, and so on, can only work with what the family has already created.

What Are the Circumstances Under Which the Learning Occurs?

This question addresses the issues of when, where, under what conditions, how, and ultimately why some individuals behave one way and other individuals behave another. For scholars such as Greenstein this question requires devoting special attention to the level of awareness of the subject, the extent to which the process is preconscious or unconscious, and the sequence in which the political orientations are acquired.[22] In other words he focuses on the internal state of the individual throughout the life cycle. To the extent that our biographical data permit we shall follow Greenstein's example.

In their study Easton and Hess also attempted to answer this broad question about the circumstances under which learning occurs. On the basis of their study of 12,000 Chicago elementary school children between the grades of two and eight, they found that political learning was well under way by the second grade. They also found that most political learning is initially personalized and related to one's feelings toward one's father. Usually the child's image of the government is affectively positive. As the child gets older the image becomes more abstract and more neutral. They found no sharp discontinuities in the socialization process. They established that the earliest and most emotional attachments are to the community level of the political system. Such attachments are principally the results of rituals such as the pledge of allegiance which cognitively have little meaning for the child, but emotionally are awe-inspiring almost to the degree of religious observance. They conclude that the American political system is in "good shape," for the allegiance patterns are formed early and are not likely to be changed with age.[23] The conclusions reached by Easton and Hess were to a large extent determined by the sample used: white, middle-class children of socially integrated members of the political community.

Robert Hess and Judith Torney used this same Chicago sample for another study. The major innovation of this work was the presentation of four basic models to explain different aspects of political socialization. The four basic explanatory frameworks are the accumulation, interpersonal transfer, identification, and cognitive development models.[24] Although the titles of these models appear to offer hope for utilization in a study of the development of female political elites, we agree with Lewis Froman[25] that they are not concerned with explaining individual variations in development. The models are narrowly focused on political beliefs, attitudes, and general substantive political content. For the purposes of this study, however, specific political beliefs held or activities undertaken are somewhat irrelevant. The models and findings, in other words, do not address our subject. Our study focuses on the atypical; earlier socialization studies were concerned primarily with the typical. We seek to find the basis for independence of action which happened to become political action but could have developed in other directions as well. We seek to explain the forces of social change leading to the development of this atypical group and the likely ripple effect of them on the system. In short, we seek to know what circumstances will produce individuals who will engage in behavior leading to social change, behavior that departs from the established patterns.

In the past decades a variety of psychological theories to explain social change have come into existence. The core of these theories has been the socialization process and how variations in this process produce personality types that will initiate social change. Two personality types have been selected, particularly by those scholars studying revolution and broad social and political change, as being key but not necessarily the only force of change. These are "(1) persons who are marginal to or unenchanted with the social order, alienated, or anomic, and (2) persons who have been frustrated or who became instruments of change through aggressive leadership."[26] For example, Howard W. Becker[27] stresses the change-prone types of persons who either have unlearned traditional values during crisis periods, the "desocialized or demoralized" type; or who have insatiable desires for variety, the "decadent or sophisticated" type; or who have dreams of constructive change, "the liberated-stable" type. Homer Barnett[28] and Robert Merton[29] also have stressed the role of the "deviant," unintegrated personality as a force for change.

Although theorists of social change have stressed the role of the unique personality, only a few have argued such personalities were the basic determiners of social change. One economist, however, Everett Hagen, has elaborated a theory of social change and economic development which attempts to identify what forces will produce creative personalities that will spearhead social and economic change.[30] He argues that the traditional, father-dominated family structure produces children with rigid, noncreative, authoritarian personalities who will cling to tradition. Using historical and anthropological data from a variety of cultures, Hagen argues that this pattern of child-rearing is broken when the family structure changes. When a strong mother and a weaker father raise children, Hagen asserts that a new, creative personality type is produced, one which will lead to entrepreneurship and greater individuality.

David C. McClelland, in *The Achieving Society*,[31] also drew attention to the importance of family structure for the creation of the entrepreneurial spirit and the need for achievement (n-Ach). His effort to explain why some individuals have a high need for achievement and others do not, rests in part upon the different roles mothers play in different families. "But lots of people break with their fathers or have ineffective or remote fathers who do not develop high ... [need for] achievement or successful entrepreneurship. The behavior and attitudes of the mother then are critical."[32] McClelland also notes that mothers who are not dominated by the fathers tend to be the ones who raise children with high need for achievement. The increase in economic activity that often takes place after major wars he attributes to the fact that the mothers were permitted by the fathers' absence to have a stronger role in the establishing of children's personality traits and values.[33]

Our review of the theories of socialization and social change shows that the interrelationship of personality traits and processes with the character and structure of cultural institutions holds the most promise of offering explanations for the development of active political women. The stress on the significance of different types of mothers and family structures for producing select personality types seems particularly noteworthy. Additionally, we found that we must look to broad, macro forces which lead to changes in family structures and relationships to find the causal link in the development of political women.

Changing the Sex-Role Ideology
of the Socialization Agents

The development of modern elite political women has parallels in the search by the unenfranchised lower-class men of ancient Athens for reasons for their exclusion, whether it was "by nature" *(physis)* or "by convention" *(nomos)*. The Sophists led the fight against traditional mores by teaching that the central quality associated with ruling *(arete)* was not one which was genetically or mystically passed on from generation to generation within the same aristocratic families, but rather a quality which could be achieved, even by previously non-political beings. We have discussed earlier the theories which contended that the absence of women from the political realm as well as from the political elites was natural and due to unalterable disqualifying traits. This topic is recalled because we believe that a necessary condition for the inclusion of women in the public realm is the recognition that all members of a society have the right and the ability to learn to function in politics—a notion first delineated in Athens.

Ernest Barker points out that specific preconditions are necessary for posing the question:[34] Is my exclusion from politics the result of my own nature or is it due to external social conventions? A certain secularity of mind is needed. The "gods" or divine forces which were believed to have decreed that things must be as they are, need to be replaced by a belief that allows the individual greater freedom and control over time and space.

In western culture, changes in the life-space of males associated with modernization (i.e., urbanization, economic development, and industrialization) have become so well accepted and legitimized in the belief system that consciously directed programs to justify men's personal and political independence are no longer necessary except for the males of previously or currently oppressed minority groups. Such is not the case for women. The ideological changes which would encourage females to have independence in acting in the political world have not yet fully occurred. Hence, in looking for the sources of change giving rise to this ideological support of female personal and political independence, we look to changing beliefs about the role and position of women.

The primordial sources of personal identification are the family, the kinship group, racial-ethnic bonds, and the religious community. Essential to the process of social change is the breakdown in one or more of these attachments as well as a definition of the "self" in private rather than group terms. Social change is so rare precisely because of the overlapping nature of these primordial relationships. To question in any way the family, kin, or the ethnic or religious community is to question them all, for they are all seemingly tied together in a fabric that appears to be of one cloth. For an external factor to wedge itself into the socialization process requires a minimal admission that the cloth does have seams and can be taken apart. It has historically been the religious community which appears to have been the weakest link in the chain. It is therefore with religious belief systems and institutions that we begin to look for changes in beliefs about women's potential for independence and subsequently their place vis-à-vis the political system.

Religion and Political Women

The relationship between religious beliefs and political participation has not been sufficiently stressed. Findings do show that countries with political regimes attached to established churches are less noted for being stable democracies than are countries where the separation of church from the state made its appearance relatively early.[35] Although the relationship between religious beliefs and individual political socialization is still largely unexplored, Dean Jaros has speculated:

> It is also possible that community-level affective socialization
> is partly an unanticipated consequence of religious teachings.

Children are typically taught that religious authority is benevolent and loving, both at home and as part of more formal church activities. If, as already suggested, children's early relationships to political authority are similar to their orientations to religious authority, it may be that some of the positive feelings toward religion are extended to political figures as well. There is some evidence that young children confuse religious ritual with patriotic observance. The similarity between hymns and national anthems, between flags and crosses, is obvious. Great sanctity can surround both realms. It is not at all surprising that U.S. children regard the pledge of allegiance as a prayer, as indeed a request to God for aid and protection.[36]

If Jaros is correct in asserting that religious beliefs and political socialization are related, then most certainly religious beliefs will have an important effect on whether or not women—and men—will consider direct, personal, independent participation by women in political decision-making a feasible option. In most existing religious systems the ministry—those supposedly closest to God and with the authority to represent Him to the people and the people to Him—is male-dominated, to say the least. When women participate in public functions of religious institutions, they almost never can expect that a female will be the minister playing the leadership role for the congregation. Historically, religious as well as political beliefs and practices have *required* that female participation in public forums be through the mediation of male figures. Independent female participation has usually had to be behind the scenes or justified by extraordinary circumstances, such as "miracles" or the lack of an appropriate male. We believe that this parallelism in religious and political authority patterns is a critical factor in understanding why so few women today as well as in the past seek political leadership.

The relationship between religion and women's place within the American legal and political system can be seen by some examples of cases presented to the U.S. Supreme Court on the status of women. In 1872 in the case of *Bradwell* v. *the State*,[37] the Court upheld an Illinois Supreme Court decision denying women the right to practice law. The male lawyer presenting Bradwell's case tried to draw a line between reasonable and unreasonable demands of women. In this case, he argued, she was not asking to usurp men's prerogatives or to enter into positions clearly proscribed by God and Nature; she was not seeking to be a minister of the Lord which would clearly be offensive to both God and man. She was seeking rather to exercise the privilege of using her skills and training by practicing law. The Court concluded the Fourteenth Amendment did not guarantee citizens the right to practice particular professions. The states could regulate who could practice law, medicine, and so on. In 1894, in the similar case of *In re Lockwood,* petitioner,[38] the Supreme Court took the next logical step to declare that the states could interpret the word "person" so as to exclude women. Even practicing law for women was offensive to man and, by extension, apparently to God as well. The role of women, according to U.S. Supreme Court decisions, has historically been decreed to be that of wife and mother; her place was supposed to be in the home under the protection of her husband or her father.[39]

Resistance to an altered position for women, a position less restricted to the private world of the family and more open to the public realm, has not been uniform within religious sects. The obvious differences between the position of women in the Judeo-Christian cultures and that of women in the Moslem and Hindu worlds need not be belabored. There are, however, even among Christian denominations differences in the degree to which their belief systems are open to an altered position for women. For example, all the countries that had granted women suffrage before World War I were predominantly Protestant: New Zealand (1893), Australia (1902), Finland (1906), and Norway (1913). Predominantly Catholic countries did not give women the right to vote until after World War II.

There are, we believe, two important ways in which Christian churches differ that could influence the type and amount of their impact on the position of women: their theological teachings and the extent to which the institution permits female leadership.

From several perspectives it would seem reasonable to believe that greater, not lesser, religious training—even in a traditional, hierarchical religion—would lead to greater, rather than lesser, political participation. To the extent that the religious teaching stresses the egalitarian aspects of the soul, regardless of the sex of its bearer, to that same extent the religious teachings ought to be positively associated with female political participation. Moral fervor and a sense of social justice based upon religious principles can be potent inspirations for political involvement. The hitch so far as the political socialization of females is concerned is the sex-role ideology that is intertwined with the religious teachings. The less traditional (Aristotelian) the sex-role ideology is, the more positively correlated is religious affiliation and training likely to be with female political participation. The sex-role ideology, not the religious teachings, is the determinant variable needing study. In societies with many religions and a modern economy the dominant societal sex-role ideology—not that unique to any one subgroup—will tend to prevail. Hence, in any large-size random sample in a country such as the United States the negative sex-role ideological effects on some individuals of any particular religious affiliation will tend to be canceled by the positive effects of its theological teachings on other individuals.

The effects of theological differences among the various Judeo-Christian faiths are probably more likely to be observed in cross-national comparisons than individual comparisons within any one nation. Religious denomination is at best a crude measure of the major thrust of an institution. If an entire country is Roman Catholic, such as Spain, and the linkage of the church to the state is quite strong, then the traditional religious sex-role ideology is likely to be pervasive; all but the most exceptional females will be private women. Those women who would wish to participate politically on their own (without being married to the head of state first, such as Eva and Isabel Peron in Argentina) would feel compelled to reject the Catholic Church, its theology and teachings as well as any institutional affiliation with it. Since participation within the existing system requires accepting the religious influence, such women would almost have to be revolutionaries. The fact that all but one of the revolutionaries studied came from countries where the Russian Orthodox, Muslim, or Roman Catholic Church was the established church lends credence to this hypothesized relationship. In other Catholic countries such as Italy and France where historical events have eroded the power of the church, a more complicated relationship between female political behavior and religious affiliation is likely to be found. In both of these countries a countervailing sex-role ideology has been promoted since World War II, in particular by their respective Communist and Socialist parties. (Women received the right to vote in France in 1945; in Italy in 1946.) Most of the female candidates for political office in these two countries have tended to be members of the Communist or Socialist parties. However, the power of competition is great. The Christian-Democratic parties in these countries, to show that they are not anti-female, have come to promote female political participation. As these interactions occur and the battle for the female vote continues, the effect of the traditional religious influence on sex-role ideology tends to be reduced.

In predominantly Protestant countries like Great Britain and the United States, the effect of the traditional religious sex-role ideology is likely to be less. The fact that it is possible for a Catholic woman to become a significant member of the political elite (Grasso and Devlin) on her own without giving up her religion illustrates the effect of these changing relationships upon women of the traditional, hierarchical religions, In predominantly Protestant or atheistic countries, where a more modern sex-role ideology tends to prevail, membership in the traditional, hierarchical religions in and of itself is not sufficient to deter female entrance into a competitively derived political elite. It is possible that in such countries, if mothers break the male mediation in the religious area by public leadership in parish matters, the impact of having all-male ministers and priests might be diminished. Support for this contention is obviously weak, but it does imply that additional research on this question is needed. More specifically, it would seem worthwhile to assess whether or not the political behavior of women who retained their religious affiliation is related to their mothers, or to themselves having been active leaders and organizers of parish social and money-raising activities. The fact that such activities are encouraged by ministers and priests and often are publicly rewarded and given sanction by a representative of God might contribute to breaking the negative effects of the religious tradition of prohibiting females in leadership roles—at least in countries where the prevailing sex-role ideology tends to be relatively enlightened.

The de facto sex-role ideology of most religions is reflected in the modes of participation it allows women in public expressions of the religious beliefs. Historically, Jewish women were not to be seen by males in the Orthodox churches; Roman Catholic women could be seen, but never heard. In 1977 the battle rages even within Protestant religions over whether or not God or just men will be offended when women become ministers. Specific and at times vitriolic rejection of female religious leaders must have an effect on any female aspiring to be a political leader or an equal to males in nonreligious areas. The hard-fought 1976 decision of the Episcopal General Assembly granting women the right to become clergy takes a step toward equality in the religious realm. Until female role models among religious clergy become more visible, however, we believe that a woman striving to achieve a public leadership role must at the minimum say to herself: "The religious restriction of female participation is confined to religious rituals. It is not transferable to political, economic, or other aspects of my life." The nature of this notion is important to stress. We are saying that it is quite possible for an active political woman to be a firm believer in a specific religion, even a rather conservative religion, so long as she has been able to cut the cord linking public participation in other areas of her life with mediation by males.

We reviewed the biographies of our thirty-six women to see if any of these tendencies to break with the pattern of male mediation in the religious area existed. Of the nine revolutionaries and five terrorists, Kollontai was the only one who did not seem to have had consistent religious institutional training. It is doubtful that she felt any need to break with a formal religious institution. As an adult she certainly was an atheist. Of the remaining eight revolutionaries and five terrorists, twelve (92 percent) broke from the religion of their childhood, most to become atheists. Some, however, like Maud Gonne and Countess Markievicz, converted from one religion to another. Because of their dedication to the Irish cause both of these women left the Anglican church to become Roman Catholics. Neither seemed to accept the theology fully, however, as both maintained an intense interest in a mystic spiritualism not condoned by the Catholic Church, such as attendance at seances. Markievicz once shocked her priest-instructor in the elements of Catholicism by expressing an admiration for Lucifer because he was a "good rebel."

The one terrorist who died while still a member of a traditional religious institution was Corday. Raised in a Roman Catholic convent, she died a Roman Catholic. However, since her death followed swiftly on her stabbing of Marat, it is not possible to assess whether or not she did make specific judgments about the relationship between religion and politics. To contemplate and commit murder, even if for a righteous purpose, requires some suspension of religious tenets.

By contrast, only one of the ten elected women changed from the religion of her parents. Lady Astor (and her husband) became Christian Scientists. The other women did not change. In part, the other elected women may not have changed religions because of the importance of religious participation to having a political career. The political significance of religious conformity as a measure of political acceptability should not be underestimated. To be a representative of the Irish Catholic in Northern Ireland one almost has to be a Roman Catholic. It is not surprising that Devlin has remained a Catholic. To be the prime minister of Israel it does not hurt to retain some of the Jewish religious practices even if one does not retain them all. In the United States if one is to be governor of Connecticut, which has a large Roman Catholic population, being a practicing Roman Catholic is a great asset. We do not wish to suggest that Devlin, Meir,[40] or Grasso are not as devout practitioners of their faiths as any other member of those religions. We wish only to point out that to become an elected official within an existing political system requires conformity in certain religious areas. Religion and politics are intimately related in structural form if not in spiritual theory and practice.

Most of the elected women seem to have ignored the lack of congruence between the public leadership roles they have played and the roles the conservative religious tradition suggests women ought to play. By having achieved in politics they reveal that they have not accepted the de facto religious prohibition against female leadership as applying beyond the religious arena. By the same token, however, they do not openly reject or attack their religious heritage. At this point we can only speculate upon the effect that women who have achieved personal political efficacy are likely to have on religious institutions.[41] Our theory that the development of efficacy results from action rather than causes it suggests that the impact may be revolutionary and dramatic. Competencies gained elsewhere are not put aside when a person enters a church.

Ethnic Background and Political Women

Most studies of socialization point out differences in political behavior based on racial/ethnic affiliation, socioeconomic status, family structure, parents' political values, and educational level. Indeed, these variables are the ones most often stressed, rather than psychological variables. In 1975 Andrew M. Greeley proposed "A Model for Ethnic Political Socialization" as depicted in Figure 4-1. To cite Greeley:

> The model hypothesizes four direct paths of political socialization within an ethnic collectivity. A child's political value may be influenced directly by the political value of his parents (X), by the family structure that is peculiar to his ethnic collectivity (VIII), by the social class background of his family (VII), and by those aspects of the ethnic subculture which are not mediated through either family structure or parents' political values (II). We also hypothesize that both family structure and parents' political value are influenced by ethnic subculture and by social class (III, IV, VI).[42]

Figure 4-1
A Model for Political Socialization Within
an Ethnic Collectivity°

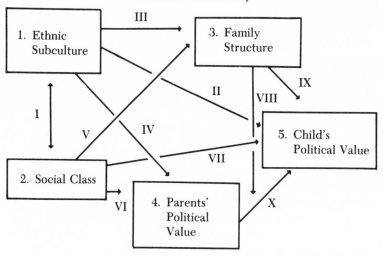

°Reprinted from Andrew M. Greeley, "A Model for Ethnic Political Socialization," *American Journal of Political Science* 19 (May 1975): 188. By permission of the Wayne State University Press and Andrew M. Greeley.

We tend to agree with Greeley that the paths of influence are as depicted in Figure 4-1. However, according to our perspective, the ethnic background is related to understanding political participation of females primarily to the extent that it determines their life-space and reflects a particular sex-role ideology, and a particular theory and practice of role relationships within the family structure.

The ethnic belief system will prescribe that certain types of persons with certain characteristics be the active persons who make the decisions. A particular family structure might not exemplify this belief system. (See Chapter Five for a detailed discussion of family structure and the development of political women.) Ethnic groups with a religious and philosophical heritage stressing strongly the traditional family relationships will have the least political participation by females, regardless of the family structure. For example, Italian and French women tend to participate politically less than Swedish or Norwegian women.[43] This relationship seems strongest when entire countries are of one ethnic and religious group and all the contributing factors converge. We suggest that Irish females will be more publicly and politically involved, even though they have a strong Roman Catholic conservative tradition, because of the great influence of England and the English legal and political system. The ethnic culture is more all-encompassing than the religious culture. Within the Irish, more so than in French and Italian cultures, there are more countervailing, perhaps even inconsistent, beliefs and practices about women. Because social change occurs where there are breaks in the socialization patterns, female political participation will tend to be greatest in cultures and subgroups that have experienced a loss of continuity and purity of ethnic and religious influences. Studies of politically active women in Chile support this thesis about participation increasing when ethnic subcultural intermarriages occur.[44] Northern European–born women who marry Latin Americans, and Chilean women who marry foreigners, tend to be more active politically than Chilean women who marry Chileans.

In general, then, whenever the ethnic subculture is penetrated, social change for women will be more probable. If an Italian woman marries an Irishman, even if both are Catholic, the probability of her participating in public and political activities should tend to be raised. If an "ethnically pure" couple moves away from its group, the probability of female political participation should tend to increase. In addition, the longer the ethnic group has been within a multiethnic society or in direct contact with different religious and/or ethnic groups and, hence, subject to heterogeneous influences, the greater the participation by females ought to be.

It seems evident that, if one's ethnic heritage stresses nonactivism and nonparticipation by the majority and by women in particular, it would be anticipated that the individual socialized in that culture would be less likely to participate as well. Unfortunately, no one has yet devised a method for rating the ethnic groups on this dimension. Nonetheless, because we stress that social change stems from breaks in the socialization chain, we believe there will be an association between ethnic mixing and female political behavior. As was the case with the religious factor, we believe it is not so much the specific ethnic background that is the key factor but how that ethnicity is incorporated into the life-space of the woman. What does the particular ethnic affiliation signify in terms of a female's gaining a sense of personal control over her life-space? Unless ethnicity affects key aspects of the psychological development, it can have no role in socialization.

Obviously, one cannot choose an ethnic affiliation as one can a religion, so the comparison between adult ethnicity and that of childhood is not possible. However, it is possible to estimate the consistency of the ethnic influence by determining whether or not the women studied personally experienced ethnic diversity, had exposure to foreign cultures, or underwent a major geographic move. Geographic moves force an awareness of alternative ways of handling personal and public relations when those moves place one in a different cultural setting. Such a major change of residence might be expected to have an effect similar to that occurring as the result of the breaking of the ethnic purity through intermarriage.

An examination of the biographies of our thirty-six women reveals that, as we expected, the private women were the least likely to have experienced any of these breaks in ethnic uniformity, while the elected/personal efficacy group, the revolutionaries, and the terrorists were the most likely. Moreover, while none of the private women had experienced the potentially diversifying effects of a cultural change due to a move or to living for extended periods in a foreign culture, four of the five wives classified as public women had. The fact that in most cases this intercultural penetration had occurred before our subjects were eighteen years of age intensified the psychological impact.

Socioeconomic Status and Political Women

Income and socioeconomic status obviously are critical in determining the life-space of a person as well as the scope and type of life chances or opportunities a child will have to change or to expand that life-space. Historically, the woman with the wealthier, higher socioeconomic status (SES) has been better educated, better traveled, and more exposed to cultures and religions other than her own. Consistent with our earlier hypotheses regarding the relationship between exposure to heterogeneous beliefs and behavior, it is reasonable to anticipate that the wealthier, middle-class women will tend to be among the political participants in greater numbers than women from the lower socioeconomic class. The existence of such practices as using women as the "conspicuous consumers" of the family to reveal the husband's earning power requires some qualification of what would otherwise be a linear relationship: the wealthiest women are not the most likely to become politicians.

As with religion and ethnicity, we believe that any significant effect of parental socioeconomic status on female political behavior has to do essentially with how it affects the family's sex-role ideology and the nature and extent of the parents' willingness to provide their daughters with personal control over their own lives. Although SES of the father can be important because of its contribution to giving greater exposure to heterogeneous beliefs and practices and to providing better health care and education for the female members of the family, it is most important due to the differential way the males and females of different classes tend to look upon and use the family psychologically. Studies have tended to show that lower working-class males look upon their jobs as simply a means of providing for their families.[45] The job is perceived as a somewhat unpleasant necessity. It is a hostile world or at best an uninviting world. Their home is their castle. Their status, prestige, ego support, and ego defense are predicated upon their remaining king and dominant in that castle. An independent, equal female threatens the foundation of this type of world.

The lower income of the family also produces the additional problem of having to cope with forced changes in the relationships if and when the wife has to go to work to supplement the family income. Facts of life objectively indicate that the male is not living up to his supposed traditional role. Because he is not, she cannot. Instead of intellectually and psychologically accepting this change, however, the lower-class working woman tends, at least initially, to reject adamantly the actual change in behavior. Her income is supplementary, a necessary evil stemming from the hostile nature of the external world. Perhaps even more than when she was not working, she stresses home, family security, and her dependence. Increased verbal and even behavioral stress upon these factors is almost essential to support the ego of the male—and indeed of the female. Their marriage began on the basis of the traditional sex roles. To change these to meet changing objective reality is not always humanly possible.

Because of these psychological factors both males and females of the lower classes on the average have a great interest in maintaining the historical relationships, that is, a dependent, submissive wife and a dominant, independent husband. The greater role that physical rather than intellectual ability plays in their occupations enhances the "need" and justification for the traditional sex roles. For these reasons the lower classes will have a greater tendency to resist any *conscious* break in the traditional relationships. We stress "conscious" because objective reality is more likely to compel a break in the idealized historical relationship in the lower classes than in the upper classes. In sum, if we looked at a representative sample of all the women in the world, we believe that SES would be found to be highly correlated with female political behavior—but only because of the effect SES has on sex-role ideology and potential for control over life-space.

To see if the SES of one's parental family is related to the adult political behavior of our thirty-six women, we compared them in terms of the socioeconomic status of their fathers. The sharpest contrast in socioeconomic status of the fathers was between the revolutionaries and the elected/personal efficacy groups of women. The revolutionaries tended to be from wealthy, aristocratic families while the political women with an early and strong sense of personal efficacy tended to come from lower middle-class families. Although this contrast existed, no clear pattern on SES for the other groups was apparent.

Sex-Role Ideology and Educational Change

As noted earlier, in the political socialization literature there is a debate as to whether the family or educational institutions are more important as socializing agents. In our judgment there is no doubt. For women, historically at least, education has definitely been second to the family in terms of influence. The function of education has been and is generally considered to be that of preparing people to fulfill their appropriate roles in society or in the family. Historically, little education was deemed necessary for girls, and often too much education was considered dangerous or harmful to their welfare or society's. Even such "great" democratic theorists as Jean-Jacques Rousseau[46] and Thomas Jefferson[47] considered women inferior beings whose main function was to serve the needs of men. In their eyes, education of women, if given at all, was essentially for the purpose of sustaining the family and its head, the father.

Obviously, one must distinguish between the status of women of different classes. Wives and daughters of the nobility and the upper classes generally had a higher status and even more power than men of lower social rank. The noble women often, but not as a rule, were given an excellent education, either through private tutoring by captive slaves, or by their fathers, brothers, or husbands. Love or self-interest of the male, however, provided the impetus for the education. Neither social status nor education was accorded to women as a right. The accident of birth or marriage determined both whether or not women would be educated and the nature of the content of that education.

People might argue that in the United States in the 1970s education figures more importantly in political socialization than it did historically. Studies do tend to show that, as Patricia Taylor notes, "the content of political socialization seems to be sex differentiated only for those with a grade school education. At higher educational levels young people of both sexes seem to learn the same political roles and values."[48] Hess and Torney[49] also report that by the seventh and eighth grades there are no sex differences in political attitudes. Orum, Cohen, Grasmuch, and Orum reported in 1974 that there were no sex differences in political knowledge and participation, political partisanship, and political affect in a sample of students in the fourth through the twelfth grade.[50] These findings were the reverse of those reported ten years earlier in a similar study by Hyman.[51]

Clearly, coeducation along with amendments giving women the right to vote and other political events such as the development of the women's liberation movement have increased the importance of education for the politicization of females. Nonetheless, the secondary importance of education in the socialization of political women is still evident. In fact, even the findings of Hess and Torney presented above prove the primacy of the family in the political socialization of girls. Until very recently *it took until junior high school to overcome the lower level of interest, knowledge, and information in politics instilled in the girls within their families at home.* It can also be argued that the schools have yet to overcome the family and cultural influence on the lower rates of participation by women in elite politics. Moreover, in 1974, at the same time it was being reported that there were no sex differences in matters relevant to political socialization, Karl Alexander and Bruce Eckland reported that the status and family origins of females were still more important in determining educational attainment than ability, a situation not true for males.[52] If women are not able to obtain the skills and pathways needed for political participation on the basis of merit and ability, how can it be argued that sex differences in political socialization have ended?

An additional problem is that what is learned in the school systems tends to focus almost totally on the individual as a *subject* within and of the political system, not as a *leader* or *decisionmaker* shaping its course. The only real political-performance role most schools encourage is recruiting individuals to vote as part of their civic obligation.[53] Some upper-class schools tend to stress becoming political and public leaders but it is precisely these upper-class schools that were the last even in the United States to be integrated by sex. Hence, although in the last quarter of the twentieth century it might be argued that formal education is of at least equal importance with the family in encouraging women to become political beings, it would be a mistake even on the basis of prima facie evidence to make such a claim for education historically—that is, up to the mid-1960s.

The women in our study were all educated before the full impact of the factors just discussed had been felt. The specifics of their educational attainment and its direction are dealt with in Chapter Six. There is, however, one change in the educational institutions which was manifested early in the twentieth century and thus had the potential to influence these women.

The change is the introduction of coeducation. This factor is particularly important for the unconscious learning of a sex-role ideology—the key determinant of female expectations about what space their life will include. The separation of the sexes at the time of initial contact with the world is an important introduction to a value system that enforces a sexual division of labor. If there are schools for boys and schools for girls, a child can readily assume that there are things that boys need to know that girls do not and vice versa. Because girls become mothers and because of tradition, it is more likely that the "girlish" things will be more related to the private world. Similarly, because boys will become soldiers, public beings, workers, and so on, their learning will focus on skills needed for these areas. Coeducation ends the more blatant aspects of this early training in the sexual division of labor.

Learning to compete with boys early in life in the school environment will have an independent effect on the feelings of competence that women have as adults. The chief effect of coeducational training is its impact on sex-role ideology. It encourages girls to think that they can grow up to do the same things boys can grow up to do. Once this activist sex-role ideology is learned, the extent and content of the education can be significant in guiding the individual girl's development. The abstract and cognitive elements of education will not overcome the lack of this more fundamental learning of activism.

A linkage of coeducation with sex-role ideology and the political socialization of girls is well illustrated by the women we have studied. Almost all the women who developed a strong sense of personal political efficacy attended coeducational elementary schools; many also attended coeducational high schools and colleges. The private women and public women, however, mostly attended all-girl schools, particularly at the elementary level. If they attended coeducational schools at all, it was at the secondary or college level—after their basic sex-role ideology had developed. (From this comparison the revolutionaries and terrorists were excluded because of the incomparability of the educational opportunities in their countries and times and those of the other women.)

Conclusion

We began this chapter by considering why most theories and empirical studies of political socialization are not relevant to our concern with the developmental processes leading to the emergence of political women. In essence, we concluded that their stress upon the typical, the traditional, and factors leading to the maintenance of the status quo prevented them from adequately addressing issues of social change. Our examination of the popularly used variables such as religious affiliation, ethnicity, and socioeconomic status and their relationship to sex-role ideology suggests we were correct in our assumptions. While such variables might be useful for studying the status quo, they do not seem to contribute to an understanding of why specific females will strive to become elite political women.[54] Breaks with the status quo, such as changing religions, stopping or reducing church attendance, geographic moves, and attendance at coeducational schools, do seem to be associated with the political women, however. The political women tended to have experienced breaks in the continuity of the types of agencies socializing them. It is important to stress, however, that these broad macro-level forces are additive and reinforcing aspects of the socialization process. Most of the sociological types of variables that most students of political socialization examine—religious affiliation, ethnicity, socioeconomic status, and educational level—can inhibit or promote the *ease of movement* of women into the public and political realms; they do not determine whether or not women will attempt to enter such realms. We believe the essential ingredient for the making of an independent political woman is the development of an activist sex-role ideology. This ideology comes primarily from her parental family. It is the family structure which interprets and applies whatever initial significance religion, ethnicity, socioeconomic status, and education have for political socialization. It is to this important question of the family and its relationship to the development of political women that we now turn.

Notes

1. Marilyn Johnson and Kathy Stanwick, *Women in Public Office: A Biographical Directory and Statistical Analysis* (New York: R. R. Bowker Company, 1976), pp. xx–xxii.

2. For a general review of this literature see Richard Dawson, "Political Socialization," ed. James A. Robinson, *Political Science Annual* 1 (1966): 2–84; Herbert Hyman, *Political Socialization: A Study in the Psychology of Political Behavior* (Glencoe, Ill.: The Free Press, 1959). Particularly noteworthy for their stress upon the social system and the status quo are the works of David Easton and Robert Hess, the collaborations of Easton and Jack Dennis, and the work of Gabriel Almond and Sidney Verba. For an excellent review of the socialization literature in general, that is, literature on the subject that is not directly related to political socialization, see Edward Zigler and Irvin L. Child, editors, *Socialization and Personality Development* (Reading, Mass.: Addison-Wesley Publishing Company, 1973), pp. 1–145. For the more recent trends in political-socialization research see D. Schwartz and S. Schwartz, eds., *New Directions in Political Socialization Research* (New York: Free Press, 1974).

3. Fred I. Greenstein, "Political Socialization," *International Encyclopedia of the Social Sciences* 14 (New York: Macmillan Co., 1968): 552–53.

4. Fred I. Greenstein, *Children and Politics* (New Haven: Yale University Press, 1965), p. 4.

5. Lester W. Milbrath, *Political Participation: How and Why Do People Get Involved in Politics?* (Chicago: Rand McNally & Company, 1965), lists a whole series of works which have found this to be the case. See p. 135.

6. E. Greenberg, ed., *Political Socialization* (New York: Aldine-Atherton, 1970).

7. Greenstein, *Children and Politics*, p. 13.

8. David Easton and Robert Hess, "The Child's Political World," *Midwest Journal of Political Science* 6 (August 1962): 235.

9. David Easton and Jack Dennis, "A Political Theory of Political Socialization," in *Socialization to Politics*, ed. Jack Dennis (New York: John Wiley & Sons, 1973), p. 42. The original concept is in David Easton and Robert Hess, "Youth and the Political System," *Culture and Social*

Character, ed. Seymour Lipset and Leo Lowenthal (Glencoe, Ill.: The Free Press, 1962), pp. 226–251.

10.   The area of psychoanalytic biography has seen attempts to look at the lives of a select few male political leaders. See for instance: L. J. Edinger, *Kurt Schumacher: A Study in Personality and Political Behavior* (Stanford, Calif.: Stanford University Press, 1964); E. Erikson, *Young Man Luther: A Study in Psychoanalysis and History* (New York: Norton, 1958); A. L. George and J. L. George, *Woodrow Wilson and Colonel House: A Personality Study* (New York: Dover, 1956); H. D. Lasswell, *Psychopathology and Politics* (New York: Viking, 1960); H. Lasswell and D. Lerner, eds., *World Revolutionary Elites* (Cambridge, Mass.: MIT Press, 1965); E. V. Wolfenstein, *The Revolutionary Personality: Lenin, Trotsky, and Gandhi* (Princeton, N.J.: Princeton University Press, 1967). None has considered thirty-six subjects; and none has included women.

11.   Gabriel Almond and Sidney Verba, *The Civic Culture* (Princeton, N.J.: Princeton University Press, 1963). In the five nations studied the schools are the focus of primary interest. The influence of Talcott Parsons and Robert Bales is evident. See the latter authors' *Family, Socialization, and Interaction Process* (Glencoe, Ill.: The Free Press, 1955).

12.   Robert Hess and Judith V. Torney, *The Development of Political Attitudes in Children* (Chicago: Aldine Publishing Company, 1967), p. 71. It is precisely because we believe it is the female's attitude toward authority, rules, and compliance which determines her later behavior that we have italicized the passage here and have stressed the family as the socializing agent of greatest import.

13.   Hyman (n. 2).

14.   Stanley Renshon, *Psychological Needs and Political Behavior: A Theory of Personality and Political Efficacy* (New York: The Free Press, 1974).

15.   James Davies, "The Family's Role in Political Socialization," *Annals of the American Academy of Political and Social Science* 361 (September 1965): 10–19.

16.   Kenneth Langton, *Political Socialization* (New York: Oxford University Press, 1969).

17.   Dean Jaros, *Socialization to Politics* (New York: Praeger, 1972), p. 88.

18. Hess and Torney, p. 71.

19. Ibid., p. 72.

20. Jean Piaget, *The Origins of Intelligence in Children* (New York: International University Press, 1952).

21. Greenstein, *Children and Politics*, pp. 67–75.

22. Ibid., esp. pp. 78–84.

23. Easton and Hess, "Youth . . ." (n. 9).

24. Hess and Torney.

25. Lewis Froman, "Learning Political Attitudes," *The Western Political Quarterly* 15 (June 1962): 306.

26. Bryce F. Ryan, *Social and Cultural Change* (New York: Ronald Press Co., 1969), p. 38.

27. Howard W. Becker, *Man in Reciprocity: Introductory Lectures on Culture, Society, and Personality* (New York: Praeger, 1956).

28. Homer Barnett, *Innovation: The Basis of Cultural Change* (New York: McGraw-Hill Book Co., 1953).

29. Robert Merton, "Science and the Economy of Seventeenth-Century England," *Science and Society* 3 (1939).

30. Everett E. Hagen, *On the Theory of Social Change* (Homewood, Ill.: The Dorsey Press, 1962).

31. David C. McClelland, *The Achieving Society* (New York: The Free Press, 1961).

32. Ibid., p. 404.

33. Ibid.

34. Ernest Barker, *The Political Thought of Plato and Aristotle* (New York: Dover Publications, 1959), pp. 28–46.

35. Seymour Lipset, *Political Man: The Social Bases of Politics* (Garden City, N.Y.: Doubleday, 1960).

36. Jaros, pp. 34–35.

37. *Bradwell v. the State*, 16 Wall. 130 (1872).

38. *In re Lockwood*, Petitioners, 154 U.S. 116 (1894).

39. Susan Kaufman Purcell, "Ideology and the Law: Sexism and Supreme Court Decisions," in *Women in Politics*, ed. Jane Jaquette (New York: John Wiley & Sons, 1974), pp. 131–153.

40. Meir writes in her autobiography, "Religion as such—to the extent that it can be separated from tradition for Jews—played very little role in our lives." Golda Meir, *My Life* (New York: G. P. Putnam's Sons, 1975), p. 15.

41. It has been noted already that the presence of female legislators has led to changing the wording of invocations and benedictions in legislatures. Jeane Kirkpatrick, *Political Women* (New York: Basic Books Publishers, 1974), p. 109.

42. Andrew W. Greeley, "A Model for Ethnic Political Socialization," *American Journal of Political Science* 19 (May 1975): 187–206. We recognize that Greeley incorporates religious affiliation into the ethnic variable, but for reasons specified in the text we feel religion is too important a factor for female political participation to obscure under the broader ethnic one.

43. Maurice Duverger, *The Political Role of Women* (Paris: UNESCO, 1955); Ralph Patai, ed., *Women in the Modern World* (New York: The Free Press, 1967); Ann Pescatello, ed., *Female and Male in Latin America* (Pittsburgh: University of Pittsburgh Press, 1973); "Women Around the World," *Annals of the American Academy of Political and Social Sciences* 375 (January 1968); Ingunn Nordeval Means, "Political Recruitment of Women in Norway," *Western Political Quarterly* 25 (September 1972): 491–521.

44. Elsa M. Chaney, "Women in Latin American Politics: The Case of Peru and Chile," *Female and Male in Latin America*, ed. Pescatello, pp. 103–140.

45. Melvin L. Kohn, "Social Class and Parent-Child Relationships: An Interpretation," in Hyman Rodman, ed., *Marriage, Family, and Society: A Reader* (New York: Random House, 1965), pp. 230–245; Arthur Besner, "Economic Deprivation and Family Patterns," *Welfare in Review* 3 (September 1965): 20–28; E. A. Wilkening, "Toward Further

Refinement of the Resource Theory of Family Power," *Sociological Focus* 2 (Winter 1968): 1–20. For a fascinating study of the relationship of the family, work, class, and their interrelationships over time, see Michael Young and Peter Willmott, *The Symmetrical Family* (New York: Pantheon Books, 1973).

46. Jean-Jacques Rousseau, *Émile* (Amsterdam, 1762).

47. Indicative of Thomas Jefferson's hesitancy about the need for educating women is the fact that the two universities he influenced the most excluded women.

48. Patricia Taylor, "Sex Differences in Voting Turnout: *The American Voter* Reconsidered," paper presented at a meeting of the Northeastern Political Science Association, Saratoga Springs, N.Y., November 7–9, 1974, p. 10.

49. Hess and Torney, Chapter 8.

50. Anthony M. Orum, Roberta S. Cohen, Sherri Grasmuch, and Amy W. Orum, "Sex, Socialization, and Politics," *American Sociological Review* 39 (April 1974): 197–209.

51. Hyman (n. 2).

52. Karl L. Alexander and Bruce K. Eckland, "Sex Differences in the Educational Attainment Process," *American Sociological Review* 39 (October 1974): 668–682.

53. Hess and Torney; Edgar Litt, "Civic Education, Community Norms and Political Indoctrination," *American Sociological Review* 28 (1963): 69–75.

54. Edinger and Searing have also found that broad background variables were not useful predictors of attitudes on the part of French and German elites. See Lewis J. Edinger and Donald D. Searing, "Social Background in Elite Analysis: A Methodological Inquiry," *American Political Science Review* 50 (June 1967): 428–45; Donald D. Searing, "The Comparative Study of Elite Socialization," *Comparative Political Studies* 4 (January 1969): 471–500; Searing, "Models and Images of Man and Society in Leadership Theory," *The Journal of Politics* 31 (February 1969): 3–31.

CHAPTER 5

Family Relations and Female Self-Images

Since the mid-1960s considerable attention has been paid to the authority structure within families and its effect upon political socialization. Indeed, as Greeley's model of ethnic political socialization (Figure 4-1) illustrates, family structure is now considered to be one of the most critical variables in political socialization. We agree that the family structure is critical. However, our rationale for linking family structure to political socialization is rather different from that of many social scientists. It follows also that our hypotheses about the effect of different types of family structure will also be different.

Our interest in family structure has to do primarily with its relationship to sex-role ideology and the extent to which it provides a girl with opportunities to gain control over her life-space. Most other studies to date have stressed the conjugal power relationship in investigating whether or not maternal dominance has a positive or negative effect upon political participation, efficacy, interest, and value orientations. In their study based upon responses to the question "Who is boss in your family?" Robert Hess and Judith Torney reported that elementary schoolboys had a lower sense of political efficacy and were less interested in politics when the mother—and not the father—dominated the family.[1] No effect on the girls was found.

The most systematic study of the conjugal power structure and its effects upon political socialization is that done by Kenneth P. Langton. On the basis of studying fatherless, mother-headed families compared to nuclear families in the Caribbean and comparable studies in the United States, Langton concludes that maternal dominance generally has "a debilitating effect upon male offspring" but relatively little effect upon females.[2] A lower sense of political efficacy was found for both males and females raised in a maternal structure with no father present. Langton found this difficult to explain.[3]

Langton also found that males from nuclear families where the mother was dominant were likely to be less politically interested, efficacious, and active than males from father-dominated families. Interestingly enough, however, this finding was strongly affected by the educational level of the family. "But among the college educated, mother dominance encourages male political involvement."[4] Langton clearly attributes this latter finding to "the greater sense of efficacy found among the more highly educated middle and upper classes [which] counteracts any differential effect mother-only families might have on the socialization of political efficacy."[5]

Langton's explanation begs what we think is the important question: "What produces political participation and political efficacy?" His references to income and education hide whatever psychological change is produced within individuals. Both indicators of social status, however, do reflect important variations among individuals in terms of sex-role ideology and the nature of their life-space and the extent to which they have control over it. A maternally dominated lower-class family whose head (the female) has little education will tend to have few skills, a narrowly circumscribed life-space, and probably repeated failure in efforts to gain control over that life-space or to expand it. Both sons and daughters, but particularly the latter, will be acutely aware of these failures. Because political efficacy is so much related to past success in participation and to competence levels, lower-class girls would predictably not have much sense of political efficacy. Middle and upper-class girls would not have their sense of efficacy lowered because the initial skill level of the mother is bound to be higher and her number of failures are lower. The fact that the mother-only family has remained in the middle or upper class in spite of the absence of a male shows a high level of competence on the part of the mother. While having a mother who holds her own might not lead to greater political efficacy and political participation, it is likely to be quite helpful in preventing a reduction in the sense of efficacy and actual participation.

The fact that sons tend to have their participation and efficacy increased by a more educated mother but that daughters do not reveals the tremendous impact that the prevailing sex-role ideology has on female behavior. Changes in the sex-role ideological content, not the level of educational attainment, are the critical factor for increasing efficacy and participation among females.[6] Increased education of mothers with a traditional sex-role ideology provides them with an increased ability to train their children to be more competent within the traditional sex roles; certainly it would not lead to increased political participation and efficacy for females in and of itself. Education can lead to increased political participation and efficacy only if it produces such skills and abilities that the nature of the life-space is changed and the need for personal control over it and the scope of the control are changed.

The question of "Who's boss?" by itself is quite unlikely to produce meaningful answers and insights into why anyone, male or female, is likely to participate in politics or feel a sense of efficacy. Without giving specific directions to the respondent, the question "Who's boss?" cannot illuminate in what areas the mother would be dominant. Children probably think in terms of who decides that they be punished. In fact, this is one of the indicators that Langton uses in his study of maternal dominance. But we still do not know who actually did the punishing, the mother or the father. We also do not know what competencies the mother had in terms of coping with the public or political world; nor do we know what type of role model she was for her children. Unless we do know these things, we cannot at all assess the impact of the mother on the daughter's behavior. We have, rather, a possible indicator of the henpecked state of the males in a family. If "maternal dominance" reduces male efficacy and participation, we suggest that it is because of the type of father the son has to imitate, not the type of mother he has. The fact that "maternal dominance" has no apparent effect on female political participation[7] substantiates this suggestion.

It is worth noting that not all scholars have found the same results on this question. Renshon, for example, using the item about who has the final rule-making authority in the family as his indicator, found no connection between "maternal dominance and a sense of personal control leading to political participation."[8] In and of itself then, "maternal dominance" is not likely to have a significant effect on female political behavior. We do agree, however, that the independence of the mother within the family structure is important for the political socialization of children. Later in this chapter we will investigate this matter. At that time we will also address the question of how the mother's role in decision-making regarding the children is related to the political development of the thirty-six women we have studied.

As this brief critique indicates, we do not believe that previous research on the relationship of the family structure to political behavior has addressed the correct questions. The questions that are important are those which investigate (1) how the various family structures contribute to producing children of both sexes who have a high need for personal independence and control over their life-space; (2) how they provide the children with the required skills, abilities, and access to needed structures and institutions to satisfy that need; and (3) how these family structures help to expand the life-space of the children so that politics becomes salient to them. Insights into these three questions can be obtained by learning more about how family structure is related to how the women included in this study became political wives, elected officials, or revolutionaries. Because of the dominating influence of sex-role ideology, we must start with learning how our subjects developed an activist (modern, if you will) sex-role ideology. We contend it has a great deal to do with the sex-role ideology and behavior of the mother.

Before delving into our analysis, however, it might be worthwhile to point out that findings concerning the parental families of our thirty-six women correspond with those of Langton which indicate that political participation is related to the intactness of the family unit.[9] Of the twenty-one women whom we have classified as achieving political women, and of the three classified as elected/mediated women, only five (21 percent) came from families which were not intact until they were at least the age of eighteen. Two of these five were terrorists (Zasulich and Corday); two were revolutionaries (Edib and Gonne); one was from the elected/personal efficacy group (Devlin). By way of contrast, of the eleven private and public wives for whom data were available, six (55 percent) came from homes broken by divorce or death. As we will point out below, however, the crucial variable is not whether or not the family was intact, but rather what type of relationships existed within the family structure if it was intact and consequences of the break for our women if it was not.

For our analysis of female sex-role development and its applicability to political behavior, we will use the theoretical framework of David B. Lynn.[10] According to Lynn, a vital difference between males and females is that females tend to identify with the culturally defined sex-role of their mothers. The mother, almost always immediately present and available, provides a direct model that girls can imitate. The learning task for girls, thus, is that of a lesson, learning by imitating, repeating on almost a one-to-one correspondence behavior they see constantly. The learning task for boys, however, requires usually a problem-solving task. Since the mother is most usually the parent who is readily available for identification, boys identify first with her just as girls do. But soon they learn that they will be punished if they imitate too closely. The question of what ought to be imitated and with whom one should identify becomes a problem.

An important consequence of the family structure that keeps the mother as the chief or sole child-rearer is, according to Lynn, that boys and girls develop different cognitive styles of thinking and different personality traits. "The little girls acquire a cognitive style that primarily involves: (1) a personal relationship, and (2) imitation rather than restructuring the field and abstracting principles. The little boy, in contrast, acquires a cognitive style that primarily involves: (1) defining the goal, (2) restructuring the field, and (3) abstracting principles."[11] These different cognitive styles, again according to Lynn, lead to women having a greater, on the average, need for affiliation with other people than men, a lower ability to solve problems, to be dependent in restructuring the field as a learning principle, and a weaker tendency to internalize moral standards. Because females do not usually need to solve the problem of what ought to be imitated and learned, they tend to be more receptive to the values and standards of others and to have less of a need to abstract and internalize moral principles. According to Lynn, the tradition which keeps the woman at home raising the children, not the conjugal power structure, is the critical factor in producing basic sex differences.

Studies identifying changes in personality characteristics and sex-role beliefs among girls tend to concentrate upon the extent to which mothers have been separated from the traditional primary role of being home to raise the children. The evidence tends to support Lynn's position that family structure and child-rearing practices, not biology or conjugal power relationships, are the critical variables determining sex differences in behavior and beliefs.

Miller found that the daughters of working mothers tend to be more aggressive, to feel they are more competent at putting puzzles together, and to have the modern sex-role ideology significantly more than the daughters of nonworking mothers.[12] Vogel, Broverman, Broverman, Clarkson, and Rosenkrantz[13] as well as Baruch[14] found that female college students of nonworking mothers tended to stereotype male and female sex roles, especially on the dimension of competence and work. Competence was associated with masculinity and therefore excluded from the female sex role by the daughters of nonworking mothers. Lipman-Blumen reports that women with the modern sex-role ideology tended to place intellectual curiosity higher in a hierarchy of values than the women with the traditional sex-role ideology.[15] The latter women stressed emotional maturity, morals, and ethics the most. It seems reasonable to assume that if imitation is so critical for the sex-role development of girls, the daughters of women with the more modern sex-role ideology will grow up with a greater sense of competence, with a higher level of skills in a wider number of areas, and with a greater problem-solving orientation than the daughters of mothers having the traditional sex-role ideology.

Because of the extreme importance of the process by which girls imitate and identify with their mothers, we hypothesize that the following patterns will be related to our ideal types of female political behavior.

1. The private women (representing the traditional woman) will have learned their sex roles by directly imitating mothers or other relevant female figures who themselves had a traditional sex-role ideology and dependence upon men. The political women and, probably, the public women will have learned their sex role by either directly imitating a mother or other relevant female figure who herself was nontraditional and unusually active in areas of life defined as "masculine," or by rejecting the

traditional role model (mother or other females) because it was either undesirable or unavailable.

2. In all of the instances where achieving political women are concerned, they will have been more distant from their mothers and other females than were the private women. This greater distance suggests that the learning of an appropriate adult role required a problem-solving approach.

> One would predict that girls who are moderately distant from their mothers would have a feminine-role identification problem to solve somewhat comparable to that for boys. One would, therefore, predict better cognitive skills (problem solving and field independence) for these girls than that typically found. This would result from their struggle to solve the feminine-role identification problem.[16]

Also pertinent is Lynn's statement, "In those rare cases, however, where there is no mother (or mother surrogate) in the home or where, if present, she is extremely detached or brutal, rather than moderately distant, one would expect such cognitive functioning to decline."[17] The relationship of distance from the same-sex parent is thus a curvilinear one. Being too close prevents problem-solving, independence, and internalization of moral principles from developing; so does too much distance.

This curvilinear relationship to one's same-sex parent suggests that intellectual differences among active political women might also be predictable. Among revolutionaries, for example, we hypothesize that the women who were most distant from their mothers will tend to be the agitators and terrorists, while those who were moderately but not extremely close will be the more theoretically oriented. For the elected political women such tendencies also probably exist, but sufficiently refined measures of cognitive differences among legislators and executives are not yet available to permit an empirical assessment of comparable hypotheses on them.

3. Mothers of the achieving political women will score higher on scales of independence within the family structure and outside the home than mothers of nonpolitical women. Indicators for these scales would include whether or not the mothers had an economic position and status separate from that of their husbands; whether or not they had different intellectual interests and independent views on political, social, economic, and

other matters from those of the husband, and so on. It is hypothesized that the mothers of achieving political women will have these capabilities more than the mothers of nonpolitical women.

In contrast to the "weaker sex" theories and Freudian approaches, the above hypotheses obviously give a substantially smaller role to the father in the psychosexual development of not only political women, but also all women. Note, however, that the primacy of the father is what is being questioned, not that he or some other comparable male figure does not play an important part in the development of their children. On the contrary, we contend that fathers play a vital part in the development of political women. The part they play in politicizing their daughters, however, begins only if girls perceive that an active, egalitarian sex role is feasible. The father's role in the psychosexual development of a daughter involves his relation with the mother more than the daughter, and with providing the daughter career alternatives or substantive interest areas which will encourage her to engage in political activity. We will also argue that fathers and brothers are critical factors in determining whether or not and the extent to which women will become "achievers," whether their field be politics or something else.

Fathers have an effect on the sex-role ideology of their daughters through their relationship with the mother and the attitudes they hold toward the family. The father who sees the family as the main support for his ego and his existence, the one chief area where he is top dog, will be the male most inclined to maintain strongly the traditional sex-role relationships and the projection of the traditional sex-role images to the children and the external world. The daughter of such a father will also tend to have a mother who accepts this situation. It would be very difficult, if not impossible, for such daughters to break with the traditional sex-role stereotype.

On the subject of fathers, we hypothesize:

1. The fathers of achieving political women will generally be men who viewed their work as interesting careers worthwhile pursuing even without the need to support a family. Conversely, the fathers of nonpolitical women will generally be men who viewed their occupations essentially as a way to feed their families and to maintain their "castles" at home.

2. The fathers of achieving political women will tend not to

care if the mothers worked; indeed, they will have encouraged them to get involved and to express their interests and abilities. Wives' entrance into the working world, even of contractual obligations, would be less threatening to the fathers of political women than to the fathers of nonpolitical women. The fathers of political women will have been more inclined to see the mothers as human beings like themselves with similar needs and interests, in contrast to the fathers of nonpolitical women. The latter will tend to see the mothers more as beings different from the males of the species, more as "baby-machines" and raisers of children than as real personalities.

3. In general, the fathers of achieving political women will have been away from home for longer periods of time than the fathers of nonpolitical women. Moreover, they will have been gone from home more frequently for purposes of self-fulfillment. The fathers of the private women will tend to view the external world as generally too hostile or at least insufficiently rewarding to get involved with.

4. Related to the latter point, but definitely separate from it, is the hypothesis that the fathers of achieving political women will have been absent more, and that these absences will have forced the mothers to perform traditionally "masculine" tasks. The decrease in the specialization of functions by sex can also develop as the result of the active participation of the father in the sharing of household chores traditionally performed by the mother. The important point is that the less the division of labor within the home, the greater the likelihood of the development of an activist sex-role ideology.

The presence of siblings also influences sex-role development. "The presence of siblings of the opposite sex might be expected to increase a subject's acquisition of characteristics of the other sex. . . . For a girl, . . . the presence of male siblings may make the prerogatives and privileges offered males particularly apparent, leading to her earlier and greater dissatisfaction with the feminine role. This might increase her likelihood of preferring, adopting, and finally identifying with characteristics of the masculine role."[18]

We hypothesize, in respect to siblings, birth order, and peers, that:

1. A higher proportion of the achieving political women than the private women will have had brothers.

2. A higher proportion of achieving political women will have older brothers than the private women. "An older cross-sex sibling has more effect than a younger one in enhancing opposite-sex-role preference, adoption, and identification."[19]

3. A higher proportion of achieving political women than private women will be later born rather than first born. Later-borns tend to imitate and to model themselves on people other than parents more than first-borns do.

4. The first-borns who do become achieving political women will have had quite unusual mothers who themselves had very active public lives. Kammeyer has found that first-born girls tend to be "conservators of the traditional culture."[20] They are much more traditionally oriented, much more religious, and much more likely to choose marriage over a career. If a first-born girl is to become a political woman, we would anticipate that the family "culture" she is preserving is one that includes an activist sex-role for women.

5. A higher proportion of the political women than private women will have been influenced by peers in their teen years. According to Lynn, "The influence of peers in shaping identification is greater for males than females."[21] This finding arises essentially because boys cannot identify immediately with the father as most girls can with their mothers. Given that we have already hypothesized that politically active women will also have had less likelihood of direct mother identification, we argue that girls who have rejected direct identification with their mothers and the prevailing female sex-role ideology or do not have that option will turn to peer groups during their adolescent years for assistance. If a peer group stresses an activist female sex role, then the girl will be inclined to adopt that sex-role ideology for herself if she has not already done so.

Sex-Role Imitation and Identification: The Mothers

Our first hypothesis states that the majority of women, regardless of adult political persuasion and behavior, will have obtained their sex-role perception from their mothers or mother-substitutes who raised them. Those women who became the traditional, private woman will have had traditional, private-women types of mothers. Most of those who became achieving political or unusual public women will have had mothers who themselves were nontraditional, activist, and independent for their time. The remainder either will not have had a close female role model available or will have rejected the one that was available as being unacceptable. In both these latter instances, the girl will have been raised more like a boy, particularly in terms of skill development and education.

The case histories of our thirty-six women tend to support these hypotheses. Of the six women classified as the traditional, private-woman type for whom information is available (De Gaulle, Eisenhower, Wilson, Stalin, Truman, and Nixon), all with the exception of Nixon had intact families, and mothers with whom these women appear to have identified. All the mothers except Nadezhda Alliluieva Stalin's presented traditional models for their daughters to emulate.

In the cases of the private women, some of the estimate of the very private nature of the lives of their mothers is based on the small amount of information on them. Madame Jacques Vendroux, the mother of Yvonne de Gaulle, came from a rather wealthy family and appears never to have worked although she did volunteer her services as a nurse during the First World War. She was a devout Catholic and her religious and patriotic beliefs were closely associated. The traditional character of her life is illustrated by her attempt to arrange the marriage of her daughter,[22] a custom very much in keeping with the social, religious, and cultural mores of France at that time. Although we have no explicit statement as to how Yvonne de Gaulle related to her mother, the characteristics of her own life and behavior approximate the model of her mother.

Elivera Carlson Doud, the mother of Mamie Eisenhower, presented a traditional, family-centered female role model for her daughter to copy. She married at the very early age of sixteen; John Doud was twenty-nine. She never worked nor does her educational attainment appear to have been great. She too was a very religious woman who had a circumscribed view of the appropriate place of women. She agreed with the decision that it was not particularly important that her daughter Mamie receive extensive schooling. Mamie Doud was not interested in continuing her education, and her parents agreed that it seemed unnecessary for her station in life.[23] Elivera Doud's lack of good health further restrained her from an activist role.

Gladys Mary Wilson's mother, Mrs. Baldwin, has been even more difficult to get significant information on than Wilson herself. We could not even learn her first name! As the wife of a Congregationalist minister, active in her husband's parish, she does not seem to have strayed too far from the accepted social mores for her status in life. The relative poverty of her family meant that Mary Wilson left home when she was eighteen to work in a factory. In doing so, she emulated her mother who also had worked because of family need prior to her marriage. The lack of material wealth of the Baldwin family was not reflected in the spiritual realm or in the strength of the familial bonds, however. The warmth and strength of the Baldwin family were nourished by a devoted, traditional, conventional woman.

The mother of Nadezhda Alliluieva Stalin was rather unusual when compared to the mothers of the other private women. Olga Fedorenko came from mixed ethnic parentage: a Ukrainian-Georgian father and a Protestant German mother. The youngest of nine children, she remained religious, if unorthodox. "She could see no difference between the Protestant, Gregorian or Armenian, and Orthodox churches and considered such distinctions a waste of time."[24] When her children were in secondary school, she had several love affairs, "with a Pole, a Hungarian, a Bulgarian, and even a Turk."[25] But in the work she performed she was traditional, "a wonderful cook and dressmaker and a splendid manager of the meager resources available to her as the wife of a Bolshevik who was in jail part of the time and always on the move from one town to another."[26] She encouraged all her children to continue their education and also joined the Bolshevik Party before the Russian Revolution. According to her granddaughter, however, her motivation seemed to be nonpolitical: "In those days my grandmother was a splendid forbearing, faithful wife."[27] When the children were older, she complained that her husband had ruined her life and "caused her 'nothing but suffering.'"[28] Although Olga Fedorenko did not commit suicide, her behavioral pattern was similar to that of her daughter, Stalin's wife. She ran away from home to marry at the age of fourteen. Nadezhda Alliluieva married at sixteen, according to one source, after having been seduced and impregnated by Stalin. Both seemed to be faithful, forbearing wives in the early years of marriage. Though both worked, neither had a distinct, separate career. Both eventually rejected their husbands: the mother by having other affairs and ultimately by living apart, the daughter by committing suicide.

The mother of Bess Truman presents a slight variation on a familiar theme. Madge Gates Wallace was known to the population of Independence, Missouri, as the "queenliest woman Independence ever produced."[29] Hailing from the wealthy aristocracy of Missouri, Madge Wallace saw herself as a lady of quality, daughter of a great industrialist and public leader.[30] As a lady she was a pillar of the social set, and hardly likely to have engaged in activities which would have given Bess Truman an active and independent model to emulate. She was an "imperious woman," the "boss" in the family.[31] She believed herself and her family to be better than Harry Truman and constantly put him down even while living in his home, including the White House. The picture presented of Madge Wallace is not one that would have fostered a modern activist sex-role ideology. It is a matter of class that differentiates Bess Truman's mother from the mothers of the other private women included in our study. It is not a matter of a break in the traditional expectations about the role of women. She merely represents the "conspicuous consumer" and "lady of leisure"—the model of traditional women among the upper classes.

The only woman among the private women we studied who did not have a family intact throughout her youth was Pat Nixon. Nixon's mother, Katherina Halberstadt Bender Ryan, died when Pat was thirteen years old. A German widow with two children when she married Pat Nixon's father, Katherina Ryan does not appear to have afforded her daughter an independent example to follow. Most of Pat Nixon's early formative years were spent in the presence of her mother who was very much tied to home and family. Additionally, Nixon assumed the role of mother to her two older brothers during the illness of first her mother and then her father, who passed away when she was eighteen; she even gave up her education to live at home and take over the duties of the household. In the case of Pat Nixon, the breakdown of the initial nuclear family led only to the acquisition of traditional female skills associated with the home and its care, not to skills transferable to the wider public realm of business or politics. The absence of her mother merely made motherhood more personally salient at an early age for Pat Nixon. For her not to have wanted to move beyond the wife/mother range of behavior in later life, even though married to a political being, should not be surprising.

Among the five wives that we classified as public women, a different pattern exists. Not one of the five reached the age of eighteen with an intact nuclear family. Two—Lady Bird Johnson and Eleanor Roosevelt—were left motherless at young ages, five and eight respectively. Nadezhda Krupskaia's father died when she was fourteen years old; the mothers of both Clementine Churchill and Jackie Kennedy divorced their husbands when the girls were still teenagers.

Lady Bird Johnson's independence as a person can hardly be questioned. Although never elected to political office herself, her support for her husband's political career was extensive; she could well have become a congresswoman from Texas herself. Her career as a businesswoman in the areas of farming and communications clearly lends support to the supposition that she might have become a political woman under different circumstances. Her skills in decision-making and problem-solving can be attributed to the attention her father gave her during the years after her mother's death. Minnie Patillo Taylor died suddenly as the result of a fall when Lady Bird, the youngest of three children, was only five. Her two brothers, eight and eleven years older than she, were sent to boarding schools. Her father tried at first to utilize neighbors as surrogate mothers but decided finally to take his daughter to his store each day rather than to be separated from her. During the day she played in the store; during the night, she slept upstairs in the store. Maids did the housework at home. Her Aunt Effie and a neighbor, Doris Powell—both more traditional sex-role models—did try to help, but Lady Bird Johnson remained closest to her father. When it came time to enter school, she attended a one-room schoolhouse near her home. Under the influence of her father she became an independent woman with the expectation that she could excel in the business world if she obtained the proper skills. In her memoirs she wrote that she took typing and shorthand in her teens because "once you got your foot in the door as a good secretary, if you had brains, personality and desire to help, you could go just about anywhere in business."[32]

Given her early and constant exposure to the business world and her father's expectation that she would participate in that world, it is perhaps not too surprising to see Lady Bird Johnson excel in business, a nontraditional, public career for women. In the case of Lady Bird Johnson, an early tragedy led to an unplanned structural opportunity to acquire "masculine" skills. She later utilized these competencies in business, after her actions were no longer mediated by her father. No other political wife included in this study had a family situation in which the mother was missing from such an early age due to death. Eleanor Roosevelt's situation does, however, approximate Lady Bird Johnson's in that her mother died when she was eight.

The role model that Anna Hall Roosevelt offered was one that Eleanor Roosevelt consciously rejected.[33] The child of a leisured gentleman from a prominent family, Anna Hall Roosevelt never had to work or be concerned with the material aspects of life. Much of her time was devoted to social activities that are associated with the upper-class traditional woman. Her memberships in such groups as the Knickerbocker Bowling Club, the Tuesday Evening Dancing Club, and her concerns with the organization of dances, cotillions, and teas were all part of the expected behavior of a woman of her class and station in life. It is this sort of hobnobbing that made Eleanor Roosevelt most uncomfortable both in her youth and her adult life. Made to feel awkward by her mother, who constantly criticized her, Roosevelt did not find her mother and her traditional manners particularly worthy of imitation. Both her mother's early death and her unpleasant experiences with her mother while she was alive seem to have convinced Roosevelt to reject those things that were most closely associated with her mother. In this case, the traditional role model was intensely disliked and rejected.

Although her father died two years after her mother, Eleanor Roosevelt was affected much more severely by his death. She greatly idolized her father and disliked her mother's evaluation of her father as worthless. Refusing to accept her mother's assessment of her alcoholic father, she created an image of her father very far removed from the reality. After his death, she continued to see herself as an outsider who identified more closely with him, the black sheep of the Roosevelt family.

By the time Eleanor Roosevelt was ten years old she had come to perceive herself as an intelligent, well-read, but ugly, awkward girl whom no one really loved or admired. Her maternal grandmother, who had been appointed her guardian after her father's death, continued the same pattern of criticism and complaint set earlier by Eleanor's mother. But the grandmother was less willing to dominate her. At the age of fourteen Eleanor

Roosevelt persuaded her grandmother to let her go to a boarding school in London. The headmistress of this school, a nonconformist interested in politics and the development of independent women, took a personal interest in her new charge. Headmistress Soutestre nourished and fostered Roosevelt's competence, self-confidence, and self-respect and provided an activist sex-role model for her. Eleanor Roosevelt had finally met and learned to admire an adult woman whom she would enjoy emulating.

As an adult Eleanor Roosevelt became extremely active in American public life and in politics. She comes the closest of our public women to being an achieving political woman even though not elected to public office. Of all the political wives, she demonstrated the greatest independent political involvement. To some, this involvement seemed so great that it was questioned at times whether it was she or Franklin Delano Roosevelt who was president.

The remaining public women/political wives (Clementine Churchill, Jackie Kennedy, and Nadezhda Krupskaia—Lenin's wife) all saw the dissolution of their nuclear family before they reached the age of eighteen. However, the father was the one missing in these three cases. The mother remained available throughout their youth and adolescence as a person to imitate. In these three cases the patterns set by the mothers seem to have been directly imitated by the daughters. The daughters' adult behavior approximates that of their mothers to a high degree.

Krupskaia was the daughter of a woman who was quite similar to herself. Krupskaia, an only child, appears to have had a very secure spot in her family. Her mother followed her father around Russia after he was dismissed from military service for his "revolutionary" views. As an adult Krupskaia also married a political revolutionary and followed him across Russia and Europe. In other words, there is no sharp contrast between Krupskaia's own adult role as Lenin's wife and her mother's role as a wife. The difference appears to be of degree, not kind. Krupskaia's mother was also a reasonably competent person. She was well-educated and earned money by teaching outside the home. When Krupskaia's father died, her mother and she did not suffer from dire financial need. Her mother fostered in her an activist sex-role ideology which included the concept of sharing the financial responsibility of providing for the family.

The mothers of Jackie Kennedy and Clementine Church-ill—Janet Lee Bouvier and Lady Blanche Hozier—have much in common. Both of the women separated from their husbands when the girls were beyond the most formative early years of childhood. In neither case did the dissolution of the marriage have a great impact on the female role model the girls had to imitate. The breakup of these two marriages did not force the women to give up the upper-class life-style to which they had become accustomed. Before and after her parents' divorce, Clementine Churchill was presented with a traditional role model to emulate. Lady Blanche Hozier was twenty-five years younger than her husband when she married him. When the marriage dissolved, she continued to maintain the aristocratic life-style with which she was familiar. Clementine Churchill thus was in a home in which the woman, though without a husband, continued to live off the wealth of her father. The dissolution of the marriage meant no severe change in sex-role expectations or established behavioral patterns.

Janet Lee Bouvier, though she too separated from her husband, Jackie Kennedy's father, was hardly left destitute. Indeed, Jackie Kennedy did not experience any great discontinuity of life-style with the separation. Living with her mother most of the year she clearly had a model to follow that has affected her entire life. Janet Lee Bouvier was the daughter of a wealthy New York family who knew all the refinements associated with the social class in which debuts, private girls' schools, and the society page were common concerns. She was an accomplished horse-woman. "Both sports and social pages during the thirties were filled with action shots of Mrs. Bouvier and her handsome mounts. Captions and headlines ran like this: 'A Picture of Grace and Skill'; 'Mrs. Bouvier turns in perfect performance with hunter at the National Horse Show.'"[34] The fame and prominence of Janet Bouvier was also closely connected with fashion. It is not at all difficult to see how Jackie Kennedy closely identified with and imitated this woman of refinement. Of course, it is also not difficult to see how her disdain for many of the grubbier aspects of politics would have developed in this environment.

The sex-role model presented to these five public women is to some degree different from that of the six private women we described. The absence of the mothers in the cases of Roosevelt and Johnson seems to have produced a vacuum with regard to a strong female role model. This lack then allowed for the development of the strong interest these women had in a more public and active life. The remaining three women—Churchill, Kennedy, and Krupskaia—had mothers to imitate and in each case the imitation of those mothers led to almost a repeat of the mothers' pattern. All three had more independent and publicly active mothers than, for example, the mothers of De Gaulle, Eisenhower, and Wilson; all three daughters became more publicly active as adults as well.

We have classified three of the thirty-six women as elected/mediated public women since their initial source of interest in politics came from their husbands' careers as politicians. These women are Nancy Astor, Leonor Sullivan, and Margaret Chase Smith. Now we turn to the lives of their mothers to see if the sex-role ideology they exhibited was in any way attributable to their mothers. If the logic of our explanatory scheme is correct, we should find that the mothers of these elected/mediated women are not as active and independent as the mothers of the achieving political women, or, as the mothers of the revolutionaries and terrorists.

Nancy Astor was named after her mother, Nancy Witcher Langhorne. Although the identification of a child with the parent for whom he or she is named does not always follow, it does appear to have been the case here. It has even been noted that the two women bore a strong physical resemblance to one another. "The older woman has all the look of one who has valiantly and cheerfully struggled through hard times, the younger the innocent expression of one with experience before her. Their mutual love is not hard to understand."[35] Nancy Langhorne was thus a model for her daughter to imitate and emulate. What was Nancy Langhorne like?

The paucity of information about Nancy Langhorne is interesting given the enormous amount of personal information about her husband who was affectionately known as "Chillie." Even within the notes of the autobiography Nancy Astor once began there is little mention of her mother. The few references that do exist are, however, revealing. Nancy Langhorne had married at the age of seventeen and bore eleven children before she died at the age of fifty-five. Nancy Astor, when recording these facts, wrote that her mother "had eleven children all unwanted." One biographer interpreted this comment as being an overstatement on Nancy Astor's part and was "possibly only referring to some repugnance for the sexual act (such as Nancy herself suffered)."[36] Despite her sense of repugnance about intercourse, Nancy Astor gave birth to six children. Although she became more independent than her mother, she was also somewhat overshadowed by her husband just as her mother had been by her father. Astor's having had five fewer children and a wealthy husband who wanted her to be a member of Parliament apparently permitted her to be less traditional than her mother.

Leonor Kretzer remained in the home of her parents until she was over thirty years old and did not marry John B. Sullivan until she was forty-four. The information available on her mother, Eleanor Jostrand Kretzer, provides a picture of a traditional, private woman. She never completed high school, though she did not marry until she was about twenty-two years old; she never worked outside the home; she was the mother of nine children. Noting that her mother had not been encouraged by her father to work, Leonor writes that "his belief was that she had enough work to guide the children and run a well-organized home where all the children had their duties and responsibilities."[37] Leonor Sullivan indicates that the decisions about family life were mutually shared by her father and mother and that theirs was a loving and sharing home. She adds in relation to political matters that "father discussed and recommended the candidates for whom to vote."[38]

The role model that Leonor Sullivan had in her mother meant that an adult resocialization to an activist role for herself was essential if she was to become politically active. It is easy to equate the role she assumed vis-à-vis her husband as most reminiscent of that her mother played vis-à-vis her father. The major difference appears to be that Leonor had no children; and she took it upon herself to "run a well-organized" office for her husband while he was alive and to keep the "home" seat of her husband occupied once he had died.

The picture presented of Carrie Chase, the mother of Margaret Chase Smith, is somewhat similar to Eleanor Kretzer's, in that she too was a "homebody" who worked only when family need made it necessary. Her work history is a mixture of odd jobs of an unskilled type taken and abandoned as the family needs altered. Smith said of her mother, "Mother was a great believer in the home. She saw to it that we always lived together as a family."[39] One of six children, two of whom died in their infancy, Smith recalls that her mother saw to it that the family did many things together and that it was this unit which was primary. Despite their low living standard, Carrie and George Chase felt that other aspects of their children's lives might well be as important as the material aspect and thus used some of their income to buy a piano and pay for lessons for their daughter. The role model with which Margaret Chase Smith had to identify as a young girl seems to be traditional. She does note, however, "We were always taught to do things for ourselves."[40]

The cases of the elected/mediated women indicate that their mothers gave them the role model of the private woman to imitate. The mothers were not any more independent or less traditional than the mothers of the public and the private women (who also married political men but who themselves were never elected to high public office). The elected/mediated women appear to be resocialized creations of their husbands and of their own adult experiences. In the cases of Sullivan and Smith, their late age at marriage, the absence of children, and their choice of husbands who strongly promoted their personal development, provided the opportunity to break with the private-woman model. Had their husbands not died, Sullivan probably would have remained a private woman and Smith a public woman. It is doubtful, however, that either would have become an elected public official without her husband's mediation. As already noted, Nancy Astor got involved in politics essentially to keep a seat for the family in Parliament; it was her husband's idea, not her own.

The elected/mediated group of women show the importance of resocialization during the adult years. The slowness of the resocialization process, however, and the chance nature of the opportunity that gave birth to these women as national legislators (that is, the premature death of their husbands) demonstrate that such resocialization is a weak reed for any women's liberation movement to rely upon. Social change would be very slow if political women were to develop from this type of resocialization process. Moreover, the fact that two of these women had no children means that any direct effects of their own resocialization could not be passed on to a new generation. Indirect role models have some importance but the mother model seems more critical.

Turning to the political women with an early sense of personal efficacy, we expect to find them to be daughters of independent and activist mothers. As we previously suggested, it is not the intactness of the family itself that makes the difference but the type of relationship existing between the mother and father. Our examination of the characters of the mothers of these seven political women produces support for this hypothesis, and especially in the lives of the two women who achieved the highest political offices within their respective countries, Golda Meir and Indira Gandhi.

Blume Mabovitch, an unusual and nontraditional woman, has been vividly described by her daughter, Golda Meir. In recounting how her mother came to marry her father, Golda notes that theirs was a very unconventional romance for Russian Jews living in Kiev in that day. Her mother had seen her father on the street and had fallen in love with him at first sight. Despite the fact that the love was not likely to be appreciated by her parents, who were thinking the customary thoughts about arranged marriages, Blume asked permission to marry the man of her choice. Poor and orphaned Moshe Yitzhak Mabovitch was not likely to impress his prospective in-laws. He was, however, educated enough to be able to read the Torah. Golda writes that "my grandfather duly took this fact into account, although I have always suspected that he was also influenced by the fact that my mother had never been known to change her mind about anything substantive."[41]

Blume Mabovitch also was less religious than one might expect. Another mark of her independence was that, when life in Kiev became particularly oppressive, she encouraged her husband to leave her and her three young daughters (Golda was only five at the time) to go to America to begin a new life for them. They were to follow. For the three years that Moshe Mabovitch was gone, his wife provided for the family. This pattern was not to change even when the family was reunited. It was Meir's mother who appears to have consistently maintained the standard of living for the family. It was she who decided to move to an apartment which included a shop below it which she opened and ran. Once again Golda Meir's own description of this occurrence is the best indication of how very independent her mother was:

ing back at my mother's decision, I can only marvel at her mination. We hadn't been in Milwaukee for more than a : or two; she didn't know one word of English; she had no ng at all of which products were likely to sell well; she had never run or even worked in a shop before. Nonetheless, probably because she was so terrified of our being as abjectly poor as we had been in Russia, she took this tremendous responsibility on herself without stopping to think through the consequences. Running the shop meant not only that she had to buy stock on credit (because obviously, we had no surplus cash), but also that she would have to get up at dawn every day to buy whatever was needed at the market and then drag her purchases back home.[42]

Meir notes that her mother's efforts had negative implications for her father's ability to provide for them. His "feelings were undoubtedly hurt by her obvious lack of faith in his ability to support us."[43] The remainder of the references to her father indicate, however, that her mother's estimation proved to be essentially correct: Golda Meir's mother rather than her father became the economic stalwart of the family. The female role model that Blume provided her daughter is definitely one of competence and independence in dealing with the world outside the home. It is not surprising that Meir found it impossible to view marriage and the family as the total focus of her life. Indeed, one might marvel at her mother's continued criticism of her daughter for her independence. Her daughter was following her example. Golda Meir was doing what her mother had done, not what her mother said she ought to do.

It would be unusual for any biographer of Indira Gandhi to write of her rise to the prime ministership of India without mentioning the role that her father, Jawaharlal Nehru, played in making politics and political matters important to her. We are not in any way suggesting that this influence was not the case, but it also ought to be recognized that her mother, Kamala Nehru, was not an ordinary, traditional housewife and mother. She gave her daughter a model of female independence and activism that contributed to Indira Gandhi's tendency to convert her dolls into soldiers fighting for the independence of India.

Much of the independence and activism of Kamala Nehru has been attributed to her ethnic background and membership in the Kashmiri Pandit family. This family had held the major native ministerial posts in the state of Jaipur and had acquired the name of Atal, or "unshakable one." Krishan Bhatia, a biographer of Indira Gandhi, believes that this title is rightly deserved by Kamala Nehru. In addition to her family background, Kamala had independence steeled into her as a result of her marriage to Jawaharlal Nehru; from the earliest years of their marriage she often was left alone and neglected by him. This was not only because of the numerous times he was in jail, but also because he did not think he needed to be at her side in times of personal illnesses or crises. On one occasion Kamala fainted just as Jawaharlal Nehru and a friend were about to leave for a political rally. "Her collapse clouded Jawaharlal's brow with worry but only briefly. He laid her on a couch and called a maid to attend to her. He would not consider canceling his engagement or even delaying his departure."[44] One might have expected a more traditional woman to complain about such neglect and to pull the mantle of the family and its sanctity more closely around her. Such was not the case for Kamala Nehru. She simply followed her husband into political activity; and on at least one occasion, she herself spent time in jail.[45]

The absence of her mother for political reasons must have added to the impressive importance attached to politics for the young Indira Gandhi, particularly since her mother's political activity was much more than a simple reflection of her father's opinions and convictions. Kamala displayed a remarkable independence of spirit and strength of character. Indira Gandhi herself recalls a demonstration of this independence when she was only four. In 1921, Mahatma Gandhi (not related to Indira Gandhi), the spiritual leader of the movement for Indian independence, had publicly

> urged everyone to discard foreign clothes and take to *khadi*. The Nehrus, their respect for the leader notwithstanding, were undecided. Motilal [Indira's grandfather] had serious doubts about the value of the gesture, and Jawaharlal procrastinated. Kamala, however, was convinced and by all accounts prodded the family into implementing Gandhi's directive. In Indira's own words, 'the whole family was against it but it was my mother's insistence that brought about the change.'[46]

Indira from her earliest days was to don the *khadi* insisted upon by her mother.

Putting the elements of the description of Kamala Nehru together reveals a woman of great inner strength. How she handled her family heritage, the hostility she met from her mother-in-law and sister-in-law, the separations from her husband, all point in the direction of courage and fortitude. She became very politically active despite her near lifelong bout with tuberculosis. She was also courageous in the face of enemy soldiers and the threat of imprisonment. This courage of Indira Gandhi's mother was seen when she delivered to a mass gathering the same speech for which her husband had been arrested a few days earlier. Kamala Nehru approached politics with the same near complete abandon as Jawaharlal Nehru's. Indira Gandhi had not only a father, grandfather, and later a husband who were public and political beings; she also had a mother who was political. The support for our hypothesis that political women develop by imitating a female whose behavior demonstrates an activist sex-role ideology is in no way diminished by this case history.

Ruby Seale St. Hill, the mother of Shirley Chisholm, also demonstrates the basic themes that we have stressed. Moreover, Chisholm as a girl had at least two activist, independent females to imitate. Between the ages of four and ten Chisholm did not live with her mother but rather with another very unconventional woman, her maternal grandmother, Emily Seale.

Charles St. Hill and Ruby Seale were Barbadians who had migrated from Barbados and met, married, and procreated three daughters in Brooklyn. The mid-1920s did not offer many opportunities to a black family. Ruby Seale felt that her children would be better off with their grandmother on her farm in Barbados. She and her husband would try to work and save for their education. In discussing her parents' decision to send her and her two younger sisters to live with their grandmother, Chisholm clearly indicates that the idea was principally her mother's. Its primary motivation was to be able to save sufficient funds for their daughters' education which Mrs. St. Hill felt was so vital.

Shirley Chisholm's grandmother was the woman essentially responsible for the formation of Chisholm's sex-role ideology between the ages of four and ten. This grandmother owned and ran her own farm. She was willing to take on the responsibility of three young girls for six years. She also accepted the children of Shirley Chisholm's Aunt Violet—four of them—for the same purposes. Of her first impressions of her grandmother, Chisholm writes: "When the bus stopped, there was Grandmother—Mrs. Emily Seale, a tall, gaunt, erect, Indian-looking woman with her hair knotted on her neck. I did not know it yet, but this stately woman with a stentorian voice was going to be one of the few persons whose authority I would never dare to defy, or even question."[47]

Although her mother's plan had been to work as a seamstress and to save money for the children's return from Barbados, the Depression wiped out most hope of making any real progress. When Shirley Chisholm did return, the economic plight of the family was not much different from when she had left. Nor was the character of her mother much altered. Just about every utterance from Chisholm's autobiography attests to the influence and impact of her mother. Chisholm writes of her mother's relation with the other women of their neighborhood:

> Most of our playmates and many of Mother's and Father's neighbors were, of course, white and Jewish. Mother's sense of humor appealed to her white friends; they would roar at her imitation of their dialect. The other women often gathered around her bench in the park when she took us there in good weather. Because she was English-speaking and could give advice about bills and other legal pitfalls of city life, she became a kind of neighborhood oracle and leader.[48]

Her mother possessed many of the problem-solving talents and skills so necessary for participation in the public, political world, and seems to have transmitted many of them to her daughter.

Chisholm also notes that her mother expected her children to move upward socially. Theirs may have been a poor lot but this was a reflection of the external circumstances and not of their natural character or station. "She [Ruby Seale St. Hill] was thoroughly British in her ideas, her manners and her plans for her daughters. We were to become young ladies—poised, modest, accomplished, educated, and graceful, prepared to take our places in the world."[49] In becoming a political woman Shirley Chisholm seems to have imitated her mother's behavior pattern and lived up to her expectation.

Ella Grasso's mother, Maria Oliva Tambussi, at first glance combines all the traits that we might expect of a woman with a very traditional sex-role ideology. She is an Italian, an ethnic group known to have strongly held beliefs about the importance of the family and the woman's place in the home. She is a devout member of the Roman Catholic faith who married at the relatively early age of eighteen, with very little formal education, completing only five years of school. Her only work experience was at a low-skill job which she gave up after her only child, Ella, was born. All these factors converge in a manner that on the surface suggests that Maria Tambussi must be a traditional, private woman. The picture given in a questionnaire graciously completed by Ella Grasso, however, presents a very different view. Grasso indicates on the questionnaire that the psychological and personal impact of her mother was not that suggested by these sociological characteristics.

Of her mother's relationship to her father Ella Grasso notes that in regard to the running of the family her mother and father shared the decision-making. Grasso also indicates that her mother kept abreast of political and economic events, discussing them with other people and her father. Her mother openly disagreed with her father on social, political, and economic matters, hardly a sign of a subordinate, traditional woman. One comment made by Grasso on our questionnaire is particularly revealing. We asked if her father encouraged her mother to work for money or to engage in contractual obligations involving money. Rather than check one of the boxes provided, Grasso wrote: "My mother did not work after I was born. She had no wish to and my father accepted any judgment *she* would have made."[50] The italics are Grasso's.

The importance of Governor Grasso's statement should not be missed. Women who remain at home and do not work are not necessarily traditional, nonactivist, dependent role models for their daughters. Maria Tambussi appears to be a concrete example of this point. She also contributes to the strength of our overall conclusion that the mothers of the personal efficacy group of women are unique and unusual women in that they have clearly presented their daughters with a model to emulate which breaks with the sex-role stereotyping so prevalent in all societies. Ella Grasso may have had an unschooled and home-oriented mother, but she did not have a nonpublic, passive, submissive, dependent mother. Her mother has encouraged and supported her throughout her political career.

The information on the mother of Martha Wright Griffiths is rather sparse. It is thus with some hesitancy that we have included Griffiths in this chapter. Some evidence exists, however, that Martha Griffiths had unusual female models to emulate and that they might well have been part of a family tradition.

Martha Griffiths' father was a rural letter carrier and her mother often served in his stead. In order to deliver the mail she would drive a double team of horses. Even for "sturdy pioneer stock,"[51] this is a bit unusual. Her paternal grandmother had been married to a man who was county sheriff and had been killed by outlaws. Undaunted by this tragedy her grandmother moved her family (three sons, one of whom was Martha's father) to the city of St. Louis "and learned to be an expert tailor. She supported her three small boys, plus establishing the precedent of a woman in a man's job."[52] This grandmother appears to have had some influence on Griffiths, who remembers her well enough to recall that one of her grandmother's ambitions in life was to live long enough to vote for a woman president.[53] Martha Griffiths also has family ties to the first woman to become a member of the legal profession in the history of Missouri. Although the information on Griffiths' own mother is minimal, the evidence clearly shows that independent, publicly active females were part of the family's tradition and value system.

On the basis of Bernadette Devlin's description of her mother in *The Price of My Soul*, it seems that her mother did not have an activist sex-role ideology. The characteristics of her mother read very much like those of Ella Grasso's mother. She was Irish rather than Italian but the family orientation of these two ethnic groups is very similar. She also is a devout Roman Catholic who had very little education and who never worked outside the home. The obvious poverty to which Devlin alludes was only heightened with the death of her father when she was nine years old. Her father even before his death had been a marginal figure. Her mother had had to make the actual day-to-day decisions for the family during much of Devlin's childhood because Devlin's father had been working in England. Because he was considered to be a "political suspect" in Northern Ireland he had been unable to find work and had been forced to leave Ireland. This left the mother to fend for herself and the children.

Devlin mentions that her mother kept abreast of the political events of the day and that she publicly disagreed with her father on political matters. The most noteworthy remembrance Devlin has of such a disagreement has to do with a political event of some import for the Irish, the Easter Rebellion. It was her father's desire to commemorate this event every year. Her mother objected that it was "over and done with" and that commemorating it was an insult to their Protestant neighbors.[54] Her mother also appears to have objected to the father's continually telling Irish nationalist stories to the children.

These indications of disagreement with her father and the need for her mother to make decisions about the family and its welfare because of the man's absence and, later, death do not in themselves lead to an image of a woman with a strong nontraditional sex-role ideology. The objective conditions for the development of an activist sex-role ideology in the daughter appear to have been present, but the sense of personal control and the desire for such control never seem to have developed in Devlin's mother. Devlin writes that her mother lost interest in her own life and lived only for her children after her husband's death.[55] With regard to Bernadette Devlin the overall assessment must be that the mother provided neither an activist orientation to the outside world nor a model of competence in dealing with it. It is possible that the weak role model was consciously rejected by Devlin just as Eleanor Roosevelt rejected the model offered by her mother. We will return to Devlin in the next chapter when we examine how her sense of personal control and competencies were developed.

It is unfortunate that for the last of our elected political women, Margaret Roberts Thatcher, there is little information available on her mother. Given the extreme independence of Margaret Thatcher herself and the elevated position she has risen to in her relatively brief career, the lack of information on her mother is felt most severely. If nothing else, our work should lead the future biographers of the ever increasing numbers of political women to include more information on these women's mothers. All we can say about Margaret Thatcher's mother is that she appears to have been present throughout Thatcher's early years and that from the lack of information to the contrary we must conclude that she was a traditional, private woman. The only reference that Russell Lewis, the biographer of Thatcher, makes to her mother, whose full name he does not even give, is that she had been a dressmaker.

All of our revolutionaries were nontraditional women who personally rejected the sex-role model of the private, nonactivist woman. Because all have clearly rejected the primacy of the mother/wife role, we hypothesized that their own mothers had to be either (1) dead or absent; (2) a woman who had rejected her daughter; or (3) a woman who herself was unusually independent, fulfilling the female role herself in an atypical way and who was perceived in meaningful ways as an equal of the father.

In the first two options the traditional mother/wife role model is removed as a source of identification and imitation. In the third the model itself is "modern." Again, the biographical data on the revolutionaries support our theses concerning the importance of both the mother figure as a role model for daughters and of sex-role ideology for female political behavior.

Two of the nine revolutionaries studied, Maud Gonne and Halide Edib, were motherless before they were four years old. Both developed unusually close relationships with their fathers, relationships which were magnified largely because of the early death of their mothers. Both fathers transferred much of their great love for the mothers to their daughters. Gonne's father, for example, made her the "lady" of his house when she was a teenager and had her accompany him as his traveling and social companion. She delighted in this role and in the fact that she and her father were sometimes taken for husband and wife. Her father's treatment of her contrasted sharply with the way her aunts were treated by her uncles. Based upon her observations of their existence, she concluded: women of that generation had a dog's life; they did not seem to have counted for anything.[56] She consciously rejected her aunts as appropriate sex-role models to imitate. Her father encouraged her to be and do whatever she wished. He allowed her as his oldest daughter to help choose the governess she and her younger sister would have. It seems fair to say that she attempted to become a type of woman for which she had no direct family role model to emulate. A single, "liberated" governess who was interested in politics and social issues seems to have provided her with a sex-role model, and was much admired and loved by Gonne. The death of Gonne's mother, Gonne's rejection of the role model offered by her aunts, and the apparent tacit approval of her father provided a background enabling Gonne to choose to identify with this less traditional woman.

Halide Edib was a most unusual revolutionary not only because she was one of the few females active in the Turkish revolution and the only woman member of the general congress of the Turkish Hearth (a secret organization supporting nationalism), but also because she never met other revolutionary writers in her early revolutionary days because "a woman's place was in the home."

Edib's father worked in the palace of Sultan Abdul Hamid II and, although busy and often away, for a Turkish father at that time he was unusually interested in his daughter. He dressed and educated her in the western style and personally supervised her diet. In order to give her the western education he desired he sent her to the American School in Constantinople. Because it was a Christian school, the sultan forbade her father to send her there. Her father, however, promised the sultan he would not ask for a promotion in the Treasury Department if the sultan would overlook his daughter's attendance at this "infidel" school. Edib admired and loved her father greatly, but she was offended deeply when he took, as was the Muslim and Turkish custom, a second wife, a young friend of hers. Edib had not minded her first stepmother, though her paternal grandmother was the woman who cared for her the most. This grandmother generally supported her son's effort to give Edib a more modern life, but the grandmother herself was a traditional Muslim woman. In her adult behavior Edib reflected both sex-role traditions. Belonging neither to a particular western culture nor to the traditional Turkish culture, she initially sought to combine being a westernized, educated, critically thinking, active person with being a traditional Muslim wife. The incompatibility of her efforts led to a nervous breakdown within a few years of married life. With her recovery came a greater stress upon her own individuality and person. Ultimately, she left her husband.

Edib most clearly illustrates the importance of socialization in developing what society will consider a "typical" woman. Her father did not change her genes or her body. He took her out of the purdah—where by custom Muslim women were secluded from the public—and changed how she dressed, what she read, and how she would think about herself and women and men in general. His conscious effort to produce a new type of Turkish woman led to her involvement in revolutionary activity; only by political and social revolution could independent, active public women become acceptable in Turkey. Even in the 1970s, fifty years after the Turkish Revolution, many Turkish women still do not feel free to appear in public, much less to remove their veils and to demand their equal rights before the law.

Four of the revolutionaries were daughters of women who,

whether by choice or accident, were thrust into nontraditional roles for women. Two of these mothers were successful businesswomen. Alexandra Kollontai's mother ran a huge estate in Finland primarily for the fun of it, even though her husband was a high-ranking general in the Russian army. Eva Broido's mother ran the family farm and forest business, because the father was so other-worldly (a Talmudic scholar) and had no interest in supporting the family. La Pasionaria's mother worked in the coal mines with her father because they needed the money. Angela Davis' mother worked as a teacher, having a career before her marriage as well as throughout it. These mothers demonstrated as much competence and independence in dealing with the "masculine" world as their husbands; in fact, some demonstrated more competence than the respective husbands.

These mothers were also loved, admired, and respected by their husbands. Kollontai's mother and father were the most romantic couple. She had been forced to marry another man against her will as a teenager, but as soon as she could she managed to divorce him to marry her first love, Kollontai. Their romance lasted throughout their marriage which, in turn, lasted until Kollontai's mother died. Alexandra Kollontai herself was never able to find a man as romantic, intelligent, and as willing to tolerate her independence and career as her father had been toward her mother. The other mothers did not have quite so romantic a love, but, nonetheless, they were loved and esteemed.

Three of the revolutionaries were raised by elite women whose leadership and role in the social life of their regions placed them in public life. Markievicz's mother, Lady Gore-Booth, married the wealthiest landowner in their section of Ireland. This wealth, along with her own charm and organizing abilities, made her the recognized social leader in the area. When Queen Victoria came to visit, the chosen head of the committee to greet her, the person who had planned and arranged for her visit, was Lady Gore-Booth. Her husband also recognized her talents, leaving her in charge of the estate during his many scientific explorations. Although by nature a gentle and just woman, she was an aristocrat and was not very concerned with the problems of the poor Irish. She had little contact with the tenants on their vast estate.

Little concerned with politics per se and generally conservative in her thinking, Lady Gore-Booth disapproved of revolutionary activities and would never appear on a public platform with her daughter Constance Markievicz. She did, however, support her other daughter Eva's efforts to obtain women's suffrage. Lady Gore-Booth wanted a more active sex-role for women within the existing system. She did not wish to overthrow the system.

Breshko-Breshkovskaia's mother was also at the center of social life in her part of Russia. Being very wealthy, she was able to have special balls and plays given on their estate. Like Markievicz's mother, her rank and station in life provided her with something of a natural public forum. She was competent, wealthy, and had many specific cultural and social responsibilities. She was also loved and respected by her husband. In spite of her basic warmth and goodness, however, she is one of the few mothers we studied who seemed to have rejected her daughter for being a girl at birth. This strong feeling of rejection was sufficiently stressed in autobiographical and biographical writings to lead us to believe that it was the key impetus leading Breshko-Breshkovskaia to strive for a sex-role that would be different, more "masculine" than that played by her mother. Breshko-Breshkovskaia was often told as a child that she had not been wanted as a baby and that her mother had hated her at birth. The mother apparently had wanted another son. By the time Breshko-Breshkovskaia was five, she was considered an almost uncontrollable rebel by her mother. Only continual effort on the part of the mother, father, and Breshko-Breshkovskaia herself enabled the family to control her "sinfulness" and willful temperament. One of the things she used to do that her mother interpreted as a deliberate act of rebellion was to take to extremes the religious teachings of her mother. Breshko-Breshkovskaia was continually giving her clothes and belongings to the peasants and defending them against floggings. Breshko-Breshkovskaia's desire to please her father, whom she dearly loved; his willingness to support, financially and otherwise, her activities to educate and help the peasants on his estate; and the esteemed status her father gave her mother were instrumental in keeping Breshko-Breshkovskaia within the "establishment" fold until her late twenties. Her mother offered her a role model of a competent, respected elite woman. If Breshko-Breshkovskaia had not felt rejected by her mother in her early years, she might have imitated her mother's role, rather than going beyond it.

Rosa Luxemburg's mother was similar to these two elite women. She was an unusually intelligent woman, respected and loved by Luxemburg's father, and a person herself interested in social philosophy. It was she who seems to have introduced the writings of Schiller to her daughter. The relationship between husband and wife seemed more intellectually equal than that of the parents of other revolutionary women. It is conceivable that such a childhood perception of intellectual equality between her parents enabled Rosa Luxemburg to later perceive herself equal to such revolutionary theorists as Lenin, Trotsky, Leibkneckt, and Kautsky. The psychological feasibility of challenging such dominant male figures certainly had to come from someplace.

Sally Davis stands out as one of the most unique of the mothers investigated. Her family relations appear to closely approximate the symmetrical family described by Young and Willmott.[57] As daughter Angela Davis notes: "The family income was earned by both my mother and father. . . . My mother who, like my father, came from a very humble background, also worked her way through college and got a job teaching in the Birmingham elementary school system. The combined salaries were nothing to boast about, yet enough to survive on, and much more than was earned by the typical southern black family. They had managed to save enough to buy the old house on the hill, but they had to rent out the upstairs for years to make the mortgage payments. Until I went to school I did not know that this was a stunning accomplishment."[58]

There is a marked similarity between the political/public activity of Sally Davis and that of her famous daughter. Angela Davis states that her mother taught her the problems of being black in America in a non-hateful way with the expectation that political action would lead to social change. The difference between the political activities of mother and daughter are more a matter of degree than kind. Indeed, for a black woman in the 1940s to have grown up in rural Alabama, "become involved, as a college student, in anti-racist movements . . . [and to have] worked to free the Scottsboro Boys and there had been whites— some of them Communists—in that struggle,"[59] may have been more radical than her daughter's actions of a generation later.

Sally Davis' courage and strength continued to be a consolation to her daughter even while Angela Davis was in jail awaiting her trial. Her mother made the trip from Alabama to New York despite the fact that she was on crutches. Frank Davis, her father, remained at home away from the public limelight and agitation on Davis' behalf. Sally Davis not only visited her daughter in prison but also agreed to participate in activities planned by the New York Committee to Free Angela Davis. Without diminishing the impact of either her father, Frank Davis, or her brother, Benny Davis of football fame, Angela Davis, in her autobiography, clearly indicates a stronger political content in the actions of all the women in the Davis family—Sally, the mother, and Angela and Fania, the daughters—than is indicated in the actions of the men in the family.

As a group the mothers of our nine revolutionaries seem to share the characteristic of being unusually loved and respected by their husbands. They clearly were independent persons within the family sphere; all but possibly La Pasionaria's mother were at least intellectually aware of the political and economic realms; and all but La Pasionaria's mother again were quite competent either within the traditional family sphere of life or in some public, "masculine" realm of life, or both. More than even the mothers of the elected political women, these mothers provided models for their daughters of female independence, achievement, competence, and self-respect. These mothers liked themselves, were loved and respected by their husbands and other men and women around them.

Among the five terrorists a very different picture of the mothers emerges. The mother of one of the terrorists, Charlotte Corday, died before she was three. In contrast to Gonne and Edib, Corday's father did not attempt to raise her but rather placed her in a convent. The nuns who raised her apparently were kind but distant and firm. No one identifiable mother-figure seemed to influence Corday. Her father visited her occasionally. Her sex-role models were certainly not that of wife/mother.

Vera Zasulich's mother lived, but her father died before she was three years old. Her mother's inability to obtain a sufficient job or income led her to give Zasulich to distant relatives to be raised. The model given by Zasulich's mother was that of a private woman whose world had collapsed with the death of her husband, forcing her to seek employment in a world she had not been prepared to enter. Her mother's incompetence in dealing with the public world had lifelong effects on Zasulich, who never felt that she belonged to any family; she never had one of her own. Zasulich's French governess, an alien in a foreign land, added to the young girl's feeling of alienation, although the governess was an important sex-role model for Zasulich. In fact, her private life as an adult approximated that of her governess' rather closely. Her governess taught her about Voltaire, the French Revolution, and gave her good mind the most disciplined training that any of the five terrorists received. Nonetheless, she could not offer a female model of competence for Zasulich. The governess was not happy personally, had no real private life, and lived in a world whose center was essentially Zasulich herself. One does not either learn a viable new sex role or easily accept an existing sex-role model in this environment.

Emma Goldman was ignored by her mother. This lack of warmth was sharply contrasted with her mother's strong attachment to her brother. The mother never defended Goldman from the beatings meted out by her father. Goldman's mother, like Sophia Perovskaia's and, to a lesser extent, Ch'iu Chin's, was oppressed by her husband. She bore the children, obeyed her husband, and suffered the various indignities women were thought to be required to bear, including being beaten. There is also no image of competence here. Nor is there a strong feeling of love between the husband and wife. While one might resign oneself to the lot of such a person, it is hard to believe that a child would desire to imitate or identify with this wife/mother model. The mother was forced to be somewhat independent within the family realm, however, because of the absences of the father.

Sophia Perovskaia's mother also was beaten by her husband. In contrast to Emma Goldman and her mother, however, Perovskaia and her mother were extremely close. Perovskaia passionately loved her mother and hated her father just as passionately. Also in contrast to Goldman, Perovskaia's mother fought back at the father. Because they were wealthy while her father was governor-general of St. Petersburg, Perovskaia and her mother often left him to live in other parts of Russia and Europe. This mother always championed her daughter, and vice versa. The sex-role model offered by Perovskaia's mother is, however, not one of competence in the public sphere or of a person respected, loved, and honored in the private sphere. If she was competent, it was in escaping from the oppressive hand of her husband and in defending her daughter. However, she did do well in handling her affairs on her trips away from her husband. She was not a weak-willed woman, but rather another relatively unskilled, defenseless, traditional woman who had the misfortune of marrying a man who was a bully and tyrant rather than the "nobleman" he was supposed to be. Her incompetence in the public realm and her subordinate legal status as a married woman made it difficult for her to free herself from the situation.

Ch'iu Chin's mother was like most Chinese women of her time, definitely subordinate to her husband, less well educated, and limited to her role as wife/mother and daughter in the clan. The family was reasonably well-off, however, and the father seemed to hold the mother in fairly high regard. The mother was interested in education and apparently competent in fulfilling her family roles and independent within her defined family sphere. She was totally dedicated to her children.

These brief descriptions of the mothers of the five terrorists present a picture of an oppressed, suppressed group of male-dominated women. While other private women previously described voluntarily and even joyfully allowed males to mediate between them and the public realm, these women had no choice. They are all traditional, private-woman types who received few visible rewards for the roles they played in life. The three terrorists whose mothers and fathers lived through their growing-up had mothers who suffered at the hands of their husbands, had little control over their own lives, and no easily found escape. The two terrorists who lost one parent in effect lost both. Women terrorists who are personally willing to kill for political reasons seem to come from emotionally crippled homes where the mother was traditional, oppressed, and unrespected as a human being.

The descriptions of the mothers of our thirty-six women show that each of the six subgroups being studied tends to have a somewhat different type of female role-model to imitate. Because it is possible that we inadvertently selected information to support our hypothesis that political women will have had more independent, activist, and nontraditional mothers than our private women, two indices of female independence were developed. The first index is one that relates to the independence of the mother within the family unit. Its purpose is to provide a measure of degree to which the mother presented to the daughter an image and role model that said that women are important people whose opinions, attitudes, and ideas are worthy of consideration within the family structure. Specifically, the concern is the extent to which the woman is likely to have played an active, independent, assertive role in the maintenance of the family. The second index reflects the extent to which the mother would and could play a similar role outside the private family unit. Important in this regard is the degree to which the mother could and did go forth into the world which men traditionally have dominated. We believe that this particular indicator is vital for the purposes of demonstrating to the daughters that the wider world can be influenced by women and that the skills necessary to do so are not instilled at birth only into the males of the species.

Attempting to identify the components of such a complex matter as independence is indeed difficult. We not only need to determine what specific patterns of action or characteristics are associated with independence, but we must also attempt to compare and rank individuals in terms of how they act within the patterns or in terms of how many of the characteristics they possess. Our task is made easier by Guttman scalogram analysis.[60]

Guttman scalogram analysis seeks to determine empirically and objectively whether or not items being related are indeed cumulative scales allowing subjects to be systematically ranked on these items. In our study the procedure quantitatively determines if having one characteristic is actually related to having a second, third, or fourth. It also permits us to assess whether or not the possession of independence within or outside the home rests upon a cumulative set of characteristics. For example, on the items we include in each index we assume that some are easier for all women to possess while others are much harder. Our assumption is that mothers who achieve a plus for possessing a greater number of the characteristics included in the scale will have provided their daughters with a more independent role model. Moreover, if the mother possesses the characteristics more difficult to obtain, she will also possess the ones less difficult to achieve. If our fundamental thesis about the importance of mothers for female political socialization is correct, then the mothers of the achieving political women should have more of the characteristics than the mothers of the nonpolitical women. Thus the Guttman scalogram analysis will permit us to determine quantitatively whether or not female independence within and outside the home is based upon a set of characteristics, each of which is consistently and cumulatively more difficult for a woman to possess. If such a set of consistent cumulative characteristics is associated with (form a Guttman scale of) female independence, then we will have produced an ordinal scale allowing us to rank the mothers into successively more independent types by the number of characteristics they possess.

Mothers' Independence Within the Family Structure

The first index, "Mother's Independence Within the Family Structure," was developed from the available biographical information on the mothers regarding six separate matters concerning their positions within the home. Mothers possessing the characteristic were given a "+." If evidence that the mother had the characteristic was not recorded in the biographical material, the mother was given a "−." No plus or minus was given in those instances where the nature of the biographical references used were themselves not comprehensive enough to cover the type of information being sought. The scoring procedures used were clearly conservative in that in no case was a "+" given on a characteristic when any doubt existed. A "−" designation was also reserved for those cases in which the source material was sufficiently extensive to warrant the conclusion that such a positive factor could not have existed. All doubtful or judgmental decisions were recorded as missing information and were excluded from the computation of the coefficients of reproducibility and scalability—the measures used by social scientists to conclude that a scale does or does not exist. The computations were based on the mothers of only twenty-nine of the thirty-six women we studied. Three mothers (those of Thatcher, Griffiths, and Khrushchev) were excluded because of the lack of information on a majority of the items. Four mothers were excluded due to either their or their husbands' death before the daughter was four years old. In these four instances (Edib, Gonne, Zasulich, and Corday) too little is known of either one or the other spouse, or the influence of the mother was too short-lived to have offered a significant role model for the daughter.

The six items used for the index of the "Mother's Independence Within the Family Structure"—in the order in which they produced an acceptable, cumulative, undimensional scale—are as follows: (1) If there is a record of the woman's having made a definite contribution to a major family decision such as what jobs would be taken, or when and if the family would move, the mother was given a "+"; if no such record exists, she was given a "−." Women participating in such decisions undoubtedly have a more equal, independent position in the family structure than those who do not; we also believe if the biographic accounts do not contain such citations that such participation by the mother was less likely to have occurred. At any rate the woman was given a positive mark *only if* a specific incident of contributing to such a decision is recorded. On this basis 76 percent of the twenty-nine mothers received a plus.

(2) The mother got a "+" if she made major decisions regarding the children, for example, if, when, and where they would go to school; if, when, why, and how they would be punished, and so on. The emphasis here is on a decision with an easily discernible impact on the child. We do not assume she made all the decisions or that she was the "boss." Unlike those who insist on the importance of the question of "Who's boss?" we feel that the factor of an activist, equal, symmetrical relationship is more important than "maternal dominance." Maternal dominance in matters that "don't count," for example, when children will go to bed or whether they will eat all their food, does not substantiate the mother's independence within the family. If there is no record of the mother's having definitely shared in decision-making about the children on noteworthy matters, she was given a "−." Forty-five percent received a "+."

(3) The woman was coded as a "+" if there is a definite record of an event when the mother openly and publicly disagreed with the father on either family or sociopolitical concerns. In either situation the woman would presumably have displayed more of an activist role model for the daughter than a woman who never disagreed with her husband. There must exist specific proof that she had this independence of spirit for her to have received a "+." Otherwise, she got a "−." Of the twenty-nine mothers 41 percent received a "+."

(4) A woman was given a "+" if her educational attainment is higher than might be expected for a woman of her social class, time, culture, and society. All women who would have had the same degree of education as most women of their time period or less than that, were coded as a "−." Clearly our "plus" code here has required the mother to possess a strong, positive factor that would have allowed her to go into the marriage with a greater

independence. Only 10 percent of the women met this requirement for receiving a "+."

(5) If the mother had a higher socioeconomic status than her husband before they married, she was given a "+." If they were the same or she belonged to a lower socioeconomic class, she received a "−." The assumption behind this coding is that women who marry men above their station in life may have chosen an acceptable means of upward social mobility but this might have been purchased at the price of independence and a sense of personal control within the home. A woman from a higher socioeconomic status who marries someone below that status is more likely to maintain independence relative to the male in the family situation even if her new socioeconomic status becomes the same as his. Again the rarity with which this occurs suggests that some strong societal pressures must exist not to break this social norm. Only 10 percent of the women for whom data were available had married men from socioeconomic conditions below their own.

Finally, (6) all the women who had a better education than their husbands were given a "+," those with the same degree of education or less were coded a "−." Again the underlying assumption is clear. To be better educated than one's husband is quite rare and is likely to afford the woman a greater sense of personal control within the family setting. Only 7 percent of the mothers were better educated.

The facts that the six items were chosen with a clear dimension in mind, that the data were collected and coded before the arrangement of items and women was known, and that the acceptable measures of undimensionality (the coefficient of reproducibility [C.R.] = .90, and the coefficient of scalability [C.S.] = .67) were found, indicate the underlying components of female independence within the family structure can be scaled and correspond to empirical reality as well as to our theoretical framework. As a descriptive summary, the index has considerable value; it reduces the amount of verbiage necessary to explain the components of female independence with the family. As a measure of empirical reality its potential might be great but further research on the scale with other samples is needed to discern if such is the case.

Having established that the six items do indeed constitute an acceptable ordinal scale of "Mothers' Independence Within the Family Structure," we then created scale types. The types were designated as those ranging from "0" (those with the fewest pluses and, hence, demonstrating the least independence within the family) to "4" (those with the most pluses and, hence, demonstrating the most independence within the family). Each mother was classified into a scale type and the mean was computed for each of the groups of women studied.

Figure 5-1 depicts graphically the results of this analysis. The mothers of the public women, the elected women with personal efficacy, and the revolutionaries had the highest mean score on this measure of the mothers' independence within the family structure. In other words these women had on the average a more independent, activist female model to imitate than the other subgroups of women even if one does not consider their behavior beyond the family sphere. The terrorists had the next most independent sex-role model to emulate, then the private women. Last were the elected/mediated women whose mothers scored the lowest on this measure of independence.

Figure 5-1
Mothers' Scores on Scale of Extent of Their Independence Within the Family Structure

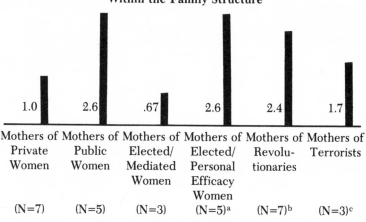

Mothers of Private Women	Mothers of Public Women	Mothers of Elected/ Mediated Women	Mothers of Elected/ Personal Efficacy Women	Mothers of Revolu- tionaries	Mothers of Terrorists
1.0	2.6	.67	2.6	2.4	1.7
(N=7)	(N=5)	(N=3)	(N=5)[a]	(N=7)[b]	(N=3)[c]

a. The mothers of Griffiths and Thatcher are excluded due to lack of data.
b. The mothers of Edib and Gonne are excluded because they died before their daughters were four years old.
c. Corday's mother and Zasulich's mother died when both our women were under four years old; hence, the mothers are excluded.

To obtain an additional guide in our exploration of the possible significance of the distributions found with this small number of cases, we completed the Student's t statistical test on various combinations of the subgroups. We found that comparing the women in terms of the common dichotomy of traditional women (the wives in the private and public women types, N = 11) and the nontraditional women (our elected/mediated, elected/personal efficacy, revolutionaries, and terrorists, N = 18) produced no statistically significant difference (Student's t = −0.781; p = .22). However, the same test comparing the private women, the elected/mediated women, and the terrorists with the public women, the elected/personal efficacy women, and the revolutionaries indicated the probability of the difference between these two groups' mean scores occurring by chance to be less than 7 in 10,000. Subanalyses comparing the two types of women who become political wives (the public versus the private women) and the two types that become elected officials (the elected/mediated women versus the elected/personal efficacy women) revealed significant differences as well (Student's t = 2.205; p = .02 and Student's t = 4.67; p = .002, respectively). The only subcategorization comparison which was not significantly different was the division of the dissident political women into revolutionaries and terrorists (Student's t = .797; p = .24). Our biographical data indicate that within the family the terrorists as a group had less activist sex-role models as mothers, but our empirical scale suggests that the revolutionaries did not have substantially more independent mothers than the terrorists.

Mothers' Independence Outside the Home

The second of our indices deals with the mother's independence outside the home. Engaging in political behavior obviously requires considerable activity outside the realm of the private family. The public/political world has traditionally been a male world. To have a mother who would venture into this world, either in its political aspects or simply in its breadwinning areas, is to have a mother who has developed skills and competencies that may not be necessary or developed in the private realm of the nuclear family.

The second index was created from the following four items of factual information: (1) Mothers who kept abreast of socioeconomic and political matters were coded as a "+" whereas those who did not were coded as a "−." Generally, we sought information on whether or not the mother was known to have had conversations about the public world and whether or not she was knowledgeable on such matters. Again, to have knowledge about the world beyond the private realm of the family is to imply that you have a "right" to be concerned with this realm, that it is of interest to you, and that you have some competence in dealing with such matters. Even a liberal definition of "keeping abreast" so as to include any mention of the mother's concern with the public realm resulted in only 52 percent of the twenty-nine mothers receiving a positive score on this item, which turned out to be the "easiest" for the women to have achieved.

(2) The mother was given a "+" if she had a regular job or career commitment during her life. She was given a "−" if she either did not work or worked intermittently at part-time jobs due solely to dire need. The need hierarchy of Maslow is pertinent to the classifications we have used on this item. We believe there is a vast difference between the psychological effects of a career obtained and worked at because of its growth-inspiring characteristics and a job at which one must work because of the fear of "starvation" or material gain only. Women who have regular jobs both because of the desire for an increased family income and because of the widening effects on their personal life-space and their sense of control are more likely to feel competent of providing for themselves. They are more likely to look upon the outside world as an environment in which they can fend for themselves and for which they have developed the problem-solving, cognitive, managerial, and other skills necessary to be successful. As such they are likely to pass this attitude on to their daughters for whom they are an immediately present and recognizable role model. Using this definition of a career commitment, only 24 percent qualified to receive a "+."

(3) Mothers were given a "+" if they had been a member of any type of public organization including religious ones. Attendance at church services was not sufficient to merit a "+," however. Only those women for whom a specific organizational link beyond simple attendance at church services was explicitly cited were given a positive mark. On this item of public organization membership and participation, only 21 percent of the mothers were credited with a "+."

Finally, (4) the mother was given a "+" if she had a career

before her marriage to her husband. She is given a "−" if she did not. In some ways this repeats the earlier item but with the important addition that the competencies she achieved were achieved at an earlier age and thus more likely to have been indicative of her personal independence and upbringing. The generational implications of this are self-evident. We assume that somewhat independent grandmothers are likely to produce somewhat more independent mothers, who in turn create more independent daughters. In our study only 7 percent of the twenty-nine mothers for whom data were available could be credited with having achieved an independent career before marriage.

Our index of "Mothers' Independence Outside the Home" was developed to assess whether or not a relationship exists between the mother's activities outside the traditional roles of wife and mother and the daughter's adult political behavior. As was the case with the first index, this index is composed of a number of items (4), leads to an acceptable ordinal scale (C.R. = .94; C.S. = .69), and allows us to arrive at scale types ranging from "0" for the least independent to "3" for the most independent.

The fact that the objective procedures of Guttman scalogram analysis produced another acceptable scale lends support to our supposition that we indeed have isolated two relatively consistent patterns. It is also noteworthy that this scale of independence outside the family found fewer cases of women meeting the criteria for independence just as our theory would suggest. This fact supports our belief that these summary indices should not be dismissed lightly. Moreover, the index scores of the twenty-nine mothers were compared to one another. Thus, for example, Eleanor Roosevelt's mother scored as a type four on the index for independence of the mothers within the family structure and as a type one on the index of mothers' independence outside the home. Utilizing "gamma" as a measure of association we found the two indices resulted in a gamma of .48. Although there is a relationship between the two indices, they do not duplicate the same dimension. Each facet of independence is separately noteworthy. Most of the relationship between the two indices is due to the fact that those mothers who were dependent outside the home were also the mothers who tended to be dependent within the home.

Figure 5-2 provides a graphic depiction of the results of our analysis of the mothers' independence outside the home. As was

Figure 5-2
Mothers' Scores on Scale of Extent of Their Independence
Outside the Home

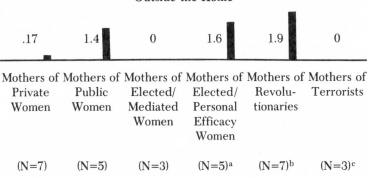

| .17 | 1.4 | 0 | 1.6 | 1.9 | 0 |

Mothers of Private Women	Mothers of Public Women	Mothers of Elected/ Mediated Women	Mothers of Elected/ Personal Efficacy Women	Mothers of Revolu- tionaries	Mothers of Terrorists
(N=7)	(N=5)	(N=3)	(N=5)[a]	(N=7)[b]	(N=3)[c]

a. The mothers of Thatcher and Griffiths are excluded due to lack of information.
b. The mothers of Edib and Gonne are excluded because they died.
c. Corday's mother died; Zasulich was given away to relatives to be raised. Both mothers are excluded.

the case with the index of the independence of the mother within the home, the hypothesized directions continue to be strong. The elected/personal efficacy group and the revolutionaries clearly were most likely to have had mothers who had achieved comfortableness in the external, public, "masculine" sphere. Next in having arrived at some level of entrance into this nonfamily domain were the mothers of the public women. The scores of the mothers of the private traditional women, the elected/mediated women, and the terrorists continue to be very similar—extremely low. Thus the trends remain strong.

As in the case of the data on the Mothers' Independence Within the Home, we applied the Student's t test to help probe the meaning of the distributions. As before, the simple comparison of the mothers by grouping the daughters according to their traditional/nontraditional behavior (the wives of famous men versus being a political actor in one's own right) was not significant (Student's t = 1.15; p = .13). However, the comparison of private women versus public women (Student's t = 2.299; p = .03), of elected/mediated versus elected/personal efficacy women (Student's t = 6.53; p = .001) and of revolutionaries versus terrorists (Student's t = 11.20; p = .0002) all resulted in significant differences. The more independent, publicly achieving women in each of the subcomparisons had more activist mothers. As Figure 5-2 and the Student's t test show, the revolutionaries and the terrorists differed the most from each other. The revolutionaries had mothers who were independent both within the family and outside the home. The terrorists had mothers who had a degree of independence within the family but little or no control over their life-space in the wider external world.

If one compares the data on Figure 5-1 with that of 5-2, some very important behavioral manifestations of the socialization process, particularly the impact of the mother, become noticeable. Throughout, the private women have had a role model to imitate that afforded them very little chance to aspire to compete with men in either the family or the public sphere of life. Their mothers tended to be neither independent within the family nor independent outside the home. It is little wonder that their daughters were not.

One of the anomalies of Figure 5-1 is the extent of the independence of the mothers of the public women in the home sphere. They scored as high as the mothers of achieving political women and revolutionaries! What then explains their reluctance to become full political participants? Figure 5-2 provides some insight on this question, for it indicates that, though the mothers of these public women may have been more independent within the home, they tended not to acquire the skills and competencies associated with the external world as did the mothers of the elected/personal efficacy and revolutionary women. In short, as our biographical data reveal, these women had demonstrated fewer of the prerequisites of public life for their daughters to imitate. The mothers continued to utilize male mediation as the primary mode of relating to the wider world. Independence in the private world of the family had not been converted into a need for personal control and independent competencies in the public world. Their daughters seemingly continued to accept this model of mediation by males relative to the political world.

Figure 5-2 is also very helpful in explaining the adult behavioral patterns of the elected/mediated women and the terrorists. Our theory would predict that the traditional private-woman types of political wives would have mothers who were not independent in their relationships outside the home. We have also suggested that the elected/mediated group would have had similar mothers. We would anticipate this nonindependence as a factor producing their acceptance of the mediation of males in their political behavior for such long periods of time. It would take some major resocialization during adult life to alter this mother-influence. The mediated/elected women literally continue to see their husbands, as long as they live, as the appropriate mediators between themselves and the world. They may be independent and equal to their husbands at home; but they do not see a way of transforming this into external competence and independence. Only after a long adult internship, in which the skills so easily acquired in youth are laboriously learned, do these women achieve a sense of personal efficacy in the political realm. Adult resocialization is much more difficult to accomplish ("You can't teach an old dog new tricks") and only an extreme and unusual convergence of structural opportunities seems to encourage this acquisition of skills.

The score of the terrorists' mothers is very similar, even if somewhat surprising. We would have logically anticipated that the terrorists, being in our achieving political category, would have had mothers similar to the revolutionaries on this scale of independence outside the home. Yet as our narrative above noted and as this scale depicts, the mothers of the terrorists are as opposite from the mothers of the revolutionaries as are the mothers of the private women. The terrorists themselves are similar to the revolutionaries in not having developed the traditional sex-role ideology but different from the revolutionaries in not having been given an alternative, positive female model to emulate. Almost all the mothers of the revolutionaries were unusually competent, atypical women, distinct, respected persons in their own right. All were admired and loved by their husbands. The same was not true for the mothers of the terrorists. In spite of the fact that the terrorists' mothers demonstrated some independence in the home, it was primarily when the husband was absent or in self-defense against his unjust beatings that they manifested this independence. What the terrorists lacked, and what the revolutionaries had, were role models who had achieved control over their personal life-space, extended it to include the public realm, and offered an example of how to behave in the public realm.

Rollo May (among others) has noted that it is often a sense of powerlessness and frustration that contributes to violence. The turning to personal acts of violence by our five terrorists does seem to be a form of frustration-aggression. The five terrorists studied seemed to want to change their sex role and behavior to a more "masculine" model. The lack of knowledge and competence to accomplish this change seems to have been a major factor motivating their violent deeds.

The importance of the competence dimension is seen further in Figure 5-2 in a direct comparison of the elected/mediated women and the terrorists. Both have quite traditional, dependent mothers in terms of the public and political realms. But key differences exist between these two types of women in the ages at which they began their independent political careers. The terrorists began quite young, usually in their teens. The elected/mediated women were married first to political men who used them as their helpmates. The husbands taught them how to compete and deal with the existing political system. A certain faith in men and the existing structure is presupposed by this behavior. These elected/mediated women began their own careers usually in their mid-thirties as mature, reasonably competent individuals. As will be demonstrated in the next chapter, the terrorists tended to hate their fathers and at least disrespect if not dislike men. The low proportion of terrorists who had fathers who viewed their mothers as equal human beings undoubtedly contributed to this lack of trust in men. In any case the combination of not having a female role model for nontraditional behavior and the dislike of males sharply reduced the likelihood that the terrorists would gain the competencies needed to engage in more "acceptable" political behavior. The revolutionaries not only had unusual role models representing competence and skills, but also had mothers who loved and respected their fathers and who were loved and respected in turn. Hence, both mother and father were able to contribute to the development of skills and competencies in these revolutionaries.

Figure 5-2 when combined with 5-1 also adds a new insight into the personal/political efficacy group and the revolutionaries. Time and time again these two groups have had the most similar traits. Both groups had mothers who were not only likely to have been independent within the home but were also comfortable in and capable of meeting the requirements of the public world. In this case the difference in their revolutionary and nonrevolutionary behavior appears to be due to the type of society and political system in which they lived. The personally efficacious, elected political women lived their lives in a time, culture, and society that recognized that women could make legitimate demands on the political system and could even fill elite positions in the political hierarchy. The revolutionaries—except for Angela Davis—did not. There is little doubt that had they done so and had they desired, they too could have been elected to the legislative bodies, cabinet posts, prime ministerships, and so on. Indeed, after their revolutions succeeded, many who still lived did hold major political positions in the new governments (for example, Kollontai, Markievicz, and La Pasionaria).

The lives of our thirty-six women clearly lead one to conclude that the adult behavior of the mother is strongly related to the daughter's adult political behavior. Because of the qualitative nature of our study, such a conclusion is obviously tentative. Repeated confirmation of such patterns and relationships is needed for such conclusions to be fully persuasive. A study conducted in 1974 by Roberta Sigel using a stratified, random sample of high school seniors attending the public schools of the Commonwealth of Pennsylvania provides one such empirical support. In her analysis she found few differences between 746 high school girls and boys in terms of their levels of political interest, levels of participation, plans for being active in politics in the future, their political evaluations, orientations, and issue preferences. The vast majority of both sexes seemed to feel political salience at the level of civic obligation. About 14 percent of the sample (105 youths) scored one full standard deviation above the average on the index of political salience, however. Of these most politicized adolescents 65 were boys (17 percent of all the boys studied) and 40 were girls (11 percent of all the girls studied). In 1974, in the public schools of Pennsylvania at least, boys still were more politicized than girls.

On the basis of a special subanalysis of this subsample of 105, Sigel concluded that "politicized girls are truly different from other girls in a great variety of ways. In this difference they also vary greatly from boys."[61] The politicized boys, however, did not seem to differ markedly from the less politicized boys. The major family difference that Sigel found between the politicized girls and boys and between the politicized and unpoliticized girls was whether or not the mother was a housewife—primarily what we have called a private woman—or a professional, career woman, which would correspond to our public woman or achieving woman with latent personal political efficacy (see Figure 2-2). As we have found in our qualitative analysis of thirty-six women in politics, Sigel found that the private type of working mother (the nonprofessional working in skilled or unskilled labor or in clerical and sales fields) raised an insignificant proportion (6 percent) of their daughters to be politicized. In contrast, the proportion of the daughters of professional women who were politicized was substantially higher—30 percent of all the daughters they produced. Just as we, Sigel also found that "No such relationships obtain for fathers' occupation and/or status."[62]

The point we have been stressing about the critical significance of the adult behavior of the same-sex parent—the mother —for female political socialization is also borne out by Sigel's empirical analysis of the relationship of the mother's occupation and the politicization of senior high school boys. She found that among the boys, regardless of the level of politicization, about forty-four percent had mothers working in semiskilled or unskilled trades while twenty-two percent had mothers in the professions. The mothers' private or public nature has no meaningful effect on the political socialization of boys, but it is a determining factor for girls!

Support in the Sigel data also exists for our contention that a mother's educational attainment alone is not a strong factor in the politicization of girls. Although almost twice as many politicized compared to unpoliticized girls had mothers with at least a college education, the actual percentage differences were very small (15 and 8 percent respectively). In contrast, among these daughters with college-educated mothers, 83 percent of the politicized girls had professionally active public women for mothers while only 25 percent of the nonpoliticized girls had such mothers.[63] The contrast between the political socialization of girls who have private and public types of women for mothers is also illustrated by Sigel's finding that "Among college graduate professional mothers 45 percent have politicized daughters; among similarly educated housewives the percentage drops to 15!"[64] Although the number of cases of politicized girls was small for these analyses in Sigel's study, both our study and Sigel's suggest that the sex-role ideology manifested by the mother, not her educational level nor her domestic dominance, is the key factor linking family structure and parental behavior to the political socialization of girls.

Distance from the Mother

According to Lynn, daughters will develop a more problem-solving, activist sex role and cognitive style of thinking if the appropriate sex-role becomes a problem, i.e., something to be deciphered rather than blindly imitated.[65] He argues that such problem-solving cognitive styles and activism will develop the less close girls are to their mothers, assuming, of course, they are not extremely distant emotionally from their mothers. The extreme emotional distance could lead to cognitive disorganization even though it might still lead to a nontraditional sex-role preference. In an effort to address this problem of distance from the mother we developed a rough estimate of how emotionally close each woman was to her mother. This estimate was based upon a scale of 1 to 10 with "10" being the closest. Subjects whose mothers died before they were four were excluded. An estimate of "5" was used if the relationship seemed normally close, neither great love nor hate. The pattern of scores of these admittedly rough estimates was generally as expected: the revolutionaries as a group were least close to their mothers, receiving a composite score of 3.7. Because their mothers were so involved in the public realm, working, or directing major social functions, they were not available to their daughters as much as most of the other mothers were. The elected/personal efficacy group came next with a 4.5 composite score; the public women had 4.5; the private women had 5.0; and the elected/mediated women had the highest composite score of 5.7, which again helps to explain why they remained relatively traditional for such a long period of their lives. The terrorists have no composite score because all had extreme love-hate complexes about their mothers, or they had no mothers at all while growing up.

The two revolutionaries and two terrorists whose mothers died before they were four also were not extremely close to the governesses, grandmothers, or nuns who raised them (Corday, Zasulich, Edib, and Gonne). The process of figuring out what being a woman meant was obviously not a simple task of imitation for them. The two women who were rejected by their mothers—Goldman and Breshko-Breshkovskaia—also saw the definition of their sex role as a problem. And Perovskaia, whose mother suffered physical beatings at the hands of her father, learned early that the traditional sex role of her mother was not for her. The question of what sex role she should adopt obviously was a problem for her too. Hence, although she was extremely close to her mother, the closeness along with the mother's extreme difficulties and dissatisfaction with her own sex role and position clearly led Perovskaia to seek some other mode of behavior than that offered by her mother.

In sum, Lynn's proposition, that atypical, more "masculine" behavior for females will be more likely when sex-role identification itself becomes a problem, is clearly supported. The case of Perovskaia suggests that the key variable is not the "distance" between the mother and daughter, but rather whether or not sex-role identification becomes a problem. Clearly other factors than "distance" can create this problem.

A subcomponent of this hypothesis on distance from the mother is that those who were most distant and experienced physical brutality in early childhood would tend to be the agitators and terrorists; Corday, Zasulich, Goldman, Perovskaia, and Ch'iu Chin contemplated or actually attempted to assassinate establishment figures. Two, Corday and Zasulich, were raised with little or no wife/mother sex-role influence, but also with no recorded physical brutality. Corday was raised in a convent. Zasulich was raised by "strangers" as she called them and a French governess. Although her mother was alive, she was most distant. Goldman's mother was alive, and quite distant. She never interfered when the father beat their daughter. Goldman's situation clearly fits the hypothesis that great distance and childhood brutalization spawn an inclination toward violence. Perovskaia's childhood clearly does not. She passionately loved her mother and was exceptionally close to her. In addition, it was not Perovskaia herself who was frequently beaten by the father, but the mother. Ch'iu Chin does not seem to have been physically brutalized either. On the contrary, she was one of the most loved and pampered of all the subjects. The chief brutalization inflicted upon her by her parents was forcing her to marry against her will in her early teens.

It seems that our hypothesis as stated is incorrect. While three of the five terrorists were distant from their mothers, only one can be said to have suffered physical brutality while at home. Becoming a female agitator or a terrorist might be related to distance from the mother, but it does not seem to be directly related to having suffered physical abuse as a child. It seems more closely related to having a mother with few skills and competencies in coping with the "male" world, that is, in not having a viable alternative female role model to emulate once the traditional one has been rejected.

Sex-Role Learning: The Fathers

As the bulk of the discussion on the mothers indicates, we believe the major impact of the fathers on the sex-role ideology of the women studied was indirect. The father's relationship to and attitude toward the mother exhibits to the child an immediate image of the "proper position" and value of women vis-à-vis men. The father provides immediate rewards and punishments to both the mother and daughter for specific sex-role behavior. Although daughters do not seem to imitate the sex-role of their fathers, they certainly do seem to reflect upon how the father and the mother interact and whether or not the sex-role behavior of the mother is rewarded by the father and is rewarding and satisfying to the mother. Not through imitation of their fathers but through cognitive reflection upon the father's interaction with and response to the mother did the young girls learn what it is to be female and how to relate to men and their world—the public arena.

There are many reasons why a woman can be independent. The death of one's spouse obviously makes for greater independence, but this type of independence is not of interest to us. As was pointed out earlier, widowhood may lead to maternal dominance in the family, but it says nothing about whether or not the woman is able to act independently and competently within the family structure or outside of it. What we need to know is whether or not these mothers were able to be independent in the presence of the husband or only when and because he was absent. A daughter's perception of the female sex-role will obviously differ depending upon the answer to this question.

According to the biographical data we reviewed, only one of the fathers of the private women was absent frequently. In addition, only one of the fathers of the elected/mediated women was often absent. The other public and achieving political women, including the terrorists, tended to have fathers who were absent more frequently. It is evident from the narrative data above that the mothers of the terrorists studied were independent primarily when they were away from their husbands. Perhaps a source of the difference in the adult behavior of our achieving political women and our terrorists is that the latter learned that female independence required the absence of a male, while the former learned that women could be independent in meaningful ways even when males were present.

For a more general assessment of the father-mother relationship, we attempted to discern from the biographical material whether or not the father viewed the mother as an equal human being. Our explicit concern was "human being," not that they played equal roles, earned identical incomes, and so on. With regard to the public women, the elected/personal efficacy women, and the revolutionaries, the pattern remains about the same. Almost all of the mothers of these women seemed to be viewed as equal human beings by their husbands. The mothers of one-half of the private women were viewed by their husbands as equal persons. Only one of the mothers of the mediated group and none of the terrorists' mothers seemed to be perceived as equal human beings by their husbands.

This material adds the attitudinal dimension of how much the mother appeared to be valued and respected by the father as a person. Figure 5-1 measures objective behavior and actual status and position regardless of how she was valued and respected. The contrast between the score of 1.7 of the mothers of the terrorists, on the scale of their independence within the family structure, and the seeming total lack of respect shown them by their husbands, the terrorists' fathers, suggests that an image inconsistency existed. On the one hand, the mothers of the terrorists exhibited some independence; on the other hand, they were not respected, much less considered as equals by the fathers. Such inconsistencies must cause a girl-child to pause, to wonder about her own value as a person. If the child thinks about the problem at all, such inconsistency is likely to lead to at least a partial rejection of the sex-role model the mother offers. The biographical data on terrorists shows this was true for them.

A critical assumption about the development of achieving political women is that the relationship of their parents was based upon at least equal footing and that the father did not dominate his wife in the home. A major subcomponent is that the fathers of these women will view their work as interesting and fun, more than just a job. This attitude will accomplish several things for the development of the daughter: (1) it will indicate that the external world is not a threatening place, that it is a place where one can demonstrate skills and abilities, enjoy oneself, and accomplish goals; and (2) it will tend to deflect the father's interests and energies away from the family, giving the mother greater freedom and independence. After reviewing the biographical material relevant to these matters, we concluded that the pattern of relationships is generally in the direction stated. Only two of the traditional private women had fathers who seemed to have a positive attitude toward their work. The terrorists also had a low proportion of such fathers. The elected/personal efficacy women, the public women, and the revolutionaries clearly had a higher proportion of fathers with positive attitudes toward their jobs and/or careers than the others. Support is thus evident for the view that a father's sense of personal control is related to his children's (here his daughter's) sense of personal control over their life-space and their willingness to engage in the public, political world.

Birth Order, Sex of Siblings, and Sex-Role Development

Studies of birth order have tended to show that the personalities of the oldest, middle, and youngest children in a family are likely to be different.[66] Studies of achievement have also suggested that first-born children, particularly sons, tend to be among society's outstanding achievers in undue proportions.[67] Altus also found a higher proportion of first-borns compared to later-borns were in college; Toman found first-borns were more concerned with achievement; and Cushna found an overrepresentation of first-borns at higher I.Q. levels.[68] Such findings might suggest we ought to hypothesize that there will be a larger proportion of first-borns or only children among our political women. However, other, usually more recent, studies strongly call into question the above findings and, as importantly, note that birth order is not a particularly useful variable when examined in isolation. The effects of birth order vary dramatically with family size, sex of siblings, social class, the family's values, the mother-father relationship, the mother's relationship to her own mother, and so on.[69] For example, with regard to family size, Nichols found that the positive effects associated with first-borns were more likely to be observed in families with three children than in families of two, four, or five children.[70] With regard to the effect of the sex of siblings, Altus reports that in two-child families both male and female first-borns with younger brothers are significantly more intelligent than those with younger sisters.[71] Yet Hodges and Ballow found that boys with learning difficulties tended to have more brothers than sisters.[72] Smelser and Stewart found that the generalization that first-borns go to college more often held only when the younger sibling was of the opposite sex.[73]

More important for our own study is the fact that the findings on birth order are not the same for males and females. To illustrate, a preference for greater complexity has been found to exist among first-born rather than later-born males, but that later-born females preferred such complexity, not first-born females.[74] McCandless and Evans also note that among "only three even tentative generalizations" which can be derived from the massive studies of birth order is the one asserting that "first-born women seem especially attracted to the company of others in a threatening situation."[75] The same generalization was not applicable to first-born men. In addition, many studies of the first-born or only female children reveal such individuals to be very traditionally socialized and desirous of a traditional female role. Kammeyer stresses that first-born girls are "conservators of tradition."[76] Sutton-Smith and Rosenberg report that girls without siblings are more "feminine" than girls with siblings.[77]

Because being a political achiever has not been a traditional value for females, we question whether or not any logical reason for assuming a relationship between birth order and female political achievement exists. In terms of traditional Western cultural standards it makes as much sense to hypothesize that the private women who married the presidents and prime ministers would perceive themselves and be perceived by the public as being the female achievers rather than the women who acted independently politically. The political wives are among the "most admired" in America because they have married men who were achievers in the "male" world. These women have the residual status of being achievers in the female world. The achieving political women we studied are achievers but from a traditional perspective they are deviants from the prescribed female sex role.

To resolve the question about birth order for our sample we

grouped the women studied into those who were only children or first-born versus those who were later-born. We found no discernible pattern that would fit any hypothesis discussed. For the various subgroups of achieving political women a majority were clearly younger members of their families but so also were the other women. To illustrate, only Mary Wilson of the private women was the oldest; she was the only child. Among the personal efficacy group of political women, Indira Gandhi and Ella Grasso were not only the oldest but they also were the only child in their families. At least in the case of Indira Gandhi the nontraditional and nonconforming behavior she displayed relative to her culture was not necessarily a violation of the norms of her own family. As an only child she could hardly escape the impact of her highly politicized family. Birth order in her case might have been the determinant of the degree to which she was the conservator and the perpetuator of the unique family tradition. In general, the data on this sample of women do not suggest that birth order and female political achievement are directly related.

Some scholars have suggested that anticipation of the mother role reduces political participation.[78] Older daughters, particularly first-born daughters, tend to receive more training for the mother role as children than other siblings because they have often been compelled to be mother-surrogates for younger brothers and sisters. Given the controversy over the relationship between motherhood and female political behavior, we examined the mother-surrogate question among our subjects. All of the women but one (Pat Nixon) who were mother-surrogates were among the elected women. Being a substitute mother as the result of being an older sister did not seem to be an impediment to these women's political behavior. Interesting, but without any clear meaning, is the fact that none of the revolutionaries or terrorists ever played the mother-surrogate role.

As was already noted, the sex of one's siblings is considered critical for sex-role development. According to Lynn, girls with brothers are likely to develop a more "masculine" sex-role preference and behavioral pattern than girls without brothers.[79] Since masculinity is usually associated with political behavior, we hypothesized that a higher percentage of the achieving political women would tend to have brothers than the nonpolitical women. Such is clearly not the case. Only seven (30 percent) of the twenty-three revolutionaries, terrorists, and elected women with personal efficacy had brothers. Five of these were revolutionaries. Of the fourteen traditional, private, public, and elected/mediated women, nine (64 percent) had brothers. We also sought to see if these women had older brothers. Again, the elected women with personal efficacy had none! One terrorist, one public woman, and three of eight (37 percent) revolutionaries had older brothers. The groups having older brothers were the traditional private women (67 percent) and the elected/mediated women (67 percent).

Having brothers, particularly older brothers, seems to retard a woman's entrance into intensive, elite political activity, not to encourage it! It is possible that when brothers exist, they are raised to be the political beings. How likely is it that Indira Gandhi would have become prime minister if she had had an older brother who wanted to follow in Nehru's footsteps? Having no brothers probably provides an opportunity structure for girls. Absence of brothers removes an important obstacle to female political participation: a male who is supposed to act for her. If politics were inherently "masculine," the pattern here would be reversed. Culture and socialization processes make politics appear to be "masculine."

Peers and Sex-Role Development

Because of their greater distance from their mothers, we have predicted that the politically active women will have turned to peer groups for solving the problem of sex-role development to a greater extent than the private or the public women. These peers will have encouraged an expanded life-space for the girls and will have broadened the girls' interest in politics. Unfortunately, few biographical sources on women examine peer groups in the same way that is done in survey research studies or even in biographies on men. Hence, we found it impossible to systematically address questions about the effect of peers on sex-role development. We have no way of judging whether the absence of references to the effect of peer groups is because of the general lack of influence they had, which would be what Lynn predicts, or whether it is another accepted omission from studies on women. In any case our overall impression is that for the private and elected/mediated women, the traditional sex-role ideology was held by all the socializing agents: the family, school, church, and peer groups. For the other political women and the public women, a more mixed picture emerges. Our impression, but it is only an impression, is that the peers of these women were likely to hold a less traditional sex-role ideology.

Conclusion

On the basis of the thirty-six women examined, it seems clear that the development of an activist sex-role ideology is a prerequisite for adult female political behavior. It also seems clear that the type and extent of independence of the mother and the scope and spheres in which she attempted to exercise her independence and personal control are critical for determining if, when, and how a girl will try to engage in elite political behavior. The women we studied who had not had mothers who were reasonably independent at least within an intact family structure were not likely to be among the independent political actors. If the mother, however, had been independent not only within the family but also outside the family, acting competently in the external, "masculine" world, the daughter demonstrated a strong tendency to become an independent political being.

The biographical data analyzed suggest that the concern with maternal and paternal dominance as the key for political socialization of girls is misplaced. Our study suggests that equal, symmetrical conjugal power relationships will be more conducive to female political participation than either maternal or paternal dominance. Additionally, the critical importance of the mother's competence in dealing with the public world cannot be overstressed. Up to this time the literature on political socialization has been extraordinary for the commonness of the finding that almost no variables examined seemed to help explain female political participation or female sense of political efficacy. We believe we have demonstrated, at least in part, why this constant "finding" has prevailed. Almost none of the literature of political socialization has seriously looked at the competencies and skills of the mother outside the home. Langton, whose contributions have drawn attention to the importance of the mother for political attitudes in the modern family, missed this basic insight. This oversight has occurred, we believe, because of the common assumption that the woman's place is in the home: if she is to become competent and independent, she does so only within the home. Within this ideological framework the question "Who's boss in the family?" seems relevant. Our study as well as Langton's shows that the political ramifications of such "maternal dominance" for girls are slight. The key to a woman's participation in politics is her mother's competence within the family structure *as well as* in the public world as an equal with males. We also were struck with how much the mothers of the elected women with personal political efficacy and the revolutionaries were admired and respected by their husbands. These mothers were not placed on a pedestal and overly protected or slighted as persons. On the contrary, the husbands encouraged these mothers' efforts to express themselves and to become involved in the public realm. Their daughters obviously grew up in a psychological environment quite different from that of the private women, the elected/mediated women, and the terrorists.

Sex-role identification with the same-sex parent has always been considered critical in political socialization literature for males. Why else do we study the occupation, education, income, status, and behavior of the father? Our mistake to date has not been in examining these variables, but rather in assuming that politics was essentially "masculine" and that, hence, the father's behavior and achievements were as critical for his daughter as for his son. They are obviously important, but in more complicated, indirect ways than previously conceived. Their importance for the daughter must be first filtered through the effect the father and his behavior have on the mother and the sex-role ideology held by the family. It is the mother's occupation, education, income, status, and behavior that directly affect the political socialization of the daughter.

It should be stressed that we are not asserting that a one-to-one correspondence between the mother and daughter exists. The role modeling, imitation, and identification that we have described do *not* involve political values, attitudes, beliefs, specific role expectations, or other substantive aspects of what is usually studied under the topics of cognitive and affective political socialization. The socialization described in this chapter is more basic: it concerns basic world views about oneself and how one relates to and is likely to be valued by the rest of the world. Such learning is the foundation for other cognitive and affective learning, particularly of a political nature. To a considerable extent, the mother-daughter patterns we have found represent learning of a psychomotor nature. Historically girls have been taught that careers and political activity are not possible for wives and mothers: procedures or methods for balancing the two roles have not been taught to girls. Although the mothers of our achieving political women did not seem to consciously teach their daughters how to blend a public life with the wife/mother role, most of the mothers were in fact doing just that by the type of lives they led. In other words, what we may have identified here is a form of psychomotor socialization that is a prerequisite for elite female political behavior. Women (and men) must not only desire a public life; they must also know how to manage their private affairs so that a public life is possible. Girls who have mothers who are already successfully combining private and public roles can learn the "how to" process by imitating their mothers, perhaps even unconsciously. Other daughters must find a sex-role model other than their own mothers; or they must "re-create the wheel." The daughter of a private woman will probably also have to fight against her mother ideologically just to try to have a career. Techniques for combining multiple roles and tasks will not be suggested by such mothers; they are likely to be suggested by mothers already engaged in public roles. It is the daughters of women with a modern sex-role ideology and competence in blending the private and public roles who have the best chance of becoming achieving political women.

Notes

1. Robert Hess and Judith Torney, *The Development of Political Attitudes in Children* (Chicago: Aldine-Atherton, 1967), pp. 100–106.

2. Kenneth P. Langton, *Political Socialization* (London: Oxford University Press, 1969), p. 51.

3. Ibid., Chapter Two, esp. p. 38.

4. Ibid., p. 51.

5. Ibid., p. 38.

6. See Chapter Four of this work for a more detailed discussion of this question.

7. Langton, pp. 50–51.

8. Stanley Renshon, *Psychological Needs and Political Behavior: A Theory of Personality and Political Efficacy* (New York: The Free Press, 1974), p. 130.

9. Langton, Chapter Two.

10. David B. Lynn, *Parental and Sex-Role Identification: A Theoretical Formulation* (Berkeley, Calif.: McCutchen Publishers Co., 1969).

11. Ibid., p. 98.

12. Shirley Matile Miller, "Effects of Maternal Employment on Sex

Role Perception, Interest, and Self-Esteem in Kindergarten Girls," *Developmental Psychology* 11 (1975): 405–406. See also Lois Wladis Hoffman, "Early Childhood Experiences and Women's Achievement Motives," *Journal of Social Issues* 28 (1972): 129ff.

13. S. R. Vogel, I. K. Broverman, D. M. Broverman, F. Clarkson, and P. S. Rosenkrantz, "Maternal Employment and Perception of Sex Roles Among College Students," *Developmental Psychology* 3 (1970): 384–391.

14. Grace K. Baruch, "Maternal Influences upon College Women's Attitudes Toward Women and Work," *Developmental Psychology* 6 (1972): 32–37.

15. Jean Lipman-Blumen, "How Ideology Shapes Women's Lives," *Scientific American* 226 (January 1972): 34–42.

16. Lynn, p. 101.

17. Ibid., p. 102.

18. Ibid., pp. 105–106.

19. Ibid., p. 106.

20. Kenneth Kammeyer, "Birth Order and the Feminine Sex Role Among College Women," *American Sociological Review* 31 (1966): 508–515.

21. Lynn, p. 107.

22. Pauline Frederick, *Ten First Ladies of the World* (New York: Meredith Press, 1967), p. 59.

23. Alden Hatch, *Red Carpet for Mamie* (New York: Henry Holt and Co., 1954), p. 24.

24. Svetlana Alliluyeva, *Twenty Letters to a Friend*, trans. Priscilla Johnson McMillan (New York: Harper & Row, 1967), p. 42.

25. Ibid., p. 45.

26. Ibid., p. 43.

27. Ibid., p. 44.

28. Ibid.

29. Alfred Steinberg, *The Man from Missouri: The Life and Times of Harry S. Truman* (New York: G. P. Putnam's Sons, 1962), p. 36.

30. Bert Cochran, *Harry Truman and the Crisis Presidency* (New York: Funk and Wagnalls, 1973), p. 41.

31. Steinberg, p. 249.

32. Lady Bird Johnson, *A White House Diary* (New York: Holt, Rinehart and Winston, 1970), p. 38.

33. Kenneth G. Richards, *Eleanor Roosevelt* (Chicago: Children's Press, 1968), pp. 36–41.

34. Mary Van Rensselaer Thayer, *Jacqueline Bouvier Kennedy* (Garden City, N.Y.: Doubleday, 1961), p. 22.

35. Christopher Sykes, *Nancy: Life of Lady Astor* (New York: Harper & Row, 1972), p. 22.

36. Ibid.

37. Sullivan questionnaire.

38. Ibid.

39. Frank Graham, Jr., *Margaret Chase Smith: Woman of Courage* (New York: The John Day Co., 1964), p. 18.

40. Ibid.

41. Golda Meir, *My Life* (New York: Putnam, 1975), p. 15.

42. Ibid., p. 32.

43. Ibid.

44. Krishan Bhatia, *Indira: A Biography of Prime Minister Gandhi* (New York: Praeger Publishers, 1974), p. 42.

45. Most biographers refer to the many years that Kamala Nehru was in jail; however, specific years are not given. Mary Carras, an associate professor of political science at Rutgers University who is completing a

biography of Indira Gandhi, believes that Nehru spent only three weeks in jail, during January 1931. This supposition was confirmed, October 1976, by the prime minister's secretariat of the government of India.

46. Bhatia, p. 40.

47. Shirley Chisholm, *Unbought and Unbossed* (Boston: Houghton Mifflin, 1970), pp. 17–18.

48. Ibid., p. 24.

49. Ibid., p. 25.

50. Grasso questionnaire.

51. Peggy Lamson, *Few Are Chosen* (Boston: Houghton Mifflin Co., 1968), p. 88.

52. Ibid., p. 87.

53. Hope Chamberlain, *A Minority of Members: Women in the U.S. Congress* (New York: Praeger, 1973), p. 262.

54. Bernadette Devlin, *The Price of My Soul* (New York: Knopf, 1969), pp. 6–7.

55. Ibid., p. 45.

56. Maud Gonne MacBride, *A Servant of the Queen* (London: Purnell and Sons, 1938).

57. Michael Young and Peter Willmott, *The Symmetrical Family* (New York: Pantheon Books, 1973).

58. Angela Davis, *An Autobiography* (New York: Random House, 1974), p. 89.

59. Ibid., p. 79.

60. In the early 1940s Louis Guttman, in one of the Social Science Research Council's series on the logic of measurement and prediction, elaborated the basic principles of his scaling technique. Guttman considered an area "scalable if responses to a set of items on that area arranged themselves in certain specified ways." (Samuel A. Stouffer, et

al., *Measurement and Prediction* 4 [New York: John Wiley and Sons, 1950], p. 5.) Critics of the Guttman technique have expressed reservations about the selection of items for scale analysis. Some argue that a preanalysis of the items to be included must be performed. However, most scholars believe that one of the main virtues of Guttman scalogram analysis is that it permits an unbiased, objective, totally quantitative method of identifying unities underlying complex variables. The purpose of the analysis is to remove subjectivity and arbitrariness. For this reason "item analysis procedures are not a necessary part of scale analysis" (Allan Edwards, *Techniques of Attitude Scale Construction* [New York: Appleton-Century Crofts, 1957], p. 178); see also Matilda White Riley, John W. Riley, Jr., and Jackson Toby, *Sociological Studies in Scale Analysis* (New Brunswick, New Jersey: Rutgers University Press, 1954); Glendon Schubert, *Quantitative Analysis of Judicial Behavior* (Glencoe, Ill.: The Free Press, 1959); and Sidney Ulmer, "Scaling Judicial Cases: A Methodological Note," *American Behavioral Scientist* (1961): 31–34.

61.   Roberta S. Sigel, "The Adolescent in Politics: The Case of American Girls," paper presented at the 1975 Annual Meeting of the American Political Science Association, San Francisco, California, September 2–5, p. 7.

62.   Ibid.

63.   Ibid., p. 8. For a broader analysis of the impact of having a mother who works, see Lois N. Hoffman and F. Ivan Nye with Stephen J. Bahr, *Working Mothers: An Evaluative Review of the Consequences for Wife, Husband, and Child* (San Francisco: Jossey-Bass, 1974).

64.   Ibid., p. 9.

65.   Lynn, Chapter Four.

66.   A. Adler, *What Life Should Mean to You* (Boston: Little, Brown and Co., 1931), esp. pp. 144–154; S. Schachter, *The Psychology of Affiliation* (Stanford University Press, 1959); Stanley Renshon, "Birth Order, Personality, and Political Socialization," *New Directions in Political Socialization*, ed. D. Schwartz and S. Schwartz (New York: The Free Press, 1974); E. E. Sampson, "The Study of the Ordinal Position," *Advances in Experimental Personality Research*, ed. B. Mayer (New York: Academic Press, 1964).

67.   J. Kagen and H. Moss, *Birth to Maturity* (New York: John Wiley and Sons, 1962).

68. W. D. Altus, "Sibling Order and Scholastic Aptitude," *American Psychologist* 17 (1962): 304, and "Birth Order and Academic Primogeniture," *Journal of Personality and Social Psychology* 2 (1965): 872–76; W. Toman, *Family Constellation* (New York: Springer, 1969); B. Cushna, "Birth Order and Verbal Mastery," paper presented at the meeting of the American Psychological Association, San Francisco, September 1968.

69. G. Mitchell and L. Schroers, "Birth Order and Parental Experience in Monkeys and Man," *Advances in Child Development and Behavior,* Vol. 8, ed. Hayne W. Reese (New York: Academic Press, 1973), pp. 159–84.

70. Cited in John Nash, *Developmental Psychology: A Psychobiological Approach* (Englewood Cliffs, N.J.: Prentice-Hall, 1970), pp. 453–55.

71. W. D. Altus, "Sibling Order and Scholastic Aptitude," *American Psychologist* 17 (1962): 304.

72. Cited in Nash, *loc. cit.*

73. W. T. Smelser and L. D. Stewart, "Where Are the Siblings? Reevaluation of the Relationship Between Birth Order and College Attendance," *Sociometry* 31 (1968): 294–303.

74. Nash, *loc. cit.*

75. Boyd R. McCandless and Ellis D. Evans, *Children and Youth: Psychosocial Development* (Hinsdale, Ill.: Dryden Press, 1973), pp. 39–40.

76. Kenneth Kammeyer, "Birth Order and the Feminine Sex-Role Among College Women," *American Sociological Review* 31 (August 1966): 508–15.

77. B. Sutton-Smith and B. G. Rosenberg, *The Sibling* (New York: Holt, 1970).

78. For examples of this literature, see Jane S. Jaquette, ed., *Women in Politics* (New York: John Wiley and Sons, 1974), and R. Darcy and Sarah Salvin Schramm, "Woman Types: Differential Responses to Politics," paper presented to the Southern Political Science Association, November 1976, Atlanta, Georgia.

79. Lynn, pp. 84–88.

CHAPTER 6

Development of
Personal Control
and Political Salience

A T THIS STAGE of our theoretical formulation we have identified the type of family structure and the type of mother and/or female model a girl needs in order to develop an activist sex-role ideology—the sine qua non in the development of achieving political women. In this chapter we pursue the second and third stages of the process of the development of achieving political women. Stage two of this development concerns developing a sense of personal control over one's life-space—over one's own activities, environment, and social relations. Stage three concerns the questions of if, when, how, and under what conditions politics becomes salient and relevant to a female's life-space.

Stage Two: Developing a Sense of Personal Control

Like many students of political socialization we believe that the family structure and emotional dynamics within that structure are critical factors in determining who will and who will not participate in political activity. Like Renshon, we argue that the linking factor for both sexes is the extent to which the family permits the child to develop a sense of personal control over his or her life-space.[1] Renshon reports that in his study of college students, more boys than girls possessed a strong sense of personal control over their lives.[2] We would anticipate this finding simply because a relatively small proportion of girls has as yet developed an activist sex-role ideology. One ought not conclude from studies such as Renshon's, however, that this lowered sense of personal control is "normal" in the sense of being the ideal, the standard to be maintained, or inherent in the female sex. We strongly expect to find in our study that the achieving political women will have demonstrated greater personal control over their life-spaces and will have the characteristics of individuals identified by Renshon as having such control.

While the activist sex-role ideology depends for its development upon the relationships between the mother and father and their respective relationships to the world external to the family, the development of a sense of personal control depends upon how the parents (or relevant substitutes) treat the individual as a child and youth.

Children are born with physiological needs that they cannot satisfy without external assistance. As Renshon notes, "the need for personal control originates in the attempt to satisfy these physiological needs, and . . . in the course of attempting to satisfy these needs, the child develops basic beliefs about the controllability of the world in general and his [her] ability to exert control in particular."[3] These basic beliefs about the control and impact one can have on the world then become the basic foundation for later learning about one's potential to participate politically. In effect, the need hierarchy of Maslow has been reintroduced. Until the first level of physiological needs has been fulfilled, the second—that of a sense of security and control— cannot become pertinent. Because of the importance of having control over the physiological level, we will examine the health and physical competence of our women before looking into the personal control issue.

Health and Elite Membership

The Maslowian need hierarchy indicates that one cannot be concerned with a higher level of need if lower need levels are still being only precariously met. In essence, this suggests that women as well as men will not become interested and concerned with political participation unless their biological needs are met and their physical well-being maintained; one is not likely to be concerned with voting if one does not have sufficient food to insure physical survival until the next election.

Because we are studying only members of an elite, it is

highly unlikely that any meaningful variation on available health indicators will appear. To be a member of the elite usually means that some control over the first need level must have already been achieved. Nonetheless, because of its possible importance to the interpretation of the other data, some assessment of our subjects' health is in order. Unless there was a concrete reference in the biographical materials to ill health of the woman as a child or as a young adult, it was assumed that the first need level had been fulfilled. Biographic accounts tend to stress only the more severe forms of ill health. Unusual illnesses, diseases, and ailments having impact upon the person's development were the ones noted.

According to the biographies, all the subjects generally had good health. The women with some record of poor health were Mary Wilson, Eleanor Roosevelt, Clementine Churchill, Nancy Astor, Indira Gandhi, Bernadette Devlin, Rosa Luxemburg, and La Pasionaria. The variations among the six subgroups of women are minimal. The only group with all members in good health as children was the terrorists. Without additional information we can only assume that even the women with poor health as children were able to achieve reasonable physiological certainty and well-being. The illnesses were not such that they could not be overcome or controlled.

Physical Competence, Sports, and Political Women

Within the traditional sex-role ideological framework an interesting contradiction exists relative to women, their attitudes and goals, and their bodies. This contradiction has been described by Jan Felshin as follows:

> Although woman and the female body particularly are conceived as "objects" almost exclusively in an extreme conception of femininity, there are implications for physical behavior. Woman is expected to be passive, of course, but not to the point of being inert; rather, she is encouraged to use her body in wholesome but decorous ways, and to be sexually attractive but not overly suggestive. In other words, role behavior in relation to physicality emanates from the feminine construct. Since it is unacceptable for women to be "masculine," the despised behaviors relate to the use of strength, activity, aggression, and too much bodily competence.[4]

Within the ideological framework alluded to here, women would appear to be required to be concerned with their bodies in two ways: (1) how they conform to societal standards of beauty and to being attractive to men, and (2) how not to get their bodies involved in physical activities that would enhance their "masculine" characteristics and make them competitive with males. Although this notion of femininity has been prevalent throughout the ages, it has not been universal by any means. At least it has been tempered by social customs and human need. Upper-class women have been expected to excel in horseback riding in some societies and in tennis in others. Lower-class women have been compelled to perform hard physical labor on farms and in factories. The conditions of life forced them to deviate from the "ideal" described by Felshin. Nonetheless, it is fair to say that these deviations from the "ideal" were relatively minor. The sports in which women engaged and the work they performed were usually viewed as being supplemental to, not competitive with, those in which their male counterparts engaged.

In the 1970s in the United States major political battles were being fought over whether or not girls should receive equal athletic treatment in the public school and recreational systems. In the past, males—boys and men—have received almost all public funds allocated for sports, particularly competitive sports. As Gerber, Felshin, Berlin, and Wyrich note, "If socialization goals are perceived in relation to maintaining socially defined sex roles, then it is logical to defend sport as a masculine preserve, and to decry the anomaly of women's participation."[5] Because of the political importance of this issue and the fact that participation in competitive sports might be indicative of a greater sense of personal control, we sought to determine if a pattern existed among our thirty-six women in terms of their involvement in competitive sports.

For several reasons we found it difficult to obtain data on the women's participation in sports. For one thing, many of our subjects were born in pre-revolutionary Russia where competitive sports were not at all stressed for women. In addition, not all biographers necessarily have the same interest in this question as we do. Hence, we can only report whether or not the biographical data read reported that the subject participated in competitive sports. We can only assume that such participation would have been sufficiently unusual for girls and women of their times that a biographer would have found it worthy of inclusion.

The results of the analysis showed that thirteen of the thirty-six women had a biographical reference to their participation in competitive sports. However, there was no clear pattern indicating that the political women were participants more than the private or public women. The individuals with references to their participation in competitive sports were: Mary Wilson, Bess Truman, Pat Nixon, Jackie Kennedy, Eleanor Roosevelt, Clementine Churchill, Nancy Astor, Margaret Chase Smith, Ella Grasso, Bernadette Devlin, Halide Edib, Angela Davis, and Constance Markievicz.

Engaging in physical fights is another type of behavior that has traditionally been associated with males. Because of its potential as an indicator of both "aggressiveness" and physical competence, we sought to learn if the achieving political women had more recorded instances of physical fights than the private or public women. Clearly, "ladies" are not given social approval for such activity. As in the case of sports, no clear pattern emerged. Of the six women for whom an instance of a physical fight was recorded, one was a private woman (Bess Truman); two were elected/mediated women (Lady Nancy Astor and Leonor Sullivan); two were in the elected/personal efficacy group (Ella Grasso and Bernadette Devlin); and one was a revolutionary (La Pasionaria). Only the public wives and the terrorists had no member with an instance of a physical fight recorded. The overall pattern is similar to that found on the question of competitive sports. No category had a significantly greater portion of its members having physical fights than another.[6]

Since we are looking for hypotheses for future empirical testing rather than proof, it might be worthwhile drawing attention to the fact that none of the terrorists was among those recorded as having fights. Given the small number of women who had such instances recorded, this fact might mean nothing. However, given the personal physical aggression they displayed as adults, it would be reasonable to assume that some of them should have committed some type of aggression against others in their childhood. But none is noted in their biographies, and no sports activity of a competitive or noncompetitive nature was recorded for them either. In any case, weak as the evidence is, the lack of such physical activity adds another suggestion that the terrorists are rather traditionally socialized women.

More systematic study of the relationship between physical activity, competitive sports, and adult political activity is obviously needed. It seems reasonable to assume that physical activity involving athletic competition between the sexes could lead to girls gaining a greater sense of personal control over their lives. The rules would have to be such, however, that size, strength, and "raw power" would not give one team an edge over the other. When one thinks of the more popular sports in the United States in particular, e.g., football, baseball, basketball, and hockey, one can see what a remarkable ideological revolution in the area of sports would have to occur before such competitions could be composed of male/female teams. There are some signs that people are thinking of such changes. In Minneapolis, Minnesota, for example, married couples have developed competitive games of slow pitch softball with new rules for an old game so that both men and women can play.[7] Family engagement in sports without regard to sex might contribute a great deal to needed social change.

Autonomy as a Child and Youth

If personal control is related to political behavior, then we should find that political women, particularly those in our achieving category, will have been given greater autonomy as children and adolescents than nonpolitical women. That autonomy ought to have been comparable to that given their siblings, particularly brothers, if they had them.

In reading the biographies, we looked for the following pieces of information to conclude that the individual had had autonomy. Could she choose to do things she wanted to do? Were all activities closely supervised by her parents? Was parental consent necessary for all activities recorded? If the answer to the first question was yes and the answer to the last two no, then a positive conclusion was reached to the question in the standard data form, "As a child, was the subject allowed to make decisions for herself?"

Our comparison of the biographical data revealed that a majority of all subgroups had recorded instances of making notable decisions for themselves. Only the private women and the elected/mediated group of women demonstrated lesser autonomy as a group. Although we anticipated this tendency, the differences between the groups are not as sharp as we would have expected. One reason for this lack of variation is that we included references to decison-making up to the age of eighteen. A few examples from the biographies themselves will indicate that for the revolutionaries and the elected/personal efficacy women, the examples of autonomy cited by biographers tended to be in the pre-teen period. The examples for the private women, in particular, tended to come from the late teen period. The later decisions also tended to concern major changes in life such as whom one might marry, or date in anticipation of marriage. The earlier decisions tended to concern where the girl would play as a child and with whom and at what. In developing a sense of personal control it seems reasonable to think that such early practice would have more far-reaching implications for the individual than the making of one major decision near adulthood.

As illustrations of the autonomy granted to the revolutionaries as children, we have selected the women whose mothers worked full-time during most of their childhood: Broido, Kollontai, La Pasionaria, and Davis. Their biographies make clear that as a consequence of their mothers' working they were left to their own devices considerably more than most girls are. Kollontai often commented on how much she was left alone as a little girl, particularly when her father was gone. Broido notes that from the age of four to the age of ten, when her mother was overwhelmed with the business, she was left to herself. She ate a hot meal with the family only when her mother returned home after a long day's work. No one apparently supervised her while her mother was gone. She ran free in the woods, playing with the other children as she desired. Her feelings of independence and her love of freedom never apparently led to any rebellion against her mother nor to any reduction of love and admiration for her. Her mother later even accompanied her to Siberia to the hard-labor prison colonies.

Because La Pasionaria was ill as a child, she did not have to join her brothers and sisters in the coal mines. Instead, she was sent to a day school located over the offices of a jail and a trade union. Although she was supposed to be supervised, the group was a rather rough-and-tumble one with many fights and nasty tricks being played upon the prisoners and other unwary adults. Her life certainly was not as constrained as that of most Spanish girls of her time.

Angela Davis also had more freedom than is typical. She was allowed to attend school in New York City away from her parents at the age of thirteen. To be away at school—not a boarding school—by oneself is not typical for most girls. Even before this time Angela Davis had had an autonomous existence because her mother had always worked and expected her to be a responsible person.

Among the elected/personal efficacy women there are some very prominent examples of unusual autonomy granted to girls. Indira Gandhi at a very early age was often left without any familial supervision. With both her parents often away for political reasons, she had to be more responsible for herself. Golda Meir also was unique in the extent to which she was accustomed to making decisions. Earlier we related how at the age of eleven she organized, ran, and spoke at a fund-raising event for schoolbooks. Additionally, at the age of fourteen she ran away from home to live with her sister in Denver. It was precisely because she was not allowed to do as she wanted and because her mother had tried to prevent her from going to school that she left home. When her sister tried to curtail her freedom and her right to make decisions for herself, she ran away from that environment as well. We could easily multiply the examples of the autonomy experienced by the political women during their early years.

The occasions of autonomous decision-making by the private women are not as numerous or dramatic, but they too can be cited. As already noted, these decisions tend to occur later in the young girls' lives. For example, Bess Truman received a plus for autonomy essentially because she insisted upon continuing to see Harry Truman despite her mother's objections. Golda Meir could have received a plus for a comparable type of decision, but even on matters such as this the contrast in the substance involved is great. To illustrate, Golda Meir dated whomever she wanted. Her expression of autonomy on the marriage question came from her decision to refuse to marry Morris Meir unless he decided to accompany her to Palestine. Because of this considerable variation in quality of the decisions being made and the age differences at which the autonomy was exercised, we tend to believe that more refined measures of autonomy would be more precise than that re-created from biographical data, and would produce findings supportive of the hypothesis we have proposed.

In relation to this question of autonomy we tried to examine the possibility that the achieving political women would have been more autonomous than their brothers or sisters. No differences between our subjects and their siblings seem to have existed. Those women possessing little autonomy as children had siblings who had little; if the women had a lot of autonomy, their siblings did also. Perhaps it is important simply that the women did not have less autonomy. More research is obviously needed.

Consistency of Rule Application

The theoretical framework outlined by Renshon suggests that consistency of rule application is critical for the development of a sense of personal control over one's life-space. In order to have control over one's domain or world, the rest of the world must be reasonably stable and predictable. Hence, we hypothesize that the application of the rules for behavior will have been more consistent within the families of the achieving political women than those of the other women. This hypothesis does not in any way assert that the achieving women were punished less than the other women but rather that regardless of the direction of the treatment, its nature or intensity, the treatment was consistent by each parent. The parents might have treated the child differently, one kindly and one harshly; the point is that each parent treated the child in a predictable fashion. We would anticipate, however, that the child who was treated most similarly by both parents would tend to be the most strongly socialized in whatever direction she ultimately went: traditional or nontraditional.

In trying to compare our thirty-six women on this variable, we sought a specific citation and/or example of the failure of rule consistency in the biographical material. Thus, the benefit of the lack of information was that consistency was assumed.

The pattern that emerges is generally as the hypothesis predicts, but with the type of exceptions that we have now come to expect. The public women, the elected/personal efficacy women, and the revolutionaries were the most likely to have experienced the security of a sense of control over their environment as children. The rules within the family were regularly applied and could lead to an anticipated range of behavior. The case of Eleanor Roosevelt illustrates the type of rule application that was negative in direction at one period, positive during another, yet consistent during both. Eleanor Roosevelt's mother, though negative to the point of diminishing Eleanor's sense of self-worth in several ways, nonetheless was consistent. Later when Roosevelt was at the London boarding school in her late teens the rule application was also consistent though what was being rewarded and punished was somewhat different. In both cases, however, she could put trust and faith in the relevant adults that they would apply the rules the way they did.

Although it is true that the private women, elected/mediated women, and the terrorists experienced less consistency of rule application than the others, the difference is not very great. With the small number of cases all we can say is that the pattern of the subgroupings is in the direction we predicted, but that the evidence is very weak. Again, however, the biographical material suggests that for the terrorists at least, some of the inconsistencies were quite extreme. For example, Ch'iu Chin knew the insecurity of having at one point been encouraged to be as independent and aggressive as her brothers. She was taught to ride horses and to do what they did—until her early teens. Suddenly her parents decided this type of behavior was improper for a young lady. Changing the rules produced an intense emotional crisis. To end their battle and to solve the problem, the parents forced her to marry. How frequently similar types of inconsistency in rule application occur for young girls today we have no idea. But there is a parallelism that exists in the United States where many families encourage their daughters to be tomboys, to compete intellectually and even physically with boys in their pre-teens and early teens, and then expect those same daughters to become "proper young ladies," married to males who continue their childhood pattern while the female is required to stay at home. We are not at all suggesting such girls will grow up to be terrorists. We are saying that such inconsistency in expectations and in what a person is rewarded and punished for is difficult to bear.

Birth Order and Personal Control

In Chapter Five we noted that some social scientists had found evidence indicating that birth order was related to variations in personality development.[8] One reason why birth order has been considered important is that it is assumed to be related to one's ability to gain control over one's life-space during childhood. According to Renshon, the lower one is in the birth order the greater the likelihood that control over one's life-space is possible.[9] A number of factors have led to this hypothesis. First, personal control as a child is closely connected to the degree to which the major authority wielders, the parents, supervise and regulate the child's behavior. The lower one is in the birth order the greater are the chances that the parents will have less direct control over his or her life. The first child is more likely to be the focus of the parent's initial attempt to arrange the rules of behavior which we expect to be more restrictive than those for younger children. Second, the first child is also likely to be the vehicle through which the parents may attempt to accomplish some of their desires and wishes. This push to achieve through the first-born is undoubtedly related to the findings that outstanding achievers tend to be the first-born.[10]

As we noted in Chapter Five when we were discussing birth order and sex-role development, a majority of all thirty-six women studied were younger members of their families. The political women were usually not the first-born, although Indira Gandhi and Ella Grasso were both only children. Although the evidence is far from overwhelming, the data on our political women suggest that if birth order is related at all to female political achievement, the relationship derives from the connection between birth order and opportunities afforded children for gaining personal control over their life-space. We include in this relationship the fact that being first-born often leads to having priority over the family's scarce resources for education, financing, and other essentials needed for achievement.[11]

Trust in One's Father

Renshon also found evidence that the amount of trust a child has in his or her parents is related to a high sense of personal control.[12] To be able to act so as to obtain a reward from a parent, the child must have a parent who is not only predictable, but also responsive. The child must find the interaction agreeable and sufficiently satisfying to pursue the relationship continually and voluntarily. Such interpersonal trust at the childhood level, Brown and Ellithrop argue, leads to a willingness to work collectively—politically and socially—later.[13] Robert Agger and co-authors also assert that trust in one's parents is related to a later sense of trust in one's government and to the feeling that one's actions can influence the government.[14] We project, therefore, that while trust is likely to be important for the development of all political women, it will be least often an ingredient present in the upbringing of the revolutionaries and the terrorists. The logic of the existing literature would suggest that these women will have lower levels of trust in both their parents or no trust in at least one, probably the father. In spite of the logic of the literature, however, in our study the consistency with which the elected/personal efficacy women and the revolutionary women group together raises the possibility that trust might be more important in predicting whether or not a woman would become revolutionary or a terrorist than whether or not a girl will become a political woman.

Studies of socialization of youths have demonstrated that their original conceptions of government tend to be very affectively positive and that the key authority figures are perceived in much the way a benevolent father-figure is.[15] The key figure is likely to be the father, and because the act of trust for a girl in her father is likely to require more of a transference than does the trust in the immediate object of imitation, the mother, such trust in her father should be related to an enhanced sense of personal control. This trust should also be particularly important for the development of a political orientation since traditionally the father is the member of the nuclear family for whom the world of politics and other collective units outside the family are relevant. Achieving political women, except for the terrorists and possibly the revolutionaries, should have a greater degree of trust in their fathers than the nonpolitical women.

To obtain a comparison of the women's trust in their fathers we rated each of them on how much trust they seemed to have had in their fathers during childhood. The scale was from 1 to 10, with "10" being the greatest amount of trust and a "1" being the least amount. A score of "5" was given unless some specific instance, example, or mention was made of either trust or distrust.

The comparison of the mean scores of the various groups reveals very little variation among the major categories—the private women, public women, elected/mediated women, the elected/personal efficacy women, and revolutionaries. The one exception is the terrorist group. In all categories of women who accepted the legitimacy of the government—including the personal efficacy women—the mean score was close to "5" (average). Although the trust variable offers insights into the affective orientation toward the regime for most of these women, it leaves unexplained not only why some became political participants and the others remained observers but also why the revolutionaries scored highest of any group in trust in their fathers.

Between those rejecting the legitimacy of the regime, the revolutionaries and the terrorists, there is a marked and highly interesting difference. These two subgroups represent the extremes of the continuum of trust in fathers. As a group, the nine revolutionaries displayed the most overall trust in their fathers whereas the terrorists displayed the least. This variation might be indicative of the factors producing the adult differences in behavior. For the revolutionaries, trust in their fathers seems to have led to a political orientation which opposed the existing regime but in a way which allowed for collective, rationalized, reasoned action. Such was not the case for the terrorists. We suspect that their lower sense of trust in their fathers led them to negatively evaluate the political regimes with which their fathers were connected. We suspect, second, that the lower trust in their fathers would have meant that their sense of personal control and predictability would have been less. As a consequence they would approach the political world with a greater degree of unpredictability and a greater sense of impotence. As noted before, the sense of powerlessness often accompanies the use of violence and terror. In most cases the violent actions of the terrorists almost appear to lack political content. Corday, for example, killed Marat, but the political significance of this act even for Corday herself does not always seem clear. At times the acts of murder, bombing, and so on appear to be more of a projection of personal frustrations suffered at the hands of their fathers than a political act directed at an oppressive regime. Sophia Perovskaia illustrates almost perfectly the Lasswellian dictum: a political woman is one who displaces private motives onto public objects and then rationalizes them in terms of the public interest.[16] It was she who insisted that the *Narodnaia Volia* (People's Will) maintain their terrorist aim of assassinating Tsar Alexander II. It was also she who maintained the will and discipline in the group to implement the deed. She seems to have hated the tsar, but much less than she hated her own father.

In our study, trust in fathers did not help to differentiate the political from the nonpolitical women. It did, however, demarcate the revolutionaries from the terrorists. The fact that it was the revolutionaries who were closest to their fathers raises an important question about much of the literature about the benevolent-father image. The question would suggest that the connection between trust toward the father and positive feelings toward a political regime might be because the samples used in such studies consisted mostly of fathers who supported the regime. In other words it might be that trust in one's father is not as directly related to regime-support as previously thought.

Primacy of the Family

In his study, Renshon also noted that the emotional closeness of the family is important for the development of a sense of personal control. He found:

> Individuals growing up in homes in which parents were perceived to have high or medium empathy were more than six times as likely than those from homes where parents were rated low in empathy, to have developed high feelings of personal control. Thus it appears that parental empathy plays at least some role in the development of personal control by providing an atmosphere in which mastery attempts may be made without excessive fear of the consequences of failure.[17]

Although empathy might well be related to personal control, it is not a variable we could examine with the type of data we have. There is one aspect of the emotional closeness component, however, that does interest us and also is more amenable to assessment by us. We are less sure than Renshon that greater amounts of emotional closeness will be positively related to political behavior for women. If the emotional closeness requires that the family always be placed first, before every other event or relationship, then it might impede female political involvement. It seems less probable that a girl raised in such a family will be able as an adult to place public meetings, events, and situations outside the family on equal footing with family activities. We are not saying that emotional closeness itself is an impediment; we are saying that there can be restrictive aspects to emotional closeness. Where the family is concerned, these restrictions are much more likely to affect girls and women than boys and men.

In contrast to the restrictive situation of such a family is the emotionally close family which permits a child the freedom to choose to attend a friend's party rather than go to a family event. We assume that such childhood choices parallel and, hence, provide training for the adult who later must choose between family and external commitments. This choice is, of course, especially difficult for a woman to make since it is she who has been historically most closely connected with the family unit. If the dominant ideology of the society requires that she find her basic meaning and value in the family, then she will be expected to give this institution and its activities the highest priority. (Men are also expected by most societies to give great importance to the family. Indeed, their purpose in life has historically been defined as the provider for the family. We in no way wish to imply that men do not give primacy to the family in many ways. We do insist, however, that the degree of the commitment and the consequences of the commitment are sharply different for men and women. Hence, although many men will also not become politically active because of the primacy of the family in their lives, the odds are much greater that women will not become active for this reason.)

To assess whether or not our women were permitted to choose nonfamily events over doing things with the family, we sought in the biographical data a positive answer to the following questions: Could the girl choose to attend a nonfamily function rather than a family one? Did the mother in particular place another value over being physically and/or emotionally close to her daughter? Once again the patterns we have so often seen emerge. As expected, the private women, who in their own adult lives placed the family over other concerns, had parental families who stressed the primacy of the family. So too did the elected/mediated group of women; had their husbands lived, they undoubtedly would never have become political actors. In contrast, relatively few of the elected/personal efficacy women, the public women, the revolutionaries, or the terrorists came from families that placed the family unit above everything else.

Because of the importance of this matter, a few concrete examples are in order. The cases of the two women who became chief executives of their countries, Gandhi and Meir, and the case of Chisholm who sought the U.S. presidency, show that they came from families that did not place togetherness and unity above all else. Socioeconomic and political matters were clearly placed above the physical intactness and closeness of the parental nuclear family.

Rather than forego their own political activity, rather than inhibit their protests against British rule, the Nehru family constantly risked imprisonment and family separation. The fact that Indira Gandhi's mother, as well as her father and grandfather, deliberately sacrificed family unity and togetherness could not but impress upon her the tremendous importance of the political realm; it must also have reduced in her mind the importance of the traditional wife/mother role. We are not suggesting that it had less general value, but rather that the wife/mother role was not as primary for her as for most women.

The case of Golda Meir is even sharper. A political decision during her prime formative years also led to the temporary dissolution of the nuclear family. Living in Kiev, Russia, the Mabovitch family had the one qualification to make life particularly difficult: they were Jewish. Moshe Mabovitch, a cabinetmaker, had moved to Kiev in the hopes of making a better life for his family. He quickly discovered that the life in Kiev was not much better than in the Pale of Settlement (the section of Russia where the Jews were to stay unless they had passed special examinations as Moshe had done). Unable to support their family, Moshe and Blume Mabovitch decided to sacrifice family unity for the possibility of a better life in the United States. Golda was five when her father left and eight when the family was reunited in Milwaukee. In her adult life Golda Meir repeated this scenario in relation to her own husband in certain respects. She refused to marry Morris Meyerson (changed to Meir) unless he was willing to go to Israel with her. As her parents before her, she often later in her political career placed an external political and/or social value above family togetherness, unity, and primacy.

The Chisholm family made comparable choices. Unable to obtain the two items that Barbadians who came to Brooklyn wanted—"a brownstone house and a college education for their children"[18]—Chisholm's mother decided to send her three daughters to their grandmother on Barbados. The parents could tolerate the division of the family unit for the sake of its members' future.

The contrast between these three political women and such private women as Mamie Doud Eisenhower could hardly be greater. In the Doud family the frequent family outings and occasions were very important. The father apparently retired at an early age so that he could spend more time with his family. Alden Hatch notes that the rule of the Doud house was that the family went to picnics and the theatre together even if some of the members did not wish to go.[19] The primacy of the family unit was never questioned. It does not seem unusual to find Mamie Eisenhower transferring this same degree of devotion to her own adult family.

Educational Attainment and Personal Control

One of the major factors in the development of personal control for everyone is the extent of educational attainment. Since women have not traditionally been expected to need skills that a formal education would provide, a woman who achieves an unusual amount of education is already being encouraged to widen the extent of her life-space, to expect some life beyond the nuclear family. This is particularly true for girls who are educated in what is considered to be unfeminine subject matter. To be educated formally in the areas of home economics, teaching, nursing, and so on only confirms the sex-role expectations that society has of women. To be educated in business administration, law, engineering, for example, is to lay the foundation for a less traditional life. We hypothesize, therefore, that achieving political women as children will have received more education than would be normal for their age, society, and social class. We also expect that they will have been more likely than the nonpolitical women to have been trained in subjects like law and engineering—nontraditional subject matter.

Figure 6-1 presents the picture of the educational attainment of the six groups of women. The possible scores that could be received were as follows: grade school or equivalent—1; high school or equivalent—2; additional training in some nonprofessional capacity (e.g., typists, clerks, midwives, practical nursing)—3; college training but not advanced professional training (included here were B.A. and B.S. degrees in elementary and secondary education)—4; and advanced degrees or professional training (e.g., pharmacists, lawyers, Ph.D.'s)—5.

The pattern in Figure 6-1 repeats the now familiar one. The public women, the personal efficacy women, and the revolutionaries are similar to one another; the private women, the elected/ mediated women, and the terrorists are similar. The former groups had obviously achieved a higher degree of education and as a consequence had been afforded the opportunity to have a wider range of expectations about the life-space they could occupy. They also would have obtained a greater sense of personal competence in the nonfamily world and a greater sense of personal control.

The elected women with a strong sense of personal political efficacy found their place where we anticipated. They were as a group the best educated of all the women studied. The revolutionaries follow closely though. As our theory also predicts, the private women have less education than the public women; and the public women are below the majority of the achieving political women. Although our original ideal types did not project that the terrorists, the elected/mediated women, and the private women would be so similar, the consistency of the finding that they are leads us not to be surprised any more. The terrorists and the elected/mediated women had lower group scores for educational attainment than the private women. The level is equivalent to high school training.

Figure 6-1
Mean Educational Attainment of the Women Studied

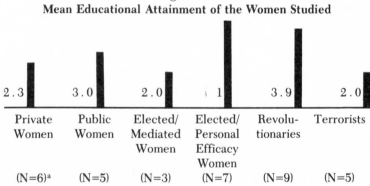

2.3	3.0	2.0	1	3.9	2.0
Private Women	Public Women	Elected/ Mediated Women	Elected/ Personal Efficacy Women	Revolutionaries	Terrorists
(N=6)[a]	(N=5)	(N=3)	(N=7)	(N=9)	(N=5)

Grade school or equivalent = 1
High school or equivalent = 2
Additional training (nonprofessional) = 3
College = 4
Advanced degrees or professional training = 5

a. Khrushchev is excluded because of lack of information.

Perhaps as important as the level of educational attainment are the subject and content which were provided during the educational experience. To have completed college or the equivalent of college but to have majored in what might be termed traditional female subject matter is not to alter substantially one's life-space or gain the competence to act successfully in the public realm. Figure 6-2 presents our findings relative to the content of the education thirty-four of these women received.

Figure 6-2
Content of Education of the Women Studied

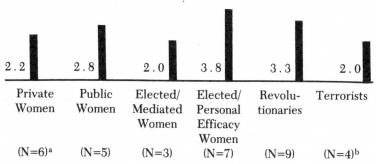

2.2	2.8	2.0	3.8	3.3	2.0
Private Women	Public Women	Elected/ Mediated Women	Elected/ Personal Efficacy Women	Revolu- tionaries	Terrorists
(N=6)[a]	(N=5)	(N=3)	(N=7)	(N=9)	(N=4)[b]

Finishing school = 1
Liberal arts = 2
Education, teaching, nursing, medicine = 3 (At doctoral level = 4)
Social or moral philosophy = 4
Business, economics, law, politics = 5

a. Khrushchev and b. Goldman are excluded because of lack of information about the content emphasis of their education.

We believe that the achieving political woman will have studied less traditional subjects than her nonpolitical counterpart and will have studied a larger number of subjects. Such education will increase her competencies, expand her life-space, and raise her sense of personal control over her life-space. In other words, the achieving political women will have been "trained" to compete with males as part of their educational process to a greater extent than the nonpolitical women. Moreover, the longer this "competition" training goes on, the greater the likelihood that females will be political participants and that larger numbers of them will become political women.

The educational content for Figure 6-2 was classified on the basis of the following criteria: if the education was mainly a finishing school for social graces, it was coded "1"; the study of liberal arts was given a "2"; "3" for the nondoctoral level of teaching, nursing, medicine (if these subjects were at the doctoral level, the score was "4" due to the emphasis social and moral philosophy receive at that level); "4" for social or moral philosophy; and "5" if the content was that of business, economics, the physical sciences, law, or politics. The direction of the classification scheme is obvious. The more nontraditional for women the education was, the higher the mean score. The higher the score the more likely the women are to have been provided with the skills necessary to compete in the public, political world, traditionally defined as "masculine."

Figure 6-2 is closely related to the findings on the levels of educational attainment. If the women with personal political efficacy and the revolutionaries were receiving higher degrees, they were also receiving this education in areas that would allow them to compete successfully with men in fields traditionally accepted as male. This variable once again finds the most politically active and astute political women (the elected/personal efficacy women and the revolutionaries) sharing the greatest similarity. Again also, the private women, the elected/mediated women, and the terrorists are similar. Educational level and content seem to contribute strongly to distinguishing most political from most nonpolitical women. They also help separate the "effective" from the "ineffective" political women: the revolutionaries and the terrorists.

The relatively low score of the elected/mediated women compared to the personal efficacy political group adds insights into their much delayed entrance into politics as independent actors. It also points to the inherent limitations of adult retooling for entrance into nontraditional careers. If these elected/mediated women had not had most unusual structural opportunities they probably would never have become politicians.

In Chapter Four we considered coeducation as a possible variable contributing to the development of political women. At that point we found similar trends. The women with personal political efficacy clearly had more coeducational training at all levels, but particularly at the elementary level, than the private, public, or elected/mediated women. It seems, thus, that the more education a woman has the more nontraditional the education is, and the more coeducational training she receives the greater the likelihood that she will become an independent political actor. The achieving political woman tends to have educational experience that extends her life-space to include the public realm and that provides her with competencies to deal with that realm.

Independent Career and Personal Control

To speak of women and careers in the same breath has historically been something of a non sequitur. The one does not necessarily follow the other. Careers are usually associated with the public/social/political world and women with the private/insular/nonpolitical world. The word "career" is rarely if ever applied to the chief adult concern of most women, being a wife and mother. One *is* a mother or a wife, but one *has* a career. Being is stressed for the mother role; doing is stressed for the career role.

As was the case with educational attainment, the historical expectation about careers for women has been a negative one. The woman desiring a career had to justify why she needed one. Her career concerns were readily accepted as legitimate if her major male mediator with the external world, either her father or husband, was no longer available or able to perform the task of supporting her. Otherwise women were not encouraged to obtain the skills required for a career.

The separation between the world of careers and the world of women is not as great as the separation between women and politics, however. Politics as an external public realm has a much longer history of sole association with the males of the species than does the economic world of jobs. The history of women's economic activity is longer than that of female political participation. Women were already a significant part of the labor force in the United States before they received even the minimal political concession of the right to vote. The necessities of economic life often overcame the niceties of the notion that women's appropriate place is in the home.

The woman with an independent career is obviously a person who has extended personal control over her life-space. We hypothesize, therefore, that the political women will have been much more likely to have attained independent careers than the nonpolitical women. They will have ventured into the male sphere prior to their political life and as a result will have acquired competencies and experiences that would make politics less foreign to them. In our scoring, to be considered as having had a career, the woman had to have worked other than part-time and to have worked for reasons other than economic hardship. Taking a job to maintain the standard of living does not constitute a career even if it is held for several years.

We reviewed the biographies to see which women had a career prior to engaging in politics. We found that the private women and the terrorists are much more similar to each other as groups than the private women and the public women are. Only one of the private women and one of the terrorists had had a career of any sort before devoting her life to, respectively, the adult family and political activity. The public women and the revolutionaries had at least a majority of their members having an independent career prior to their marriage and subsequent entrance into politics. The one anomaly appears to be the relatively low number of the women with personal political efficacy having careers. We expected that more of their numbers would have had independent careers than the public women or the elected/mediated women. Three women of the personal efficacy group, Golda Meir, Indira Gandhi, and Bernadette Devlin, account for all the members in this group who did not have an independent career before their political career. In each of these cases there was no independent career because politics was their first and earliest commitment. From their early youth these women had been in politics. Meir was raising funds for causes from the age of eleven years. Devlin became a member of Parliament straight from college. Gandhi's political involvement was almost from birth. Politics was so extraordinarily salient to these women at such an early age that it became their career from the outset.

As in the case of education, the nature of the career is likely to be as important as having a career. The societal division of labor into male and female jobs even within the public business world is far too well-known to require an extensive discourse on the matter here. We considered it a plus if the women studied had a career which could be considered one in which men would be the more frequent participants. For example, the occupations of nurse, elementary school teacher, seamstress, and governess would clearly be traditional for women whereas those of Margaret Thatcher would be nontraditional—first a chemist and later a barrister specializing in tax law.

The information on the types of career our thirty-six women had is even more indicative of the pattern we have come to expect. Neither the private women nor the terrorists had careers in fields nontraditional for women. Those who had independent careers apparently did not have ones that altered their life-space substantially or increased their control over it. The public women, the elected women with personal efficacy, and the revolutionaries were all in nontraditional careers. Only one of the elected/mediated women had a nontraditional career. Thus the achieving political women, excluding the terrorists, had attained competencies and skills that were transferable to the political realm. By contrast, none of the private women had such training. The public women who did achieve some independence in their adult lives relative to their famous husbands all had had some earlier career that made an independent life-style a possibility.

Personal Control and the Development of Political Women

By way of summary we attempted to formulate a Guttman scale and resulting index for personal control over life-space utilizing the twelve distinct items previously discussed: autonomy as a child, rule consistency, birth order, primacy of family, trust in one's father, an independent career, a nontraditional career, physical health, physical fights, participation in competitive sports, educational attainment, and "femininity" or "masculinity" of the educational content. The attempt proved futile (the C.R. for this scale was only .85 and the C.S. was only .55, both below acceptable levels). Upon re-examination we realized that the twelve items contained the foundation for a comparison of the women's personal control within their parental nuclear family and their potential for personal control in an expanded life-space. In short, it seemed that two scales comparable to those created for the mothers of the women (see Chapter Five) lay dormant here: (a) a scale of "Personal Control Within the Childhood Family," and (b) a scale of "Potential for Personal Control Outside the Home."

The scale "Personal Control Within the Childhood Family" was derived from the following four items: (1) the woman was given a "+" if a record of having had autonomy as a child existed—79 percent of the thirty-four women for whom information was available possessed this trait as children (Khrushchev and Griffiths were excluded because of no data); (2) 74 percent of the women received a "+" for having achieved a score of 5 or more for trust in their fathers; (3) for having experienced rule consistency within the family, 68 percent of the thirty-four women were given a "+"; finally (4) 50 percent of the women's biographical data allowed us to code them as "+" because the primacy of the family was not always foremost, that is, as girls, they were allowed on occasion to attend other events when a family and another social event conflicted.

A Guttman scalogram analysis of these four items produced coefficients of reproducibility and scalability of .91 and .61 respectively. Scale types ranging from "3" for the women with the most personal control within the family to "0" for those with the least control were then assigned. Figure 6-3 presents the mean score for each of the types on this dimension.

Figure 6-3
Mean Scores for the Women's Sense of Personal Control Within the Childhood Family

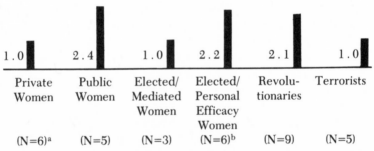

1.0	2.4	1.0	2.2	2.1	1.0
Private Women	Public Women	Elected/ Mediated Women	Elected/ Personal Efficacy Women	Revolu- tionaries	Terrorists
(N=6)[a]	(N=5)	(N=3)	(N=6)[b]	(N=9)	(N=5)

a. Khrushchev and b. Griffiths are excluded due to lack of information.

Figure 6-3 shows that the familiar patterns once again emerge. As was the case with the scaling of the mothers' independence within the family, certain groups cluster together. The private, elected/mediated, and terrorist groups of women received precisely the same mean score. The three other groups—the public women, the personal efficacy women, and the revolutionaries—have similar scores.

As in the case of the scales developed in Chapter Five, we applied the Student's t test to the various subcategorizations depicted in Figure 6-3. The tests indicated that the classifying of the women into traditional (political wives) and nontraditional (the political actors) categories produced no significant difference. The contrasts between the private and the public women and the revolutionaries and terrorists were significant, however, at the .001 and .03 levels respectively. The comparison of the mean scores of the elected/mediated women and the elected/personal efficacy women indicated that the probability of the distribution found could occur by chance 7 out of 100 times. The difference between the mean scores of the women with the lowest group scores on this scale of personal control within the childhood family (the private women, elected/mediated women, and terrorists) and the mean scores of the women with the highest group scores (the elected/personal efficacy women, the public women, and the revolutionaries) indicated the probability of the distribution occurring by chance to be less than .00006.

The second scale "Potential for Personal Control Outside the Home" also consists of four items. Pluses were given if the woman studied had a career, if this career was of a nontraditional nature, if the education received was greater than expected for a girl of the time and culture, and if the content of that education was in areas more closely associated with "masculinity" than "femininity." The order of these items was as they have just been presented. The percentages of women scoring a "+" on each of the items were 51, 43, 40, and 29 percent, respectively. The measures of unidimensionality for this scale were even higher. The C.R. was .98 and the C.S. .80.

Figure 6-4 illustrates the composite scores of the groups on this scale. The range was from "0" to "4." Those with most potential for personal control in an expanded life-space received a "4."

As was the case in the previous scale, the same groups cluster together. The terrorists have the lowest potential for exerting personal control over an expanded life-space, according to this index. The private women and elected/mediated women have the next lowest potential. The public women, although having almost twice the score of the elected/mediated women, are still below the revolutionaries and elected women with personal efficacy.

The application of the Student's t test to the various sub-

Figure 6-4
Mean Scores for the Women's Potential for Personal Control
Outside the Home

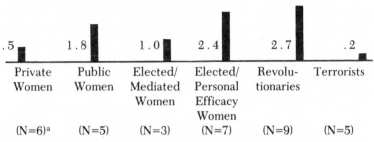

Private Women	Public Women	Elected/ Mediated Women	Elected/ Personal Efficacy Women	Revolutionaries	Terrorists
.5	1.8	1.0	2.4	2.7	.2
(N=6)[a]	(N=5)	(N=3)	(N=7)	(N=9)	(N=5)

a. Khrushchev is excluded due to lack of information.

groups indicated again that the classification of the women into just two groups on the basis of traditional versus nontraditional behavior (being a political wife versus being a political actor oneself) was not statistically significant (p = .098). The comparison between the private and public women subgroups also was not (p = .10). The probability of the difference in mean scores of the elected/mediated women and the elected/personal efficacy women occurring by chance was .07, while for the revolutionaries and terrorists it was .009.

Clearly the characteristics of these real women both illustrate the validity of our ideal types and provide support for our assertion that it is the variations in the socialization experiences that have produced the sharp differences in political behavior.

The Mother's Independence and the Daughter's Personal Control

In the multivariate analysis of all the family-related variables, Renshon found that the parent's level of personal control was the greatest predictor of the child's level of personal control.[20] We have already agreed with this conclusion in our earlier assertions about the effect of the mother and father on a girl's sex-role ideology. If the mother exhibited personal control over her life within the family structure and outside of it in particular, then a daughter, we argued, was likely to obtain the impression that she too could exercise control over her life. As for the fathers, we argued that the political women were more likely to have as fathers men who were externally oriented, men who viewed the world as a playground for their self-fulfillment and achievement, not as a hostile arena from which they ought to retreat. With the development of these two scales on the personal control our thirty-six women experienced as children, we can now systematically attempt to obtain additional insights into the extent to which the mothers' level of personal control (independence) are related not only to development of their daughters' personal control over life-space, but also to the development of political women.

A visual comparison of the configurations of the types of women in Figure 6-3 and of the mothers by each type in Figure 5-1 reveals graphically how very similar are the scores on the index of "Mothers' Independence Within the Family" to the daughters' scores on the index of "Personal Control Within the Childhood Family." The gamma measure of association between these scores of the mothers and daughters is .64. A visual comparison of the configuration in Figure 6-4 with that in 5-2 shows that the mothers' scores on the index of "Mothers' Independence Outside the Home" and the daughters' scores on the index of "Potential for Personal Control Outside the Home" are also very similar. The gamma measure of the association between these two mother-daughter indices is .71. The picture seems clear. Mothers who have independence and control over their life-space tend to produce daughters with great potential for achieving comparable independence and control. Mothers who do not possess such independence and control produce daughters who will not be likely to obtain independence and control. These comparisons between mothers and daughters also add support for our view that obtaining an activist sex-role ideology must precede expanding and obtaining control over a girl's life-space.

Stage Three: Becoming Aware of the Salience of Politics

Up to this point in our theoretical model of the four stages of the development of political women we have discussed those two stages which we believe to be essential to the development of a nontraditional woman: stage one, the development of an activist—modern, if you will—sex-role ideology, and stage two, the development of a sense of personal control over one's life-space, and the abilities to implement such control. The data in Chapters Five and Six so far support our contention that the variables underlying the stage-one and stage-two developments are foremost in explaining why many women in the world will no longer remain in the strictly private realm of the family and home. What remains to be determined is why some of these women with an activist sex-role ideology become involved in politics while others do not. Why, in brief, does political rather than economic activity, for example, attract these women? Again it is to the specifics of the socialization process of our subjects that we must look to find the answers to these queries.

Politics becomes important to a person because of the rewards or punishments it has to offer. It has thus a very strong affective component. Following Piaget's model for human intellectual development,[21] we would not expect children under the age of ten to have strong, intellectually defensible stands on politics. We would expect, nonetheless, that they would be aware of whether or not politics and the government were important to their parents and peers. If it were important to individuals who in turn were important to the child, we would expect that politics would be more likely to be important to him or her. It is of utmost importance for us to stress, however, that the conviction that politics is important alone is not sufficient to produce political activity on the part of women. A girl coming from a highly politicized family (such as the Kennedys, for example), in which politics has directly impinged upon her life, need not become an independent political being. Without the prior conditions specified in stages one and two, no direct, personal, independent political behavior is likely to occur. Many a highly politicized family has seen the continued relegation of its female members to the strictly private realm of the family. If females in this situation do become involved, their participation tends to be in supportive and wifely ways. The salience of politics alone does not produce Indira Gandhis, Golda Meirs, Margaret Thatchers, and Ella Grassos.

The specific hypotheses about how political salience develops are rather straightforward. They seek to identify whatever political, social, or economic situations or events might have occurred or existed within the life of the subjects as children to make politics salient to them. We will first discuss these variables within the family situation and then discuss the impact of more macro-level events and situations.

Parental Discussion of Politics and Political Salience

Because of emotional importance of the parents to most children, we hypothesized that the parents (or substitutes) of the political women would have discussed political or related social and moral issues with them with a higher degree of frequency and intensity in the pre-adolescent years than the parents of the nonpolitical women.

It is clear from the biographical data that a higher proportion of the parents of the elected/personal efficacy women and the revolutionaries discussed such topics with them. The terrorists and the elected/mediated women did not have this conscious parental introduction to politics. One of the terrorists, Vera Zasulich, did have discussions about Voltaire and other social thinkers with her governess, but the discussions were not about politics per se. In her memoirs she clearly states that she had no conception of politics until her late teens and early twenties.[22] In the case of the elected/mediated women, this lack of discussion by the parents conforms with our suggestion that it was an adult association with their husbands which made politics salient to them. It also helps us understand why adult resocialization was needed.

The types of discussions that led to politics' becoming salient to the personal efficacy women as children can be illustrated with a few examples. Gandhi's life, as previously noted, was constantly filled with political discussions. In a British Broadcasting Corporation interview, Gandhi commented on her childhood as follows: "As a child, when the freedom struggle was on, the house was being constantly raided by police, our goods and chattels being confiscated, we were being arrested and having to hide contraband and literature, and I was all part of it . . . . I was part of the processions and the meetings and it was an extremely insecure childhood. One did not know from day to day who would be alive, who would be in the house, and what would happen next."[23] Bernadette Devlin recalls her father telling her bedtime stories and singing songs with Irish nationalist and revolutionary themes. Golda Meir described the family fights in her early childhood because of the revolutionary associations Sheyna, her sister, had in Russia. Her mother was constantly seeking to force Sheyna to give up these friends for fear that they might make their father's search for work even more difficult than it was. Sheyna, however, persisted. Shirley Chisholm notes the occasions on which she and her father discussed the political movement of Marcus Garvey and its significance for the black minority in the United States. Margaret Thatcher also came from a family environment in which politics was often discussed. Her father was a grocer by trade, but he served on the Grantham Council for twenty-five years and rose to become its mayor. In their home "there was always plenty of interest in what her father was doing, for he was at the centre of anything of consequence going on in the town."[24] Grasso as well indicates that political discussions were common between her and her parents during her childhood.

Six of the revolutionaries also had such discussions. Edib's father was a westernizer in a traditional Turkish culture. His efforts to raise Edib as a western woman led to discussions about political and social change. Gonne's father was a liberal in outlook and supported the Irish, though an officer in the British army. Gonne, who adored her father, discussed the situation of the Irish with him frequently during her childhood and youth. As an adult her sympathy went further than his had, but for years, until his death, she was unable to advocate the taking up of arms against the British soldiers. This position was undoubtedly related to the fact that her father had been a British officer.

Luxemburg's father was a well-educated man of culture and intelligence, determined to give all his children a good education. He was sympathetic to the national-revolutionary movement in Poland and dedicated to improving the Polish school system. Coming from an emotionally close family with an intelligent, well-read mother, Luxemburg benefited from discussions on politics while young. Kollontai's father was away from home much of the time because of his job as a general in the army. When he was home, he spent much of his time writing the history of the Bulgarian Wars. He was quite liberal for his time; indeed, he was radical. He helped write Bulgaria's first constitution which was accepted over the objection of the tsar. As a small child, Kollontai often heard her mother express the fear that the tsar would arrest her father. Fearing his loss, the little girl often burst out in criticism of the tsar and the autocracy.

Breshko-Breshkovskaia was very close to her father. A man of broad, liberal ideas, he encouraged her to read many books on social and moral philosophy. By sixteen she said she knew the French Revolution by heart.[25] Since she had been taught French, German, and Russian early, she read them in the original with him. She traveled with him as he supervised his estate. Together they sought ways of helping the peasant and of seeking reform within the autocracy. Both were particularly interested in the *zemstvo*, the first Russian effort at representative government. After spending two and one-half years in St. Petersburg as a governess in a nobleman's house and being active in liberal circles, she returned home at her father's request. Knowing she wanted to be independent from him, he assisted her in opening a boarding school for wealthy girls and also built a cottage so she could teach the peasant children at no charge. Only after she was twenty-eight years old did she break with her father, her husband, and family to engage in revolutionary activity. The early father-daughter discussions led to politics becoming salient, but it took the repressiveness of the autocracy itself to make her a revolutionary. Angela Davis also had political discussions as a child with her family. It is evident from the examples given for both the elected women with personal political efficacy and the revolutionaries that the discussions were not simply abstract intellectual ones; the interest in the political discussion was great because politics had a special meaning and consequence for the parents, particularly the fathers.

Three other women (one private, Alliluieva Stalin, and two public women, Clementine Churchill and Nadezhda Krupskaia) also had a record of political discussions in their homes but these discussions were not so intensely personal. Alliluieva's father, though a Marxist, did not seem to try to involve his daughter emotionally or intellectually with his revolutionary activities. In spite of the Marxian ideology the family seemed to assume that females were not as interested in politics as males. The salience Alliluieva developed was the type that makes a girl interested in political men, such as the man she married, Stalin.

In the public-woman category Clementine Churchill and Nadezhda Krupskaia are the two subjects with whom the parents discussed politics. Some readers might be surprised that Eleanor Roosevelt is not among these women. The reason she is not is that the biographical materials clearly indicate that until she reached the boarding school in London in her mid-teens, politics was always considered to be a man's concern. The activities of her uncle, Teddy Roosevelt, were discussed but more because he was a relative than because politics was a topic considered relevant or pertinent to Eleanor Roosevelt or her parents.

The grandmother and aunts of Clementine Churchill discussed politics with her. The discussion was of a more abstract nature than that most of the political women had. Neither her mother nor her father was rewarded or punished for political beliefs and activities. The discussions were not of the type that would seem to call forth a personalized response from Clementine Churchill as a little girl. The situation again was very different from that of the others whose fathers and/or mothers were actually affected by political events.

The case of Krupskaia is more comparable to the revolutionaries and political women with personal political efficacy. Her father was also somewhat radical for his time. He was forced to leave government service for suspected unapproved political activity. Although Krupskaia does not dwell upon his actual activities, her father's subsequent forcible removal from his good government job seems to have made the Russian political situation more salient to her. She of all the public women is also the most consistently involved in politics throughout her life.

It seems clear that personalized discussions about politics and their potential impact upon the girl and her life is critical to the development of the political woman. The nature of the discussions described in the biographies suggest that abstract intellectualized discussions are not sufficient to make politics strongly salient for little girls. Again, additional research is needed.

Salience as the Result of a Special Love/Hate for a Parent

With few exceptions most of the subjects had neither a special love nor hate for their parents. We would expect if politics were particularly important to a parent who was especially loved or hated that it would become much more salient to the child. Three of the political women with personal efficacy, Chisholm, Thatcher, and Devlin, seemed to have had a special love for their fathers. The fact that the fathers were particularly concerned about politics and its impact upon their lives and the lives of others undoubtedly intensified its salience to the daughters. Among the revolutionaries, Kollontai, Edib, Gonne, and

Breshko-Breshkovskaia had special loves for their fathers. As was already noted above, this love seemed to help intensify the salience of politics. Perovskaia had a special, intense love for her mother and a most intense hatred for her father. The fact that her father was a descendant of the Russian tsars and that he was at various times a high-level government official, including being the governor-general of St. Petersburg, made her aware of politics. The probability is very high that her effort to assassinate Tsar Alexander II was emotionally connected with this hatred of her father.

As was suggested earlier in this chapter when we were discussing the girl's trust of her father, our data on this variable of special love and hate do not seem to be related to regime-support or regime-rejection in general. The love and admiration for the father in these instances seems to determine whether or not the girl will try to perpetuate his beliefs and views. If the father was supportive of the existing status quo and regime and the daughter loved him especially much, she too stayed within the system. If the father wanted social and political change and was punished by the regime or it seemed he might be, the daughter with special love for him tended to become a revolutionary opposing the existing order. In other words, the emotional attachment to one's father and the perception of his benevolence or lack of it is more related to the acceptance and rejection of his political values than it is to regime-support.

Special Events Leading to Political Salience

We also sought information as to whether or not a special historical event with political significance occurred that was personalized for the girl. We found that this situation was much more likely to have existed for the revolutionaries than any other group. Some of the examples have already been given in our discussions of the daughters and their fathers. Kollontai was personally affected by the Bulgarian constitution. Edib's entire life was altered because of the attempts to westernize Turkey. The other examples are less directly related to the fathers.

Three of the girls from Jewish families were made aware of the political situation because of the requirement that their families live in certain areas and that they go to certain schools: Broido, Luxemburg, and Meir. The oppressiveness of the Russian autocracy for Jewish people was personally recognized by these individuals, but it is obvious, however, that such recognition is not sufficient to produce political behavior.

Angela Davis as a child experienced the shock of having known and been friends with several of the young black children who were murdered in a church bombing. The political, social, and economic discrimination against blacks in the United States was obviously made emotionally salient to her.

La Pasionaria, because she was sick as a child, was sent to a day school over the offices of a trade union and a jail. She heard frequent comments about the oppressiveness of the Spanish government and how inhuman the working conditions of most laborers were. She vividly recalls how much it pained her to see her father standing in cold water up to his chest working in the coal mines. The trade union movement became personally relevant to her because of her father's suffering. Indeed, her mother suffered from the same type of problems.

Gonne and Markievicz had special political events become salient to them because of their special relationships to the Irish peasants on their fathers' estates. During both of their childhoods it was the custom to forcibly remove the Irish—men, women, and children—from specific lands and to burn their houses. Many of them died; all suffered. The parents of these two girls did not approve of this policy and refused to carry it out themselves. The daughters tried to help the peasants who were their friends. This emotional involvement and opposition to the British policy as children clearly underlay much of their adult activity.

It is evident that the intrusion of political events in the lives of these children produced more negative than positive feelings toward the government in power. Politics became salient for its punishment potential. Because of the similarity of these examples to those in the early life of Indira Gandhi, it is worth pointing out that her father ended up having a successful career as the first Indian prime minister. The change of government changed the salience of politics from a punishment to a reward motif.

The School, the Peer Group, and Political Salience

The peer groups and school environment might also be the source of the development of political salience. Numerous scholars believe these two socializing agents are more important than the family. Although we certainly don't agree with that conclusion so far as achieving political women are concerned, it is highly probable that the school and peer environments do contribute to the development of political salience. Our efforts to learn if the achieving political women were educated in a more political school environment than is typical for girls revealed that only the elected women with personal political efficacy had this politicized school environment. As was pointed out in Chapter Four, it was this group of women that also had coeducational training at the elementary level much more frequently than the other groups of women. These elected/personal efficacy women were clearly experiencing a very different socialization process than the private, public, elected/mediated, and terrorist women.

Although it was not possible to make comparative judgments about the revolutionaries, since they tended to be tutored by governesses, it is clear from their biographies that peer-group influence was very important for getting them involved in political activities. Almost all of the Russian revolutionaries and terrorists became involved in their late teens with student or worker study groups. These groups considered the sexes to be equal. They also argued that critically thinking individuals had to become active. Women as well as men had to try to produce social change.[26] Rosa Luxemburg's school, consisting of Jewish compatriots, was teeming with anti-Russian and anti-government sentiment. Halide Edib had political discussions at the American University in Beirut, Lebanon. Angela Davis also had intensive political discussions with her peers.

The pattern on this question of the impact of the peer group is essentially a repeat of that found earlier in the study. Politics became salient to the revolutionaries and to the elected women with political efficacy in several ways. There is clearly a cumulative buildup of the salience. As girls, most of these women were encouraged to talk and think about politics not only at school or among their peers, but also at home in the family. Having not only one's parents but also one's teachers and peers discuss politics must have helped to legitimize the notion that politics was not only an area that girls could become interested in, but also one in which they ought to become interested. Having the most important individuals in one's life-space from several different age groups and institutions stressing the importance of politics for girls is most unusual.

It is important to stress once again, for girls who have not successfully passed through stage one (development of an activist sex-role ideology) and stage two (development of a need and ability to exercise personal control over an expanded life-space), that stage three (the realization of the salience of politics) is likely to result in political salience on the level of civic obligation. They might vote on this level, but are not likely to seek to influence the political system by direct, independent, unmediated action, or even by making specific demands to participate.

Conclusion

This chapter provides support for the contention that political efficacy and political participation develop as the result of the need for and ability to exercise personal control over one's life-space. In our investigation we found that the elected women with personal political efficacy and the revolutionaries were likely to have had the experiences and characteristics that would provide them greater personal control over their lives. These women were also more likely to have achieved the skills necessary to expand their life-space to the point of including the political realm. The elected/mediated women and the terrorists failed in their youth to develop the skills and competencies associated with achievement in the political world. For the elected/mediated women this failure meant that they were faced with a slow and arduous resocialization process in their adult years in order to become effective political achievers. Except for Vera Zasulich, the terrorists did not become political achievers. Most terrorists were executed for their violence in their mid-twenties. Thus they were political actors only in a limited and fleeting sense. They never had the option of being resocialized. In all cases the private nonpolitical women were least likely to have achieved a need for and a sense of personal control over their life-space. The public women had achieved more personal control over their existence within the family environment than the private women, but were as unlikely to have gained the abilities and traits to expand this life-space as the private women.

Politics became salient to the elected women with personal political efficacy initially by means of their discussions with their parents, particularly their fathers. But more than one group of individuals and institutions stressed the importance of politics.

Hence, one cannot say that one socialization agency was more important than the other. The revolutionaries tended to have their impetus toward politics more affected by broad social events than the elected/personal efficacy women, but they too were subject to the political influences of many institutions and relevant persons at different stages in their lives.

The second and third stages of our theoretical model of the political socialization of women have continued to demonstrate the remarkable similarity between what we have termed the private traditional women and the women whom one might believe to be the most committed to their political causes and activities, the terrorists. As we have progressed through our analyses, it has become evident that the terrorists we studied were quite traditionally socialized. It also seems that their violent acts were as much acts of frustration and powerlessness as acts with deep political content. These women seem to have developed an active sex-role ideology, but were never given the needed skills and competencies to implement that ideology. Ultimately, our analysis has shown that the elected women with personal political efficacy are the most similar to the revolutionaries in the way they were socialized, and that the private women have backgrounds most in common with the terrorists. This conclusion was surely not a finding we had anticipated at the start of our study.

We would like to remind the reader that there is a stage four in our theory which stipulates that a human being must have a history of successful participation in politics at various stages of the life cycle in order to continue the effort. Although stages three and four are important for the development of political women, it should be clear from our discussion that stages one and two are much more critical. Women can become elected national officials by means of resocialization even though they skipped stages one and two in their youth, but such adult resocialization is most rare—in our study it seems to require the ghoulish prerequisite of having one's husband die while holding political office. Then, after a husband's death, it may take several years for the woman to realize the full potential of both herself and her office. Such resocialization is likely neither to increase the proportion of women in the national political elite nor to produce prime ministers and presidents.

Notes

1. Stanley Allen Renshon, *Psychological Needs and Political Behavior: A Theory of Personality and Political Efficacy* (New York: The Free Press, 1974).

2. Ibid., p. 145.

3. Ibid., p. 64.

4. Jan Felshin, "The Dialectics of Women and Sport," *The American Woman in Sport*, by Ellen W. Gerber, Jan Felshin, Pearl Berlin, and Wanum Wyrich (Reading, Mass.: Addison-Wesley Publishing Company, 1974), p. 198.

5. Ibid., p. 201.

6. It should be noted that biographers do not seem to pay much attention to this matter for girls. Data for two of the six who we know engaged in fist fights came from women completing our questionnaire.

7. Personal conversations with Jerry Cawley and Sandy Ahlfors Cawley in Minneapolis, Minnesota.

8. A. Adler, *What Life Should Mean to You* (Boston: Little, Brown and Co., 1931), esp. pp. 144–54; S. Schachter, *The Psychology of Affiliation* (Stanford, Calif.: Stanford University Press, 1959); Stanley Renshon, "Birth Order, Personality, and Political Socialization," *New Directions in Political Socialization*, ed. D. Schwartz and S. Schwartz (New York: The Free Press, 1974); E. E. Sampson, "The Study of Ordinal Position," *Advances in Experimental Personality Research*, ed. B. Mayer (New York: Academic Press, 1964).

9. Renshon, *Psychological Needs*, p. 127.

10. J. Kagen and H. Moss, *Birth to Maturity* (New York: John Wiley and Sons, 1962).

11. G. Mitchell and L. Schroers also note the greater allocation of resources to first-borns. See their "Birth Order and Parental Experience in Monkeys and Man," in *Advances in Child Development and Behavior*, Vol. 8, ed. Hayne Reese (New York: Academic Press, 1973), pp. 159–84.

12. Renshon, *Psychological Needs*, pp. 135–40.

13. Steve Brown and John Ellithrop, "Emotional Experiences in Polit-

ical Groups: The Case of the McCarthy Phenomenon," *American Political Science Review* 64 (1970): 349–66.

14. Robert Agger et al., "Political Cynicism: Measurement and Meaning," *Journal of Politics* 23 (1961): 477–506.

15. Fred I. Greenstein, "The Benevolent Leader: Children's Images of Political Authority," *American Political Science Review* 54 (December 1960): 934–43; Fred I. Greenstein, "The Benevolent Leader Revisited: Children's Images of Political Leaders in Three Democracies," *American Political Science Review* 69 (December 1975): 1371–1398.

16. H. D. Lasswell, *Psychopathology and Politics* (Chicago: University of Chicago Press, 1930).

17. Renshon, *Psychological Needs*, p. 139.

18. Shirley Chisholm, *Unbought and Unbossed* (New York: Avon Books, 1970), p. 17.

19. Alden Hatch, *Red Carpet for Mamie* (New York: Henry Holt & Co., 1954), pp. 145–48.

20. Renshon, *Psychological Needs*, p. 240.

21. Jean Piaget and A. Weil, "The Development in Children of the Idea of the Homeland and a Relation with Other Countries," *International Social Science Bulletin* 3 (1951): 561–78. For a summary of Piaget's work see John H. Flavell, *The Developmental Psychology of Jean Piaget* (Princeton, N.J.: Van Nostrand, 1963).

22. Vera Zasulich, "Vospominania," *Byloe, 1919*, No. 14, pp. 89–107.

23. Quoted in Krishan Bhatia, *Indira: A Biography of Prime Minister Gandhi* (New York: Praeger Publishers, 1974), p. 43.

24. Russell Lewis, *Margaret Thatcher: A Personal and Political Biography* (London: Routledge & Kegan Paul, 1975), p. 13.

25. E. Breshko-Breshkovskaia, "Iz moikh vospominanii," *Vestnik russkoi revoliutsii*, 1905, No. 4, pp. 187–224.

26. For an excellent and detailed description of the political thought and activity of such young Russians during this period, see Franco Venturi, *Roots of Revolution: A History of the Populist and Socialist Movements in Nineteenth-Century Russia*, trans. Francis Haskell (New York: Alfred A. Knopf, 1960).

Chapter 7

Conclusions, Summary Profiles, and Implications of the Study

E BEGAN THIS endeavor with the deliberate intent of reconceptualizing current thinking—popular and that of social scientists—about the socialization of women to specialized elite political roles. In general, we have been discussing how girls are socialized to become achievers as adults in roles that traditionally were foreclosed to them because of their sex. Our approach has been to combine the inductive and deductive methods of analysis in the hopes that an examination of the real lives of female members of the political elite would enlighten and sharpen our hypothesis-generating and theory-building enterprise.

By way of conclusion and summary we feel that it is appropriate to investigate three major themes. First, to what extent has our theoretical model of the socialization of female political elites afforded us insights into the real-life activity, motivation, and behavior of these thirty-six women? In addition, have we been able to isolate any concrete, empirical referents for the ideal types theoretically formulated? Are there factual differences in these women's life experiences which would help to explain whether or not they engaged in political activity, or would differentiate among their styles and the intensity and salience of politics to them? In short, does our theoretical model provide any explanation for the differences in the adult political behavior of our thirty-six women?

Second, what are the implications of our study for the future study of women and politics? Does our conceptual approach and methodology hold any promise for future usage on a wider scale? Can the results of our study be replicated with a sample of political women with greater claim to representativeness? What significance does our approach have for research being conducted in related disciplines?

Finally, what, if anything, does our study of the development of these thirty-six elite women have to indicate about public policy? If we assume or accept the assumption that political participation is a desired goal, that women add a valuable dimension to the political world and therefore that an increase in their numbers should be encouraged, are there any policies our study would suggest for encouraging these things? We obviously are in no position to substantiate any broad policy changes but we believe that the results of our study do raise some vital questions about the socialization of girls.

Conclusions About Our Theoretical Framework

Our theoretical framework of the socialization of political women is built upon four stages of development. First, the child must develop an activist sex-role ideology; second, she must gain personal control over her life-space, gaining needed competencies and abilities to maintain control as the life-space expands; third, politics must become personally salient to her; and fourth, at various points of the life cycle her efforts at political participation must have been sufficiently rewarded and her experiences sufficiently successful to encourage her to continue. Our theory requires that these stages must be passed through sequentially; that is, the conditions of stage one must successfully be met before stage two will be possible. Any reversal of the sequence will do little to produce independent political women. In other words, politics can become salient to girls and women, but if they have not developed an activist sex-role ideology that permits them to perceive female political activity separate from male mediation, then such salience will not impel them into the political world. We should also add, however, that a girl can have successfully traversed stages one, two, and three, only to find that the opportunity for female achievement in politics is nonexistent or is extremely restricted.

The four stages require us to examine an individual's life

longitudinally. Although we believe that childhood socialization is most important for the first two stages particularly, we do not rule out the possibility of adult resocialization. Our feeling on the basis of the biographies of the thirty-six women we have studied is that adult resocialization of sex-role ideology is extraordinarily difficult and will be successful—regardless of the direction of the resocialization—in very few cases. The sex-role ideology and the gaining of a sense of personal control are so intimately related for girls that the squelching of an activist, independent ideology seems to lead almost automatically to a restricted female life-space and to the reduction of the opportunities for education and other means needed both to extend the life-space and to gain the abilities required to control that expanded life-space, particularly as it extends to the public/political realm.

In our judgment the four-stage model of the socialization of achieving political women has been supported by the biographical data on the thirty-six women we have studied. The private women, the public women, and the achieving political women do appear to be on a continuum not only in terms of their adult political behavior, but also in terms of how many of the four stages of the socialization process they have traversed. The private women as a group did not reach even stage one; they did not develop an activist sex-role ideology. The public women developed a more activist ideology, but, like their mothers before them, the activism did not extend to gaining the type of competencies and abilities needed to participate as equals with men in politics. The political women tended as a group (excluding the terrorists) to have passed through all four stages. The most succinct way of summarizing how well our framework helps to differentiate the socialization processes leading to specific types of female political behavior is to give brief profiles of each of the groups studied. These profiles summarizing our findings clearly indicate that our theoretical framework of female political socialization does provide a viable explanation for the differences in adult political behavior of our thirty-six women.

By developing a typology of female political behavior based upon three key dimensions of the theoretical framework (activist sex-role ideology, control over life-space, salience of politics), we have been able to identify mutually exclusive categories of female behavior that we would never have come up with had we considered behavior only on the basis of actual political status and achievement. Had someone made a study of merely the socialization of our three groups—political wives, elected female officials, and female revolutionaries—no insights would have been revealed. For in each of these three groups are women who behave differently: the political wives consist of both "private" and "public" women; the elected officials include "public" and "private" women resocialized, and political women who early in their lives had a strong sense of political efficacy. In the revolutionary group, the terrorists acted differently than the achieving revolutionaries. Without our theoretical framework and the typology, such differences in the political types of women would not have been easily identified and no consistent patterns would have become apparent. Findings on the private political wife would have canceled those on the public political wife. The findings on elected/mediated women would cancel those on the elected/personal efficacy women, and those on the terrorists would eliminate the insights on the revolutionaries.

Summary Profiles of the Types of Political Women

The Private, Traditional Women

The private woman is one whose adult life-space does not include much room for the political sphere. If anything, her concern for this area is one marked by civic obligation. She participates because it is her duty to participate. Duty does not imply much activity. She votes; she listens; and when major political events directly interfere with her life, she resents the intrusion. Politics has little or no salience for her. Conflicts between the roles of wife/mother and those of public being with civic responsibilities are minimal, for the definition of duty is minimal. For her, severe conflict between the two spheres is rare. The dominance and priority given to the family is so great that the pull of auxiliary matters meets with little sympathy or awareness.

The private woman is the daughter of an equally private woman. Her mother, in relation to her father, is likely to have adhered rigidly to a strict sexual division of labor. The mother has accepted the limitation of her world to that of the family. Within the family she is not likely to have had much authority relative to her husband; the major decisions about the home and the family are his. He is recognized as the legitimate and only truly competent judge of what is good for the family. Inequality of status, stature, authority, and power are the marks of this family. The male and the contribution he makes to the family are more highly valued than those of the female. Although she may be more closely linked with the family and its internal maintenance, his decisions even in this realm are supreme. The assumption that the woman's prime concern should be the family is so marked that any change that would endanger this unit is looked upon with extreme skepticism. The father in the childhood family of the private woman is the ultimate rule-maker and he is more likely than not to be constantly concerned with this realm rather than a more public one. He too looks upon the "outside world" as hostile and finds his home to be his "castle." He may more readily respond to the call of duty, for instance in the time of war, but he does this not out of interest in the political but out of sense of duty which is closely aligned with his protective role vis-à-vis the family.

Of primary importance in the negation of the political realm for women is a mother who has maintained a traditional sex-role ideology. Through imitation of this key female role model, the daughter has learned that no higher role can be given a woman than to devote herself totally and without compromise to her husband and children. Within and outside the family, the mother of such a woman is highly dependent on males and male mediation. She neither recognizes nor accepts the importance of personal independence for herself either within the family or without in the wider world. She is "protected" from the need to be concerned with these matters because of her man.

The mother of the private woman is not likely to have gained significant control over her life-space, which in her case is her family. She accepts her position within this sphere as most important and she does not seek to go beyond its confines. Consequently, she is not likely to have discussed politics, been particularly aware of its influence, nor notably concerned with enhancing her knowledge of and interest in it. These attitudes and behavioral patterns tend to be picked up by her daughter. Her daughter, unless she is presented with an alternative activist sex-role model to imitate that can replace the mother's model, will most certainly tend to repeat the patterns already set by her mother.

The private woman is also not likely to have been given the training or educational opportunities which would lead her to expect a different life-style from that of her mother. As a child expected to achieve in roles and patterns acceptable to her parents, she will tend to define her personal goals, like her mother, in terms of the primacy of her family. She is not likely to feel that training for a career or an extended life-space is necessary. She is willing to accept the sex division found within her childhood family; thus, she is not likely to see any reason to complain when her brothers are given the training necessary for them to repeat the pattern set by the father. From the earliest she is acquainted with, and acceptive of, the definition of certain activities as "unladylike" and not appropriate for her. Sports, physical activity, aggressive behavior, and any attempt to gain direct and personal control over one's immediate environment will be disapproved, punished, or not contemplated. Her personal definition of a successful and worthwhile life is one which calls for an early marriage to a man of slightly higher socioeconomic status than her father, and procreation of children.

With a private-woman role model for a mother, with education and peer encouragement to reinforce that model, nothing short of a major political event directly impinging on the woman's life-space will propel her to hear or respond to the call of public awareness or political life. At most she will accept a determination by the relevant male in her life of the relative importance she should place on the wider public/political world. Outside of broad socioeconomic modernization factors which are propelling a more active acceptance of a political role for females, her interest in politics is not likely to be any greater than that of her own mother. Circumstances of marriage to a "political male," that is, one who has decided to make politics his career, may require that she be more interested in politics than she might want; but like her mother before her, she believes that the dominant and perhaps even sole obligation of a woman is to her husband and children. Thus, she will attempt to be of assistance in the political life he has chosen, but she is also likely to resent its interference in what she would prefer to remain a private matter. This particular problem is never faced by the vast majority of traditional women for they marry men who have not found their career and life in politics. For those traditional women who have by their own self-conception the "misfortune" to be married to a man whose public life makes their private life less private, their consuming concern is to keep the political realm as distant as possible. They often envy the solitude of the life their mothers have lived, but they also realize as their mothers before them the necessity to do what they can to assist and help their husbands.

The private women we have included in our study illustrate how little import adult opportunities have for women if prior socialization has not equipped them to want to seize the opportunities. When presented with the circumstances which would make politics personally salient to them and in which they could have some impact, they merely resented and rejected the intrusion of politics into their private lives. By contrast, when the political women were faced with obstacles to their political participation, whether emanating from the regime itself or from persons in their immediate environment, they would not be dissuaded. One might conclude from this that it is the impact of what was learned early that counts, and that "what" is not political in nature—it is an activist or contemporary sex-role ideology.

The Terrorists

It was with astonishment that we greeted the socialization data pertaining to the terrorists included in our study. Having anticipated that they would be generally like the other political women, particularly the revolutionaries, we were continually surprised to find that the group they most closely approximated was the traditional private women.

This was the only group for which the Lasswellian, and ultimately Freudian-based, theory of personal displacement of private frustrations onto public objects seemed to hold any explanatory promise. Here were women we initially believed to be the most intense in their political commitment, for most of them ultimately laid down their lives for a political cause. The significance of a hypothesis-generating exercise which looks at *real* people is borne out here. Had we built upon a theory never tied to reality even tenuously because of the lack of a representative sample, this "surprise" would not have been forthcoming. Our terrorists turned out to be not very political at all. As a group they were not very skilled, knowledgeable, or competent as political actors. In many cases these women did not even give a political meaning to the act for which they were subsequently executed or gave their lives.

The patterns in the stages of socialization that were most apparent with the private women were repeated with the terrorists. The one major difference was that the terrorists developed an activist sex-role ideology within the confines of the private family. Physical necessity was more likely to have demanded that the mothers of terrorists engage in what might be termed nontraditional female activity; it was not as result of their own sense of personal control that they became active in fields outside the traditional female one.

The mothers of the terrorists were very similar to those mothers of the private women (and elected/mediated group) in the dimension we have labeled independence outside of the family. They had none. They differed from the mothers of the elected/mediated women, however, in that they were generally oppressed within the family by their husbands and unrespected for the roles they did play.

In stage two of our theory the terrorists scored as low as the private women. Not encouraged in their youth to believe that they could or would ever be able to control their own life situation, they were also not given the skills and training that might have made this option a possibility. As adults with the foundation for a nontraditional sex-role ideology, the terrorists were faced with seemingly contradictory demands. Nontraditional women by desire, but not capable of handling the strains of a nontraditional life, they became involved in revolutionary and terrorist activity which seems to have been mainly an outlet for their pent-up emotions and frustrations.

Displacement of personal frustrations onto public objects may well explain their political activity. However, the explanation of the terrorists' lives is as well-founded in our theory of personal development as it is any Freudian or Lasswellian one. Indeed, since we can differentiate various types of political behavior and find causal links to explain them, we would suggest that our theory is of much wider relevance and potential. There must be an explanation for behavior that leads to social changes, and for its opposite as well, the maintenance of social patterns. We believe that our theory has provided the framework for such an investigative study.

The Public Women

The category of public women/political wives revealed the importance of variations in the role-model offered by the mother. Expecting to discover that the mothers of these political wives would be more similar to than different from the private women's mothers, we were initially unaware of the degree to which the differences between them formed a pattern. The mothers of the public women were much more likely than the mothers of the private women to have been considered the equal partner in the family environment. They were women who had achieved a much greater control over their life-space. This added control was primarily exercised in the family environment but at least in this realm the daughter had a female to imitate who was not passive, not primarily submissive, and not unconsulted in decisions having to do with the family itself.

The greater independence of the mother within the home was for the most part closely aligned with an altered pattern of expectations on the part of the father. They did not seem to need the dominance of the private realm to offset a feeling of impotence in relation to the wider world. Nevertheless, for the daughter, the relationship of mother to father did not alter the expectation that the major link between the female and that wider world of politics would be through the mediation of a male, more precisely a husband. These daughters in their adult life would accept the mediation of their political husbands as their mothers had accepted the mediation of their fathers. But like their mothers, they would have a greater control over their immediate family life-space and their dependence on males would be less than that of the traditional woman.

Inherent in the lives of the public women is an explanation of why these highly visible females never desired a political career of their own. Although these women were more likely to have had mothers who were the equals of their husbands in the home, they also were mothers who for the most part had no personal experience with independence in the public realm. Without the training and skill development that would establish their independence and equality in the male spheres of economics, education, and politics, the mothers of these women gave them no direct model of working in the world to imitate. As adults, public women continued to need the mediation of males, their husbands. They outdid their mothers in the degree to which they extended their life-space to include public areas, but this development was an adult acquisition. Formed later and with few chances to achieve the rewards of successful participation without male mediation, they seldom developed into women with a sense of personal political efficacy. One senses, however, that in most cases the adult structural opportunity presented by the death or demise of their husbands might have led to the personal use of the skills and talents they had developed during their adult apprenticeship.

Public women demonstrated more personal control as youths than their private-woman counterparts. More likely to have been educated to a nontraditional sex role, they were better equipped to meet the challenges of public life as the wife of a chief executive. They were also more likely to have had all the elements we have noted to define a sense of personal control. On this count they are much closer to the political women than the private women and terrorists.

The public woman differs significantly from the private woman, and we believe that this type may represent a transitional role for an increasing number of women advancing toward greater political awareness and interest. Mediation by males may provide the initial nature of the involvement in politics, but once activated, these experiences may accumulate so as to transform the public being into a political one. Since the public women in our study were wives of chief executives, we were unable to investigate the conversion process necessary to transform, for instance, a public experience in an organization like the League of Women Voters or within the party infrastructure into a sense of personal political efficacy sufficiently well-developed to lead to standing for public office. We can only suggest that women who are the products of family environments wherein the mother has achieved independence within the family and wherein they themselves have begun to acquire the skills which would facilitate participation in the public sphere are the most likely to convert these experiences into a sense of personal political efficacy.

The Elected/Mediated Women

In several respects the profile of the elected/mediated woman closely approximates that of the political wives who were public women. In other elements the profile is much closer to that of the private women and the terrorists. Convinced that there was a substantive difference between the woman who has achieved an elective political office as the result of the insistence, encouragement, or death of a politically active male, and the woman who personally planned for and engaged in political activity, we kept the data on these two groups separate, although the women in both groups ultimately attained similar elective status.

Once again the major determinant of the behavior of the adult woman seems to have been the sex-role ideology presented by the mother. Perhaps most surprising was the degree to which the elected/mediated group were women with traditional mothers. Their mothers were very much like the mothers of the private women and terrorists. They were even more traditional than the mothers of the other public women.

The mothers of the women who achieved high political office through the mediation of their husbands possessed few of the characteristics we consider essential for the transmission of an activist orientation toward the public world. Neither particularly independent in their own homes nor particularly inclined to have acquired the skills necessary for advancement in the public realm, these mothers presented traditional role-models for their daughters. Measures of the mothers' independence appear to have been slightly higher than the mothers of the private women but not as high as those of public women. (Given the same opportunities as the elected/mediated women, the public women probably would have parlayed them into a more fully developed sense of personal political efficacy than these elected officials did.)

These patterns confirm the primacy of the early socialization experience. The adult resocialization which these women underwent to convert them from nonpolitical, private beings into political helpmates to their political husbands and later into independent political actors themselves did not so easily overcome the expectation patterns of a lifetime. One senses that the length of apprenticeship grows directly with the degree to which the adult pattern is contrary to the youth pattern. The more traditional the initial socialization process, the more concentrated or protracted must be the adult resocialization to overcome this earlier pattern.

The attitudes of the fathers of these elected/mediated women are closer to those of the fathers of the private women than to the fathers of the public women. These were men who made their home their primary concern and considered their job and economic activity as a means to support their family rather than as an expression of themselves.

The elected/mediated women were less likely to have

gained significant control over their life-spaces as children. Their ability to take the confidence achieved in the family sphere and extend it to a wider realm was not great, and they probably would not have become political women without the adult mediation of their political husbands. Simply to hear opportunity knocking requires some ability to conceive of its possibilities and its beneficial consequences. For the most part the mediated/elected group achieved the characteristics necessary to "hear the knock"—but only when they were well into adulthood.

Their initial attraction to politics appears to have been the direct result of their adult life. No prior preparation in their childhood family appears to have been available. With a less well-developed sense of their own personal control, they approached the political world with a hesitancy as marked as that of the traditional wives of political men. The salience of politics to them was a derivative of their relationship to their husbands. Moreover, the political actions these women engaged in continued to be mediated. To some degree we believe this helps explain the relatively minor accomplishments and social changes initiated by the vast majority of women elected to political office. Since most women elected to office have come to their positions as the result of the mediation of their political husbands, and without personally derived goals and desires associated with the political realm, they are less likely to formulate personal directions for their political activity. Circumstances seem to rule them rather than their making the circumstances. Initiatives and new formulations are rare. Deriving their interests from their political husbands and often seeing this as a way of replicating their own mothers' devotion to and dependence on their fathers, they tend to continue to take stances and policy positions very much in keeping with those of their husbands. Just as the initial demand for the extension of the vote to females should not have caused the "power elite" any great worry, so too the political behavior of elected/mediated women should cause no upset, for it tends to duplicate the positions taken by the relevant male in their lives.

Achieving Political Women: Elected/Personal Efficacy Group

The most famous of the women included in our study appear

in this category. The profile of their socialization experience lends considerable weight to the theory underlining our study. For no other group save the revolutionaries has there been the consistency of the findings relative to the four stages of female political socialization. It is most appropriate that the achievers in our study have most closely approximated the model we anticipated would explain female political behavior. Undoubtedly, there is great need for further investigation and study but the hypothesis-generating and theory-building exercise we have undertaken here found support in the biographic material concerning these real women. Certainly the sample is not sufficiently large nor is it representative enough of the universe of political women, but we are nevertheless impressed with the consistency of the patterns which we found among this group.

Perhaps the strongest case can be made with this group for the essential influence of the first role-model for a young girl, her mother. The mothers of these most unusual and public women were for the most part also most unusual and public women. Taught early to expect an active role in the family and its decision-making through imitation of a mother who definitely played such a role, these political achievers had accepted the idea that they could be both female and competent. Once one adds that their mothers were also likely to have begun the process of extending the life-space they occupied to include some public sphere traditionally defined as "masculine," we find yet more support for the view that the development of an activist, modern sex-role ideology is the necessary determinant in the development of political women.

It may seem repetitive to cite the primacy of the model of the mother but we believe that this factor is so important that it bears underlining. Women who achieved a personal sense of efficacy about directing their lives had an effective model very early in life. This model did not have to have been connected with politics, but only to have gained control over her life-space, primarily the family, and to have begun the process of developing an extended life-space. The mothers of the political women refused to equate their total life with the private aspects of the family. They maintained the importance of the family unit without seeing the sexual division of labor in socially accepted stark terms. They as well as their husbands had responsibilities to support, enhance, and promote the family. They as well as their husbands had skills and competencies which would make their participation in the "public male spheres" profitable for themselves and their family. They refused to accept the social stigma of being "unfeminine" as a restraint on their activities. Strong women with a sense of their own worth, confident of their abilities as well as cognizant of their limitations, created an atmosphere in which sex stereotyping did not limit options for their daughters from the day of their birth. The display of a world view rather than of a parochial one and the example of activism are the major contributions these mothers made to their famous daughters.

The second stage of the developmental model, the development of a sense of personal control, is as strongly displayed by the elected/personal efficacy group as the first stage was. The data on the childhood experiences of these women are remarkable for the consistency of the pattern presented. Encouraged by the presence of an unusually active mother to expect a nontraditional role for themselves, they were led early into areas that were not familiar to most young girls. They saw few limitations to what they could be. They did not learn that being female meant that they could not be political beings. And no obstacle was going to prevent them from gaining the skills and competencies which would make such a possibility real. They experienced very early in their lives the liberating effect of making decisions for themselves and accepting the concurrent responsibility. Their early life was no more mediated by males than their later political life would be. They would not be "anti-male" but they would also not be so consumed by the presumed restraints of being a wife and/or mother that they would recognize limitations to what they could do.

These women were afforded the training and the life experiences necessary for them to develop the sense that their immediate life-space was within their control. They were afforded the opportunity to learn rational problem-solving approaches. They learned early to compete with males and to assume that that competition would never find them defeated simply because they were girls. Any attempt to restrict their skill training or their own sense of competence would meet with the belligerent response of one who has expected no insurmountable restraints to personal development, and who refuses to accept the legitimacy of any.

These attitudes are carried into their adult life, and they see no necessity for giving up marriage and children in order to pursue their goals. A family is a real obstacle only to those who have some personal doubt about their own definition of their mission. They may wish that the social structure made more provisions for their admixture of public and private existence. The society's refusal to afford them the social approval associated with the woman who totally dedicates herself to her family does not deter them, however. The sense of personal control they have achieved in their youth has expanded their life-space and changed the personal psychological meaning of each of Maslow's need levels. Self-definition and self-concept have expanded. Also noteworthy is their seeming immunity to the hubris of those women who have broken with a socially approved pattern but who lack a sense of the righteousness of this break. These latter women need to negate, diminish, and belittle the socially approved model of wife/mother at home. The personal efficacy group has enough confidence in themselves and the choices they have made not to need to deny the importance of the family and the importance of the mother's role. This may be the greatest testimony of appreciation they could provide for their own mothers.

The first two stages of our model have laid the foundations for an atypical role outside the family but have not explained why the realm of this role would be political. The third stage provides this explanation, and the facts about our achieving political women provide once again strong foundations for believing that our theoretical framework does explain the empirical reality.

In every case of women who accepted the legitimacy of the regime, stood for election to a political office, achieved a sense of personal efficacy, and received rewards from operating in the political realm, politics had been a discussion topic during their childhood. Such family talk, especially when it occurs in early childhood, legitimates the child's interest in the subject and makes this realm personally important and significant. Here the importance of the father and male siblings is a factor to consider. Most of the political women in our study came to an interest in politics as a result of male influence. But male influence and male mediation are two different and distinct things. These women in the personal efficacy group were not told what they were to believe, how to vote, or how to act. The political realm was in that sense an unmediated realm. Just as their mothers before them had put aside the need for male mediation in the generalized "public" realm, they may have become interested in politics as the result of political discussions with adults in their families, as the result of their fathers' and/or mothers' political activity, or as the result of a significant life-experience with political overtones, but in all these cases the motivation for responding as they did appeared to be their own independence and sense of personal control.

The Revolutionaries

One of the discoveries in our investigation is the degree to which the findings we have just cited relative to the elected/personal efficacy women are also true of the revolutionaries. These results too lend strong support to our model of the socialization of political women. Obviously, the same disclaimers as to the representativeness and paucity of cases need to be made here. But once again one is struck by the degree to which the patterns found with the elected political achievers are repeated.

The mothers of the revolutionaries were women who had achieved a high degree of independence both within the family and within public life. Accepted generally as the equals of their husbands, these mothers laid the foundation for the revolutionaries' expectations that they too would play an equally responsible and important role as the men with whom they might become involved in their adult life whether in the private or the public realm. The daughters also learned that they must have skills and competencies to enter the public world. Their mothers had looked upon the public world as an anxiously anticipated and accepted challenge and so too their daughters looked upon this excursion with some pleasure. The public realms were not unknown; they could not, therefore, elicit the same type of fear and dread they seemed to hold for many private women. The public realms promised change and challenge; these women were as eager as their mothers before them to meet that challenge.

The revolutionaries also demonstrated a highly developed sense of personal control. Indeed, of all the groups they were the most likely in their childhood years to have been led to the belief that their need for personal control was acceptable and that its extension to a traditionally nonfemale realm was also legitimate. Influences of their youth all pointed in the same direction. There were few clearly defined and restricted areas labeled "for boys only." Allowed to feel that they could be and do generally what they wanted, they would not as adults settle for a private-woman life-style. One of the marks of their determination in this regard is the revolutionary nature of their political behavior. One might well assume, given the basic similarity between this group and the political achievers, that had the revolutionaries been born in another time and place, they too would have overcome the societal obstacles to female political participation and have gone on to significant elective offices.

The only major difference found to explain the diversity of political behavior between the elected achievers and the revolutionaries (outside of the general time and societal ones just noted) is in regard to the third stage. Politics for the revolutionaries was certainly no less salient than it was for the elected women, nor were the revolutionaries any more likely to have accepted male mediation in this realm, but their expression was against the regime instead of in support of it. The reason appears to rest in how politics became salient to them. The revolutionaries more than any other group had been on the punishment end of politics as a direct result of a personally disruptive event. To have a tragedy befall one and to be able to attribute at least partial blame to the political system is certainly conducive to producing political behavior which is regime-negating.

The examination of the socialization process for the revolutionaries included in our study demonstrates the value of a theoretical framework aimed at explaining social change. With the exception of Angela Davis, all of our revolutionaries began their activities in the nineteenth century. For women in their day and age to have been concerned with politics foretold of a major break in the socialization process. This break was occasioned by the examples of an activist mother and a father liberated from male chauvinism. Its political import, however, was supplied by events that led them to question the legitimacy of the political regime itself. These factors coalesced to foster a revolutionary approach to the content, intensity, and direction of their political behavior.

Research Implications

For the most part the biographical data on the lives of the thirty-six women whom we have studied do fall into the patterns of our theoretical framework. This framework has allowed us the possibility of not only categorizing the adult behavior of real women, but also of specifying the types of political and nonpolitical learning, and the socialization processes needed to produce given adult political behavior. This initial success leads us to conclude that this study has a variety of implications for future research—on socialization in general, political socialization in particular, social movements, specific types of political behavior, and, of course, the study of female behavior.

Social science stresses hypothesis-testing which, in turn, suggests the primacy of the deductive approach to the study of a subject matter. One presumably starts with a theory to explain and simplify the more complex and corrugated reality, collects data which are observable and measurable, and then puts the theory to the test. Then the researcher is either led to a still firmer belief in the theory (seemingly not a subjectively unimportant consequence) or, much less frequently, to a revision or a reconsideration of the theory. We would very much like to emphasize the limitations of this strictly deductive approach particularly as it relates to the subject of women. The pervasiveness of sexism and the concomitant inability to conceive of women in non-sexist terms means that research in this area is fraught with difficulties. Rare indeed is the theoretical model that does not have a preconceived notion of what is the appropriate response of women as opposed to men. Rare indeed are the research designs and measuring instruments which do not structure into themselves preconceived expectations about women which then are fulfilled in the process of research.

As Thomas Kuhn has pointed out in his discussion of the discovery procedures in the physical sciences, contradictory instances and unexplained aberrations from a scientific paradigm must become very numerous before those who have a vested interest in the continuation of a familiar and traditional explanation schema will find the restructuring of the paradigm necessary.[1] As noted time and time again, changes in physical science paradigms encounter less general resistance for they hardly ever touch the society at large. Social theories, however, are much more likely to meet the resistance of the layperson—as well as those researchers using the schema. This resistance is particularly likely to arise if the language and conceptualization of the subject matter are being questioned. The study of women constitutes such a case.

The mere inclusion of women in the study of political behavior required a major social science breakthrough just as the inclusion of women in the voting population required a major societal breakthrough. Because the nature of the subject matter is so tainted with preconceived and predetermined patterns of expectation, almost any theoretical model is likely to create a bias toward the continuation of the explanatory schemas that have excluded women from the study of politics. Since female members of the political elite have been so few, they have been largely ignored or studied as the exception. Until there are attempts to study this "unique" phenomenon with theories that must explain the behavior of this female elite as something other than a deviation from the expected, current theories must be preceded by an "openness" to the complicated nature of the reality. Reality must speak to us first. We must look and listen before hypotheses capable of understanding and explaining the behavior in question can be formulated, much less tested. Facts not only do not speak for themselves; theories also do not. They too are applied and interpreted within a broader world outlook that contains hidden assumptions and agendas. It is not at all clear that studies of random, representative samples of college students or some other "typical" population used to "test" these theories are likely to reach accurate conclusions about the nature of the prerequisites for elite participation or for identifying sources of social change.

Biographers are as much a captive of their own images of what a woman is and what is "unusual" about the women they study as the rest of us are. They too seek information and record its presence within the ideologically accepted conceptual framework. Time and time again, in reading the biographies of the women in our study, we were struck by the implicit evaluation that it was the information about the father which was thought to be essential for explaining the political development of the daughter. When a woman had not achieved a personal political position, the father remained a key figure for examination but there was much more likelihood that the mother would receive more attention. If the woman was "unusual" and political, it was clearly within the expectation of the biographers to look for this development as a result of the influence of the males in the woman's life. In most cases the fact that the biographers could not ignore the "unusual" nature of the political woman's mother is the best testimony to the very nontraditional and activist women they were. Rarely do the biographers attribute political significance to this. The inherent lack of a comparative framework in biographies makes it almost impossible to overcome the biases inherent in the prevailing sex-role ideology.

We would hope that biographers of achieving women, whether in the political or some other realm, would seek to include information more systematically on the variables that were found pertinent in this study. It would be helpful to know much more, for example, about the biographee's mother and the mother's relationship to the father. The mother's competencies and abilities in the public realm are likely to be as critical as those of the father's for a daughter, yet they are seldom mentioned.

We have employed Maslow's need hierarchy and Renshon's application of it to political efficacy as the theoretical framework to investigate the relatively new phenomenon of elite political women. Although such women have existed in the past, for the most part they were the daughters of royal or aristocratic families for whom the family circumstance necessitated participation. The emergence of females in politics, elected in their own right, is a twentieth-century phenomenon.

Maslow's need hierarchy is based on an evaluation of the human species which does not accept that the sex differences among its members are key determinants to need and behavioral patterns. It does not recognize one need hierarchy for men and another for women. The societal division of labor and distribution of roles which are consistently found to differentiate between the male and female of the species cannot be attributed to the existence of two separate and distinct natural need hierarchies. The same need hierarchy applies to women as well as to men. The sequence of need development and fulfillment is the same for men and women. Men who have not achieved a degree of physical health, physiological and biological well-being, cannot move to the second level of the need hierarchy—personal control. It is only at this second level that political matters can become salient as a means of fulfilling a human need. Unless men have gained some sense of well-being about their day-to-day existence, they cannot be particularly concerned with politics. The same applies to women.

The applicability of the *same* need hierarchy (and the same sequence of development) to both men and women has implications for future research. Although some of these implications appear so self-evident that they should not need mentioning, sexism and the expectations of the behavioral differences between the two genders in the political arena are so pervasive that even the most basic facts require stressing.

First, as already noted, politics is not inherently a "masculine" activity. Research on politics and political behavior should drop the assumption that it is.

Second, political scientists, politicians, and the public should stop assuming that having women in public office or as active participants in the political system will eventually lead to a basic change in public policy or in definition of the public interest. Almost none of the elected women with personal political efficacy or the revolutionaries were women who would have actively sought the title "feminists." Although none opposed the feminist movement, very few actively crusaded on its behalf. One even voted against the Equal Rights Amendment to the U.S. Constitution. These women who "have made it" gained the acceptance of the male-dominated structure. They seem to have also gained similar "virtues" and "vices" that their male counterparts have. We cannot accept the perspective that says "Give women the reins of power, and then watch war, corruption, hunger, and misery disappear." This assumption of the consequence of the development of political women accepts a basic theory of human nature which assumes that the male and female of the species are really different by nature. The nonsexist nature of the Maslowian need hierarchy suggests that we ought to refute this assumption. The question needing to be researched is not how sex is related to public policy preferences but rather how variations in life-space and competencies are related to public policy preferences. In the past, sex as a research variable has been useful because it has succinctly summarized variations in the male/female life-space and experiences. As the twenty-first century approaches, this variable is likely to lose much of its usefulness.

Third, we believe that recent research on political women has too often fallen into the acceptance of the sexist theories underlying the societal understanding of the "proper place" of women. Expecting to see a role conflict between her roles as wife and mother and those of her political career, these works have concentrated on these impediments to political achievement by women. We do not wish to suggest that these obstacles are not real, nor do we want in any way to diminish the impediment they present to real women. We do believe, however, that the very nature of the perception of role conflict is contingent upon the socialization processes occurring considerably earlier. Thus we would like to suggest that, for the women whom Jeane Kirkpatrick, in her 1974 study entitled *Political Women*, found unable to manage the conflict between their roles as wife/mother and state legislator, the problem for these women is predicated on their less well-developed activist sex-role ideology, a lessened sense of personal control, and the failure of politics to have attained the "self-defining" character it has for women who have achieved significant political success. Less research is needed to ascertain what it is about women and their role conflicts per se that does not allow them to engage in certain types of activities; more research is needed on what characterizes in positive terms the women who have engaged in such activity. To study the "why" of female nonparticipation in traditionally defined male spheres only confirms the previously known and legitimated sex stereotyping. To study the "why" of participation by women in nontraditional, formerly "male" roles, requires a look at the things that bring changes to society rather than a concern for the past or the status quo.

Fourth, because the Maslowian framework does not have built-in biases on the basis of race, color, or creed any more than sex, it would seem quite worthwhile to investigate subcultural and subgroup variations in political participation in the elite using the framework outlined here for women. The basic conceptual variation for these studies from what we have done here would be the identification and investigation of the uniqueness of the life-space of the particular subgroup being studied. An important question we have not really touched in this study is the impact that one's ethnicity and race have on the development of the activist ideology and on the definition, nature, and scope of one's life-space. An examination of ethnicity and race in this framework might lead to a major breakthrough in our knowledge of how ethnicity and political behavior are related. The same four stages of the socialization process outlined in this study on women will have to be traversed by males as well as females if they are to enter the political elite. Stage one, the development of an activist ideology, that is, learning how to relate to the world, to time, to others, and to oneself in an active, outgoing, public way, lies at the core of this process. Social scientists need to learn more about this type of learning, and political scientists, in particualr, need to do more research on how the members of political elites learn this activist ideology and how it relates to political behavior.

Fifth, the assumptions made about human nature in this study have not been limited by time or specific cultures. We have assumed—and the patterns we have found by types of adult behavior performed seem to support the view—that human nature at its core is relatively constant. What has changed over time to produce variations in human behavior and culture—the manifestations of human nature—is not human nature itself but rather the experiences, the competencies, and the opportunities that human beings have. The socialization processes in some cultures and times foster human development, that is, allow persons to advance to higher need levels. In all cultures and in all times a selection process occurs indicating that only a given proportion of individuals benefit from the type of sequential socialization needed to become achievers.

This brings us to a major question raised at the beginning of this book. Why at this point in history have so many female political achievers developed? Is their existence an aberration or is it likely to continue and to expand? Although much more research is obviously needed on these questions, we believe reasonable answers to them do exist.

The thirty-six women we studied were not "unnatural" women. Indeed, many of the political women, including revolutionaries, were among the most cultured, beautiful, and desired women of their times. Political activity is clearly not unnatural for women. There is nothing intrinsic in the political realm that militates against the participation of women. Tradition and custom, mores, and social expectations are the primary determinants of the historical nonparticipation of women. Theories of the "weaker" sex will not and cannot account for lesser participation. The fact that there are increasing numbers of political women suggests that they are not freaks of nature. The fact that there are explanatory factors for their increasing numbers, for their emergence at this time and in the countries they are found most often, means that they cannot be aberrations, accidents, in the course of history.

In our judgment there are macro-level developments which

indicate that the numbers of female political participants should continue to multiply. The technological and economic foundations of our culture, the striving of the masses for equality of condition, status, and experience, rest upon industrialization. The mass production needed to provide sufficient goods and services to meet basic human needs and human wants did not exist before the Industrial Revolution. Although this material foundation has as important ramifications for the lives of women as of men, the effect of industrialization upon the family has had the greatest impact on the lives of women. As Thompson has noted, "Each stage in industrial differentiation and specialization struck also at the family economy, disturbing customary relations between man and wife, parents and children, and differentiating more sharply between 'work' and 'life.'"[2] This disturbing of the family has given rise to several different types of families especially in terms of the role and status of women. As our discussion in Chapter One of Michael Young's and Peter Willmott's *The Symmetrical Family*[3] and their theory of types of families has indicated, it is the increase in the proportion of families based on companionate love, mutual esteem and respect, that leads to our optimism about future female political participation.

This kind of family—the stage-three type—seems to have been most rare in history. It is this type of family (and the societies which allow and encourage such families to develop) that permits the girl-child to develop her full human potential. As was also noted in Chapter One, all three types of families have surely existed throughout history; indeed, there are undoubtedly other types of families as well. The point we wish to make is that the proportion of the families at each of these stages at various times in history has varied substantially. Young and Willmott stress strongly that it is only in the twentieth century that the proportion of stage-three families has been sufficiently large to have an effect upon the society as a whole.

We see a clear relationship between this stage-three type of family and the development of political women. The elected women with personal political efficacy and the revolutionaries whom we studied came from families based upon companionate love and mutual esteem, with a basic equality between the mother and the father. With few exceptions both parents seemed able to have personal control over their lives and to have expanded life-spaces. The mother and father were not identical, but they were equal in meaningful ways. So long as the macro-level economic and technological developments encourage this type of family, the number of achieving public and political women will, we believe, increase.

Sixth, we have noted the critical importance of the same-sex parent, the mother, as a predictor of the daughter's behavior. It seems logical to assume that if the mother is so important, then a major reason for the rise and fall of various feminist movements might well have been identified. To the extent that feminists are less likely to marry and raise daughters who then are socialized in an activist ideological framework, to that degree does the feminist cause take on rise-and-fall character. Feminist and women's liberation movements like most other social movements have tended to stress "consciousness," have tried to make specific issues salient to women and girls. Most, in other words, have conducted campaigns at what we call stage three of our socialization hierarchy. Social movements have a difficult time in actually changing the life-space and competencies of individuals. Wars, depressions, geographical moves, technological advances, and similar major events can lead to such changes, but social movements cannot. Social movements tend to arise after major life-space changes occur.

Making people aware of politics or of a specific issue alone may produce an enlarged social movement, but it is not likely to produce lasting social change. Although activist sex-role models other than the mother can exert some influence in leading women to politics, our impression is that the import of non-mother sex-role models is secondary. In other words, our study strongly suggests to us that daughters with activist sex-role ideologies and nontraditional female behavior patterns develop as a direct consequence of having had mothers who tended toward having either an activist sex-role ideology and/or chose or were forced to engage in nontraditional female behavior. If this is so to the extent we believe it to be, then the multiplying of women in politics—indeed, the expansion of the feminist movement—is highly dependent upon the child-bearing and child-rearing patterns of already liberated women. Historically and currently many "liberated" women have tended not to marry, not to have children, and if they had them, not to raise them. We wonder how lasting the gains made for women will be if it is primarily the private, traditional women who raise the children. We also wonder if the rise and fall of the various feminist movements in history is not directly related to the inherent contradiction between women's becoming "liberated" from the family and children and the need to perpetuate their own kind. If the liberated women do not multiply and reproduce themselves, then the expansion of their numbers is dependent upon macro-level forces or accidents of history.

Our study, like that of many others, found that the political achievers came from an intact family based upon love, esteem, and respect, as well as equality. The women's liberation movement in the United States in the 1970s is credited by many for the upsurge of single-parent families, a doubling of the divorce rate, and a sharp increase in the numbers of women who live alone. If the findings of our study and other studies are correct, that female achievers tend to come from and apparently require a stage-three family environment, then not only all women but also all men ought to be concerned about correcting those features of society and its ideologies that give rise to the current sharp increase in negative socialization environments. Stage-one and stage-two families do not generate achieving types of women. Our society needs to develop public policies that will promote and support the stage-three type of family. We believe that women from this kind of family will expand their life-spaces and will extend personal control over their lives. Families or men per se are not hindrances to the liberation of women; only certain types of families and men are hindrances.

Public-Policy Implications

The public-policy implications of our study are probably even more numerous than its research implications. It is with great caution that we approach this section for we are fully cognizant of the exploratory nature of our investigation and the verification that it still requires. To suggest that we could encourage a particular orientation in public policy as the result of our investigation of thirty-six women would be audacious if not foolhardy. We would, however, feel remiss if we did not at least indicate that our theory of the socialization of political females has profound and severe implications in this area.

Implied in this assertion is a basic assumption that humans grow according to how they are socialized. There are vast variations in the types of people a society produces. If we understand that socialization creates the kinds of people in the society, resignation to the will of a supernatural being or to a noncontrollable process is less possible. Ignorance of social processes allows for the continued belief that responsibility rests outside the control of ourselves. It also attributes a mystical power to institutional forms which through misunderstanding are felt to be beyond human control. But as the processes shaping the human being become more understood, the responsibility for acting with and upon this knowledge is more pronounced, and social change is made more possible. We begin to see the value implications of the public choices that are or are not made.

If one starts with the assumption that it is important for *all* members of the society to be public beings, to be active members of the political system, then one also must project an altered pattern of expectation about the private world of women and the family because females will now be included in the public world —a sphere mainly closed to them in the past. The implications for public policy are quite clear. If stage-one and stage-two families impede or foreclose political participation by women, do public policies supporting such families violate women's civil liberties? If so, they are unconstitutional, are they not? The potential implications of this study for public policy regarding the family and parental relationships are extensive indeed. Should the government encourage the working mother by policies designed to make full-time work less of a burden and more of a joy? Should fathers be encouraged to assume some of the nurturant and socializing roles traditionally restricted to the role of mother? If we want girls to become political participants equal to men, the answer seems to be yes. Policies relating to salaries but also to maternity leave, child-care facilities, paternity leave, and other economically related benefits become primary. The work of Safilios-Rothschild[4] should be consulted to develop more fully some of the implications relative to the internal structure of the family and its relationship to the public realm.

Although our work would point to the primacy of the family as the major source of political socialization, educational institutions clearly have an impact. Educational environments which foster the belief that there are naturally separate "male and female" areas perpetuate sex-role differences. Our study suggests that girls denied equal treatment in the educational process are quite unlikely to become independent political participants. A longitudinal study of the changes in U.S. women's sex-role attitudes, 1964–1974, found, as we have, that "educational attainment and employment are among the most important predictors of attitudes at a given point in time."[5] Clearly, a nation that seeks to promote political participation by women—or even an activist sex-role ideology in women—must certainly end the unequal allocation of educational resources by sex in both the curricular and extracurricular areas. To produce political women, restrictions against females in professional training *must* end. Further, cultural norms and laws which encourage girls to marry several years earlier than boys and, therefore, to end or interrupt their education, should be reconsidered.

Religion has provided most people with a key component of their basic world outlook. Most religions have a sharply restricted view of the public role of women. The major religions have tended to place women in subordinate positions on earth while usually granting that women can be equal in heaven—but not all do even that. Since the churches throughout history have conferred a grudging citizenship on women—one always mediated by males—might not this historical religious conditioning be a major obstacle for women to become independent actors in the political realm? If the present exclusion of females from the ministry in most churches is confirmed by other studies to be linked to nonparticipation or to a reduction in female political participation, then a constitutional question of major proportion will have been raised. Does separation of church and state require the state to tolerate sexually segregated systems in religions if this segregation is clearly linked to a reduction of a group's civil and political liberties? If religious beliefs provide the basic ideological support for a subordinate female sex-role ideology and that ideology is at the core of women's nonparticipation and inability to exercise their civil and political rights, then what responsibility does the state have to alter that view?

In the final analysis the basic questions raised by the women's liberation movement must be asked again. Do we want to encourage the development of the activist egalitarian sex-role ideology among the female population? Is the belief that women should be as free as men to pursue educational and occupational goals one that we really want to promote? Is the equal sharing of responsibilities and rights within and outside the home a public policy which we desire? If there is nothing in the nature of woman that necessitates her remaining a nonpublic, nonpolitical being, do we want to follow up on the implications of our study for the development of political women? If we do not, then perhaps we should not be so hypocritical as to proclaim that our democracy is of the people, for the people, and by the people. Unless, of course, we wish to deny that women are people.

Notes

1. Thomas S. Kuhn, *The Structure of Scientific Revolutions* (Chicago: University of Chicago Press, 1962), pp. 52–65.

2. E. P. Thompson, *The Making of the English Working Class* (London: Gollancz, 1963), p. 416.

3. Michael Young and Peter Willmott, *The Symmetrical Family* (New York: Pantheon Books, 1973).

4. Constantina Safilios-Rothschild, *Women and Social Policy* (Englewood Cliffs, N.J.: Prentice-Hall, 1974).

5. Karen Oppenheim Mason, John L. Czajka, and Sara Arber, "Change in U.S. Women's Sex-Role Attitudes, 1964–1974," *American Sociological Review* 41 (August 1976): 573.

Data Form: The Making of Political Women°

I. General background data

1. Subject's full name (include maiden if any) _____

   _____

2. Date of birth _____

3. Date of death _____

4. Major type of political behavior (more than one item may be checked):

   ____a. political wife

   ____b. elected political official

   ____c. political revolutionary

5. Nationality (ethnic affiliation) _____

   _____

6. Race _____

7. Country of birth _____

8. Country or countries where political behavior occurred. If more than one country, describe in detail what activity was performed in each country. _____

   _____

9. On a separate sheet, list the specific political activities engaged in, any offices held, years of involvement, and other specific political or nonpolitical achievements that this woman accomplished.

10. Type of political system of country when the woman became active politically (check one):

    ____a. traditional autocracy

    ____b. modern autocracy, but not communist

    ____c. East European communist (including USSR)

    ____d. Western European and U.S. type of constitutional liberal democracy

11. Age at which the woman first became involved in political activity:

    ____a. 19 or under   ____e. 35 to 39

    ____b. 20 to 24   ____f. 40 to 44

°This is a copy of the biographic data form used for each of the women included in our study.

    _____c. 25 to 29   _____g. 45 to 49

    _____d. 30 to 34   _____h. 50 and over

12. Age first elected to office or first became revolutionary:

    _____a. 19 or under   _____e. 35 to 39

    _____b. 20 to 24   _____f. 40 to 44

    _____c. 25 to 29   _____g. 45 to 49

    _____d. 30 to 34   _____h. 50 and over

13. Length of time engaged in political activity, from entrance to death or present:

    _____a. 2 years or less   _____e. 16 to 20 yrs.

    _____b. 3 to 5 yrs.   _____f. 21 to 25 yrs.

    _____c. 6 to 10 yrs.   _____g. 25 yrs. and over

    _____d. 11 to 15 yrs.

II. Composition of the family during subject's childhood

1. Was the nuclear family intact throughout childhood (up to age 18 were both parents living)?

    _____yes   _____no

    a. If no, which parent was absent?

        _____mother   _____father   _____both

    b. Did that parent die or leave?

        _____died when the child was _____years old

        _____left when the child was _____years old

    c. Describe in some detail the circumstances of the death or departure. What was the major cause of the death or departure? In particular could this event have been attributed by the subject to political factors? Elaborate as much as possible. _____

    _____

    _____

2. How many siblings were in the childhood family? _____

    a. How many brothers? _____

        (1) how many were older brothers? _____

        (2) how many were younger brothers? _____

    b. How many sisters? _____

        (1) how many older sisters? _____

        (2) how many younger sisters? _____

3. Birth order _____ (give exact position in family if known)

_____a. oldest part of family
_____b. middle part of family
_____c. youngest part of family

4. If mother or father left or died, describe the effect of the death or departure on who raised the subject and on how she was raised. Provide as much detail as possible.

_____

_____

III. Characteristics of subject's mother

1. Mother's full name _____

2. Highest level of education achieved by mother:
   _____a. no formal education
   _____b. grade school or equivalent—at least literate
   _____c. high school or equivalent
   _____d. additional training of a skill type (nonprofessional, e.g., midwife, clerk, typist, secretary, etc.)
   _____e. college training, but not professional training (include here elementary and secondary education degrees for teaching and other nonprofessional white collar jobs)
   _____f. professional training and advanced degrees (e.g., pharmacy, law, medicine, M.A., and Ph.D.)
   _____check if had Ph.D.
   _____g. Don't know

3. Main subjects studied by mother:
   _____a. business, economics, law, political economy or politics
   _____b. social or moral philosophy
   _____c. education, teaching, nursing
   _____d. best described as "general liberal arts"
   _____e. mainly finishing school, social-graces type

4. Were any of the schools attended by the mother coeducational?   _____yes   _____no
   If yes, which ones? _____

   _____

5. How old was the subject's mother when she married her father? _____

6. What was the religious affiliation of the mother? _____

   a. Was the mother an active and devoted practitioner of this faith? ____yes   ____no
   b. Did she participate regularly in any church organization (once a week or more)?
      ____yes   ____no
      If yes, briefly describe this activity. _____

7. To which ethnic group did the subject's mother belong? _____

8. Race of the mother _____
9. What was the occupation of the mother's father? _____

10. Would you say the mother came from a:
    ____a. lower socioeconomic family
    ____b. lower middle socioeconomic family
    ____c. upper middle socioeconomic family
    ____d. upper class socioeconomic family
11. Which of the categories best decribes the work history of the mother prior to her marriage?
    ____a. never worked, married young
    ____b. never worked, lived off father's wealth
    ____c. never worked, independently wealthy
    ____d. worked in low-skill trade
    ____e. worked as a semiprofessional (e.g. teacher, nurse, etc.)
    ____f. worked as a professional
12. If the mother worked prior to the marriage to the subject's father, what was the main occupation that she worked at? _____

13. Which of the categories best describes the work history of the mother after her marriage?
    ____a. never worked for money or under contract
    ____b. worked part-time, because of family need
    ____c. worked full-time, because of family need
    ____d. worked part-time because of desire for self-expression or outside stimulation
    ____e. worked full-time because of desire for self-expression or outside stimulation

14. If the mother worked after her marriage, what was the main occupation that she worked at? _____

15. If the subject's mother had a career prior to and after her marriage, did she keep it up after the child or other children were born? ____yes ____no

16. List any organizations of which the subject's mother was a member. _____

_____

Indicate any offices held in these organizations: _____

_____

17. Did the mother keep abreast of political events in her country?

____yes ____no ____don't know

18. Did the mother keep abreast of economic events in her country?

____yes ____no ____don't know

19. Did the mother contribute to decisions about the economic life of the family? For example, did she help decide whether or not a job should be changed or a geographic move made?

____yes ____no ____don't know

20. Did the mother ever openly disagree with the father on social, political, or economic matters?

____yes ____no

If yes, give specific instances. _____

_____

_____

21. Was the mother the final authority in the family regarding the establishing of rules and behavior requirements for the children? Choose the category which best describes the relationship:

____a. yes, definitely, father played almost no role

____b. yes, father may have disagreed but almost always lost out to mother

____c. no, mother and father mutually shared the decision-making

____d. father dominated, but did consider mother's views

____e. father definitely dominated no matter what mother thought or did

22. Did the mother mete out the physical punishment to the children?

_____a. yes, always; father seldom or never did

_____b. yes, sometimes, along with father

_____c. no, seldom or never; father responsible

_____d. no physical punishment seems to have been used

_____e. don't know

IV. Characteristics of the subject's father

1. Father's full name _____

2. Highest level of education achieved by father:

_____a. no formal education

_____b. grade school or equivalent—at least literate

_____c. high school or equivalent

_____d. additional training of a skill or trade type (nonprofessional, e.g., carpentry, skilled labor, military, etc.)

_____e. college training, but not professional in nature

_____f. professional training and advanced degrees (e.g., law, medicine, M.A., and Ph.D.)

_____check if had Ph.D.

_____g. don't know

3. Main subjects studied by father:

_____a. business, economics, law, political economy or politics

_____b. social or moral philosophy

_____c. skill and technical training

_____d. best described as "general liberal arts"

4. Were any of the schools attended by the father coeducational? _____yes   _____no

If yes, which ones? _____

_____

5. How old was the subject's father when he married her mother? _____

6. What was the religious affiliation of the father? _____

_____

a. Was the father an active and devoted practitioner of this faith? _____yes   _____no

b. Did he participate regularly in any church organization (once a week or more)?

_____yes   _____no

If yes, briefly describe this activity. _____

_____

7. To which ethnic group did the subject's father belong?

8. Race of the father _____

9. Was the race of the father different from that of the mother? ____yes ____no

10. Was the ethnic stock of the father different from that of the mother? ____yes ____no

11. Did the family live within a geographic area which was inhabited by a special racial/ethnic group? ____yes ____no

12. Did the father have the same religious affiliation as the mother? ____yes ____no

13. Were the religious beliefs of the father and mother similar? ____yes ____no

14. What was the occupation of the father's father? _____

15. Would you say the father came from a:
    ____a. lower socioeconomic family
    ____b. lower middle socioeconomic family
    ____c. upper middle socioeconomic family
    ____d. upper class socioeconomic family

16. Does the father appear to have:
    ____a. raised his socioeconomic status as an adult (upward mobility)
    ____b. stayed the same in socioeconomic status
    ____c. lowered his socioeconomic status (downward mobility)

17. How does the father's socioeconomic status compare with that of the subject's mother's family? His was:
    ____a. lower
    ____b. the same
    ____c. higher

18. What was the father's chief occupation? _____

19. Which of the following best characterizes the father's attitude toward his work or career?
    ____a. job only; worked because needed the money
    ____b. job, but also enjoyed it
    ____c. would have done the work even if he hadn't needed the money

20. Was the father gone from home frequently?
    ____a. yes, several days at a time and quite frequently
    ____b. no
    If yes, explain the reasons for the absences and any effects the absence of the father had on how the child was raised. _____

21. To what extent would you say that this subject's father would have agreed with the following statement: "My home is my castle and I am king of it."
    ____a. would strongly   ____c. would some-
    agree   what disagree
    ____b. would somewhat   ____d. would strongly
    agree   disagree

22. To what extent would you say that this subject's father would have agreed with the following statement: "I am really comfortable and powerful only when I am at home, away from the outside world."
    ____a. would strongly   ____c. would some-
    agree   what disagree
    ____b. would somewhat   ____d. would strongly
    agree   disagree

23. Did the father encourage the mother to express her views on social, political, and/or economic matters?
    ____a. yes, definitely did
    ____b. vaguely seems to have
    ____c. not sure, but don't think so
    ____d. no, definitely did not

24. Did the father encourage the mother to be involved and to participate in nonfamily, nonchurch matters?
    ____a. yes, definitely did
    ____b. vaguely seems to have
    ____c. not sure, but don't think so
    ____d. no, definitely did not

25. List any organizations in which the subject's father was a member. _____

    Indicate any offices held in these organizations. _____

26. Did the father encourage the mother to work for

money or to engage in contractual obligations involving money?

    ____a. yes, definitely did, thought it would be good for her

    ____b. accepted her working because she insisted on it

    ____c. accepted her working because family needed money

    ____d. definitely discouraged her working

    ____e. family so wealthy the issue was never considered

27. Did the subject's father ever perform "female" jobs around the house such as cleaning, cooking, caring for children, etc.?

    ____a. yes, regularly

    ____b. often

    ____c. occasionally

    ____d. seldom

    ____e. never

V. Characteristics of the subject's childhood

1. Highest level of education achieved by subject:

    ____a. no formal education

    ____b. grade school or equivalent—at least literate

    ____c. high school or equivalent

    ____d. additional training of a skill type (nonprofessional: e.g., midwife, clerk, typist, secretary, etc.)

    ____e. college training, but not professional training

    ____f. professional training and advanced degrees (e.g., pharmacy, law, medicine, M.A., and Ph.D.)

        ____check if had Ph.D.

    ____g. don't know

2. Main subjects studied:

    ____a. business, economics, law, political economy or politics

    ____b. social or moral philosophy

    ____c. education, teaching, nursing

    ____d. best described as "general liberal arts"

    ____e. mainly finishing school, social-graces type

3. If the woman had no formal education or did not go on to higher schooling, state why. Did she receive additional education or job training later by other means? Describe the circumstances of her education in some detail. _____

_____

_____

4. Type of elementary school:
   ____a. no school, governess or family-centered
   ____b. religious, church or special ethnic school
   ____c. private, elite, but nonreligious school, nonethnic
   ____d. public school

5. Type of secondary school:
   ____a. no school, governess or family-centered
   ____b. religious, church or special ethnic school
   ____c. private, elite, but nonreligious school, nonethnic
   ____d. public school

6. Type of higher education school (give name if possible): _____

_____

   ____a. none
   ____b. religious or ethnic private school
   ____c. private, elite, but nonreligious, nonethnic
   ____d. public, state college
   ____e. public, state university

7. To what extent was her education coeducational?
   ____a. not at all
   ____b. elementary school only
   ____c. secondary school only
   ____d. college only
   ____e. elementary and secondary
   ____f. elementary and college
   ____g. secondary and college
   ____h. elementary, secondary, and college

8. Briefly describe the extent to which the content of the education received during childhood concerned political issues and problems. _____

_____

9. For a girl of her time, was that education:
   ____a. unusually political   ____c. typical
   ____b. somewhat political   ____d. less political

10. To what extent was the education of the subject similar to that given male children at that time, especially her brothers if she had any?
    ___a. exactly the same
    ___b. similar in matters pertaining to literature, religion, history but not similar otherwise
    ___c. very different (if possible specify) _____
    _____

11. Religion the subject was raised in:
    ___a. none, raised as atheist or agnostic or without any institutionalized religious beliefs
    ___b. religious denomination which does not refer to a personal God, e.g., Unitarian, Deist, etc.
    ___c. reformed "modern" Protestant
    ___d. reformed Jewish
    ___e. Orthodox Jewish
    ___ f. Protestant fundamentalist
    ___g. Roman Catholic
    ___h. Greek Orthodox
    ___ i. Russian Orthodox

12. Importance of religious philosophy and beliefs in home:
    ___a. very important   ___c. somewhat unimportant
    ___b. somewhat impor-   ___d. very unimportant
           tant

13. Did the girl ever have physical fights as a child?
    ___a. none that were specifically noted
    ___b. yes, with both boys and girls
    ___c. yes, but with girls only
    ___d. no, and strong parental tones against such things

14. If the girl did have physical fights, did the parents punish or reprimand her for her aggressive behavior?
    ___a. yes, physically spanked her and/or withdrew desired goods
    ___b. yes, reprimanded her verbally
    ___c. parents did nothing, though knew of it
    ___d. parents never learned of the fight(s)
    ___e. parents supported the action as "justified"

15. To what extent did sports play an important role in her life as a child?

_____a. very important, she was a tomboy, competed with boys (must have direct citation)
_____b. important, but competed only with girls
_____c. was spectator only
_____d. did not particularly like sports, especially competitive ones
_____e. don't know, no mention of sports

16. Describe any sports activity the girl participated in.

_____

17. Were there any ways in which the child appeared to be different from other girls of her age at her time?
_____yes   _____no
If yes, specify. _____

_____

18. Was the health of the subject as a child generally:
_____a. excellent   _____c. fair
_____b. good   _____d. poor

19. If health was only fair or bad, explain circumstances.

_____

20. Did the child ever act as a surrogate mother for a younger child or anyone?
_____yes   _____no
If yes, describe the circumstances. _____

21. As a child, was the subject allowed to make decisions for herself?
_____yes   _____no   _____don't know
If yes, give a specific example of such a decison.

_____

22. In relation to her siblings was the subject:
_____a. more autonomous than other members of her family
_____b. more autonomous than sisters, but not brothers
_____c. about the same as the others
_____d. less autonomous than brothers
_____e. less autonomous than both brothers and sisters
_____f. had no siblings

23. Were the rules of behavior applied in a consistent manner during the subject's childhood? For example, if she were spanked for behavior today, would she be spanked for it tomorrow?

_____a. parents both consistent and in same direction

_____b. parents both consistent, but in different directions

_____c. father inconsistent

_____d. mother inconsistent

_____e. both inconsistent

24. Did the child discuss the rules of behavior with her parents? _____yes _____no _____don't know

25. Generally speaking, was the subject's family close emotionally?

_____a. yes, the whole family was close

_____b. subject was close to parents but not siblings

_____c. subject was close to one parent, but not to other parent or to siblings

_____d. subject was close to siblings, but not parents

_____e. subject was close to only one or two siblings, but not to others

_____f. no, family was not close at all, didn't even like each other

26. Did the family do many things together when the subject was a child (work, play, picnic, sing, talk, etc.)?

_____yes _____no _____don't know

If yes, describe such occasions. _____

_____

27. Did the subject seem to feel safe and secure within her family framework?

_____a. yes, trusted both parents, felt them responsive

_____b. trusted only mother, father hostile or gone

_____c. trusted only father, mother hostile or gone

_____d. no, did not feel safe or secure or trust either

_____e. insecure childhood but due to factors other than parents (explain) _____

_____

28. Did the child feel loved by her parents?

_____a. generally felt loved by both parents

_____b. generally felt loved by only one (which_____)

_____c. did not feel loved by parents

29. If child felt hated, unliked, unloved or ignored which parent was it who made her feel this way?
_____father _____mother _____both

30. To which parent did the child seem most attached?
_____a. both equally
_____b. father mostly
_____c. mother mostly

31. Did the child feel she could talk to her parents about the things that concerned her the most?
_____a. yes, to both
_____b. mother only
_____c. father only
_____d. neither

32. Was the family placed above all other activities and friends by the mother? _____yes _____no
Give examples to support your conclusion. _____

33. Was the family placed above all other activities and friends by the father? _____yes _____no
Give examples to support your conclusion. _____

34. Was the subject as a child expected to place family events, gatherings, and parties above all other activities?
_____yes _____no _____don't know
Give examples to support your conclusion._____

35. Did the parents discuss politics or social issues with the subject as a child?
_____yes _____no _____don't know
If yes, must be able to cite instance. _____

36. Did the parental family associate with people of different religious beliefs and faiths?
_____yes _____no _____don't know
If yes, would you say the association was:
_____frequent _____occasional
_____intermittent

37. Did the parental family associate with people of different ethnic backgrounds?

____yes ____no ____don't know

If yes, would you say the association was:

____frequent ____occasional

____intermittent

38. Would you say the subject as a child believed that she could grow up to be or do whatever she chose or wanted?

____a. definitely yes

____b. somewhat yes

____c. somewhat no

____d. definitely no

39. Are there any special circumstances or relationships which occurred in this subject's childhood that can be directly linked with her development as a political or nonpolitical woman? ____yes ____no

If yes, specify. _____

_____

VI. Family and work situation as an adult

1. At what age did the woman leave her parents' or guardian's home? _____

2. Explain the circumstances of her leaving for the first time. _____

_____

3. Did the woman legally marry?

____yes ____no

If yes, which of the following best describes the marriage?

____a. married for love and stayed married to the same man and in love throughout her life

____b. married for love, but it did not work out so got a divorce

____c. married for love, but it did not work out, so just left

____d. married for love, love died but stayed married anyway

____e. did not marry out of love but to escape (specify) _____

_____

____f. other (specify) _____

_____

4. Did the woman ever have a common-law relationship?

____yes ____no ____don't know

5. On a separate sheet, describe in some detail the marital or common-law relationships the woman had as an adult.

6. Is there any evidence that as a child or young adult this subject seriously considered not marrying?

____yes ____no

Give specific citation if evidence exists. _____

7. At what age did she marry or have common-law relationship? _____

8. Did the subject work before she married?

____yes ____no ____don't know

9. Describe work history of subject prior to her marriage.

10. In characterizing this work history before her marriage would you say this constituted a "career"?

____a. definitely yes

____b. yes, somewhat

____c. not really, but foundations were being built

____d. definitely not

11. Was the woman engaged in political activity before her marriage? ____yes ____no

12. To what extent was the marriage instrumental in getting the woman interested and active in politics?

____a. no connection at all

____b. because of boredom or desire for outlets, got involved; wanted to do something besides being wife and mother

____c. husband or partner encouraged her and pushed her into politics

____d. event affecting married family made politics salient (explain) _____

13. What was the age of the husband or partner at the time of marriage? _____

14. What is the age difference between the husband and wife? _____

15. What was the husband's major occupation? _____

16. What was the ethnic background of the husband? ____

17. Was the ethnic background of the husband the same or different from the subject's?
    ____same   ____different

18. Religion the subject practiced as an adult:
    ____a. none, an atheist, agnostic, or nonpractitioner
    ____b. denomination which does not refer to a personal God
    ____c. reformed "modern" Protestant
    ____d. reformed Jewish
    ____e. Orthodox Jewish
    ____f. Protestant fundamentalist
    ____g. Roman Catholic
    ____h. Greek Orthodox
    ____i. Russian Orthodox

19. Religion the husband of subject practiced as an adult:
    ____a. none, an atheist, agnostic, or nonpractitioner
    ____b. denomination which does not refer to a personal God
    ____c. reformed "modern" Protestant
    ____d. reformed Jewish
    ____e. Orthodox Jewish
    ____f. Protestant fundamentalist
    ____g. Roman Catholic
    ____h. Greek Orthodox
    ____i. Russian Orthodox

20. Was his religious affiliation the same or different from hers?   ____same   ____different

21. As an adult did the subject practice religion in an institutionalized setting?
    ____a. yes, very faithfully (attends church at least once a week)
    ____b. yes, usually (attends church a couple of times a month)
    ____c. occasionally and sporadically attends
    ____d. not really, though she maintains general philosophy
    ____e. definitely not

22. Is her adult faith the same as the one she was raised in?
    ____yes   ____no

23. Do you note any change in the religious intensity of the

subject throughout her life? Be specific, give direct citation. _____

_____

24. What was the highest educational attainment by husband?
    ____a. no formal education
    ____b. grade school or equivalent—at least literate
    ____c. high school or equivalent
    ____d. additional training of a skill type (nonprofessional, e.g., carpentry, skilled labor, military, etc.)
    ____e. college training, but not professional in nature
    ____f. professional training and advanced degrees (e.g., law, medicine, M.A., Ph.D.)
    ____check if had Ph.D.
    ____g. don't know
25. Main subjects studied by husband or partner:
    ____a. business, economics, law, political economy or politics
    ____b. social or moral philosophy
    ____c. skill and technical training
    ____d. best described as "general liberal arts"
    ____e. other (specify) _____
26. Was the subject's educational level higher than her husband's?
    ____higher   ____the same   ____lower
27. Did the woman work after her marriage other than in political activity? ____yes   ____no
    If yes, describe the work history of the subject after her marriage. _____

    _____

28. In characterizing this work history after her marriage would you say this constituted a "career"?
    ____a. definitely yes
    ____b. yes, somewhat
    ____c. not really, but foundation for one was there
    ____d. definitely not
29. If the subject had not worked after or before her marriage, does she have sufficient salable skills to support herself and her family if her husband died?
    ____yes   ____no

Explain conclusion. _____

_____

30. List any organizations in which the subject was a member. _____

_____

Indicate any offices held in these organizations. _____

_____

31. How many children does the subject have? _____
32. How old was the oldest when she began her political activity? _____
33. How old was the youngest when she began her political activity? _____
34. Does the husband help with the housework?
    ____yes   ____no, he won't
    ____no, maid does it
35. Does the husband care for the children?
    ____yes   ____no, he won't
    ____no, hired help does
36. Does evidence exist to indicate that the subject's marriage and family responsibilities have kept her from engaging in activities or actions she would have liked to have done? ____yes   ____no
    Give specific information to justify conclusion. _____

_____

37. Does evidence exist to indicate that the spouse "suffered" unduly from the subject's activities?
    ____yes   ____no
    Give specific information to justify conclusion. _____

_____

38. Does evidence exist to indicate that the children "suffered" unduly from the subject's activities?
    ____yes   ____no
    Give specific information to justify conclusion. _____

_____

39. Specify any other characteristics about the subject's childhood family and environment, or her adult family and environment, which you believe might help explain the subject's political or nonpolitical activity.

Mary A. Boutilier, Ph.D. is assistant professor of government at Seton Hall University. She is primarily responsible for political theory and methodology courses taught by the department.

Rita Mae Kelly, Ph.D. is associate professor in the Department of Urban Studies at Rutgers. She has published two books, *Community Control of Economic Development: American Entrepreneurship in Poverty Environments* and *The Pilot Police Project: A Description and Assessment of an OEO Experiment in Police-Community Relations.*